40 Model Essays

A Portable Anthology

40
Model Essays

A Portable Anthology
Second Edition

JANE E. AARON

ELLEN KUHL REPETTO

Bedford/St. Martin's   BOSTON ◆ NEW YORK

For Bedford/St. Martin's

Senior Executive Editor: Leasa Burton
Developmental Editor: Kate Mayhew
Senior Production Editor: Gregory Erb
Production Supervisor: Lisa Chow
Executive Marketing Manager: Molly Parke
Associate Editor: Alyssa Demirjian
Copy Editor: Hilly van Loon
Permissions Manager: Kalina K. Ingham
Senior Art Director: Anna Palchik
Text Design: Sandra Rigney and Janis Owens
Cover Design: Donna Lee Dennison
Cover Photo: Bridge by Anne McAulay. Lensmodern Ltd.
Composition: Cenveo Publisher Services
Printing and Binding: Malloy Lithographing, Inc.

President, Bedford/St. Martin's: Denise B. Wydra
Presidents, Macmillan Higher Education: Joan E. Feinberg
    and Tom Scotty
Editor in Chief: Karen S. Henry
Director of Marketing: Karen R. Soeltz
Production Director: Susan W. Brown
Associate Production Director: Elise S. Kaiser
Managing Editor: Elizabeth M. Schaaf

Manufactured in the United States of America.
1   2   3   4   5   6   15   14   13   12

For information, write: Bedford/St. Martin's, 75 Arlington Street,
    Boston, MA 02116 (617-399-4000)

ISBN 978-1-4576-1024-0 (paperback)
ISBN 978-1-4576-3842-8 (High School Edition)

Acknowledgments
Acknowledgments and copyrights appear at the back of the book on pages 390–93, which
constitute an extension of the copyright page. It is a violation of the law to reproduce these
selections by any means whatsoever without the written permission of the copyright holder.

Preface for Instructors

40 Model Essays: A Portable Anthology is a brief and affordable rhetorically arranged reader. With about half the usual number of selections and for about half the price of similar books, *40 Model Essays* provides a manageable collection of carefully chosen readings and clear, concrete guidance on reading and writing.

As before, this second edition offers a selection of classic and contemporary readings proven to be successful in the classroom. Joining favorites by such writers as E. B. White, Joan Didion, and Anna Quindlen are newer voices including Dagoberto Gilb, Cheryl Peck, and Bill McKibben. The selections vary in length to accommodate different teaching needs, but all are clear, well-crafted models of the rhetorical methods.

EDITORIAL FEATURES

Concise, effective reading and writing instruction supports the selections that form the core of the book:

- **A general introduction helps students become better critical readers and writers.** To demonstrate the reading process, the introduction includes a sample passage annotated by a student and a detailed analysis of a professional essay. The discussion of the writing process guides students through each stage, from considering subject, purpose, audience, and thesis through revising and editing.
- **Chapter introductions offer detailed, practical instruction** in the ten methods of development: description, narration, example, division or analysis, classification, process analysis, comparison and contrast, definition, cause-and-effect analysis, and argument and persuasion. Each introduction discusses basic concepts and then suggests strategies for starting, focusing,

organizing, drafting, revising, and editing an essay using the method.

- **Apparatus helps students make good use of the selections.** Each reading includes a separate headnote for the writer and for the essay. Following each selection are four sets of detailed questions on meaning, purpose and audience, method and structure, and language. A question labeled "Other Methods" highlights the writer's use of combined rhetorical methods. Finally, several writing topics after each selection guide students in creating their own essays.

- **Additional writing topics at the end of each chapter** list further ideas for applying the chapter's method of development.

- **A glossary at the end of the book** defines and illustrates more than a hundred terms, with specific cross-references to longer discussions in the text.

NEW TO THIS EDITION

The second edition of *40 Model Essays* retains the book's emphasis on excellent writing while updating the selections and refining the editorial support.

- **Fourteen new readings** touch on interesting topics that will enliven class discussion and spark good writing. Every chapter now includes at least one recent essay to complement the classic choices, and the chapter on argument has been thoroughly overhauled to reflect current issues. Ranging in subjects from food and culture to new media and the environment, the new selections represent both emerging writers—such as Jennifer Finney Boylan and Firoozeh Dumas—and established favorites such as William Least Heat-Moon, Walter Mosley, and Francine Prose.

- **Updated discussion of critical reading.** A highlight of the fresh readings is the new essay in the general introduction. Contemporary, short, and accessible, Edward P. Jones's "Shacks" anchors a new, simplified sample analysis that shows students how asking a series of questions about a work can help them reach a critical understanding of its elements and its writer's strategies.

- **More emphasis on developing a thesis.** To help students focus their writing, the general introduction also offers an expanded discussion of forming and expressing a thesis. The introduction to each rhetorical method now breaks out the discussion of thesis as well, emphasizing the importance of writing with a purpose and making the advice easy to locate.
- **New writing topics.** The suggestions for writing at the end of each chapter have been refreshed too, with anywhere from two to five new ideas for writing with the method.

ADDITIONAL HELP FOR LEARNING AND TEACHING

40 Model Essays doesn't stop with a book. Several online resources help students get more out of the book and teachers do more with the course.

At *Re:Writing* (*bedfordstmartins.com/rewriting*), students can visit *Exercise Central* and practice editing with over nine thousand interactive writing and grammar exercises, find advice on citing sources in *Research and Documentation Online* by Diana Hacker, view sample papers and designed documents, take the *St. Martin's Tutorial on Avoiding Plagiarism*, watch videos of writers talking about writing, and learn about reading and using visuals.

Students' books can also be packaged with a variety of innovative tools at a significant discount. *VideoCentral* is a growing collection of videos that capture real-world, academic, and student writers talking about how and why they write. *Re:Writing Plus* upgrades the basic version of *Re:Writing* with hundreds of model documents, the first ever peer-review game, and full access to *VideoCentral*. And the *i-series* offers online interactive exercises on key rhetorical and visual concepts (*ix*), multimedia argument tutorials (*i-claim*), and hands-on practice with research and source citation (*i-cite*).

The instructor's manual for *40 Model Essays* aims to help teachers integrate the text into their courses and use it in class. It is available bound into the book and as a downloadable PDF at *bedfordstmartins.com/40modelessays/catalog*, and includes an overview of the book's organization and chapters, ideas for combining the reader with other course materials, tips for teaching with each essay, and detailed possible answers for all of the critical reading questions in the student text.

Bedford/St. Martin's also provides several digital teaching tools at no charge. *Teaching Central* (*bedfordstmartins.com/teachingcentral*) offers the entire list of Bedford/St. Martin's print and online professional resources—landmark reference works, source books on pedagogical issues, award-winning collections, and practical advice for the classroom—all for free and all in one place. *Bits* (*bedfordbits.com*) collects creative ideas from a community of teachers, scholars, authors, and editors in an easily searchable blog; topics include revision, research, grammar and style, technology, peer review, and much more. And *Bedford Course Packs* (*bedfordstmartins.com/coursepacks*) make it easy to integrate course-specific digital materials into the popular course management systems *Blackboard, WebCT, Angel,* and *Desire2Learn.*

To learn more about any of these resources, contact your sales representative, e-mail sales_support@bfwpub.com, or visit *bedfordstmartins.com/40modelessays/catalog.*

ACKNOWLEDGMENTS

Many instructors helped to shape this edition of *40 Model Essays*, offering insight from their experience and suggestions for improvement. Grateful thanks to Lisa Alvarez, Irvine Valley College; James Anderson, University of Michigan–Flint; Irma Ned Bailey, San Antonio College; Jessica Baldanzi, Goshen College; Judy Bello, Lander University; Mary Ellen Bertolini, Middlebury College; Cynthia Bily, Macomb Community College; Roseanne Camacho, Providence College; William Carr, Trocaire College; David Cassick, Los Angeles Trade Technical College; Chitralekha Duttagupta, Utah Valley University; Kelley McKay Fuemmeler, Missouri Valley College; Sandra Kay Heck, Walters State Community College; Charlyn Ingwerson, Drury University; Krista Jackman, University of New Hampshire; Laura Jeffries, Florida State College at Jacksonville; James Kosmicki, Central Community College; Nathan Leslie, Virginia Community College; Amy Mansfield, North Georgia College & State University; Daiva Markelis, Eastern

Illinois University; Barbara McClure, Santa Rosa Junior College; Mark Ristroph, Augusta Technical College; Laura Smith, University of New Hampshire; Robert White, Piedmont Virginia Community College; Margaret Wye, Rockhurst University; and Jeannie Zeck, MacMurray College.

And once again happy thanks go to the talented and supportive folks at Bedford/St. Martin's, who this time saw the need for an updated *40 Model Essays* and helped to shape it: Joan Feinberg, Denise Wydra, Karen Henry, Steve Scipione, Maura Shea, Molly Parke, Andrea Cava, Amanda Legee, and especially Kate Mayhew, Regina Tavani, and Gregory Erb.

Contents

Chapter 2
NARRATION

Chapter 3
EXAMPLE

Chapter 6
PROCESS ANALYSIS

Chapter 8
DEFINITION

Chapter 9
CAUSE-AND-EFFECT ANALYSIS

Chapter 10
ARGUMENT AND PERSUASION

Introduction

READING AND WRITING

This collection of essays has one purpose: to help you become a better reader and writer. It combines examples of good writing with explanations of the writers' methods, questions to guide your reading, and ideas for your own writing. In doing so, it shows how you can adapt the processes and techniques of others as you learn to communicate clearly and effectively on paper.

Writing well is not an inborn skill but an acquired one: you will become proficient only by writing and rewriting, experimenting with different strategies, listening to the responses of readers. How, then, can it help to read the work of other writers?

- *Reading others' ideas can introduce you to new information and give you new perspectives on your own experience.* Many of the essays collected here demonstrate that personal experience is a rich and powerful source of material for writing. But the knowledge gained from reading can help pinpoint just what is remarkable in your experience. And by introducing varieties of behavior and ways of thinking that would otherwise remain unknown to you, reading can also help you understand where you fit in the scheme of things. Such insight not only reveals subjects for writing but also improves your ability to communicate with others whose experiences naturally differ from your own.

- *Reading exposes you to a broad range of strategies and styles.* Just seeing that these vary as much as the writers themselves should assure you that there is no fixed standard of writing, while it should also encourage you to find your own strategies and style. At the same time, you will see that writers do make choices to suit their subjects, their purposes, and especially their readers.

Writing is rarely easy, even for the pros; but the more options you have to choose from, the more likely you are to succeed at it.

- *Reading makes you sensitive to the role of audience in writing.* As you become adept at reading the work of other writers critically, discovering intentions and analyzing choices, you will see how a writer's decisions affect you as audience. Training yourself to read consciously and critically is a first step to becoming a more objective reader of your own writing.

The rest of this introduction offers strategies for making the most of your reading and writing for this course and elsewhere. But first you should understand the book's organization. The essays are arranged by chapter to introduce ten methods of developing a piece of writing:

description	process analysis
narration	comparison and contrast
example	definition
division or analysis	cause-and-effect analysis
classification	argument and persuasion

These methods correspond to basic and familiar patterns of thought and expression, common in our daily musings and conversations as well as in writing for all sorts of purposes and audiences: college term papers, lab reports, and examinations; blogs, social-networking pages, and online discussion boards; business memos and reports; letters to the editors of newspapers; articles in popular magazines. The methods provide a context for critical reading and also stimulate writing by helping you generate and shape ideas. Detailed chapter introductions explain each method and give advice for using it to develop your own essays. The essays that follow provide clear examples that you can analyze and learn from (with the help of specific questions) and can refer to while writing (with the help of specific writing suggestions).

READING

When we look for something to watch on television or listen to on the radio, we often tune in to one station after another, pausing just long enough each time to catch the program or music being broadcast before settling on one choice. Much of the reading we do is similar: we skim a newspaper, magazine, or Web site, noting headings and scanning text to get the gist of the content. But such skimming is not really reading, for it neither involves us deeply in the subject nor engages us in interaction with the writer.

Reading Critically

To get the most out of reading, we must invest something of ourselves in the process, applying our own ideas and emotions and attending not just to the substance but also to the writer's interpretation of it. This kind of reading is **critical** because it looks beneath the surface of a piece of writing. (The common meaning of *critical* as "negative" doesn't apply here: critical reading may result in positive, negative, or even neutral reactions.)

Critical reading can be enormously rewarding, but of course it takes care and time. A good method for developing your own skill in critical reading is to prepare yourself beforehand and then read the work at least twice to uncover what it has to offer. Preparation can involve just a few minutes as you form some ideas about the author, the work, and your likely response to the work:

- *What is the author's background, what qualifications does he or she bring to the subject, and what approach is he or she likely to take?* The biographical information provided before each essay in this book should help answer these questions; many periodicals, books, and Web sites include similar information on their authors.

- *What does the title convey about the subject and the author's attitude toward it?* Note, for instance, the quite different attitudes conveyed by these three titles on the same subject: "Safe Hunting," "In Touch with Ancient Spirits," and "Killing Animals for Fun and Profit."

- *What can you predict about your own response to the work?* What might you already know about the subject? Based on the title and other clues, are you likely to agree or disagree with the author's views?

After developing some expectations about the piece of writing, read it through carefully to acquaint yourself with the subject, the author's reason for writing about it, and the way the author presents it. (Each essay in this book is short enough to be read in one sitting.) Try not to read passively, letting the words wash over you, but instead interact directly with the work to discover its meaning, the author's intentions, and your own responses.

One of the best aids to active reading is to make notes on separate sheets of paper or, preferably (if you own the book), on the pages themselves. As you practice making notes, you will probably develop a personal code meaningful only to you. As a start, however, try this system:

- *Underline or bracket passages* that you find particularly effective or that seem especially important to the author's purpose.
- *Circle words you don't understand* so that you can look them up when you finish.
- *Put question marks in the margins* next to unclear passages.
- *Jot down associations that occur to you*, such as examples from your own experience, disagreements with the author's assumptions or arguments, or connections to other works you've read.

When you have finished such an active reading, your annotations might look like those below. (The paragraph is from the end of the essay reprinted on pp. 6–8.)

> I learned, once the world became larger than Sandra Walker and me and Worcester, Massachusetts, that we are born with few tools with which to build our little shacks of life, and we are born with even less knowledge of how to use those tools. I don't know what I would have done if I hadn't had it in me to write those letters, those stories, to Sandra. I was able to crawl into December, and I woke up one day and knew, without a letter from Sandra, without anyone telling me so, that wherever in the universe Sandra Walker would end up I would not be there with her. I made peace with that, and I think I had a sense that I wasn't really eighteen anymore, but fast going on twenty.

Marginal annotations: true? | ? | like a toddler | ✓ | why? | so he grew up, but just a little bit?

Before leaving the essay after such an initial reading, try to answer your own questions by looking up unfamiliar words and figuring out the meaning of unclear passages. Then let the essay rest in your mind for at least an hour or two before approaching it again.

When rereading the essay, write a one- or two-sentence summary of each paragraph—in your own words—to increase your mastery of the material. Aim to answer the following questions:

- *Why did the author choose this subject?*
- *Who is the intended audience?* What impression did the author wish to make on readers?
- *What is the author's point?* Can you find a direct statement of the thesis, or main idea, or is the thesis implied?
- *What details does the author provide to support the thesis?* Is the supporting evidence reliable? complete? convincing?
- *How does the author organize ideas?* What effect does that arrangement have on the overall impact of the essay?
- *What do language and tone reveal about the author's meaning, purpose, and attitude?*
- *How successful is the essay as a whole, and why?*

A procedure for such an analysis—and the insights to be gained from it—can best be illustrated by examining an actual essay. The annotated paragraph on the previous page comes from "Shacks" by Edward P. Jones. The entire essay is reprinted on the next pages in the same format as other selections in the book, with a note on the author and a note on the essay.

EDWARD P. JONES

Born in 1950, Edward P. Jones has been hailed as a major voice of Southern literature. Although his childhood in Washington, DC, was marked by poverty and instability, Jones showed an early love for reading and won a scholarship to the College of the Holy Cross. He completed a BA in 1972 and went through a period of homelessness before obtaining a clerical job with Science *magazine and publishing his first short story in* Essence—*both in the same week. Jones went on to earn an MFA from the University of Virginia, and for eighteen years he proofread tax newsletters during the day while writing fiction in his spare time. His tales of urban life—collected in* Lost in the City *(1992) and* All Aunt Hagar's Children *(2006)—have won popular and critical acclaim, and his novel* The Known World *(2003), about black slaveholders, was awarded the Pulitzer Prize and the National Book Critics Circle Award. Now a professor of English at George Washington University, Jones has also taught at Princeton, the University of Maryland, and the University of Virginia. He lives in Arlington, Virginia.*

Shacks

In this essay written for a special "Starting Out" issue of the New Yorker *in 2011, Jones reflects on a life lesson he stumbled on in his first semester of college. By engaging in an eager yet futile effort to build a romance, Jones discovered a talent he hadn't known he had.*

In my first months as a college freshman, I cared more than any- 1 thing about a young woman with whom I'd gone to high school— Sandra Walker, a thin, brown-skinned woman who might not have been pretty enough for the rest of the universe but was more than pretty enough for me. She was at college in Atlanta and I was in Worcester, Massachusetts. I had never kissed her, for she was true to someone else. I don't think I'd even so much as touched the back of her hand, but I cared for her, and the only way I knew how to express what I felt at that point in my life was to write letters, and write letters I did. Three and four and five a week I wrote. All of them were more than five pages long and many went to fifteen pages—so thick once they had been folded that I had to reinforce the envelopes with tape. I had always written legibly, but the fear was so great that Sandra Walker might not be able to decipher even one syllable I had written that I began printing everything, and to this day the only cursive writing I do is my signature.

Things like that get in the blood, and they become who you 2 are. I never received a strongly positive response from Sandra, but the crumbs, the letters sharing with me only the minutiae of her life, were enough to keep me writing—September and October and November. There wasn't much beyond the crumbs. Imagining as best I could what a young woman at the front door of the rest of her life might want to hear from a young man, I put all the hope I had into each letter, using the limited language of an eighteen-year-old who knew books of mathematics but not much else. It is amazing the little shacks of life we can build when it seems that so much is at stake. Before it was all over, the letters—from what I can remember, for I have not seen any of them since the day I sent them off—became grand and fanciful creations about some marvellous future that Sandra Walker and I could have. It was a world of fiction, of course, a place conjured up in my imagination, because, as my mother could have told Sandra, I could barely take care of myself and would not have known what to do with, first, a girlfriend, and then a wife and all the children we were supposed to have.

But I was alone in the wilderness in Worcester, away from 3 Washington, DC, my home, for the first time, and I needed some shack of life. I know now that had I been someone who knew only how to paint pictures, I would have done that. I would have made my case with painting after painting, wrapping them with care and sending them off to Atlanta. Or if I had known how to carve little figures in wood I would have carved Sandra and me and our happy future in oak or maple or whatever wood I could salvage in Worcester. Or I would have weighed poor Sandra down with volumes of poetry or tapes of songs with her name in every title.

I learned, once the world became larger than Sandra Walker 4 and me and Worcester, Massachusetts, that we are born with few tools with which to build our little shacks of life, and we are born with even less knowledge of how to use those tools. I don't know what I would have done if I hadn't had it in me to write those letters, those stories, to Sandra. I was able to crawl into December, and I woke up one day and knew, without a letter from Sandra, without anyone telling me so, that wherever in the universe Sandra Walker would end up I would not be there with her. I made peace with that, and I think I had a sense that I wasn't really eighteen anymore, but fast going on twenty.

Even read quickly, Jones's essay would not be difficult to comprehend: the author draws on a story from his time as a college student to make a point at the end about talent. In fact, a quick reading might give the impression that Jones produced the essay effortlessly, artlessly. But close, critical reading reveals a carefully conceived piece whose parts work independently and together to achieve the author's purpose.

Asking Questions

One way to uncover the underlying intentions and relations in a piece of writing is to answer a series of questions about the work. The following questions proceed from the general to the specific—from overall meaning through purpose and method to word choices—and they parallel the more specific questions after the essays in this book. Here the questions come with possible answers for Jones's essay. (The paragraph numbers can help you locate the appropriate passages in Jones's essay as you follow the analysis.)

Meaning

What is the main idea of the essay—the chief point the writer makes about the subject, to which all other ideas and details relate? What are the subordinate ideas that contribute to the main idea?

Jones states his main idea near the end of his essay: "we are born with few tools with which to build our little shacks of life, and we are born with even less knowledge of how to use those tools" (paragraph 4). As we grow up, he is saying, we discover our talents and desires and learn what to do with them. (Writers sometimes postpone stating their main idea, as Jones does here. Perhaps more often, they state it near the beginning of the essay. See p. 17.) Jones leads up to and supports his idea by narrating an episode from his own life—his obsessive writing of letters to a young woman he longed for during his first semester of college (1–2)—and contemplating other ways he might have approached her (3) to reach a larger truth. The story is developed with specific details from Jones's memory—the bulk of the envelopes (1), descriptions of the raw talents he had (writing letters, persisting, and imagining, 1–2)—and with examples of the talents he lacked—taking care of himself (2), painting, carving, and writing poetry (3).

Purpose and Audience

Why did the author write the essay? What did the author hope readers would gain from it? What did the author assume about the knowledge and interests of readers, and how are these assumptions reflected in the essay?

Jones seems to have written his essay for two interlocking reasons: to show, and thus explain, that we all feel an inherent need to do something meaningful with our lives—to construct our "shacks"—and to argue gently that individual talents must be identified and developed before they can be used to full advantage.

Jones assumes that his readers, like him, are people who have gone to college, people to whom the emotional turmoil of freshman year will feel familiar. He comments, for instance, on the doubts of "an eighteen-year-old who knew books of mathematics but not much else" (paragraph 2), the reality that he "could barely take care of [him]self" (2), and the loneliness of being away from "home . . . for the first time" (3). But he also expresses hopes of being "at the front door of the rest of . . . life" (2) and reveals an imagination full of "grand and fanciful creations about some marvellous future" (2), taking pains to show (with some hint of embarrassment) the lengths to which he practiced his only skill—letter writing—to try to secure that future for himself.

At the same time, Jones seems to expect that readers of the *New Yorker*—with its emphasis on culture and the arts—will be aware that he is now an established fiction writer and therefore will grasp that his youthful letters, the "stories" (4) he conjured and sent out, built the foundation for his future life. However, readers who do not recognize this point are still likely to understand and appreciate his main idea.

Method and Structure

What method or methods does the author use to develop the main idea, and how do the methods serve the author's subject and purpose? How does the organization serve the author's subject and purpose?

As writers often do, Jones develops his main idea with a combination of the methods discussed in this book. The primary support for his idea consists of narration (Chapter 2), a story about courtship. The narrative is developed with description (Chapter 1), especially of the letters Jones wrote (as in paragraphs 1–2), and with classification (Chapter 5) and examples (Chapter 3) of the forms of expression he might have tried if he had the talent (3). Jones relies on division or analysis (Chapter 4) to tease apart the elements of his messages to Sandra Walker, and he uses comparison and contrast (Chapter 7) to show the differences between his letters and her responses (2). In addition, he draws on definition (Chapter 8) to give meaning to the "shacks" metaphor that shapes the essay (title, 2–4). (See "Language," below, for further discussion of Jones's figures of speech.)

While using many methods to develop his idea, Jones keeps his organization fairly simple. He does not begin with a formal introduction or a statement of his idea but instead starts right off with his story, the inspiration for his idea. In the first paragraph he narrates and describes his efforts to connect with a former high school classmate by writing letters to her. Then in paragraph 2 he explains why he persisted despite her lack of enthusiasm and suggests that those letters may have served an as-yet undiscovered purpose in his life. Still delaying a statement of his main idea, Jones contrasts his writing with other forms of communication, which he sees as talents different from his own (3). Finally, he relates his awakening to the truth of his situation and zeroes in on his main idea (4). Although he has withheld this idea until the end, we see that everything in the essay has been controlled by it and directed toward it.

Language

How are the author's main idea and purpose revealed at the level of sentences and words? How does the author use language to convey his or her attitudes toward the subject and to make meaning clear and vivid?

Perhaps Jones's most striking use of language to express and support his idea is in his **figures of speech**, creative expressions that imply meanings beyond or different from their literal meanings. (See the Glossary.) As is often the case, you may need to puzzle over some of his words before you can fully understand their meaning. This is particularly true of Jones's central metaphor, "shacks of life" (title and paragraphs 2–4). A metaphor compares two unlike things by saying one is the other: Jones equates a physical shelter to the framework that a person creates to shape his or her existence. The **connotations** of the word "shack" add more layers of meaning: shacks are simple structures, often temporary or unstable, and they tend to be associated with people of limited means. Jones's idea, it seems, is that a person doesn't need much to build a life, just enough "tools" (4)—a metaphor for skills or talents—to survive.

The essay includes several other inventive figures of speech as well. In paragraph 2 alone Jones uses three metaphors—the behaviors "that get in the blood," the "crumbs" offered by his female correspondent, and "the front door of the rest of her life"—separate from, but cleverly echoing, the "shacks" metaphor. Calling the small city of Worcester, Massachusetts, a "wilderness" (3) is hyperbole, or deliberate exaggeration, suggesting the author's emotional isolation more than the physical reality of place (and again, echoing the "shacks" theme). And finally, the last paragraph depends on contrasting **images** of infancy (captured in the words "born" and "crawl") and adulthood (not "eighteen anymore, but fast going on twenty") to reinforce Jones's admission that his maturation and understanding were incomplete.

Jones's ideas gain additional impact with **parallelism**, the use of similar grammatical form for ideas of equal importance. (See the Glossary.) For instance, every sentence of paragraph 3, except the first, uses the phrase "I would have," building rhythm and stressing the young man's desperate need to communicate. The phrase "those letters, those stories" (4) clarifies that his missives were an early form of fiction writing. Similarly, the repetition of "we are born with" (4) emphasizes both the author's lingering immaturity and his point that raw talents in their infancy must be nurtured in order to thrive.

These notes on Jones's essay show how one can arrive at a deeper, more personal understanding of a piece of writing by attentive, thoughtful analysis. Guided by the questions at the end of each essay and by your own sense of what works and why, you'll find similar lessons and pleasures in all of this book's readings.

WRITING

An analysis like the preceding one is valuable in itself, helping you better understand and appreciate whatever you read. But it can make you a better writer, too, by showing you how to read your own work critically, broadening the range of strategies available to you, and suggesting subjects for you to write about.

Accompanying the questions on the essays in this book are writing topics—ideas for you to adapt and develop into essays of your own. Some of these call for your analysis of the essay; others lead you to examine your own experiences or outside sources in light of the essay's ideas. At the end of each chapter is an additional set of writing topics that provides a range of subjects for using the chapter's method of development.

To help you develop essays using the various methods, each chapter's introduction gives specific advice arranged by stages of the writing process described below: getting started, forming a thesis, organizing, drafting, and revising and editing. Actually, these stages are quite arbitrary, for writers do not move in straight lines through fixed steps. Instead, just as they do when thinking, writers continually circle back over covered territory, each time picking up more information or seeing new relationships, until their meaning is clear to them and can be made clear to readers. No two writers proceed in exactly the same way, either. Still, viewing the process in stages does help sort out its many activities so that you can develop the process or processes that work best for you.

Getting Started

Every writing situation involves several elements: you communicate a *thesis* (a central idea) about a subject to an *audience* of readers for a particular *purpose*. At first you may not be sure of your idea or your purpose. You may not know how you want to approach your readers, even when you know who they are. Your job in getting started, then, is to explore options and make choices.

Subject and Purpose

A **subject** for writing may arise from any source, including your own experience or reading, a suggestion in this book, or an assignment from your instructor. Whatever its source, the subject should be something you care enough about to probe deeply and to stamp with your own perspective.

This personal stamp comes from your **purpose**, your reason for writing. The purpose may be one of the following:

- *To explain* the subject so that readers understand it or see it in a new light.
- *To persuade* readers to accept or reject an opinion or to take a certain action.
- *To entertain* readers with a humorous or exciting story.
- *To express* the thoughts and emotions triggered by a revealing or instructive experience.

A single essay may sometimes have more than one purpose: for instance, a writer might both explain what it's like to have a disability and try to persuade readers to respect special parking zones for people with disabilities. Your reasons for writing may occur to you early on, arising out of the subject and its significance for you. But you may need to explore your subject for a while—even to the point of writing a draft—before you know what you want to do with it.

Audience

Either very early, when you first begin exploring your subject, or later, as a check on what you have generated, you may want to make a few notes on your anticipated **audience**. The notes are optional, but thinking about audience definitely is not. Your topic and purpose—as well as your thesis, supporting ideas, details and examples, organization, style, tone, and language—should reflect your answers to the following questions:

- *What impression do you want to make on readers?*
- *What do readers already know about your subject? What do they need to know?*
- *What are readers' likely expectations and assumptions about your subject?*
- *How can you build on readers' previous knowledge, expectations, and assumptions to bring them around to your view?*

These considerations are obviously crucial to achieve the fundamental purpose of all public writing: communication. Accordingly, they come up again and again in the chapter introductions and the questions after each essay.

Invention

Ideas for your writing—whether your subject itself or the many smaller ideas and details that contribute to what you have to say about it—may come to you in a rush, or you may need to search for them. Writers use a variety of searching techniques, from jotting down thoughts while they pursue other activities to writing concentratedly for a set period. Here are a few techniques you might try.

Journal writing.   Many writers keep a **journal**, a record of thoughts and observations. Whether in a notebook or in a computer file, journal entries give you an opportunity to explore ideas just for yourself, free of concerns about readers who will judge what you say or how you say it. Regular journal entries can also make you more comfortable with the act of writing and build your confidence. Indeed, writing teachers often require their students to keep journals for these reasons.

In a journal you can write about whatever interests, puzzles, or disturbs you. For example, you might analyze a relationship that's causing you problems, explore your reactions to a movie or a song, or confide your dreams and fears. Any of this material could provide a seed for a writing assignment, but you can also use a journal deliberately to develop ideas for assignments. For instance, after reading Edward Jones's "Shacks" (p. 6), you might explore your feelings about loneliness or romance, recount a particular episode from your own first months of college, examine your attitudes toward writing, or respond to Jones's ideas about talent. Writing for yourself, you will feel free to explore what is on your mind without worrying about correctness.

Freewriting.   Another effective invention technique is **freewriting**, exploratory writing in which you write without stopping for ten or fifteen minutes, following ideas wherever they lead, paying no attention to completeness or correctness or even sense. Like journal writing, freewriting is rough: the tone is usually informal; thoughts might be left dangling; some sentences might be shapeless or incomplete; words can be misspelled. But none of this matters because the freewriting is just exploratory.

Using the methods of development.   The methods of development discussed in this book can also be useful tools for probing a subject. They suggest questions that can spark ideas by opening up different approaches.

- *Description:* How does the subject look, sound, smell, taste, and feel?
- *Narration:* What is the story in the subject? How did it happen?
- *Example:* How can the subject be illustrated? What are instances of it?
- *Division or analysis:* What are the subject's parts, and what is their relationship or significance?
- *Classification:* What groups can the subject be sorted into?
- *Process analysis:* How does the subject work, or how does one do it?
- *Comparison and contrast:* How is the subject similar to or different from something else?
- *Definition:* What are the subject's characteristics and boundaries?
- *Cause-and-effect analysis:* Why did the subject happen? What were or may be its consequences?
- *Argument and persuasion:* Why do I believe as I do about the subject? Why do others have different opinions? How can I convince others to accept my opinion or believe as I do?

Forming a Thesis

Have you ever read a work of nonfiction and wondered, "What's the point?" Whether consciously or not, we expect a writer to have a point, a central idea that he or she wants readers to take away from the work. We also expect that idea to determine the content of the work—so that everything relates to it—and we expect the content in turn to demonstrate or prove the idea.

Arriving at a main idea, or **thesis**, is thus an essential part of the writing process. Sometimes it will occur to you at the moment you hit on your subject. More often, you will need to explore your thoughts for a while—even to the point of writing a draft—before you pin down your main idea. To find a workable thesis, keep narrowing your focus until you have something to say about a subject. For example, one writer decided to write about family but quickly discovered that the topic is too broad to work with. She then narrowed the subject to adoptive families, but even that covered too much territory. As she continued to tighten her focus, she first thought she would discuss adopted children who try to contact their birth parents, then she considered explaining how adoptees can locate the necessary information about their adoption, and in the end she decided to discuss how legal and other barriers can impede adoptees' efforts to find their birth parents. In a few steps, the writer turned a broad subject into a manageable idea worth pursuing. The process isn't always simple, but it is a necessary first step in finding a thesis.

Once you've narrowed your subject and have a reason to write about it, the best way to focus on your thesis is to sketch it out in a **thesis sentence** (or sentences): an assertion that makes your point. Edward Jones states his thesis near the end of his essay "Shacks" (p. 7):

> [W]e are born with few tools with which to build our little shacks of life, and we are born with even less knowledge of how to use those tools.

Jones's thesis statement, while poetic, nonetheless ties together all of the other ideas and details in his essay; it also reflects his purpose in writing the essay and focuses his readers on a single point. All effective thesis sentences do this: they go beyond generalities or mere statements of fact to express the writer's unique perspective on the subject.

Because the point of an essay may change over the course of the writing process, your thesis sentence may change as well, sometimes considerably. Even so, it's a good idea to draft it early because it can help keep you focused as you generate ideas and organize your thoughts. The following thesis sentences show how the writer discussed earlier moved from an explanatory to a persuasive purpose between the early stages of the writing process and the final draft.

> TENTATIVE Adopted children can contact their birth parents, although sometimes the process is difficult.

> TENTATIVE Adopted children often need persistence to locate information about their birth parents.

> FINAL Laws and traditions unfairly hamper adopted children from seeking information about their birth parents.

The first two sentences identify the subject of the essay, but they are broad and bland and neither clearly focuses on the writer's interest: the impediments to obtaining information. In contrast, the final sentence makes a definitive assertion and clearly conveys the persuasive purpose and opinion. Thus the sentence lets readers know what to expect: an argument that adopted children should be treated more fairly when they seek information about their birth parents. Readers will also expect some discussion of the "laws and traditions" that hamper adoptees' searches, what is "unfair" and "fair" in this situation, and what changes the author proposes.

In college writing, the thesis is commonly stated near the beginning of an essay, sometimes in the first paragraph, where it serves as a promise to examine a particular subject from a particular perspective. But the thesis sentence may come elsewhere as long as it controls the whole essay, as Jones's does. The thesis may even go unstated, as some essays in this book illustrate, but it must govern every element of the work as if it were announced.

Organizing

Writers vary in the extent to which they arrange their material before they begin writing, but most do establish some plan. The plan may consist of a list of key points, a fuller list including specifics as well, or even a detailed formal outline—whatever gives order to your ideas and provides some direction for your writing. You will find that some subjects and methods of development demand fuller plans than others: a chronological narrative of a personal experience, for instance, would not require as much pre-arrangement as a comparison of two complex social policies. Most of the methods of development also suggest specific structures, as you will find in reading the chapter introductions and essays.

Most essays consist of three parts: an introduction and a conclusion (discussed below) and the **body**, the most substantial and longest part that develops the main idea or thesis. As you explore your subject, you will discover both ideas that directly support your thesis and more specific examples, details, and other evidence that support these ideas. Each supporting idea, or subpoint, may take a paragraph or more to develop with specifics.

When you seek a plan in your ideas, look first for your subpoints, the main supports for your thesis. Use these as your starting points to work out your essay one chunk (or paragraph) at a time. You can fill in the supporting evidence in your organizational plan, or you can wait until you begin drafting to get into the specifics.

As you plan the body of your essay, you can also be thinking of how you want to begin and end it. An effective opening or closing may not become apparent until after you have drafted the body of the essay. But considering how you want to approach readers and what you want to leave them with can help channel your thoughts while you draft.

- The **introduction** draws readers into the essay and focuses their attention on the main idea and purpose—often stated in a thesis sentence.
- The **conclusion** ties together the elements of the essay and provides a final impression for readers to take away with them.

These basic forms allow considerable room for variation. Especially as you are developing your writing skills, you will find it helpful to state your thesis sentence near the beginning of the essay; but sometimes you can place it effectively at the end, or you can let it direct what you say in the essay but never state it at all. One essay may need two paragraphs of introduction but only a one-sentence conclusion, whereas another essay may require no formal introduction but a lengthy conclusion. How you begin and end depends on your subject and purpose, the kind of essay you are writing, and the likely responses of your readers. Specific ideas for opening and closing essays are included in each chapter introduction and in the Glossary under *introductions* and *conclusions*.

Drafting

However detailed your organizational plan is, you should not view it as a rigid taskmaster while you are drafting your essay. If you are like most writers, you will discover much of what you have to say while putting your thoughts into sentences and paragraphs. In fact, if your subject is complex or difficult for you to write about, you may need several drafts just to work out your ideas and their relationships.

While drafting, remember: write first; then revise. Concentrate on *what* you are saying, not on *how* you are saying it. Awkwardness, repetition, wrong words, grammatical errors, spelling mistakes—these and other more superficial concerns can be attended to in a later draft. The same goes for considering your readers' needs. Like many writers, you may find that attention to readers during the first draft inhibits the flow of ideas. If so, postpone that attention until the second or third draft.

You may find it helpful to start your draft with your thesis sentence—or to keep it in front of you as you write—as a reminder of your purpose and main idea. But if you find yourself pulled away from the thesis by a new idea, you may want to let go and follow your train of thought, at least for a while. After all, drafting is your opportunity to find what you have to say. If your purpose and main idea change as a result of such exploration, you can always revise your thesis accordingly.

Revising and Editing

In a rough draft you have the chance to work out your meaning without regard for what others may think. Eventually, though, you must look critically at a draft. In this stage, called **revision** (literally, "re-seeing"), you see the draft as a reader sees it, mere words on a page that are only as clear, interesting, and significant as you have made them. To gain something like a reader's distance from your work, try one or more of the following techniques:

- *Put your first draft aside for at least a few hours—preferably overnight—before attempting to revise it.* You may have further thoughts in the interval, and you will be able to see your work more objectively when you return to it.
- *Ask another person to read and comment on your draft.* Your teacher may ask you and your classmates to exchange drafts so that you can help each other revise. But even without such a procedure, you can benefit from others' responses. Keep an open mind to your readers' comments, and ask questions when you need more information.
- *Make an outline of your draft by listing what you cover in each paragraph.* Such an outline can show gaps, overlaps, and problems in organization.
- *Read the draft out loud.* Speaking the words and hearing them can help to create distance from them and can make errors easier to spot.
- *Imagine you are someone else—*a friend, perhaps, or a particular person in your intended audience—and read the draft through that person's eyes, as if for the first time.
- *Print a double-spaced copy of your draft.* It's much easier to read text on paper than on a computer screen, and you can spread out printed pages to see the whole paper at once. Once you've finished revising, transferring changes to the computer requires little effort.

For most writers, revision actually divides into two phases: one for fundamental changes in content and structure; and the other for more superficial changes in style, grammar, and the like. In the first phase, you might ask yourself the following questions:

- *Is the purpose clear and consistent?*
- *Do subordinate points relate to the thesis sentence and support it fully?*
- *Have you provided enough facts, examples, and other evidence for readers to understand your meaning and find your ideas convincing?*

- *Does your organization channel readers' attention as you intended?*
- *Does each sentence and each paragraph relate clearly and logically to the ones before and after?*

In **editing** you turn from what the text says to how it sounds and looks:

- *Are transitions smooth between paragraphs and sentences?*
- *Are sentences clear and concise, and do their lengths and structures vary to suit your meaning and purpose?*
- *Do concrete, specific words sharpen your meaning?*
- *Are details vivid enough to help your readers see your subject as you want them to?*
- *Are grammar, punctuation, and spelling correct?*

Once you are satisfied that your essay achieves your purpose and is as clear as possible, prepare the final draft, the one you will submit. Proofread the draft carefully to correct spelling errors, typographical mistakes, and other minor problems.

By finishing with revising and editing, we have circled back to the beginning of this chapter. Good writers are good readers. Reading the essays in this book will give you pleasure and set you thinking. But analyzing and writing about them will also increase your flexibility as a writer and train you to read your own work critically.

Chapter 1

DESCRIPTION

USING THE METHOD

Whenever you use words to depict or re-create a scene, an object, a person, or a feeling, you use **description**. You draw on the perceptions of your five senses—sight, hearing, smell, taste, and touch—to understand and communicate your experience of the world. A mainstay of conversation between people, description is likely to figure in almost any writing situation: an e-mail home may describe a new roommate's spiky purple hair; a laboratory report may describe the colors and odors of chemicals; a business memo may distinguish between the tastes of two competitors' chicken potpies.

Your purpose in writing and your involvement with the subject will largely determine how objective or subjective your description is.

- In **objective description** you strive for precision and objectivity, trying to convey the subject impersonally, without emotion. This is the kind of description required in scientific writing— for instance, a medical diagnosis or a report on an experiment in psychology—where cold facts and absence of feeling are essential for readers to judge the accuracy of procedures and results. It is also the method of news reports and of reference works such as encyclopedias.

- In **subjective description**, in contrast, you draw explicitly on your emotions, giving an impression of the subject filtered through your experience of it. Instead of withdrawing to the background, you invest feelings in the subject and let those feelings determine which details to describe and how to describe them. Your state of mind—perhaps loneliness, anger, or joy—can be re-created by reference to sensory details such as numbness, heat, or sweetness.

In general, you should favor objective description when your purpose is explanation and subjective description when your purpose is self-expression or entertainment. But the categories are not exclusive, and most descriptive writing mixes the two. A news report on a tropical storm, for instance, might objectively describe bent and broken trees, fallen wires, and lashing rains, but your selection of details would give a subjective impression of the storm's fearsomeness.

Whether objective or subjective or a mixture of the two, effective description requires a **dominant impression**—a central theme or idea about the subject to which readers can relate all the details. The dominant impression may be something you see in the subject, such as the apparent purposefulness of city pedestrians or the expressiveness of an actor. Or it may derive from your emotional response to the subject, perhaps pleasure (or depression) at all the purposefulness, perhaps admiration (or disdain) for the actor's technique. Whatever its source, the dominant impression serves as a unifying principle that guides your selection of details and the reader's understanding of the subject.

One aid to creating a dominant impression is a consistent **point of view**, a position from which you approach the subject. Point of view in description has two main elements:

- A real or imagined *physical* relation to the subject: you could view a mountain, for instance, from the bottom looking up, from fifteen miles away across a valley, or from an airplane passing overhead. The first two points of view are fixed because you remain in one position and scan the scene from there; the third is moving because you change position.

- A *psychological* relation to the subject, a relation partly conveyed by pronouns. In subjective description, where your feelings are part of the message, you might use *I* and *you* freely to narrow the distance between yourself and the subject and between yourself and the reader. But in the most objective, impersonal description, you will use *one* ("One can see the summit") or avoid self-reference altogether in order to appear distant from and unbiased toward the subject.

Once you establish a physical and psychological point of view, readers come to depend on it. Thus a sudden and inexplicable shift from one view to another—zooming in from fifteen miles away to the foot of a mountain, abandoning *I* for the more removed *one*—can disorient readers and distract them from the dominant impression you are trying to create.

DEVELOPING A DESCRIPTIVE ESSAY

Getting Started

The subject for a descriptive essay may be any object, place, person, or state of mind that you have observed closely enough or experienced sharply enough to invest with special significance. A chair, a tree, a room, a shopping mall, a movie actor, a passerby on the street, a feeling of fear, a sense of achievement—anything you have a strong impression of can prompt effective description.

Observe your subject directly, if possible, or recall it as completely as you can. Jot down the details that seem to contribute most to the impression you're trying to convey. You needn't write the description of them yet—that can wait for drafting—but you do want to capture the possibilities in your subject.

You should start to consider the needs and expectations of your readers early on. If the subject is something readers have never seen or felt before, you will need enough objective details to create a complete picture in their minds. A description of a friend, for example, might focus on his distinctive voice and laugh, but readers will also want to know something about his appearance. If the subject is essentially abstract, like an emotion, you will need details to make it concrete for readers. And if the subject is familiar to readers, as a local shopping mall or an old spruce tree on campus probably would be, you will want to skip obvious objective information in favor of fresh observations that will make readers see the subject anew.

Forming a Thesis

When you have your subject, specify in a sentence the impression that you want to create for readers. The sentence will help keep you on track while you search for the sensory details that will make your description concrete and vivid. It should evoke a quality or an atmosphere or an effect, as these examples do:

> His fierce anger at the world shows in every word and gesture.

> The mall is a thoroughly unnatural place, like a space station in a science-fiction movie.

Such a sentence can serve as the thesis of your essay. You don't necessarily need to state it outright in your draft; sometimes you may prefer to let the details build to a conclusion. But the thesis should hover over the essay nonetheless, governing the selection of every detail and making itself as clear to readers as if it were stated.

Organizing

Though the details of a subject may not occur to you in any particular order, you should arrange them so that readers are not confused by your shifts among features. You can give readers a sense of the whole subject in the introduction to the essay: objective details of location or size or shape, the incident leading to a state of mind, or the reasons for describing a familiar object. In the introduction, also, you may want to state your thesis—the dominant impression you will create.

The organization of the body of the essay depends partly on point of view and partly on dominant impression. If you take a moving point of view—say, strolling down a city street—the details will probably arrange themselves naturally. But a fixed point of view, scanning a subject from one position, requires your intervention. When the subject is a landscape, a person, or an object, you'll probably want to use a spatial organization: near to far, top to bottom, left to right, or vice versa. Other subjects, such as a shopping mall, might be better treated in groups of features: shoppers, main concourses, insides of stores. Or a description of an emotional state might follow the chronological sequence of the event that aroused it (thus overlapping description and narration, the subject of the next chapter). The order itself is not important, as long as there is an order that channels readers' attention.

Drafting

The challenge of drafting your description will be bringing the subject to life. Whether it is in front of you or in your mind, you may find it helpful to consider the subject one sense at a time—what you can see, hear, smell, touch, taste. Of course, not all senses will be applicable to all subjects; a chair, for instance, may not have a noticeable odor, and you're unlikely to know its taste. But proceeding sense by sense can help you uncover details—such as the smell of a tree or the sound of a person's voice—that you may have overlooked.

Examining one sense at a time is also one of the best ways to conceive of concrete words and figures of speech to represent sensations and feelings. For instance, does *acid* describe the taste of fear? Does an actor's appearance suggest the smell of soap? Does a shopping mall smell like new dollar bills? In creating distinct physical sensations for readers, such representations make meaning inescapably clear.

Revising and Editing

When you are ready to revise and edit, use the following questions as a guide.

- *Have you in fact created the dominant impression you intended to create?* Check that you have plenty of specific details and that each one helps to pin down one crucial feature of your subject. Delete irrelevant details that may have crept in. What counts is not the number of details but their quality and the strength of the impression they make.
- *Are your point of view and organization clear and consistent?* Watch for confusing shifts from one vantage point or organizational scheme to another. Watch also for confusing and unnecessary shifts in pronouns, such as from *I* to *one* or vice versa. Any shifts in point of view or organization should be

clearly essential for your purpose and for the impression you want to create.

- *Have you used the most specific, concrete language you can muster?* Keep a sharp eye out for vague words like *delicious, handsome, loud,* and *short* that force readers to create their own impressions, or worse, leave them with no impression at all. Use details that call on readers' sensory experiences, say why delicious or why handsome, how loud or how short. At the same time, cut or change fancy language that simply calls attention to itself without adding to your meaning.

E. B. WHITE

With an infallible ear for language and a keen eye for detail, Elwyn Brooks White earned a place among America's finest writers. White was born in 1899 in Mount Vernon, New York, where he also grew up. After graduating from Cornell University in 1921, he traveled for a time in the West before heading back to settle in Manhattan. In 1927 he joined the staff of the New Yorker, *which was a little over a year old, and for decades his contributions of essays, poems, editorials, and cartoon captions helped shape the magazine. With his wife, Katharine Sergeant White (herself an influential* New Yorker *editor), and their son, Joel, White moved in 1938 to Maine, where he took up farming and animal husbandry while continuing to write. Among his nineteen books are many essay collections; three works for children, including the classic* Charlotte's Web *(1952); and* The Elements of Style *(50th anniversary ed., 2008), his revision of the composition textbook he used at Cornell, by his teacher William Strunk, Jr. In his last decade, White published his* Letters *(1976),* Essays *(1977), and* Poems and Sketches *(1981), and he edited a collection of Katharine White's essays on gardening, published two years after her death in 1977. White died in 1985 on the Maine farm they had shared.*

Once More to the Lake

Probably White's best-known essay, "Once More to the Lake" was written in 1941 and collected in One Man's Meat *(1944) along with White's other contributions to* Harper's Magazine. *Mingling past and present, reflection and observation, poetic images, and spoken rhythms, the essay describes White's visit to a scene of his boyhood, a place "linking the generations in a strong indestructible chain."*

One summer, along about 1904, my father rented a camp on 1
a lake in Maine and took us all there for the month of August.
We all got ringworm from some kittens and had to rub Pond's

Extract on our arms and legs night and morning, and my father rolled over in a canoe with all his clothes on; but outside of that the vacation was a success and from then on none of us ever thought there was any place in the world like that lake in Maine. We returned summer after summer—always on August 1 for one month. I have since become a salt-water man, but sometimes in summer there are days when the restlessness of the tides and the fearful cold of the sea water and the incessant wind that blows across the afternoon and into the evening make me wish for the placidity of a lake in the woods. A few weeks ago this feeling got so strong I bought myself a couple of bass hooks and a spinner and returned to the lake where we used to go, for a week's fishing and to revisit old haunts.

I took along my son, who had never had any fresh water up his 2 nose and who had seen lily pads only from train windows. On the journey over to the lake I began to wonder what it would be like. I wondered how time would have marred this unique, this holy spot—the coves and streams, the hills that the sun set behind, the camps and the paths behind the camps. I was sure that the tarred road would have found it out, and I wondered in what other ways it would be desolated. It is strange how much you can remember about places like that once you allow your mind to return into the grooves that lead back. You remember one thing, and that suddenly reminds you of another thing. I guess I remembered clearest of all the early mornings, when the lake was cool and motionless, remembered how the bedroom smelled of the lumber it was made of and of the wet woods whose scent entered through the screen. The partitions in the camp were thin and did not extend clear to the top of the rooms, and as I was always the first up I would dress softly so as not to wake the others, and sneak out into the sweet outdoors and start out in the canoe, keeping close along the shore in the long shadows of the pines. I remembered being very careful never to rub my paddle against the gunwale for fear of disturbing the stillness of the cathedral.

The lake had never been what you would call a wild lake. 3 There were cottages sprinkled around the shores, and it was in farming country although the shores of the lake were quite heavily wooded. Some of the cottages were owned by nearby farmers, and you would live at the shore and eat your meals at the farmhouse. That's what our family did. But although it wasn't wild, it was a fairly large and undisturbed lake and there were places in it that, to a child at least, seemed infinitely remote and primeval.

I was right about the tar: it led to within half a mile of the 4 shore. But when I got back there, with my boy, and we settled into a camp near a farmhouse and into the kind of summertime I had known, I could tell it was going to be pretty much the same as it had been before—I knew it, lying in bed the first morning, smelling the bedroom and hearing the boy sneak quietly out and go off along the shore in a boat. I began to sustain the illusion that he was I, and therefore, by simple transposition, that I was my father. This sensation persisted, kept cropping up all the time we were there. It was not an entirely new feeling, but in this setting it grew much stronger. I seemed to be living a dual existence. I would be in the middle of some simple act, I would be picking up a bait box or laying down a table fork, or I would be saying something, and suddenly it would be not I but my father who was saying the words or making the gesture. It gave me a creepy sensation.

We went fishing the first morning. I felt the same damp moss 5 covering the worms in the bait can, and saw the dragonfly alight on the tip of my rod as it hovered a few inches from the surface of the water. It was the arrival of this fly that convinced me beyond any doubt that everything was as it always had been, that the years were a mirage and that there had been no years. The small waves were the same, chucking the rowboat under the chin as we fished at anchor, and the boat was the same boat, the same color green and the ribs broken in the same places, and under the floorboards the same freshwater leavings and débris—the dead helgramite, the wisps of moss, the rusty discarded fishhook, the dried blood from yesterday's catch. We stared silently at the tips of our rods, at the dragonflies that came and went. I lowered the tip of mine into the water, tentatively, pensively dislodging the fly, which darted two feet away, posed, darted two feet back, and came to rest again a little farther up the rod. There had been no years between the ducking of this dragonfly and the other one—the one that was part of memory. I looked at the boy, who was silently watching his fly, and it was my hands that held his rod, my eyes watching. I felt dizzy and didn't know which rod I was at the end of.

We caught two bass, hauling them in briskly as though they [6]
were mackerel, pulling them over the side of the boat in a busi-
nesslike manner without any landing net, and stunning them
with a blow on the back of the head. When we got back for a
swim before lunch, the lake was exactly where we had left it, the
same number of inches from the dock, and there was only the
merest suggestion of a breeze. This seemed an utterly enchanted
sea, this lake you could leave to its own devices for a few hours
and come back to, and find that it had not stirred, this constant
and trustworthy body of water. In the shallows, the dark, water-
soaked sticks and twigs, smooth and old, were undulating in clus-
ters on the bottom against the clean ribbed sand, and the track of
the mussel was plain. A school of minnows swam by, each min-
now with its small individual shadow, doubling the attendance,
so clear and sharp in the sunlight. Some of the other campers
were in swimming, along the shore, one of them with a cake of
soap, and the water felt thin and clear and unsubstantial. Over
the years there had been this person with the cake of soap, this
cultist, and here he was. There had been no years.

Up to the farmhouse to dinner through the teeming, dusty [7]
field, the road under our sneakers was only a two-track road. The
middle track was missing, the one with the marks of the hooves
and the splotches of dried, flaky manure. There had always been
three tracks to choose from in choosing which track to walk
in; now the choice was narrowed down to two. For a moment I
missed terribly the middle alternative. But the way led past the
tennis court, and something about the way it lay there in the sun
reassured me; the tape had loosened along the backline, the alleys
were green with plantains and other weeds, and the net (installed
in June and removed in September) sagged in the dry noon, and
the whole place steamed with midday heat and hunger and emp-
tiness. There was a choice of pie for dessert, and one was blue-
berry and one was apple, and the waitresses were the same country girls, there having been no passage of time, only the illusion of
it as in a dropped curtain—the waitresses were still fifteen; their
hair had been washed, that was the only difference—they had
been to the movies and seen the pretty girls with the clean hair.

Summertime, oh, summertime, pattern of life indelible, the [8]
fadeproof lake, the woods unshatterable, the pasture with the
sweetfern and the juniper forever and ever, summer without end;

this was the background, and the life along the shore was the design, the cottagers with their innocent and tranquil design, their tiny docks with the flagpole and the American flag floating against the white clouds in the blue sky, the little paths over the roots of the trees leading from camp to camp and the paths leading back to the outhouses and the can of lime for sprinkling, and at the souvenir counters at the store the miniature birchbark canoes and the postcards that showed things looking a little better than they looked. This was the American family at play, escaping the city heat, wondering whether the newcomers in the camp at the head of the cove were "common" or "nice," wondering whether it was true that the people who drove up for Sunday dinner at the farmhouse were turned away because there wasn't enough chicken.

It seemed to me, as I kept remembering all this, that those 9 times and those summers had been infinitely precious and worth saving. There had been jollity and peace and goodness. The arriving (at the beginning of August) had been so big a business in itself, at the railway station the farm wagon drawn up, the first smell of the pine-laden air, the first glimpse of the smiling farmer, and the great importance of the trunks and your father's enormous authority in such matters, and the feel of the wagon under you for the long ten-mile haul, and at the top of the last long hill catching the first view of the lake after eleven months of not seeing this cherished body of water. The shouts and cries of the other campers when they saw you, and the trunks to be unpacked, to give up their rich burden. (Arriving was less exciting nowadays, when you sneaked up in your car and parked it under a tree near the camp and took out the bags and in five minutes it was all over, no fuss, no loud wonderful fuss about trunks.)

Peace and goodness and jollity. The only thing that was 10 wrong now, really, was the sound of the place, an unfamiliar nervous sound of the outboard motors. This was the note that jarred, the one thing that would sometimes break the illusion and set the years moving. In those other summertimes all motors were inboard; and when they were at a little distance, the noise they made was a sedative, an ingredient of summer sleep. They made one-cylinder and two-cylinder engines, and some were make-and-break and some were jump-spark, but they all made a sleepy sound across the lake. The one-lungers throbbed and fluttered, and the twin-cylinder ones purred and purred, and that was a quiet sound, too. But now the campers all had outboards. In the daytime, in the hot mornings, these motors made a petulant, irritable sound; at night, in the still evening when the afterglow lit the water, they whined about one's ears like mosquitoes. My boy loved our rented outboard, and his great desire was to achieve single-handed mastery over it, and authority, and he soon learned the trick of choking it a little (but not too much), and the adjustment of the needle valve. Watching him I would remember the things you could do with the old one-cylinder engine with the heavy flywheel, how you could have it eating out of your hand if you got really close to it spiritually. Motorboats in those days didn't have clutches, and you would make a landing by shutting off the motor at the proper time and coasting in with a dead rudder. But there was a way of reversing them, if you learned the trick, by cutting the switch and putting it on again exactly on the final dying revolution of the flywheel, so that it would kick back against compression and begin reversing. Approaching a dock in a strong following breeze, it was difficult to slow up sufficiently by the ordinary coasting method, and if a boy felt he had complete mastery over his motor, he was tempted to keep it running beyond its time and then reverse it a few feet from the dock. It took a cool nerve, because if you threw the switch a twentieth of a second too soon you would catch the flywheel when it still had speed enough to go up past center, and the boat would leap ahead, charging bull-fashion at the dock.

We had a good week at the camp. The bass were biting well and the sun shone endlessly, day after day. We would be tired at night and lie down in the accumulated heat of the little bedrooms after the long hot day and the breeze would stir almost imperceptibly outside and the smell of the swamp drift in through the rusty screens. Sleep would come easily and in the morning the red squirrel would be on the roof, tapping out his gay routine. I kept remembering everything, lying in bed in the mornings — the small steamboat that had a long rounded stern like the lip of a Ubangi, and how quietly she ran on the moonlight sails, when the older boys played their mandolins and the girls sang and we ate doughnuts dipped in sugar, and how sweet the music was on the water in the shining night, and what it had felt like to think about girls then. After breakfast we would go up to the store and the things were in the same place—the minnows in a bottle, the plugs and spinners disarranged and pawed over by the youngsters from the boys' camp, the Fig Newtons and the Beeman's gum. Outside, the road was tarred and cars stood in front of the store. Inside, all was just as it had always been, except there was more Coca-Cola and not so much Moxie and root beer and birch beer and sarsaparilla. We would walk out with the bottle of pop apiece and sometimes the pop would backfire up our noses and hurt. We explored the streams, quietly, where the turtles slid off the sunny logs and dug their way into the soft bottom; and we lay on the town wharf and fed worms to the tame bass. Everywhere we went I had trouble making out which was I, the one walking at my side, the one walking in my pants.

One afternoon while we were there at the lake a thunder- 12 storm came up. It was like the revival of an old melodrama that I had seen long ago with childish awe. The second-act climax of the drama of the electrical disturbance over a lake in America had not changed in any important respect. This was the big scene, still the big scene. The whole thing was so familiar, the first feeling of oppression and heat and a general air around camp of not wanting to go very far away. In midafternoon (it was all the same) a curious darkening of the sky, and a lull in everything that had made life tick; and then the way the boats suddenly swung the other way at their moorings with the coming of a breeze out of the new quarter, and the premonitory rumble. Then the kettle drum, then the snare, then the bass drum and cymbals, then crackling light against the dark, and the gods grinning and licking their chops in the hills. Afterward the calm, the rain steadily rustling in the calm lake, the return of light and hope and spirits, and the campers running out in joy and relief to go swimming in the rain, their bright cries perpetuating the deathless joke about how they were getting simply drenched, and the children screaming with delight at the new sensation of bathing in the rain, and the joke about getting drenched linking the generations in a strong indestructible chain. And the comedian who waded in carrying an umbrella.

When the others went swimming, my son said he was going 13
in, too. He pulled his dripping trunks from the line where they
had hung all through the shower and wrung them out. Languidly,
and with no thought of going in, I watched him, his hard little
body, skinny and bare, saw him wince slightly as he pulled up
around his vitals the small, soggy, icy garment. As he buckled the
swollen belt, suddenly my groin felt the chill of death.

Meaning

1. The main idea of White's essay is fully revealed only in the last paragraph. What is this idea? Why, after White had identified so closely
with his son, reliving his own boyhood, does he suddenly feel the
"chill of death"?

2. In the opening paragraph White mentions that he sought escape
from "the restlessness of the tides and the fearful cold of the sea water and the incessant wind" to the "placidity of a lake in the woods."
His escape seems complete but for the "creepy sensation" (paragraph 4) and the "dizzy" feeling (5) accompanying the illusion that
time has stood still since his boyhood. What causes these uneasy
feelings, and how do they relate to the main idea of the essay?

3. Why do you think it disturbs White momentarily that the road offers only two tracks to choose from, not the three of his boyhood
(paragraph 7)? How does this observation relate to the main idea of
the essay?

Purpose and Audience

1. Do you think White's purpose is solely to express his feelings, or does
he want to explain something as well? If so, what does he want to
explain?

2. To what extent does White seem to consider readers unlike himself — say, young adults with no children and no experience of lake-
side vacations? Does he succeed in making you identify with the perceptions and feelings prompted by his experience? What details or
passages do you find particularly effective or ineffective, and why?

3. Why do you think White devotes such detail to boat handling (paragraph 10)? In answering, consider especially the significance of the
idea of getting "really close to [the boat] spiritually," the many undefined boating terms, and the context of comparison between inboard
and outboard motors and between his son's experiences and his own.

Method and Structure

1. Why do you think White chose mainly subjective description to explore the themes of this essay? Would objective description have the same effect? Why, or why not?

2. Locate the many flashbacks in which White remembers being a boy at the lake. (See p. 63 for an explanation of *flashback*.) What events in the present trigger these flashbacks? Note that in some passages (paragraph 8, for instance) the time is neither clearly present nor clearly past. Why?

3. OTHER METHODS   Though primarily a descriptive essay, "Once More to the Lake" is also developed by narration and by comparison and contrast. Locate examples of both methods just in paragraph 12, and analyze what they contribute to the essay as a whole.

Language

1. How would you characterize White's tone? What, for example, is the effect of "holy," "sweet," and "cathedral" (paragraph 2), "sleepy" (10), and similar words throughout the essay? (If necessary, see *tone* in the Glossary.)

2. White's sense that time has stood still is repeated or restated many times throughout the essay—not only explicitly, as in "There had been no years" (paragraph 5), but also in single words, such as "indelible" (8). Locate both the restatements and the single words in paragraphs 4–11. How does White intensify this theme in his description of the oncoming storm (12)? How do the figures of speech in the description of the storm and the lingering over the "deathless joke" forecast the essay's last sentence? (If necessary, consult the Glossary for *figures of speech*.)

Writing Topics

1. Think of a situation in which you observed a child undergoing an experience or making a decision that recalls your own childhood. (The child may be a brother, sister, son, daughter, cousin, neighbor, or even a stranger.) Write a narrative essay linking your observations with your memories, making sure that you lead the reader to see the insights you gained.

2. Recall a time when you accompanied a parent or other adult (aunt, uncle, grandparent, and so on) to a place he or she knew well but you were seeing for the first time. It could be a place where the person grew up, went to school, lived for a time, or vacationed. Write an essay in which you compare your reactions to the place with what you remember of the adult's reactions or what, with hindsight, you think the adult's reactions might have been.

WILLIAM LEAST HEAT-MOON

In his extensive sojourns across the United States travel writer William Least Heat-Moon has attended closely to the distinctive people and places he has encountered in small towns and little-known byways. Born William Lewis Trogdon in 1939 in Kansas City, Missouri, to parents of Irish-English and Osage extraction, he changed his name to Least Heat-Moon to honor his Native American background. After graduating from the University of Missouri at Columbia in 1961, he stayed on to earn a PhD in literature and a BA in photojournalism. He has contributed narratives of his journeys to many periodicals, including the Atlantic, Esquire, *the* New Yorker, *the* New York Times, *and* Whole Earth Review. *Heat-Moon is best known, however, for his meticulously researched travelogues:* Blue Highways *(1982),* Prairy-Erth *(1991),* This Land Is Your Land *(1997),* River-Horse *(1999), and most recently* Roads to Quoz *(2008). When he's not meandering about the country, Heat-Moon makes his home in Columbia, Missouri.*

Dance of the Hobs

In Roads to Quoz *Heat-Moon chronicles the sixteen-thousand-mile quest he and his wife, "Q," made in search of American "quoz," an archaic term for "anything strange, incongruous, or peculiar." They found one such instance in the Quapaw Ghost Light—a legendary apparition that reportedly floats above a valley at the border of Missouri and Oklahoma. In this essay, adapted from a chapter of the same name, he describes the exhilaration of doubting one's own eyes.*

Perhaps somewhere in Missouri or Oklahoma exists a local 1 newspaper or magazine never to have carried an item about the Quapaw Light, more commonly known in the old mining area as the Hornet Spook Light. Reports, both in print and from people I spoke to, claimed the phantasm sometimes appeared briefly or not at all, and on other occasions would shine till dawn. Generally, it had a constancy rather alien in the realm of ghosts. "It's reliable enough, especially on cloudy nights," a librarian told me, "and I never heard of it harming anybody, unless scaring the dickens out of you is harmful—you know, out there in the dark, getting a whack put on your ticker."

In both Jasper and Ottawa counties, I came upon nobody 2 unaware of the thing, about half saying they'd seen it, and most of them believing it not yet properly explained by science. But one fellow, ignoring the many photographs of it, called it "the Hornet Spoof Light." I asked had he seen it, and he replied, "How does a sane person see what isn't there?"

Based upon no physical evidence except declarations written 3 and spoken, and in spite of the sanity question, I still believed in the possibility of something spectral: not a specter perhaps but maybe a manifestation of a spectrum out on the wooded slope above the Spring River on the western edge of the Ozark Plateau. I further believed Q and I would encounter nothing, yet we nevertheless went forth, interested not so much in debunking as merely observing. We headed south as the sky was clearing just enough to reveal a frail, crescent moon setting beyond the prairie of eastern Oklahoma. The Devil's Promenade was a wooded vale dropping down to the Spring River to the west. The lane was less forested than formerly but yet woodsy and remote enough, despite a couple of tumbledown dwellings and a farm near the river, to create good darkness for a light show. Still, steady electrification had recently caused a few visitors—those managing to find the proper lane—to watch some electrical radiant and entirely miss the Ghost Light. Or so we were told.

The customary accounts concurred on the phenomenon ear- 4 lier appearing in another location not far distant, but for the past half century it had taken its shine to E-50. "She jiggles around a little, but she don't go straggling across the county," said an old fellow tottering through the library. "She's a homebody. You just got to sit real quiet like you was in Granny's parlor."

At Halloween, he'd often known the road to be lined with 5 cars, but on the March evening Q and I drove to the hollow, no one else was around, and our expectation was tempered only by a sense we'd not be lucky enough to glimpse the whatever. I rolled us along slowly over the new asphalt running as straight west as a surveyor's transit can lay a lane down, the engineered perfection having relief only in its rise and fall over low hills of blackjack oaks. Melodious calls of toads roused the darkness, and the damp air smelled of spring.

Right after we crossed the Missouri line and entered the 6 Promenade, a small light appeared in the distance on the left of the road. My anticipation apparently got the better of me, and I blurted out something to which Q said, "You're seeing some kind of vehicle way ahead of us," and a pickup did pass by soon after. I pulled to the side, shut off the engine, got out of the car. In a darkness so deep I could see down only to my knees, I began walking as if I were wading the night. When I returned, my sudden emergence from the thick obscurity caused Q to jump.

In a whisper, as if the Powers of Spectral Illumination have 7 ears, she asked for explanations I'd read that afternoon: ball lightning, will-o'-the-wisp, marsh gas, mine gas, fox fire, Saint Elmo's fire, sunspots, glowing minerals, static electricity, ionized plasma; headlights from automobiles, billboards, a water tower, a landing field, a farm; and, of course, those ectoplasmic souls in search of craniums — theirs or yours.[1]

Thirty minutes passed, and no emanation of any sort appeared, 8 so I drove back eastward to a higher spot with a longer view. A van had arrived, with four intent faces staring into the west. I stopped far enough away not to block their view, then walked to them. A woman of middle years and three teenage girls glanced at me only to ascertain I was possessed of a more or less standard head lacking any luminescence and in the accustomed location.

Had they seen it? Without looking my way, the woman mur- 9 mured slowly, uneasily, "It's there right now."

I turned to the west. Blackness. Soot, pitch, ebony, the inside 10 of a crow. Otherwise, zilch. She whispered, eyes still fixed forward, "In thirty years, this is the best I've ever seen it." I looked again. Nothing. Spoof Light.

[1]In an earlier part of *Roads to Quoz* Heat-Moon explains that local legends about the light include "yarns of a vicious, captured Civil War sergeant — vengefully decapitated by being stood in front of a cannon — who spends eternity hunting his head; of a lady walking moonless nights with a ball of fire where her noddle should be; of a miner following his shaking carbide lamp in quest of a lost you-name-it." [Editors' note.]

Then, as if I'd suddenly regained lost vision, the dark got 11
punctured—a white-hot poker thrust through a black tent. The
whiteness rose above the distant road, waxed brighter, dimmed,
then again brighter, its edge tinged blood-red. A not-of-this-Earth
gleaming seemed to float a mile or two away, slightly shifting lat-
erally, like an animal moving its head side to side as it fixes on its
quarry. Great Caesar's Ghost!

I was at last seeing the Quapaw Light! I started off down the 12
black road to tell Q, but I couldn't keep from turning around to
assure that nothing was coming up from behind. Holy Willie! A
Nodgort[2] had found a crack in my rationality, and the pesky hob
was dancing, mocking. I forced myself to stand still for a moment
to prove reason yet prevailed, even if a bit equivocally. *There,*
I thought, *that's a moment, that's enough.* But I had to restrain
an impulse to quickstep back to the safety of the car. (Oh, reader,
do you shake your head? Well, consider this: A jokester jumping
out of the scrub at that moment could have put a whack on my
ticker.)

"What's wrong?" Q asked, and I nodded westward, and she 13
looked that way. "What am I supposed to be seeing?" The road
was black again. "I don't see any—oh! Is that it?" It was it: wax-
ing, pendulating, waning, throwing out a bubble of redness, sucking it back in, vanishing only to show itself again, making a tiny
zig to set up a zag.

The thing glimmered and shimmered, twinkled and blinked, 14
flickered and fluttered, glistened and winked. We stared so long I
began to believe our eyes were playing tricks, so we corroborated
what the little dazzler was doing: Tell me what you're seeing, I
said, and Q answered, "It just moved left." Yes. "Coming back the
other way." Yes. "Getting reddish again." Yep. "Oops, just disappeared—no, it's back—and brighter." Exactly.

It was doing the pixy peekaboo. "The thing's playful," Q said. 15
"No wonder people are fond of it—it's a Tinker Bell." In my
satanic voice I rasped, No, my pretty—mistake not a tool of the
Devil. Then, changing to a falsetto, I repeated the librarian's wise-
crack: "Around here, we take it lightly."

Spooky, as it's sometimes called, resembled an evening star 16
low in the sky on a clear night, but it upended astrophysics in

---

[2]"Trogdon," the author's former last name, spelled backward. [Editors' note.]

its shifting from a red dwarf to a white giant, although it was never bigger than a bright planet seen with moderate-power binoculars.

A farm truck came from behind and passed, and we watched 17 to see whether it would spook the Light, but the globe bravely continued its performance. I started the engine and went slowly forward to get closer; I was an infant reaching out to touch the first star he ever sees. At our approach, the gleaming kept its distance as does a rainbow or mirage, then it winked out. We turned around to go back to where we'd been, and again there it was, hanging above the lane. If we couldn't close the distance on it, then that eliminated explanations like will-o'-the-wisp or lights from a tower—anything with a fixed location. Q: "It's not a figment of the imagination. It's actually there—or somewhere. Something's somewhere. It's real as a rainbow. Maybe not as beautiful, but a lot more lively."

We gaped at it for nearly two hours because it was what we 18 had wanted to find: an authentic optical phenomenon reportedly unexplained by science. A merry spectral puzzle. Observing it was like stepping back into the Dark Ages when nature was full of phantasmagoria, when mysteries overwhelmed explications and ignorance transcended illumination, a time when superstition could extinguish enlightenment, when priestly obfuscations manipulated folk into blind faiths where charms and potions, spells and incantations, holy relics and amulets, were defenses against hobgoblins going thumpity-bump in the night or rising in the woods to flicker their mischief.

The Light was less spectacular than suggested by the most 19 fanciful claims, so much so that had someone not initially observed it prior to the electrification of the county, the phenomenon might not be noticed today. In fact, when we arrived, I *had* seen it, only to be convinced by Q that it was a moving vehicle. As we were leaving, she said, "It's my first UFO," adding before I could cavil, "Unexplained Flickering Orb."

The Quapaw Ghost Light is remarkable but not incredible, 20 modest but worth its myth, possessed of the power of the peculiar, and among the many phantasms of the Ozarks, Spooky is one of the few to come forth predictably and allow examination. You can't hear, touch, smell, or taste it, but you can't doubt seeing it if your patience allows.

Meaning

1. Why is Heat-Moon fascinated by the idea of the Quapaw Light? What does it represent to him?
2. What does Heat-Moon mean when he says he hoped to see "not a specter perhaps but maybe a manifestation of a spectrum" (paragraph 3)?
3. Does "Dance of the Hobs" have a thesis? What is Heat-Moon's point?

Purpose and Audience

1. How would you describe Heat-Moon's purpose in this essay?
2. What do you think the light looks like, based on Heat-Moon's description? What dominant impression of the phenomenon does he create?
3. Does Heat-Moon assume that his readers believe in ghosts and apparitions, or does he expect that they will be skeptical? How does he ensure that readers won't write him off as crazy?

Method and Structure

1. In paragraph 3 Heat-Moon says that he was "interested not so much in debunking as merely observing," suggesting that he will describe his experience with the objectivity of a scientist. Is this, in fact, what he does? Would you say that his description is mainly objective or subjective? Why?
2. Point to a few sentences in the essay that make particularly effective use of concrete details and figures of speech to describe Heat-Moon's experience of searching for and seeing the light. (If necessary, see the Glossary for a definition of *figures of speech*.)
3. In his first paragraph, Heat-Moon quotes a librarian, who warns of "getting a whack put on your ticker." What does that mean? Where in his essay does Heat-Moon return to this notion, and what is the effect of the repetition?
4. OTHER METHODS "Dance of the Hobs" is as much narration as it is description. How does Heat-Moon use dialogue to structure his story and add interest?

Language

1. How would you describe Heat-Moon's diction? What does his language contribute to the overall effectiveness of his essay? (For a definition of *diction*, see the Glossary.)

2. Why do you suppose Heat-Moon chose to capitalize "Powers of Spectral Illumination" (paragraph 7) and "Light" (19)?

3. What is the effect of the first sentence of paragraph 14?

Writing Topics

1. Every region of the United States has its share of mysteries and urban legends like the flickering orb Heat-Moon seeks out: gravity hills, hitchhiking ghosts, buried treasures, and so forth. Explore the function of such folklore. Where do legends come from? What purpose do they serve in contemporary American culture? How do they compare to other forms of mythology?

2. Answer the question posed by Heat-Moon's informant in paragraph 2: "How does a sane person see what isn't there?" Have you ever seen something you couldn't explain? In an essay, consider how expectation and context might shape a person's perception of reality. Draw on Heat-Moon's experience as well as your own.

3. Although a nonfiction essay, "Dance of the Hobs" is told like a ghost story. Analyze how Heat-Moon crafts his tale. How does he move from one stage of his quest to the next? Does the story seem to build in a particular way? What strategies does the author use to build suspense?

JOAN DIDION

One of America's leading nonfiction writers, Joan Didion consistently applies a journalist's eye for detail and a terse, understated style to the cultural dislocation pervading modern American society. She was born in 1934 in Sacramento, a fifth-generation Californian, and graduated from the University of California at Berkeley in 1956. Her essays have been collected in Slouching Towards Bethlehem *(1968),* The White Album *(1979),* Salvador *(1983),* Essays and Conversations *(1984),* Miami *(1987),* After Henry *(1992),* Political Fictions *(2001),* Fixed Ideas: America Since 9.11 *(2003), and* We Tell Ourselves Stories in Order to Live *(2006). Didion has published five novels:* Run River *(1963),* Play It As It Lays *(1970),* A Book of Common Prayer *(1977),* Democracy *(1984), and* The Last Thing He Wanted *(1996). With her husband, the writer John Gregory Dunne, she wrote screenplays for movies, among them* Panic in Needle Park *(1971),* A Star Is Born *(1976),* True Confessions *(1981), and* Up Close and Personal *(1996). Didion's most recent books are memoirs of devastating loss:* The Year of Magical Thinking *(2005) recounts her emotional state in the wake of her husband's sudden death, and* Blue Nights *(2011) explores her feelings upon losing their daughter to an extended illness not long afterward.*

The Santa Ana

In describing the violent effects of a hot, dry wind on Los Angeles, Didion ranges typically outward from herself to the people figuring in local news reports. "The Santa Ana" first appeared in the Saturday Evening Post *in 1967 and later appeared as part of "Los Angeles Notebook," an essay collected in* Slouching Towards Bethlehem.

There is something uneasy in the Los Angeles air this after- 1
noon, some unnatural stillness, some tension. What it means is
that tonight a Santa Ana will begin to blow, a hot wind from the

northeast whining down through the Cajon and San Gorgonio Passes, blowing up sandstorms out along Route 66, drying the hills and the nerves to the flash point. For a few days now we will see smoke back in the canyons, and hear sirens in the night. I have neither heard nor read that a Santa Ana is due, but I know it, and almost everyone I have seen today knows it too. We know it because we feel it. The baby frets. The maid sulks. I rekindle a waning argument with the telephone company, then cut my losses and lie down, given over to whatever it is in the air. To live with the Santa Ana is to accept, consciously or unconsciously, a deeply mechanistic view of human behavior.

I recall being told, when I first moved to Los Angeles and was 2 living on an isolated beach, that the Indians would throw themselves into the sea when the bad wind blew. I could see why. The Pacific turned ominously glossy during a Santa Ana period, and one woke in the night troubled not only by the peacocks screaming in the olive trees but by the eerie absence of surf. The heat was surreal. The sky had a yellow cast, the kind of light sometimes called "earthquake weather." My only neighbor would not come out of her house for days, and there were no lights at night, and her husband roamed the place with a machete. One day he would tell me that he had heard a trespasser, the next a rattlesnake.

"On nights like that," Raymond Chandler[1] once wrote about 3 the Santa Ana, "every booze party ends in a fight. Meek little wives feel the edge of the carving knife and study their husbands' necks. Anything can happen." That was the kind of wind it was. I did not know then that there was any basis for the effect it had on all of us, but it turns out to be another of those cases in which science bears out folk wisdom. The Santa Ana, which is named for one of the canyons it rushes through, is a *foehn* wind, like the *foehn* of Austria and Switzerland and the *hamsin* of Israel. There are a number of persistent malevolent winds, perhaps the best known of which are the mistral of France and the Mediterranean sirocco, but a *foehn* wind has distinct characteristics: it occurs on the leeward slope of a mountain range and, although the air begins as a cold mass, it is warmed as it comes down the mountain and appears finally as a hot dry wind. Whenever

---

[1]Chandler (1888–1959) is best known for his detective novels featuring Philip Marlowe. [Editors' note.]

and wherever a *foehn* blows, doctors hear about headaches and nausea and allergies, about "nervousness," about "depression." In Los Angeles some teachers do not attempt to conduct formal classes during a Santa Ana, because the children become unmanageable. In Switzerland the suicide rate goes up during the *foehn*, and in the courts of some Swiss cantons the wind is considered a mitigating circumstance for crime. Surgeons are said to watch the wind, because blood does not clot normally during a *foehn*. A few years ago an Israeli physicist discovered that not only during such winds, but for the ten or twelve hours which precede them, the air carries an unusually high ratio of positive to negative ions. No one seems to know exactly why that should be; some talk about friction and others suggest solar disturbances. In any case the positive ions are there, and what an excess of positive ions does, in the simplest terms, is make people unhappy. One cannot get much more mechanistic than that.

Easterners commonly complain that there is no "weather" at 4 all in Southern California, that the days and the seasons slip by relentlessly, numbingly bland. That is quite misleading. In fact the climate is characterized by infrequent but violent extremes: two periods of torrential subtropical rains which continue for weeks and wash out the hills and send subdivisions sliding toward the sea; about twenty scattered days a year of the Santa Ana, which, with its incendiary dryness, invariably means fire. At the first prediction of a Santa Ana, the Forest Service flies men and equipment from northern California into the southern forests, and the Los Angeles Fire Department cancels its ordinary nonfirefighting routines. The Santa Ana caused Malibu to burn the way it did in 1956, and Bel Air in 1961, and Santa Barbara in 1964. In the winter of 1966–67 eleven men were killed fighting a Santa Ana fire that spread through the San Gabriel Mountains.

Just to watch the front-page news out of Los Angeles during 5 a Santa Ana is to get very close to what it is about the place. The longest single Santa Ana period in recent years was in 1957, and it lasted not the usual three or four days but fourteen days, from November 21 until December 4. On the first day 25,000 acres of the San Gabriel Mountains were burning, with gusts reaching 100 miles an hour. In town, the wind reached Force 12, or hurricane force, on the Beaufort Scale; oil derricks were toppled and people ordered off the downtown streets to avoid injury from flying objects. On November 22 the fire in the San Gabriels was out of control. On November 24 six people were killed in automobile accidents, and by the end of the week the Los Angeles *Times* was keeping a box score of traffic deaths. On November 26 a prominent Pasadena attorney, depressed about money, shot and killed his wife, their two sons, and himself. On November 27 a South Gate divorcée, twenty-two, was murdered and thrown from a moving car. On November 30 the San Gabriel fire was still out of control, and the wind in town was blowing eighty miles an hour. On the first day of December four people died violently, and on the third the wind began to break.

It is hard for people who have not lived in Los Angeles to 6 realize how radically the Santa Ana figures in the local imagination. The city burning is Los Angeles's deepest image of itself: Nathanael West perceived that, in *The Day of the Locust*; and at the time of the 1965 Watts riots what struck the imagination most indelibly were the fires.[2] For days one could drive the Harbor Freeway and see the city on fire, just as we had always known it would be in the end. Los Angeles weather is the weather of catastrophe, of apocalypse, and, just as the reliably long and bitter winters of New England determine the way life is lived there, so the violence and the unpredictability of the Santa Ana affect the entire quality of life in Los Angeles, accentuate its impermanence, its unreliability. The wind shows us how close to the edge we are.

Meaning

1. Does Didion describe purely for the sake of describing, or does she have a thesis she wants to convey? If so, where does she most explicitly state this thesis?

2. What is the dominant impression Didion creates of the Santa Ana wind? What effect does it have on residents of Los Angeles?

3. Explain what Didion means by a "mechanistic view of human behavior" (paragraph 1). What would the opposite of such a view of human behavior be?

4. How might Didion's last sentence have two meanings?

---

[2]*The Day of the Locust* (1939), a novel about Hollywood, ends in riot and fire. The August 1965 disturbances in the Watts neighborhood of Los Angeles resulted in millions of dollars in damage from fires. [Editors' note.]

Purpose and Audience

1. Why do you think Didion felt compelled to write about the Santa Ana? Consider whether she might have had a dual purpose.

2. What kind of audience is Didion writing for? Primarily people from Los Angeles? How do you know? Does Didion identify herself as an Angelina?

Method and Structure

1. Didion doesn't describe the Santa Ana wind itself as much as its effects. Why does she approach her subject this way? What effects does she focus on?

2. Didion alternates between passages of mostly objective and mostly subjective description. Trace this movement throughout the essay.

3. What is the function of the quotation from Raymond Chandler at the beginning of paragraph 3? How does it serve as a transition?

4. OTHER METHODS   The essay is full of examples of the wind's effects on human beings. How do these examples help Didion achieve her purpose?

Language

1. Note Didion's frequent use of the first person (*I* and *we*) and of the present tense. What does she achieve with this point of view?

2. What is the effect of the vivid imagery in paragraph 2? In what way is this imagery "surreal" (fantastic or dreamlike)?

Writing Topics

1. Using Didion's essay as a model, write a descriptive essay about something that annoys you, frightens you, or even causes you to come unhinged. Your subject could be a natural phenomenon, such as the one Didion describes, or something else: bumper-to-bumper traffic at rush hour, long lines at the department of motor vehicles or another government agency, lengthy automated voice-mail systems that come to dead ends. You may use examples from your own experience and observation, from experiences you have read or heard about, or, like Didion, from both sources.

2. Didion tries to explain the Santa Ana phenomenon scientifically in paragraph 3 as having something to do with an excess of positive ions in the air. But she admits that nobody knows why there are

more positive than negative ions or why that fact should translate into human unhappiness. To what extent do you think moods can be explained by science? Are emotions simply the by-products of brain chemistry, as some scientists would suggest? Write an essay, using description and narration, about someone you know (or know of) whose moods are affected by forces beyond his or her control. Be sure to include enough detail to create a vivid portrait for your readers.

3. Didion perceives the Santa Ana as a cultural phenomenon in Los Angeles that affects the attitudes, relationships, and activities of residents "just as the reliably long and bitter winters of New England determine the way life is lived there" (paragraph 6). Consider a place you know well and describe how some aspect of the climate or weather affects the culture, "the way life is lived," not only during a particular event or season but throughout the year.

JUDITH ORTIZ COFER

Judith Ortiz Cofer, who was born in Puerto Rico in 1952, is a writer and a professor of literature and writing at the University of Georgia in Athens. Her works include The Latin Deli *(1993),* The Meaning of Consuelo *(2003), and many other books of poems and stories. She has been anthologized in* The Best American Essays, The Norton Book of Women's Lives, The Pushcart Prize, *and the* O. Henry Prize Stories. *She received a PEN/Martha Albrand Special Citation in nonfiction for* Silent Dancing *(1990) as well as the Anisfield Wolf Book Award for* The Latin Deli. *She also coedited an anthology of essays,* Sleeping with One Eye Open: Women Writers and the Art of Survival *(1999). Cofer has received fellowships from the National Endowment for the Arts and the Witter Bynner Foundation for poetry. Her most recent books include the novel* If I Could Fly *(2011), the poetry collection* A Love Story Beginning in Spanish *(2005), and several works for young adults.*

Silent Dancing

Describing old home movies and fragments of dreams, Cofer re-creates her childhood in an immigrant family that moved from Puerto Rico to New Jersey when she was three years old. The essay was first published in the Georgia Review *and later appeared as the title essay in Cofer's collection* Silent Dancing.

We have a home movie of this party. Several times my mother and 1 *I have watched it together, and I have asked questions about the silent revelers coming in and out of focus. It is grainy and of short duration, but it's a great visual aid to my memory of life at that time. And it is in color—the only complete scene in color I can recall from those years.*

We lived in Puerto Rico until my brother was born in 1954. 2 Soon after, because of economic pressures on our growing family, my father joined the United States Navy. He was assigned to duty on a ship in Brooklyn Yard—a place of cement and steel that was to be his home base in the States until his retirement more than twenty years later. He left the Island first, alone, going to New York City and tracking down his uncle who lived with his family across the Hudson River in Paterson, New Jersey. There my father found a tiny apartment in a huge tenement that had once housed Jewish families but was just being taken over and transformed by Puerto Ricans, overflowing from New York City. In 1955 he sent for us. My mother was only twenty years old, I was not quite three, and my brother was a toddler when we arrived at El Building, as the place had been christened by its newest residents.

My memories of life in Paterson during those first few years 3 are all in shades of gray. Maybe I was too young to absorb vivid colors and details, or to discriminate between the slate blue of the winter sky and the darker hues of the snow-bearing clouds, but that single color washes over the whole period. The building we lived in was gray, as were the streets, filled with slush the first few months of my life there. The coat my father had bought for me was similar in color and too big; it sat heavily on my thin frame.

I do remember the way the heater pipes banged and rattled, 4 startling all of us out of sleep until we got so used to the sound that we automatically shut it out or raised our voices above the racket. The hiss from the valve punctuated my sleep (which has always been fitful) like a nonhuman presence in the room—a dragon sleeping at the entrance of my childhood. But the pipes were also a connection to all the other lives being lived around us. Having come from a house designed for a single family back in Puerto Rico—my mother's extended-family home—it was curious to know that strangers lived under our floor and above our heads, and that the heater pipe went through everyone's apartment. (My first spanking in Paterson came as a result of playing tunes on the pipes in my room to see if there would be an answer.) My mother was as new to this concept of beehive life as I was, but she had been given strict orders by my father to keep the doors locked, the noise down, ourselves to ourselves.

It seems that Father had learned some painful lessons about 5 prejudice while searching for an apartment in Paterson. Not until years later did I hear how much resistance he had encountered with landlords who were panicking at the influx of Latinos into a neighborhood that had been Jewish for a couple of generations. It made no difference that it was the American phenomenon of ethnic turnover which was changing the urban core of Paterson, and that the human flood could not be held back with an accusing finger.

"You Cuban?" one man had asked my father, pointing at 6 his name tag on the navy uniform—even though my father had the fair skin and light brown hair of his northern Spanish background, and the name Ortiz is as common in Puerto Rico as Johnson is in the United States.

"No," my father had answered, looking past the finger into 7 his adversary's angry eyes. "I'm Puerto Rican."

"Same shit." And the door closed. 8

My father could have passed as European, but we couldn't. 9 My brother and I both have our mother's black hair and olive skin, and so we lived in El Building and visited our great-uncle and his fair children on the next block. It was their private joke that they were the German branch of the family. Not many years later that area too would be mainly Puerto Rican. It was as if the heart of the city map were being gradually colored brown—*café con leche*[1] *brown. Our color.*

The movie opens with a sweep of the living room. It is "typical" 10 *immigrant Puerto Rican decor for the time: The sofa and chairs are square and hard-looking, upholstered in bright colors (blue and yellow in this instance) and covered with the transparent plastic that furniture salesmen then were so adept at convincing women to buy. The linoleum on the floor is light blue; where it had been subjected to spike heels, as it was in most places, there were dime-size indentations all over it that cannot be seen in this movie. The room is full of people dressed up: dark suits for the men, red dresses for the women. When I have asked my mother why most of the women are in red that night, she has shrugged and said, "I don't remember. Just a coincidence." She doesn't have my obsession for assigning symbolism to everything.*

[1]Spanish for "coffee with milk." [Editors' note.]

The three women in red sitting on the couch are my mother, 11
my eighteen-year-old cousin, and her brother's girlfriend. The novia[2]
is just up from the Island, which is apparent in her body language.
She sits up formally, her dress pulled over her knees. She is a pretty
girl, but her posture makes her look insecure, lost in her full-skirted
dress, which she has carefully tucked around her to make room for
my gorgeous cousin, her future sister-in-law. My cousin has grown
up in Paterson and is in her last year of high school. She doesn't
have a trace of what Puerto Ricans call la mancha *(literally, the*
stain: the mark of the new immigrant—something about the pos-
ture, the voice, or the humble demeanor that makes it obvious to
everyone the person has just arrived on the mainland). My cousin is
wearing a tight, sequined, cocktail dress. Her brown hair has been
lightened with peroxide around the bangs, and she is holding a ciga-
rette expertly between her fingers, bringing it up to her mouth in a
sensuous arc of her arm as she talks animatedly. My mother, who
has come up to sit between the two women, both only a few years
younger than herself, is somewhere between the poles they represent
in our culture.

It became my father's obsession to get out of the barrio, and 12
thus we were never permitted to form bonds with the place or
with the people who lived there. Yet El Building was a comfort
to my mother, who never got over yearning for *la isla.*[3] She felt
surrounded by her language: The walls were thin, and voices
speaking and arguing in Spanish could be heard all day. *Salsas*
blasted out of radios, turned on early in the morning and left on
for company. Women seemed to cook rice and beans perpetu-
ally—the strong aroma of boiling red kidney beans permeated
the hallways.

Though Father preferred that we do our grocery shopping 13
at the supermarket when he came home on weekend leaves, my
mother insisted that she could cook only with products whose
labels she could read. Consequently, during the week I accompanied her and my little brother to La Bodega—a hole-in-the-wall
grocery store across the street from El Building. There we squeezed
down three narrow aisles jammed with various products. Goya

[2]Fiancée, or a girl just arrived from Puerto Rico. [Editors' note.]
[3]The island. [Editors' note.]

and Libby's—those were the trademarks that were trusted by her *mamá*, so my mother bought many cans of Goya beans, soups, and condiments, as well as little cans of Libby's fruit juices for us. And she also bought Colgate toothpaste and Palmolive soap. (The final *e* is pronounced in both these products in Spanish, so for many years I believed that they were manufactured on the Island. I remember my surprise at first hearing a commercial on television in which "Colgate" rhymed with "ate.") We always lingered at La Bodega, for it was there that Mother breathed best, taking in the familiar aromas of the foods she knew from Mamá's kitchen. It was also there that she got to speak to the other women of El Building without violating outright Father's dictates against fraternizing with our neighbors.

Yet Father did his best to make our "assimilation" pain- 14 less. I can still see him carrying a real Christmas tree up several flights of stairs to our apartment, leaving a trail of aromatic pine. He carried it formally, as if it were a flag in a parade. We were the only ones in El Building that I knew of who got presents on both Christmas and *día de Reyes*, the day when the Three Kings brought gifts to Christ and to Hispanic children.

Our supreme luxury in El Building was having our own tele- 15 vision set. It must have been a result of Father's guilt feelings over the isolation he had imposed on us, but we were among the first in the barrio to have one. My brother quickly became an avid watcher of Captain Kangaroo and Jungle Jim, while I loved all the series showing families. By the time I started first grade, I could have drawn a map of Middle America as exemplified by the lives of characters in *Father Knows Best, The Donna Reed Show, Leave It to Beaver, My Three Sons,* and (my favorite) *Bachelor Father,* where John Forsythe treated his adopted teenage daughter like a princess because he was rich and had a Chinese houseboy to do everything for him. In truth, compared to our neighbors in El Building, *we* were rich. My father's navy check provided us with financial security and a standard of living that the factory workers envied. The only thing his money could not buy us was a place to live away from the barrio—his greatest wish, Mother's greatest fear.

In the home movie the men are shown next, sitting around a 16 *card table set up in one corner of the living room, playing dominoes.*

The clack of the ivory pieces was a familiar sound. I heard it in many houses on the Island and in many apartments in Paterson. In Leave It to Beaver, *the Cleavers played bridge in every other episode; in my childhood, the men started every social occasion with a hotly debated round of dominoes. The women would sit around and watch, but they never participated in the games.*

Here and there you can see a small child. Children were always 17 *brought to parties and, whenever they got sleepy, were put to bed in the host's bedroom. Babysitting was a concept unrecognized by the Puerto Rican women I knew: A responsible mother did not leave her children with any stranger. And in a culture where children are not considered intrusive, there was no need to leave the children at home. We went where our mother went.*

Of my preschool years I have only impressions: the sharp bite 18 of the wind in December as we walked with our parents toward the brightly lit stores downtown; how I felt like a stuffed doll in my heavy coat, boots, and mittens; how good it was to walk into the five-and-dime and sit at the counter drinking hot chocolate. On Saturdays our whole family would walk downtown to shop at the big department stores on Broadway. Mother bought all our clothes at Penney's and Sears, and she liked to buy her dresses at the women's specialty shops like Lerner's and Diana's. At some point we'd go into Woolworth's and sit at the soda fountain to eat.

We never ran into other Latinos at these stores or when eat- 19 ing out, and it became clear to me only years later that the women from El Building shopped mainly in other places—stores owned by other Puerto Ricans or by Jewish merchants who had philosophically accepted our presence in the city and decided to make us their good customers, if not real neighbors and friends. These establishments were located not downtown but in the blocks around our street, and they were referred to generically as La Tienda, El Bazar, La Bodega, La Botánica. Everyone knew what was meant. These were the stores where your face did not turn a clerk to stone, where your money was as green as anyone else's.

One New Year's Eve we were dressed up like child models 20 in the Sears catalogue: my brother in a miniature man's suit and bow tie, and I in black patent-leather shoes and a frilly dress with several layers of crinoline underneath. My mother wore a bright red dress that night, I remember, and spike heels; her long black hair hung to her waist. Father, who usually wore his navy uniform during his short visits home, had put on a dark civilian suit for the occasion: We had been invited to his uncle's house for a big celebration. Everyone was excited because my mother's brother—Hernan—a bachelor who could indulge himself with luxuries—had bought a home movie camera, which he would be trying out that night.

Even the home movie cannot fill in the sensory details such 21 a gathering left imprinted in a child's brain. The thick sweet-ness of women's perfumes mixing with the ever-present smells of food cooking in the kitchen: meat and plantain *pasteles*, as well as the ubiquitous rice dish made special with pigeon peas—*gan-dules*—and seasoned with precious *sofrito* sent up from the Island by somebody's mother or smuggled in by a recent traveler. *Sofrito* was one of the items that women hoarded, since it was hardly ever in stock at La Bodega. It was the flavor of Puerto Rico.

The men drank Palo Viejo rum, and some of the younger 22 ones got weepy. The first time I saw a grown man cry was at a New Year's Eve party: He had been reminded of his mother by the smells in the kitchen. But what I remember most were the boiled *pasteles*, plantain or yucca rectangles stuffed with corned beef or other meats, olives, and many other savory ingredients, all wrapped in banana leaves. Everybody had to fish one out with a fork. There was always a "trick" *pas-tel*—one without stuffing—and whoever got that one was the "New Year's Fool."

There was also the music. Long-playing albums were treated 23 like precious china in these homes. Mexican recordings were popular, but the songs that brought tears to my mother's eyes were sung by the melancholy Daniel Santos, whose life as a drug addict was the stuff of legend. Felipe Rodríguez was a particu-lar favorite of couples, since he sang about faithless women and broken-hearted men. There is a snatch of one lyric that has stuck in my mind like a needle on a worn groove: *De piedra ha de ser mi cama, de piedra la cabezera . . . la mujer que a mi me quiera . . . ha de quererme de veras. Ay, Ay, Ay, corazón, porque no amas . . .* I must have heard it a thousand times since the idea of a bed made of stone, and its connection to love, first troubled me with its dis-turbing images.

The five-minute home movie ends with people dancing in a [24] circle—the creative filmmaker must have set it up, so that all of them could file past him. It is both comical and sad to watch silent dancing. Since there is no justification for the absurd movements that music provides for some of us, people appear frantic, their faces embarrassingly intense. It's as if you were watching sex. Yet for years, I've had dreams in the form of this home movie. In a recurring scene, familiar faces push themselves forward into my mind's eye, plastering their features into distorted close-ups. And I'm asking them: "Who is *she*? Who is the old woman I don't recognize? Is she an aunt? Somebody's wife? Tell me who she is."

"See the beauty mark on her cheek as big as a hill on the lunar [25] landscape of her face—well, that runs in the family. The women on your father's side of the family wrinkle early; it's the price they pay for that fair skin. The young girl with the green stain on her wedding dress is *la novia*—just up from the Island. See, she lowers her eyes when she approaches the camera, as she's supposed to. Decent girls never look at you directly in the face. *Humilde*, humble, a girl should express humility in all her actions. She will make a good wife for your cousin. He should consider himself lucky to have met her only weeks after she arrived here. If he marries her quickly, she will make him a good Puerto Rican–style wife; but if he waits too long, she will be corrupted by the city, just like your cousin there."

"She means me. I do what I want. This is not some primitive [26] island I live on. Do they expect me to wear a black mantilla on my head and go to mass every day? Not me. I'm an American woman, and I will do as I please. I can type faster than anyone in my senior class at Central High, and I'm going to be a secretary to a lawyer when I graduate. I can pass for an American girl anywhere—I've tried it. At least for Italian, anyway—I never speak Spanish in public. I hate these parties, but I wanted the dress. I look better than any of these *humildes* here. My life is going to be different. I have an American boyfriend. He is older and has a car. My parents don't know it, but I sneak out of the house late at night sometimes to be with him. If I marry him, even my name will be American. I hate rice and beans—that's what makes these women fat."

"Your *prima*[4] is pregnant by that man she's been sneaking around [27] with. Would I lie to you? I'm your *tía política*,[5] your great-uncle's

[4]Cousin. [Editors' note.]
[5]Aunt-in-law. [Editors' note.]

common-law wife—the one he abandoned on the Island to go marry your cousin's mother. *I* was not invited to this party, of course, but I came anyway. I came to tell you that story about your cousin that you've always wanted to hear. Do you remember the comment your mother made to a neighbor that has always haunted you? The only thing you heard was your cousin's name, and then you saw your mother pick up your doll from the couch and say: 'It was as big as this doll when they flushed it down the toilet.' This image has bothered you for years, hasn't it? You had nightmares about babies being flushed down the toilet, and you wondered why anyone would do such a horrible thing. You didn't dare ask your mother about it. She would only tell you that you had not heard her right, and yell at you for listening to adult conversations. But later, when you were old enough to know about abortions, you suspected.

"I am here to tell you that you were right. Your cousin was grow- 28
ing an *americanito* in her belly when this movie was made. Soon after, she put something long and pointy into her pretty self, thinking maybe she could get rid of the problem before breakfast and still make it to her first class at the high school. Well, *niña*,[6] her screams could be heard downtown. Your aunt, her *mamá*, who had been a midwife on the Island, managed to pull the little thing out. Yes, they probably flushed it down the toilet. What else could they do with it—give it a Christian burial in a little white casket with blue bows and ribbons? Nobody wanted that baby—least of all the father, a teacher at her school with a house in West Paterson that he was filling with real children, and a wife who was a natural blonde.

"Girl, the scandal sent your uncle back to the bottle. And guess 29
where your cousin ended up? Irony of ironies. She was sent to a village in Puerto Rico to live with a relative on her mother's side: a place so far away from civilization that you have to ride a mule to reach it. A real change in scenery. She found a man there—women like that cannot live without male company—but believe me, the men in Puerto Rico know how to put a saddle on a woman like her. *La gringa*,[7] they call her. Ha, ha, ha. *La gringa* is what she always wanted to be . . ."

The old woman's mouth becomes a cavernous black hole I 30
fall into. And as I fall, I can feel the reverberations of her laughter. I hear the echoes of her last mocking words: *la gringa, la gringa!* And the conga line keeps moving silently past me. There is no music in my dream for the dancers.

[6]Child. [Editors' note.]
[7]Foreigner or outsider, especially a North American or Briton. [Editors' note.]

When Odysseus visits Hades to see the spirit of his mother,[8] 31
he makes an offering of sacrificial blood, but since all the souls
crave an audience with the living, he has to listen to many of
them before he can ask questions. I, too, have to hear the dead
and the forgotten speak in my dream. Those who are still part of
my life remain silent, going around and around in their dance.
The others keep pressing their faces forward to say things about
the past.

My father's uncle is last in line. He is dying of alcohol- 32
ism, shrunken and shriveled like a monkey, his face a mass
of wrinkles and broken arteries. As he comes closer I realize
that in his features I can see my whole family. If you were to
stretch that rubbery flesh, you could find my father's face, and
deep within *that* face—my own. I don't want to look into those
eyes ringed in purple. In a few years he will retreat into silence,
and take a long, long time to die. *Move back, Tío, I tell him. I
don't want to hear what you have to say. Give the dancers room
to move. Soon it will be midnight. Who is the New Year's Fool
this time?*

Meaning

1. Of her father, Cofer writes, "The only thing his money could not
   buy us was a place to live away from the barrio—his greatest wish,
   Mother's greatest fear" (paragraph 15). Why was moving her father's
   greatest wish? Why did her mother fear it? What passages from the
   essay support your answer?
2. Are the quoted speeches in paragraphs 25–29 real or imagined? Use
   evidence from the essay to support your answer.

Purpose and Audience

1. What do you think is Cofer's purpose in this essay? Does she have
   something specific she wants the reader to understand?
2. What assumptions does Cofer make about her audience? How familiar do readers have to be with Puerto Rican culture in order to
   understand Cofer's dominant impression?

---

[8]An episode in the *Odyssey*, usually attributed to the ancient Greek poet Homer.
In Greek mythology, Hades rules the underworld. [Editors' note.]

Method and Structure

1. What does Cofer's description of Paterson and her childhood apartment (paragraphs 3–4) tell us about Cofer herself as a child?

2. What are the contents of the passages in italics (paragraphs 1, 10–11, 16–17) and the ones in smaller type (25–29)? How do these passages work with those in regular type? What is their effect?

3. How well does the observation in paragraph 24, "It is both comical and sad to watch silent dancing," convey the dominant impression of Cofer's essay? What, if anything, would you add to "comical and sad"?

4. OTHER METHODS   Paragraph 11 offers three examples of Puerto Rican women: Cofer's mother, her assimilated cousin, and the cousin's brother's girlfriend. How do these three examples illustrate a cultural shift Puerto Rican immigrants were experiencing at the time the home movie was made?

Language

1. How might "silent dancing" serve as a metaphor for memory? (If necessary, see the Glossary for a definition of *metaphor*.)

2. What larger meaning can we infer from this sentence in paragraph 23: "Long-playing albums were treated like precious china in these homes"?

Writing Topics

1. In an essay, describe a dream you've had that stays with you. Try to interpret the dream in the context of your life at the time. What do you think it meant? Why did you have it when you did? What did it tell you?

2. Have you had the experience of being isolated from your surroundings, whether because of language or culture or because of some other barrier—being new in town, feeling friendless, or even just having to study when everyone else was having fun? Describe the experience in an essay, using plenty of details to help your readers understand your feelings.

3. Analyze the different tones of Cofer herself, her cousin (paragraph 26), and her *tía política* (25, 27–29). How do their tones convey the different experiences and expectations of these three women?

Writing with the Method

DESCRIPTION

Select one of the following topics, or any topic they suggest, for an essay developed by description. Be sure to choose a topic you care about so that description is a means of communicating an idea, not an end in itself.

People

1. An exceptionally neat or messy person
2. A person whose appearance and mannerisms are at odds with his or her real self
3. A person you admire or respect
4. An annoying neighbor

Places and Scenes

5. A frightening place
6. A place you daydream about
7. A prison cell, police station, or courtroom
8. A neighborhood devastated by foreclosures
9. The scene at a concert

Animals and Things

10. A work of art
11. A pet or an animal in a zoo
12. A prized possession or favorite childhood toy
13. A saxophone or other musical instrument

Sensations

14. The look and taste of a favorite or detested food
15. Waiting for important news
16. Sneezing
17. Skating, running, bodysurfing, skydiving, or some other activity
18. Extreme hunger, thirst, cold, heat, or fatigue

Chapter 2

NARRATION

USING THE METHOD

To **narrate** is to tell a story, to relate a sequence of events that are linked in time. We narrate when we tell of a funny experience, report a baseball game, or trace a historical event. By arranging events in an orderly progression, we illuminate the stages leading to a result.

Sometimes the emphasis in narration is on the story itself, as in fiction, biography, autobiography, some history, and much journalism. But often a narrative serves some larger point, as when a paragraph or a brief story about an innocent person's death helps to strengthen an argument for stricter handling of drunk drivers. When used as a primary means of developing an essay, such pointed narration usually relates a sequence of events that led to new knowledge or had a notable outcome. The point of the narrative—the idea the reader is to take away—then determines the selection of events, the amount of detail devoted to them, and their arrangement.

Though narration arranges events in time, narrative time is not real time. An important event may fill whole pages, even though it took only minutes to unfold; and a less important event may be dispensed with in a sentence, even though it lasted hours. Suppose, for instance, that a writer wants to narrate the experience of being mugged in order to show how courage came unexpectedly to his aid. He might provide a slow-motion account of the few minutes' encounter with the muggers, including vivid details of the setting and of the attackers' appearance, a moment-by-moment replay of his emotions, and exact dialogue. At the same time, he will compress events that merely fill in background or link main events, such as how he got to the scene of the mugging or the follow-up questioning by a police detective. And he will entirely omit many events, such as a conversation overheard at the police station, that have no significance for his point.

The point of a narrative influences not only which events are covered and how fully but also how the events are arranged. There are several possibilities:

- A straight chronological sequence is usually the easiest to manage because it relates events in the order of their actual occurrence. It is particularly useful for short narratives, for those in which the last event is the most dramatic, or for those in which the events preceding and following the climax contribute to the point being made.

- The final event, such as a self-revelation, may come first, followed by an explanation of the events leading up to it.

- The entire story may be summarized first and then examined in detail.

- **Flashbacks**—shifts backward rather than forward in time—may recall events whose significance would not have been apparent earlier. Flashbacks are common in movies and fiction: a character in the midst of one scene mentally replays a different scene.

In addition to providing a clear organization, you can also help readers by adopting a consistent **point of view**, a position relative to the events, conveyed in two main ways:

- Pronouns indicate your place in the story: the first-person *I* if you are a direct participant; the third-person *he, she, it,* and *they* if you are an observer or reporter.

- Verb tense indicates your relation in time to the sequence of events: present (*is, run*) or past (*was, ran*).

Combining the first-person pronoun with the present tense can create great immediacy ("I feel the point of the knife in my back"). At the other extreme, combining third-person pronouns with the past tense creates more distance and objectivity ("He felt the point of the knife in his back"). In between extremes, you can combine first person with past tense ("I felt . . .") or third person with present tense ("He feels . . ."). The choice depends on your actual involvement in the narrative and on your purpose.

DEVELOPING A NARRATIVE ESSAY

Getting Started

You'll find narration useful whenever relating a sequence of events can help you make a point, sometimes to support the thesis of a larger paper, sometimes *as* the thesis of a paper. If you're assigned a narrative essay, probe your own experiences for a situation such as an argument involving strong emotion, a humorous or embarrassing incident, a dramatic scene you witnessed, or a learning experience like a job. If you have the opportunity to do research, you might choose a topic dealing with the natural world (such as the Big Bang scenario for the origin of the universe) or an event in history or politics (such as how a local activist worked to close down an animal-research lab).

Explore your subject by listing all the events in sequence as they happened. At this stage you may find the traditional journalist's questions helpful: *Who was involved? What happened? When did it happen? Where did it happen? Why did it happen? How did it happen?* These questions will lead you to examine your subject from all angles. Then you need to decide which events should be developed in great detail because they are central to your point; which merit compression because they merely contribute background or tie the main events together; and which should be omitted altogether because they add nothing to your point and might clutter your narrative.

While you are weighing the relative importance of events, consider also what your readers need to know in order to understand and appreciate your narrative.

- *What information will help locate readers in the narrative's time and place?*
- *How will you expand and compress events to keep readers' attention?*
- *What details about people, places, and feelings will make the events vivid for readers?*
- *What is your attitude toward the subject* —lighthearted, sarcastic, bitter, serious? —and how will you convey it to readers in your choice of events and details?

- *What should your point of view be?* Do you want to involve readers intimately by using the first person and the present tense? Or does that seem overdramatic, less appropriate than the more detached, objective view that would be conveyed by the past tense or the third person or both?

Forming a Thesis

Whatever your subject, you should have some point to make about it: Why was the incident or experience significant? What does it teach or illustrate? If you can, phrase this point in a sentence before you start to draft. For instance:

> I used to think small-town life was boring, but one taste of the city made me appreciate the leisurely pace of home.
>
> A recent small earthquake demonstrated the hazards of inadequate civil-defense measures.

Sometimes you may need to draft your story before the point of it becomes clear to you, especially if the experience had a personal impact or if the event was so recent that writing a draft will allow you to gain some perspective.

Whether to state your main point outright in your essay, as a thesis sentence, depends on the effect you want to have on readers. You might use your introduction to lead to a statement of your thesis so that readers will know from the start why you are telling them your story. Then again, to intensify the drama of your story, you might decide to withhold your thesis sentence for the conclusion or omit it altogether. Remember, though, that the thesis must be evident to readers if it isn't stated: the narrative needs a point.

Organizing

Narrative essays often begin without formal introductions, instead drawing the reader in with one of the more dramatic events in the sequence. But you may find an introduction useful to set the scene for your narrative, to summarize the events leading up to it, to establish the context for it, or to lead to a thesis statement if you want readers to know the point of your story before they start reading it.

The arrangement of events in the body of your essay depends on the actual order in which they occurred and the point you want to make. To narrate a trip during which one thing after another went wrong, you might find a strict chronological order most effective. To narrate an earthquake that began and ended in an instant, you might sort simultaneous events into groups—say, what happened to buildings and what happened to people—or you might arrange a few people's experiences in order of increasing drama. To narrate your experience of city life, you might interweave events in the city with contrasting flashbacks to your life in a small town, or you might start by relating one especially bad experience in the city, drop back to explain how you ended up in that situation, and then go on to tell what happened afterward. Narrative time can be manipulated in any number of ways, but your scheme should have a purpose that your readers can see, and you should stick to it.

Let the ending of your essay be determined by the effect you want to leave with readers. You can end with the last event in your sequence, or the one you have saved for last, if it conveys your point and provides a strong finish. Or you can summarize the aftermath of the story if it contributes to the point. You can also end with a formal conclusion that states your point—your thesis—explicitly. Such a conclusion is especially useful if your point unfolds gradually throughout the narrative and you want to emphasize it at the finish.

Drafting

Drafting a narrative can be less of a struggle than drafting other kinds of papers, especially if you're close to the events and you use a straight chronological order. But the relative ease of storytelling can be misleading if it causes you to describe events too quickly or to write without making a point. While drafting, be as specific as possible. Tell what the people in your narrative were wearing, what expressions their faces held, how they gestured, what they said. Specify the time of day, and describe the weather and the surroundings (buildings, vegetation, and the like). All these details may be familiar to you, but they won't be to your readers.

At the same time, try to remain open to what the story means to you, so that you can convey that meaning in your selection and description of events. If you know before you begin what your thesis is, let it guide you. But the first draft may turn out to be a search for your thesis, in which case you'll need another draft to make it evident in the way you relate events.

In your draft you may want to experiment with dialogue — quotations of what participants said, in their words. Dialogue can add immediacy and realism, as long as it advances the narrative and doesn't ramble beyond its usefulness. In reconstructing dialogue from memory, try to recall not only the actual words but also the sounds of speakers' voices and the expressions on their faces — information that will help you represent each speaker distinctly. And keep the dialogue natural sounding by using constructions typical of speech. For instance, most speakers prefer contractions like *don't* and *shouldn't* to the longer forms *do not* and *should not*; and few speakers begin sentences with *although*, as in the formal-sounding "Although we could hear our mother's voice, we refused to answer her."

Whether you are relating events in strict chronological order or manipulating them for some effect, try to make their sequence in real time and the distance between them clear to readers. Instead of signaling sequence with the monotonous *and then . . . and then . . . and then* or *next . . . next . . . next*, use informative transitions that signal the order of events (*afterward, earlier*), the duration of events (*for an hour, in that time*), or the amount of time between events (*the next morning, a week later*). (See the Glossary under *transitions* for a list of such expressions.)

Revising and Editing

When your draft is complete, revise and edit it by answering the following questions.

- *Is the point of your narrative clear, and does every event you relate contribute to it?* Whether or not you state your thesis, it should be obvious to readers. They should be able to see why you have lingered over some events and compressed others, and they should not be distracted by insignificant events and details.

- *Is your organization clear?* Be sure that your readers will understand any shifts backward or forward in time.

- *Have you used transitions to help readers follow the sequence of events?* Transitions such as *meanwhile* or *soon afterward* serve a dual purpose: they keep the reader on track, and they link sentences and paragraphs so that they flow smoothly.
- *If you have used dialogue, is it purposeful and natural?* Be sure all quoted speeches move the action ahead. And read all dialogue aloud to check that it sounds like something someone would actually say.

LANGSTON HUGHES

A poet, fiction writer, playwright, critic, and humorist, Langston Hughes described his writing as "largely concerned with depicting Negro life in America." He was born in 1902 in Joplin, Missouri, and grew up in Illinois, Kansas, and Ohio. After dropping out of Columbia University in the early 1920s, Hughes worked at odd jobs while struggling to gain recognition as a writer. His first book of poems, The Weary Blues *(1926), helped seed the Harlem Renaissance, a flowering of African American music and literature centered in the Harlem district of New York City during the 1920s. The book also generated a scholarship that enabled Hughes to finish college at Lincoln University. In all of his work—including* The Negro Mother *(1931),* The Ways of White Folks *(1934),* Shakespeare in Harlem *(1942),* Montage of a Dream Deferred *(1951),* Ask Your Mama *(1961), and* The Best of Simple *(1961)—Hughes captured and projected the rhythms of jazz and the distinctive speech, subtle humor, and deep traditions of African American people. He died in New York City in 1967.*

Salvation

A chapter in Hughes's autobiography, The Big Sea *(1940), "Salvation" is a simple yet compelling narrative about a moment of deceit and disillusionment for a boy of twelve. As you read Hughes's account, notice how the opening two sentences set up every twist of the story.*

I was saved from sin when I was going on thirteen. But not really 1 saved. It happened like this. There was a big revival at my Auntie Reed's church. Every night for weeks there had been much preaching, singing, praying, and shouting, and some very hardened sinners had been brought to Christ, and the membership of the church had grown by leaps and bounds. Then just before the revival ended, they held a special meeting for children, "to bring the young lambs to the fold." My aunt spoke of it for days ahead. That night, I was escorted to the front row and placed on the mourner's bench with all the other young sinners, who had not yet been brought to Jesus.

My aunt told me that when you were saved you saw a light, 2 and something happened to you inside! And Jesus came into your life! And God was with you from then on! She said you could see and hear and feel Jesus in your soul. I believed her. I have heard a great many old people say the same thing and it seemed to me they ought to know. So I sat there calmly in the hot, crowded church, waiting for Jesus to come to me.

The preacher preached a wonderful rhythmical sermon, all 3 moans and shouts and lonely cries and dire pictures of hell, and then he sang a song about the ninety and nine safe in the fold, but one little lamb was left out in the cold. Then he said: "Won't you come? Won't you come to Jesus? Young lambs, won't you come?" And he held out his arms to all us young sinners there on the mourner's bench. And the little girls cried. And some of them jumped up and went to Jesus right away. But most of us just sat there.

A great many old people came and knelt around us and 4 prayed, old women with jet-black faces and braided hair, old men with work-gnarled hands. And the church sang a song about the lower lights are burning, some poor sinners to be saved. And the whole building rocked with prayer and song.

Still I kept waiting to *see* Jesus.   5

Finally all the young people had gone to the altar and were 6 saved, but one boy and me. He was a rounder's[1] son named Westley. Westley and I were surrounded by sisters and deacons praying. It was very hot in the church, and getting late now. Finally Westley said to me in a whisper: "God damn! I'm tired o' sitting here. Let's get up and be saved." So he got up and was saved.

Then I was left all alone on the mourner's bench. My aunt 7 came and knelt at my knees and cried, while prayers and songs swirled all around me in the little church. The whole

[1]Local Methodist preacher. [Editors' note.]

congregation prayed for me alone, in a mighty wail of moans and voices. And I kept waiting serenely for Jesus, waiting, waiting—but he didn't come. I wanted to see him, but nothing happened to me. Nothing! I wanted something to happen to me, but nothing happened.

I heard the songs and the minister saying: "Why don't you 8 come? My dear child, why don't you come to Jesus? Jesus is waiting for you. He wants you. Why don't you come? Sister Reed, what is this child's name?"

"Langston," my aunt sobbed. 9

"Langston, why don't you come? Why don't you come and be 10 saved? Oh, Lamb of God! Why don't you come?"

Now it was really getting late. I began to be ashamed of 11 myself, holding everything up so long. I began to wonder what God thought about Westley, who certainly hadn't seen Jesus either, but who was now sitting proudly on the platform, swinging his knickerbockered legs and grinning down at me, surrounded by deacons and old women on their knees praying. God had not struck Westley dead for taking his name in vain or for lying in the temple. So I decided that maybe to save further trouble, I'd better lie, too, and say that Jesus had come, and get up and be saved.

So I got up. 12

Suddenly the whole room broke into a sea of shouting, as 13 they saw me rise. Waves of rejoicing swept the place. Women leaped in the air. My aunt threw her arms around me. The minister took me by the hand and led me to the platform.

When things quieted down, in a hushed silence, punctuated 14 by a few ecstatic "Amens," all the new young lambs were blessed in the name of God. Then joyous singing filled the room.

That night, for the last time in my life but one—for I was 15 a big boy twelve years old—I cried. I cried, in bed alone, and couldn't stop. I buried my head under the quilts, but my aunt heard me. She woke up and told my uncle I was crying because the Holy Ghost had come into my life, and because I had seen Jesus. But I was really crying because I couldn't bear to tell her that I had lied, that I had deceived everybody in the church, that I hadn't seen Jesus, and that now I didn't believe there was a Jesus anymore, since he didn't come to help me.

Meaning

1. What is the main point of Hughes's narrative? What change occurs in him as a result of his experience?
2. What finally makes Hughes decide to get up and be saved? How does this decision affect him afterward?
3. What do you make of the title and the first two sentences? What is Hughes saying here about "salvation"?

Purpose and Audience

1. Why do you think Hughes wrote "Salvation" as part of his autobiography more than two decades after the experience? Was his purpose simply to express feelings prompted by a significant event in his life? Did he want to criticize his aunt and the other adults in the congregation? Did he want to explain something about childhood or about the distance between generations? What passages support your answer?
2. What does Hughes seem to assume about his readers' familiarity with the kind of service he describes? What details help make the procedure clear?
3. How do dialogue, lines from hymns, and details of other sounds (paragraphs 3–10) help re-create the increasing pressure Hughes feels? What other details contribute to this sense of pressure?

Method and Structure

1. Why do you think Hughes chose narration to explore the themes of this essay? Can you imagine an argumentative essay (Chapter 10) that would deal with the same themes? What might its title be?
2. Where in his narrative does Hughes insert explanations, compress time by summarizing events, or jump ahead in time by omitting events? Where does he expand time by drawing moments out? How does each of these insertions and manipulations of time relate to Hughes's main point?
3. In paragraph 1 Hughes uses several transitions to signal the sequence of events and the passage of time: "for weeks," "Then just before," "for days ahead," "That night." Where does he use similar signals in the rest of the essay?
4. OTHER METHODS Hughes's narrative also explains a process: we learn how a revival meeting works. Why is this process analysis essential to the essay?

Language

1. What does Hughes's language reveal about his adult attitudes toward his experience? Does he feel anger? bitterness? sorrow? guilt? shame? amusement? What words and passages support your answer?

2. Hughes relates his experience in an almost childlike style, using many short sentences and beginning many sentences with *And*. What effect do you think he is trying to achieve with this style?

3. Hughes expects to "see" Jesus when he is saved (paragraphs 2, 5, 7), and afterward his aunt thinks that he has "seen" Jesus (15). What does each of them mean by *see*? What is the significance of the difference in Hughes's story?

Writing Topics

1. Write a narrative essay about a time when others significantly influenced the way you thought, looked, or acted—perhaps against your own true beliefs or values. What was the appeal of the others' attitudes, appearance, or behavior? What did you gain by conforming? What did you lose? Use specific details to explain how and why the experience affected you.

2. Hughes says, "I have heard a great many old people say the same thing and it seemed to me they ought to know" (paragraph 2). Think of a piece of information or advice that you heard over and over again from adults when you were a child. Write a narrative essay about an experience in which you were helped or misled by that information or advice.

3. It seems that Hughes wants to be saved largely because of the influence of his family and his community. Westley (paragraphs 6 and 11) represents another kind of influence, peer pressure, that often works against family and community. Think of an incident in your own life when you felt pressured by peers to go against your parents, religion, school, or another authority. Write a narrative essay telling what happened and making it clear why the situation was important to you. What were the results?

ANNIE DILLARD

A poet and essayist, Annie Dillard (born 1945) is part naturalist, part mystic. Growing up in Pittsburgh, she was an independent child given to exploration and reading. After graduating from Hollins College in the Blue Ridge Mountains of Virginia, Dillard settled in the area to investigate her natural surroundings and to write. She demonstrated her intense, passionate involvement with the world of nature and the world of the mind early in her career with Pilgrim at Tinker Creek *(1974), a series of related essays that earned her a Pulitzer Prize. Dillard's prolific output since then has spanned several genres, including poetry in volumes such as* Tickets for a Prayer Wheel *(1974) and* Mornings Like This *(1995); essays collected in* Teaching a Stone to Talk *(1982),* The Writing Life *(1989), and* For the Time Being *(1999); literary criticism in* Living by Fiction *(1982) and* Encounters with Chinese Writers *(1984); and, most recently, a novel,* The Maytrees *(2007). In 1999 she was inducted into the American Academy of Arts and Letters. Dillard now lives in North Carolina and is professor emeritus at Wesleyan University.*

The Chase

In her autobiography, An American Childhood *(1987), Dillard's enthusiasm for life in its many forms colors her recollections of her own youth. "The Chase" (editors' title) is a self-contained chapter from the book that narrates a few minutes of glorious excitement.*

Some boys taught me to play football. This was fine sport. You thought up a new strategy for every play and whispered it to the others. You went out for a pass, fooling everyone. Best, you got to throw yourself mightily at someone's running legs. Either you brought him down or you hit the ground flat out on your chin, with your arms empty before you. It was all or nothing. If you hesitated in fear, you would miss and get hurt: you would take a hard fall while the kid got away, or you would get kicked in the face while the kid got away. But if you flung yourself whole-heartedly at the back of his knees—if you gathered and joined body and soul and pointed them diving fearlessly—then you likely wouldn't get hurt, and you'd stop the ball. Your fate, and your team's score, depended on your concentration and courage. Nothing girls did could compare with it.

Boys welcomed me at baseball, too, for I had, through enthu- 2
siastic practice, what was weirdly known as a boy's arm. In win-ter, in the snow, there was neither baseball nor football, so the boys and I threw snowballs at passing cars. I got in trouble throw-ing snowballs, and have seldom been happier since.

On one weekday morning after Christmas, six inches of new 3
snow had just fallen. We were standing up to our boot tops in snow on a front yard on trafficked Reynolds Street, waiting for cars. The cars traveled Reynolds Street slowly and evenly; they were targets all but wrapped in red ribbons, cream puffs. We couldn't miss.

I was seven; the boys were eight, nine, and ten. The oldest 4
two Fahey boys were there—Mikey and Peter—polite blond boys who lived near me on Lloyd Street, and who already had four brothers and sisters. My parents approved of Mikey and Peter Fahey. Chickie McBride was there, a tough kid, and Billy Paul and Mackie Kean too, from across Reynolds, where the boys grew up dark and furious, grew up skinny, knowing, and skilled. We had all drifted from our houses that morning looking for action, and had found it here on Reynolds Street.

It was cloudy but cold. The cars' tires laid behind them on the 5
snowy street a complex trail of beige chunks like crenellated cas-tle walls. I had stepped on some earlier; they squeaked. We could have wished for more traffic. When a car came, we all popped it one. In the intervals between cars we reverted to the natural soli-tude of children.

I started making an iceball—a perfect iceball, from perfectly 6
white snow, perfectly spherical, and squeezed perfectly translu-cent so no snow remained all the way through. (The Fahey boys and I considered it unfair actually to throw an iceball at some-body, but it had been known to happen.)

I had just embarked on the iceball project when we heard 7
tire chains come clanking from afar. A black Buick was moving

toward us down the street. We all spread out, banged together some regular snowballs, took aim, and, when the Buick drew nigh, fired.

A soft snowball hit the driver's windshield right before the 8 driver's face. It made a smashed star with a hump in the middle.

Often, of course, we hit our target, but this time, the only 9 time in all of life, the car pulled over and stopped. Its wide black door opened; a man got out of it, running. He didn't even close the car door.

He ran after us, and we ran away from him, up the snowy 10 Reynolds sidewalk. At the corner, I looked back; incredibly, he was still after us. He was in city clothes: a suit and tie, street shoes. Any normal adult would have quit, having sprung us into flight and made his point. This man was gaining on us. He was a thin man, all action. All of a sudden, we were running for our lives.

Wordless, we split up. We were on our turf; we could lose 11 ourselves in the neighborhood backyards, everyone for himself. I paused and considered. Everyone had vanished except Mike Fahey, who was just rounding the corner of a yellow brick house. Poor Mikey, I trailed him. The driver of the Buick sensibly picked the two of us to follow. The man apparently had all day.

He chased Mikey and me around the yellow house and up 12 a backyard path we knew by heart: under a low tree, up a bank, through a hedge, down some snowy steps, and across the grocery store's delivery driveway. We smashed through a gap in another hedge, entered a scruffy backyard and ran around its back porch and tight between houses to Edgerton Avenue; we ran across Edgerton to an alley and up our own sliding woodpile to the Halls' front yard; he kept coming. We ran up Lloyd Street and wound through mazy backyards toward the steep hilltop at Willard and Lang.

He chased us silently, block after block. He chased us silently 13 over picket fences, through thorny hedges, between houses, around garbage cans, and across streets. Every time I glanced back, choking for breath, I expected he would have quit. He must have been as breathless as we were. His jacket strained over his body. It was an immense discovery, pounding into my hot head with every sliding, joyous step, that this ordinary adult evidently knew what I thought only children who trained at football knew:

that you have to fling yourself at what you're doing, you have to point yourself, forget yourself, aim, dive.

Mikey and I had nowhere to go, in our own neighborhood 14 or out of it, but away from this man who was chasing us. He impelled us forward; we compelled him to follow our route. The air was cold; every breath tore my throat. We kept running, block after block; we kept improvising, backyard after backyard, running a frantic course and choosing it simultaneously, failing always to find small places or hard places to slow him down, and discovering always, exhilarated, dismayed, that only bare speed could save us—for he would never give up, this man—and we were losing speed.

He chased us through the backyard labyrinths of ten blocks 15 before he caught us by our jackets. He caught us and we all stopped.

We three stood staggering, half blinded, coughing, in an obscure 16 hilltop backyard: a man in his twenties, a boy, a girl. He had released our jackets, our pursuer, our captor, our hero: he knew we weren't going anywhere. We all played by the rules. Mikey and I unzipped our jackets. I pulled off my sopping mittens. Our tracks multiplied in the backyard's new snow. We had been breaking new snow all morning. We didn't look at each other. I was cherishing my excitement. The man's lower pants legs were wet; his cuffs were full of snow, and there was a prow of snow beneath them on his shoes and socks. Some trees bordered the little flat backyard, some messy winter trees. There was no one around: a clearing in a grove, and we the only players.

It was a long time before he could speak. I had some dif- 17 ficulty at first recalling why we were there. My lips felt swollen; I couldn't see out of the sides of my eyes; I kept coughing.

"You stupid kids," he began perfunctorily. 18

We listened perfunctorily indeed, if we listened at all, for the 19 chewing out was redundant, a mere formality, and beside the point. The point was that he had chased us passionately without giving up, and so he had caught us. Now he came down to earth. I wanted the glory to last forever.

But how could the glory have lasted forever? We could have 20 run through every backyard in North America until we got to Panama. But when he trapped us at the lip of the Panama Canal, what precisely could he have done to prolong the drama of the chase and cap its glory? I brooded about this for the next few years. He could only have fried Mikey Fahey and me in boiling oil, say, or dismembered us piecemeal, or staked us to anthills. None of which I really wanted, and none of which any adult was likely to do, even in the spirit of fun. He could only chew us out there in the Panamanian jungle, after months or years of exalting pursuit. He could only begin, "You stupid kids," and continue in his ordinary Pittsburgh accent with his normal righteous anger and the usual common sense.

If in that snowy backyard the driver of the black Buick had 21 cut off our heads, Mikey's and mine, I would have died happy, for nothing has required so much of me since as being chased all over Pittsburgh in the middle of winter—running terrified, exhausted—by this sainted, skinny, furious red-headed man who wished to have a word with us. I don't know how he found his way back to his car.

Meaning

1. What lesson did Dillard learn from the experience of the chase? Where is her point explicitly revealed?

2. In paragraph 2 Dillard writes, "I got in trouble throwing snowballs, and have seldom been happier since." What exactly is Dillard saying about the relationship between trouble and happiness? Do you think she is recommending "getting in trouble" as a means to happiness? Why, or why not?

Purpose and Audience

1. What seems to be Dillard's purpose in "The Chase": to encourage children to get into trouble? to encourage adults to be more tolerant of children who get into trouble? something else?

2. In her first paragraph, Dillard deliberately shifts from the first-person point of view (using *me*) to the second (using *you*). What is the effect of this shift, and how does it contribute to Dillard's purpose?

Method and Structure

1. Why do you think Dillard chose narration to illustrate her point about the difference between children and adults? What does she gain from this method? What other methods might she have used?

2. In this straightforward narrative, Dillard expands some events and summarizes others: for instance, she provides much more detail about the chase in paragraph 12 than in paragraphs 13 and 14. Why might she first provide and then pull back from the detail in paragraph 12?

3. How does the last sentence of paragraph 2—"I got in trouble throwing snowballs, and have seldom been happier since"—serve to set up the story Dillard is about to tell?

4. OTHER METHODS   Dillard makes extensive use of description. Locate examples of this method and analyze what they contribute to the essay as a whole.

Language

1. How would you characterize Dillard's style? How does the style reflect the fact that the adult Dillard is writing from a child's point of view?

2. What does Dillard mean by calling the man who chases her "sainted" (paragraph 21)? What is her attitude toward this man? What words and passages support your answer?

3. Consider Dillard's description of cars: traveling down the street, they looked like "targets all but wrapped in red ribbons" (paragraph 3), and their tires in the snow left "a complex trail of beige chunks like crenellated castle walls" (5). What is the dominant impression created here?

Writing Topics

1. Write a narrative essay about a time you misbehaved as a child. Use the first-person *I*, strong verbs, and plenty of descriptive details to render vividly the event and its effects on you and others.

2. Write a narrative essay about a time you discovered that "an ordinary adult" knew some truth you thought only children knew. What was that truth, and why did you believe until that moment that only children knew it? What did this adult do to change your mind?

3. Though Dillard focuses on a time when no harm was done, the consequences of throwing snowballs at moving cars could be quite serious. Rewrite the essay from the point of view of someone who would *not* glorify the children's behavior—the man driving the Buick, for instance, or one of the children's parents. How might one of these people narrate these events? On what might he or she focus?

JENNIFER FINNEY BOYLAN

Jennifer Finney Boylan is a prolific writer whose work is filled with wry observations about the human condition. Born James Boylan in 1958 in Valley Forge, Pennsylvania, her youth was marked by confusion—as a boy and a young man Boylan felt the tug of female identity, yet married Deirdre "Grace" Finney in 1988 and settled down to a more or less conventional life. Though she has written more than a dozen novels, collections of short stories, and (under a pseudonym) books for young adults, Boylan is best known for She's Not There *(2003), a poignant memoir that deals with transgender issues, her decision to undergo sex-change surgery in her early forties, and the response of those around her (especially Finney, to whom she remains happily married with two children). Boylan is also a contributing writer for* Condé Nast Traveler, *has written articles for publications ranging from the* New York Times *to* Martha Stewart Living, *and appears regularly on television and radio. A graduate of Wesleyan University, she has taught at Johns Hopkins University, University College Cork in Ireland, Ursinus College, and Colby College in Waterville, Maine, where she is a professor of creative writing and American literature.*

In the Early Morning Rain

A recent spate of suicides by lesbian, gay, bisexual, and transgendered teenagers inspired a group of openly gay adults to launch It Gets Better, *a growing collection of* YouTube *videos and personal essays meant to assure LGBT youth that the bullying and self-loathing they might endure through high school and college will not torment them forever. "In the Early Morning Rain," a revised passage from* She's Not There, *is Boylan's contribution to the project.*

When I was young there was a time when I figured, the hell with 1 it. I'd never even said the word *transgender* out loud. I couldn't imagine saying it, ever. I mean, please.

So instead, one day a few years after I got out of college, I 2
loaded all my things into the Volkswagen and started driving. I
wasn't sure where I was going, but I knew I wanted to get away
from the Maryland spring, with its cherry blossoms and its bursting tulips and all its bullshit. I figured I'd keep driving farther and
farther north until there weren't any people. I wasn't sure what I
was going to do then, but I was certain something would occur
to me that would end this transgender business once and for all.

I set my sights on Nova Scotia. I drove to Maine and took a 3
ferry out of Bar Harbor. I drove onto the SS *Bluenose* and stood
on the deck and watched America drift away behind me, which as
far as I was concerned was just fine.

There was someone walking around in a rabbit costume on 4
the ship. He'd pose with you and they'd snap your picture and an
hour or so later you could purchase the photo of yourself with
the rabbit as a memento of your trip to Nova Scotia. I purchased
mine. It showed a sad-looking boy—*I think that's a boy*—with
long hair reading a book of poetry as a moth-eaten rabbit bends
over him.

In Nova Scotia I drove the car east and north for a few days. 5
When dusk came, I'd eat in a diner, and then I'd sleep either in the
car or in a small tent that I had in the back. There were scattered
patches of snow up there, even in May. I kept going north until
I got to Cape Breton, which is about as far away as you can get
from Baltimore and still be on dry land.

In Cape Breton I hiked around the cliffs, looked at the ocean. 6
At night I lay in my sleeping bag by the sea as breezes shook the
tent. I wrote in my journal, or read the poetry of Robert Frost, or
grazed around in the Modern Library's *Great Tales of Terror and
the Supernatural.* I read one up there called "Oh, Whistle, and I'll
Come to You, My Lad."[1]

In the car I listened to the Warlocks sing "In the Early Morn- 7
ing Rain"[2] on the tape deck. I thought about this girl I knew, Grace
Finney. I thought about my parents. I thought about the clear,

[1]A short story by English writer M. R. James (1862–1936). In the tale, a lonely
professor on a seaside vacation inadvertently summons a ghost that manifests
itself as a strong wind. [Editors' note.]

[2]The Warlocks were an early incarnation of the Grateful Dead. The song, written by Gordon Lightfoot, is about a traveler who misses a loved one but lacks the
means to make the trip home. [Editors' note.]

inescapable fact that I was female in spirit and how, in order to be whole, I would have to give up on every dream I'd had, save one.

I stayed in a motel one night that was officially closed for 8 the season, but which the operator let me stay in for half price. I opened my suitcase and put on my bra and some jeans and a blue knit top. I combed my hair out and looked in the mirror and saw a perfectly normal-looking young woman. *This is so wrong?* I said to myself in the mirror. *This is the cause of all the trouble?*

I thought about settling in one of the little villages around 9 here, just starting life over as a woman. I'd tell everyone I was Canadian.

Then I lay on my back and sobbed. Nobody would ever 10 believe I was Canadian.

The next morning I climbed a mountain at the far northern 11 edge of Cape Breton Island. I climbed up to the top, trying to clear my head, but it wouldn't clear. I kept going up and up, past the tree line, past the shrub line, until at last there was just moss.

There I stood, looking out at the cold ocean, a thousand miles 12 below me, totally cut off from the world.

A fierce wind blew in from the Atlantic. I leaned into it. I saw 13 the waves crashing against the cliff below. I stood right at the edge. My heart pounded.

I leaned over the edge of the precipice, but the gale blowing 14 into my body kept me from falling. When the wind died down, I'd start to fall, then it would blow me back up again. I played a little game with the wind, leaning a little farther over the edge each time.

Then I leaned off the edge of the cliff at a sharp angle, my 15 arms held outward like wings, my body sustained only by the fierce wind, and I thought, *Well all right. Is this what you came here to do?*

Let's do it then. 16

Then a huge blast of wind blew me backward and I landed 17 on the moss. It was soft. I stared straight up at the blue sky, and I felt a presence.

Are you all right, son? said the voice. *You're going to be all* 18 *right. You're going to be all right.*

Looking back now, I am still not sure whose voice that was. 19 My guardian angel? The ghost of my father? I don't know. Does it really change things all that much, to give a name to the spirits that are watching out for us?

Still, from this vantage point—over twenty-five years later— 20 my heart tells me that was the voice of my future self, the woman that I eventually became, a woman who, all these years later, looks more or less like the one I saw in the mirror in the motel. Looking back on the sad, desperate young man I was, I am trying to tell him something. *It will get better. It will not always hurt the way it hurts now. The thing that right now you feel is your greatest curse will someday, against all odds, turn out to be your greatest gift.*

It's hard to be gay, or lesbian. To be trans can be even harder. 21 There have been plenty of times when I've lost hope.

But in the years since I heard that voice—*Are you all right,* 22 *son? You're going to be all right*—I've found, to my surprise, that most people have treated me with love. Some of the people I most expected to lose, when I came out as trans, turned out to be loving, and compassionate, and kind.

I can't tell you how to get here from there. You have to figure 23 that out for yourself. But I do know that instead of going off that cliff, I walked back down the mountain that morning and instead began the long, long journey toward home.

Meaning

1. What main idea does Boylan hope readers will take from this very personal story?

2. What does the author mean by "in order to be whole, I would have to give up on every dream I'd had, save one" (paragraph 7)? What one dream could the young Boylan keep? Why would keeping it require giving up everything else?

Purpose and Audience

1. Notice the shift in point of view from *I* throughout the essay to *you* in the last paragraph. What does this switch reveal about Boylan's imagined audience and her reasons for writing?

2. How do you think Boylan expects her audience to react to her story? Does she seem to assume readers will find her experience and feelings strange, or does she assume some other response? What in the essay makes you think as you do?

Method and Structure

1. Boylan offers more concrete and vivid details in paragraphs 11 to 17 than she does elsewhere. What is she describing here, and why does she focus on this particular episode? What function does this passage serve in the narrative?

2. What effect does the author's use of internal dialogue (in *italics*) have on her narrative?

3. OTHER METHODS   Besides narration, Boylan also uses definition to explore the meaning of *transgender*. How does she define the term as it applies to her? What do *you* understand it to mean?

Language

1. Comment on the irony in paragraphs 9 and 10. How does Boylan use humor to lighten the mood of her story? (If necessary, consult the Glossary for the definition of *irony*.)

2. To what extent are the statements in paragraphs 18 and 19 to be taken literally? Does Boylan really believe that a spiritual presence spoke out loud? How can you tell?

Writing Topics

1. Write a narrative based on some transformative experience of your own, still vivid in your memory.

2. In an essay, explain what *man* or *woman* means to you. Does your definition correspond to traditional assumptions about gender or is it more fluid, like Boylan's? What characteristics does your definition *not* include?

3. Locate Gordon Lightfoot's lyrics to the song "Early Morning Rain" and a copy of M. R. James's story "Oh, Whistle, and I'll Come to You, My Lad." Read both closely, then write an analysis that explores the parallels between them and Boylan's narrative. Why do you suppose Boylan references these obscure works in her story? How does knowing their content affect your understanding of her experience?

GEORGE ORWELL

A masterful novelist, essayist, journalist, and critic, George Orwell was a highly political writer with little tolerance for authoritarianism, deceit, or pretension. He was born Eric Arthur Blair in 1903 in Bengal, India, where his father held a position in the British civil service. After attending school in England, in 1922 Orwell returned to the East as an officer with the British police in Burma. Five years later he left government service with a lasting contempt for the injustices of imperialism. He had believed since childhood that he should be a writer, so he returned to Europe to become one. His next years of wandering, odd jobs, and poverty were chronicled in Down and Out in Paris and London *(1933), his first book and the occasion for assuming his pen name. Other books followed, including* Burmese Days *(1934), a novel based on his colonial experiences, and* Homage to Catalonia *(1938), a memoir of fighting against the fascists in the Spanish Civil War in 1936. Orwell's best-known works are two satirical novels,* Animal Farm *(1945) and* Nineteen Eighty-Four *(1949), both attacks on totalitarian government. He wrote, he said, largely from political purpose, from a "desire to push the world in a certain direction, to alter other people's ideas of the kind of society that they should strive for." Orwell died in 1950, at the age of forty-six. The four-volume* Collected Essays, Journalism, and Letters of George Orwell, *coedited by his widow, Sonia Orwell, was published in 1968.*

Shooting an Elephant

In this essay, Orwell recounts a difficult decision he faced as a police officer in Burma working for the oppressive British government. The selection is from Shooting an Elephant and Other Essays *(1950).*

In Moulmein, in Lower Burma, I was hated by large numbers 1
of people—the only time in my life that I have been important
enough for this to happen to me. I was subdivisional police officer

of the town, and in an aimless, petty kind of way anti-European feeling was very bitter. No one had the guts to raise a riot, but if a European woman went through the bazaars alone somebody would probably spit betel juice over her dress. As a police officer I was an obvious target and was baited whenever it seemed safe to do so. When a nimble Burman tripped me up on the football field and the referee (another Burman) looked the other way, the crowd yelled with hideous laughter. This happened more than once. In the end the sneering yellow faces of young men that met me everywhere, the insults hooted after me when I was at a safe distance, got badly on my nerves. The young Buddhist priests were the worst of all. There were several thousands of them in the town and none of them seemed to have anything to do except stand on street corners and jeer at Europeans.

All this was perplexing and upsetting. For at that time I had   2 already made up my mind that imperialism was an evil thing and the sooner I chucked up my job and got out of it the better. Theoretically—and secretly, of course—I was all for the Burmese and all against the oppressors, the British. As for the job I was doing, I hated it more bitterly than I can perhaps make clear. In a job like that you see the dirty work of Empire at close quarters. The wretched prisoners huddling in the stinking cages of the lockups, the grey, cowed faces of the long-term convicts, the scarred buttocks of the men who had been flogged with bamboos—all these oppressed me with an intolerable sense of guilt. But I could get nothing into perspective. I was young and ill-educated and I had had to think out my problems in the utter silence that is imposed on every Englishman in the East. I did not even know that the British Empire is dying, still less did I know that it is a great deal better than the younger empires that are going to supplant it. All I knew was that I was stuck between my hatred of the empire I served and my rage against the evil-spirited little beasts who tried to make my job impossible. With one part of my mind I thought of the British Raj[1] as an unbreakable tyranny, as something clamped down, in *saecula saeculorum*,[2] upon the will of prostrate peoples; with another part I thought that the greatest joy in the

---

[1]British imperial government. *Raj* in Hindi means "reign," a word similar to *rajah*, "ruler." [Editors' note.]

[2]Latin, "world without end." [Editors' note.]

world would be to drive a bayonet into a Buddhist priest's guts. Feelings like these are the normal by-products of imperialism; ask any Anglo-Indian official, if you can catch him off duty.

One day something happened which in a roundabout way 3 was enlightening. It was a tiny incident in itself, but it gave me a better glimpse than I had had before of the real nature of imperialism—the real motives for which despotic governments act. Early one morning the subinspector at a police station the other end of town rang me up on the phone and said that an elephant was ravaging the bazaar. Would I please come and do something about it? I did not know what I could do, but I wanted to see what was happening and I got on to a pony and started out. I took my rifle, an old .44 Winchester and much too small to kill an elephant, but I thought the noise might be useful *in terrorem*.[3] Various Burmans stopped me on the way and told me about the elephant's doings. It was not, of course, a wild elephant, but a tame one which had gone "must." It had been chained up, as tame elephants always are when their attack of "must" is due, but on the previous night it had broken its chain and escaped. Its mahout,[4] the only person who could manage it when it was in that state, had set out in pursuit, but had taken the wrong direction and was now twelve hours' journey away, and in the morning the elephant had suddenly reappeared in the town. The Burmese population had no weapons and were quite helpless against it. It had already destroyed somebody's bamboo hut, killed a cow and raided some fruit stalls and devoured the stock; also it had met the municipal rubbish van and, when the driver jumped out and took to his heels, had turned the van over and inflicted violences upon it.

The Burmese subinspector and some Indian constables 4 were waiting for me in the quarter where the elephant had been seen. It was a very poor quarter, a labyrinth of squalid bamboo huts, thatched with palmleaf, winding all over a steep hillside. I remember that it was a cloudy, stuffy morning at the beginning of the rains. We began questioning the people as to where the elephant had gone and, as usual, failed to get any definite information. That is invariably the case in the East; a story always sounds clear enough at a distance, but the nearer you get to the scene of

---

[3]Latin, "to give warning." [Editors' note.]
[4]Keeper or groom, a servant of the elephant's owner. [Editors' note.]

events the vaguer it becomes. Some of the people said that the elephant had gone in one direction, some said that he had gone in another, some professed not even to have heard of any elephant. I had almost made up my mind that the whole story was a pack of lies, when we heard yells a little distance away. There was a loud, scandalized cry of "Go away, child! Go away this instant!" and an old woman with a switch in her hand came round the corner of a hut, violently shooing away a crowd of naked children. Some more women followed, clicking their tongues and exclaiming; evidently there was something that the children ought not to have seen. I rounded the hut and saw a man's dead body sprawling in the mud. He was an Indian, a black Dravidian coolie, almost naked, and he could not have been dead many minutes. The people said that the elephant had come suddenly upon him round the corner of the hut, caught him with its trunk, put its foot on his back and ground him into the earth. This was the rainy season and the ground was soft, and his face had scored a trench a foot deep and a couple of yards long. He was lying on his belly with arms crucified and head sharply twisted to one side. His face was coated with mud, the eyes wide open, the teeth bared and grinning with an expression of unendurable agony. (Never tell me, by the way, that the dead look peaceful. Most of the corpses I have seen looked devilish.) The friction of the great beast's foot had stripped the skin from his back as neatly as one skins a rabbit. As soon as I saw the dead man I sent an orderly to a friend's house nearby to borrow an elephant rifle. I had already sent back the pony, not wanting it to go mad with fright and throw me if it smelled the elephant.

The orderly came back in a few minutes with a rifle and five 5 cartridges, and meanwhile some Burmans had arrived and told us that the elephant was in the paddy fields below, only a few hundred yards away. As I started forward practically the whole population of the quarter flocked out of the houses and followed me. They had seen the rifle and were all shouting excitedly that I was going to shoot the elephant. They had not shown much interest in the elephant when he was merely ravaging their homes, but it was different now that he was going to be shot. It was a bit of fun to them, as it would be to an English crowd; besides they wanted the meat. It made me vaguely uneasy. I had no intention of shooting the elephant—I had merely sent for the rifle to defend myself

if necessary—and it is always unnerving to have a crowd following you. I marched down the hill, looking and feeling a fool, with
the rifle over my shoulder and an ever-growing army of people
jostling at my heels. At the bottom, when you got away from the
huts, there was a metalled road and beyond that a miry waste of
paddy fields a thousand yards across, not yet ploughed but soggy
from the first rains and dotted with coarse grass. The elephant
was standing eight yards from the road, his left side towards us.
He took not the slightest notice of the crowd's approach. He was
tearing up bunches of grass, beating them against his knees to
clean them and stuffing them into his mouth.

I had halted on the road. As soon as I saw the elephant I   6
knew with perfect certainty that I ought not to shoot him. It is a
serious matter to shoot a working elephant—it is comparable to
destroying a huge and costly piece of machinery—and obviously
one ought not to do it if it can possibly be avoided. And at that
distance, peacefully eating, the elephant looked no more dangerous than a cow. I thought then and I think now that his attack of
"must" was already passing off; in which case he would merely
wander harmlessly about until the mahout came back and caught
him. Moreover, I did not in the least want to shoot him. I decided
that I would watch him for a little while to make sure that he did
not turn savage again, and then go home.

But at that moment, I glanced round at the crowd that had   7
followed me. It was an immense crowd, two thousand at the least
and growing every minute. It blocked the road for a long distance
on either side. I looked at the sea of yellow faces above the garish
clothes—faces all happy and excited over this bit of fun, all certain
that the elephant was going to be shot. They were watching me as
they would watch a conjuror about to perform a trick. They did
not like me, but with the magical rifle in my hands I was momentarily worth watching. And suddenly I realized that I should have
to shoot the elephant after all. The people expected it of me and I
had got to do it; I could feel their two thousand wills pressing me
forward, irresistibly. And it was at this moment, as I stood there
with the rifle in my hands, that I first grasped the hollowness, the
futility of the white man's dominion in the East. Here was I, the
white man with his gun, standing in front of the unarmed native
crowd—seemingly the leading actor of the piece; but in reality
I was only an absurd puppet pushed to and fro by the will of those

yellow faces behind. I perceived in this moment that when the white man turns tyrant it is his own freedom that he destroys. He becomes a sort of hollow, posing dummy, the conventionalized figure of a sahib. For it is the condition of his rule that he shall spend his life in trying to impress the "natives," and so in every crisis he has got to do what the "natives" expect of him. He wears a mask, and his face grows to fit it. I had got to shoot the elephant. I had committed myself to doing it when I sent for the rifle. A sahib has got to act like a sahib; he has got to appear resolute, to know his own mind and do definite things. To come all that way, rifle in hand, with two thousand people marching at my heels, and then to trail feebly away, having done nothing—no, that was impossible. The crowd would laugh at me. And my whole life, every white man's life in the East, was one long struggle not to be laughed at.

But I did not want to shoot the elephant. I watched him beat- 8 ing his bunch of grass against his knees, with that preoccupied grandmotherly air that elephants have. It seemed to me that it would be murder to shoot him. At that age I was not squeamish about killing animals, but I had never shot an elephant and never wanted to. (Somehow it always seems worse to kill a *large* animal.) Besides, there was the beast's owner to be considered. Alive, the elephant was worth at least a hundred pounds; dead, he would only be worth the value of his tusks, five pounds, possibly. But I had got to act quickly. I turned to some experienced-looking Burmans who had been there when we arrived, and asked them how the elephant had been behaving. They all said the same thing: He took no notice of you if you left him alone, but he might charge if you went too close to him.

It was perfectly clear to me what I ought to do. I ought to 9 walk up to within, say, twenty-five yards of the elephant and test his behavior. If he charged, I could shoot; if he took no notice of me, it would be safe to leave him until the mahout came back. But also I knew that I was going to do no such thing. I was a poor shot with a rifle and the ground was soft mud into which one would sink at every step. If the elephant charged and I missed him, I should have about as much chance as a toad under a steamroller. But even then I was not thinking particularly of my own skin, only of the watchful yellow faces behind. For at that moment, with the crowd watching me, I was not afraid in the ordinary sense, as I would have been if I had been alone. A white man mustn't be frightened in front of "natives"; and so, in general, he isn't frightened. The sole thought in my mind was that if anything went wrong those two thousand Burmans would see me pursued, caught, trampled on, and reduced to a grinning corpse like that Indian up the hill. And if that happened it was quite probable that some of them would laugh. That would never do. There was only one alternative. I shoved the cartridges into the magazine and lay down on the road to get a better aim.

The crowd grew very still, and a deep, low, happy sigh, as of 10 people who see the theater curtain go up at last, breathed from innumerable throats. They were going to have their bit of fun after all. The rifle was a beautiful German thing with cross-hair sights. I did not then know that in shooting an elephant one would shoot to cut an imaginary bar running from ear-hole to ear-hole. I ought, therefore, as the elephant was sideways on, to have aimed straight at his ear-hole; actually I aimed several inches in front of this, thinking the brain would be further forward.

When I pulled the trigger I did not hear the bang or feel the 11 kick—one never does when a shot goes home—but I heard the devilish roar of glee that went up from the crowd. In that instant, in too short a time, one would have thought, even for the bullet to get there, a mysterious, terrible change had come over the elephant. He neither stirred nor fell, but every line of his body had altered. He looked suddenly stricken, shrunken, immensely old, as though the frightful impact of the bullet had paralyzed him without knocking him down. At last, after what seemed a long time—it might have been five seconds, I dare say—he sagged flabbily to his knees. His mouth slobbered. An enormous senility seemed to have settled upon him. One could have imagined him thousands of years old. I fired again into the same spot. At the second shot he did not collapse but climbed with desperate slowness to his feet and stood weakly upright, with legs sagging and head drooping. I fired a third time. That was the shot that did for him. You could see the agony of it jolt his whole body and knock the last remnant of strength from his legs. But in falling he seemed for a moment to rise, for as his hind legs collapsed beneath him he seemed to tower upward like a huge rock toppling, his trunk reaching skywards like a tree. He trumpeted, for the first and only time. And then down he came, his belly towards me, with a crash that seemed to shake the ground even where I lay.

I got up. The Burmans were already racing past me across 12 the mud. It was obvious that the elephant would never rise again, but he was not dead. He was breathing very rhythmically with long rattling gasps, his great mound of a side painfully rising and falling. His mouth was wide open. I could see far down into caverns of pale pink throat. I waited a long time for him to die, but his breathing did not weaken. Finally I fired my two remaining shots into the spot where I thought his heart must be. The thick blood welled out of him like red velvet, but still he did not die. His body did not even jerk when the shots hit him, the tortured breathing continued without a pause. He was dying, very slowly and in great agony, but in some world remote from me where not even a bullet could damage him further. I felt I had got to put an end to that dreadful noise. It seemed dreadful to see the great beast lying there, powerless to move and yet powerless to die, and not even to be able to finish him. I sent back for my small rifle and poured shot after shot into his heart and down his throat. They seemed to make no impression. The tortured gasps continued as steadily as the ticking of a clock.

In the end I could not stand it any longer and went away. I 13 heard later that it took him half an hour to die. Burmans were bringing dahs and baskets even before I left, and I was told they had stripped his body almost to the bones by the afternoon.

Afterwards, of course, there were endless discussions about 14 the shooting of the elephant. The owner was furious, but he was only an Indian and could do nothing. Besides, legally I had done the right thing, for a mad elephant has to be killed, like a mad dog, if its owner fails to control it. Among the Europeans opinion was divided. The older men said I was right, the younger men said it was a damn shame to shoot an elephant for killing a coolie, because the elephant was worth more than any damn Coringhee coolie. And afterwards I was very glad that the coolie had been killed; it put me legally in the right and it gave me sufficient pretext for shooting the elephant. I often wondered whether any of the others grasped that I had done it solely to avoid looking a fool.

Meaning

1. Why did Orwell shoot the elephant?
2. Describe the epiphany that Orwell experiences in the course of the event he writes about. (An *epiphany* is a sudden realization of a truth.)
3. In the last paragraph of his essay, Orwell says he was "glad that the coolie had been killed." How do you account for this remark?

Purpose and Audience

1. What is the purpose of this essay? What does Orwell seem to want readers to think or do as a result of reading the essay?
2. What does "Shooting an Elephant" gain from having been written years after the events it recounts?

Method and Structure

1. In addition to serving as an introduction to Orwell's essay, what function is performed by paragraphs 1 and 2?
2. From what circumstances does the irony of Orwell's essay spring? (For the definition of *irony*, consult the Glossary.)
3. OTHER METHODS How do the examples in paragraphs 1 and 2 illustrate Orwell's conflict about his work as a police officer in Burma?

Language

1. What do you understand by Orwell's statement that the elephant had "gone 'must'" (paragraph 3)? Look up *must* or its variant *musth* in an unabridged dictionary.
2. How effective is Orwell's use of adjectives in describing the death of the elephant? How do these adjectives convey Orwell's feelings about his decision?

Writing Topics

1. Write a narrative essay about a time when you acted against your better judgment in order to save face in front of others. Tell the story of your action, and consider what the results were, what you might have done differently, and what you learned from the experience.

2. With what examples of governmental face saving are you familiar? If none leaps to mind, read a newspaper or watch the news on television or online to catch public officials in the act of covering themselves. (Not only national government but local or student government may provide examples.) In an essay, analyze two or three examples: What do you think was really going on that needed covering? Did the officials succeed in saving face, or did their efforts fail? Were the efforts harmful in any way?

3. Orwell is honest with himself and his readers in acknowledging his mistakes as a government official. Write an essay that examines the degree to which confession may, or may not, erase blame for misdeeds. Does Orwell remain just as guilty as he would have been if he had not taken responsibility for his actions? Why, or why not? Feel free to supplement your analysis of Orwell's case with examples from your own life or from the news.

NARRATION

Select one of the following topics, or any other topic they suggest, for an essay developed by narration. Be sure to choose a topic you care about so that narration is a means of communicating an idea, not an end in itself.

Friends and Relations

1. Gaining independence
2. A friend's generosity or sacrifice
3. A wedding or funeral
4. An incident from family legend

The World around You

5. An interaction you witnessed while taking public transportation
6. A storm, a flood, an earthquake, or another natural event
7. The history of your neighborhood
8. A community event, such as a meeting, demonstration, or celebration
9. A time when a poem, story, film, song, or other work changed you

Lessons of Daily Life

10. A time when you confronted authority
11. A time when you had to deliver bad news
12. A time when a long-anticipated possession proved disappointing
13. Your biggest social blunder

Firsts

14. Your first day of school, as a child or more recently
15. The first time you met someone who became important to you
16. The first performance you gave

Adventures

17. An episode of extrasensory perception
18. An intellectual journey, such as pursuing a new field or solving a mystery
19. A trip to an unfamiliar place

Chapter 3

EXAMPLE

USING THE METHOD

An **example** represents a general group or an abstract concept or quality. Steven Spielberg is an example from the group of movie directors. A friend's calling at 2:00 a.m. is an example of her inconsiderateness—or desperation. We habitually use examples to bring general and abstract statements down to earth so that listeners or readers will take an interest in them and understand them.

The chief purpose of examples is to make the general specific and the abstract concrete. Since these operations are among the most basic in writing, it is easy to see why illustration or exemplification (the use of example) is among the most common methods of writing. Examples appear frequently in essays developed by other methods. In fact, as diverse as they are, all the essays in this book employ examples for clarity, support, and liveliness. If the writers had not used examples, we might have only a vague sense of their meaning or, worse, might supply mistaken meanings from our own experiences.

While nearly indispensable in any kind of writing, exemplification may also serve as the dominant method of developing an essay. When your primary goal is to convince readers of the truth of a generalization—whether a personal observation or a controversial assertion—using examples is a natural choice. Any of the following general statements, for instance, might form the central assertion of an essay:

EXAMPLE   97

Facebook has changed the way people relate to one another.

Some fans at the championship game were more competitive than the players.

A mental hospital is no place for the mentally ill.

A funeral benefits the dead person's family and friends.

Generalizations such as these beg for examples: as many as necessary to support the idea.

How many examples are necessary to support a generalization? That depends on your subject, your purpose, and your intended audience. Two basic patterns are possible:

- A single **extended example** of several paragraphs or several pages fills in needed background and gives the reader a complete view of the subject from one angle. For instance, the purpose of a funeral might be made clear with a narrative and descriptive account of a particular funeral, the family and friends who attended it, and the benefits they derived from it.
- **Multiple examples**, from a few to dozens, illustrate the range covered by the generalization. The competitiveness of a team's fans might be captured with three or four examples. But supporting the generalization about mental hospitals might demand many examples of patients whose illnesses worsened in the hospital or (from a different angle) many examples of hospital practices that actually harm patients.

Sometimes a generalization merits support from both an extended example and several briefer examples, a combination that provides depth along with range. For instance, half the essay on mental hospitals might be devoted to one patient's experiences and the other half to brief summaries of the experiences of others.

DEVELOPING AN ESSAY BY EXAMPLE

Getting Started

You will need examples whenever your experiences, observations, or reading lead you to make a general statement: the examples give readers evidence for the statement so that they see its truth.

An appropriate subject for an example paper is likely to be a general idea you have formed about people, things, the media, or any other feature of your life. Say, for instance, that you have noticed while watching television that many programs aimed at teenagers deal with sensitive topics such as drug abuse, domestic violence, or chronic illness. There is a promising subject: teen dramas that address controversial social issues.

After choosing a subject, you should make a list of all the pertinent examples that occur to you. This stage may take some thought and even some further reading or observation. While making the list, focus on identifying as many examples as you can, but keep your intended readers at the front of your mind: what do they already know about your subject, and what do they need to know in order to accept your view of it?

Forming a Thesis

Having several examples of a subject is a good starting place, but you will also need a thesis that ties the examples together and gives them a point. A clear thesis is crucial for an example paper because without it readers can only guess what your illustrations are intended to show.

To move from a general subject to a workable thesis, try making a generalization based on what you know of individual examples, for instance:

> Some teen dramas do a surprisingly good job of dramatizing and explaining difficult social issues.

> Some teen dramas trivialize social issues in their quest for higher ratings.

Either of these statements could serve as the thesis of an essay, the point you want readers to take away from your examples.

Avoid the temptation to start with a broad statement and then try to drum up a few examples to prove it. A thesis such as "Teenagers do poorly in school because they watch too much television" would require factual support gained from research, not the lone example of your brother. If your brother performs poorly in school and you attribute his performance to his television habits, then narrow your thesis so that it accurately reflects

EXAMPLE   99

your evidence—perhaps "In the case of my brother, at least, the more time spent watching television, the poorer the grades."

After arriving at your thesis, you should narrow your list of examples down to those that are most pertinent, adding new ones as necessary to persuade readers of your point. For instance, in illustrating the social value of teen dramas for readers who believe television is worthless or even harmful, you might concentrate on the programs or individual episodes that are most relevant to readers' lives, providing enough detail about each to make readers see the relevance.

Organizing

Most example essays open with an introduction that engages readers' attention and gives them some context to relate to. You might begin the paper on teen dramas, for instance, by briefly narrating the plot of one episode. The opening should lead into your thesis sentence so that readers know what to expect from the rest of the essay.

Organizing the body of the essay may not be difficult if you use a single example, for the example itself may suggest a distinct method of development (such as narration) and thus an arrangement. But an essay using multiple examples usually requires close attention to arrangement so that readers experience not a list but a pattern. Some guidelines:

- *With a limited number of examples*—say, four or five—use a climactic organization, arranging examples in order of increasing importance, interest, or complexity. Then the strongest and most detailed example provides a dramatic finish.
- *With many examples*—ten or more—find some likenesses among examples that will allow you to treat them in groups. For instance, instead of covering fourteen teen dramas in a shapeless list, you might group them by subject into shows dealing with family relations, those dealing with illness, and the like. (This is the method of classification, discussed in Chapter 5.) Covering each group in a separate paragraph or two would avoid the awkward string of choppy paragraphs that might result from covering each example independently,

and arranging the groups themselves in order of increasing interest or importance would further structure your presentation.

To conclude your essay, you may want to summarize by elaborating on the generalization of your thesis now that you have supported it. But the essay may not require a conclusion at all if you believe your final example emphasizes your point and provides a strong finish.

Drafting

While you draft your essay, remember that your examples must be plentiful and specific enough to support your generalization. If you use fifteen different examples, their range should allow you to treat each one briefly, in one or two sentences. But if you use only three examples, say, you will have to describe each one in sufficient detail to make up for their small number. And, obviously, if you use only a single example, you must be as specific as possible so that readers see clearly how it illustrates your generalization.

Revising and Editing

To be sure you've met the expectations that most readers hold for examples, revise and edit your draft by considering the following questions.

- *Is your generalization fully supported by your examples?* If not, you may need to narrow your thesis statement or add more evidence to prove your point.
- *Are all examples, or parts of a single example, obviously relevant to your generalization?* Be careful not to get sidetracked by interesting but unrelated information.
- *Are the examples specific?* Examples bring a generalization down to earth only if they are well detailed. For an essay on the social value of teen dramas, for instance, simply naming representative programs and their subjects would not demonstrate their social value. Each drama would need a plot summary that shows how the program fits and illustrates the generalization.

EXAMPLE   101

- *Do the examples, or the parts of a single example, cover all the territory mapped out by your generalization?* To support your generalization, you need to present a range of instances that fairly represents the whole. An essay would be misleading if it failed to acknowledge that not *all* teen dramas have social value. It would also be misleading if it presented several shows as representative examples of socially valuable teen programming when in fact they were the *only* instances of such television.

PERRI KLASS

Perri Klass is a pediatrician, a writer, and a knitter. She was born in 1958 in Trinidad and grew up in New York City and New Jersey. Klass obtained a BA from Harvard University in 1979, finished Harvard Medical School in 1986, and teaches journalism and pediatrics at New York University. Her publications are extensive: short stories and articles in Mademoiselle, Antioch Review, *the* New England Journal of Medicine, *and other periodicals; several novels, including* Other Women's Children *(1990) and* The Mercy Rule *(2008); five essay collections; a memoir,* Every Mother Is a Daughter: The Neverending Quest for Success, Inner Peace, and a Really Clean Kitchen *(2006); and the nonfiction books* Quirky Kids: Understanding and Helping Your Child Who Doesn't Fit In *(2003) and* Treatment Kind and Fair: Letters to a Young Doctor *(2007). Klass is the president and medical director of Reach Out and Read, a nonprofit group that works with pediatricians to distribute books to disadvantaged children.*

She's Your Basic LOL in NAD

Most of us have felt excluded, confused, or even frightened by the jargon of the medical profession—that is, by the special terminology and abbreviations for diseases and procedures. In this essay Klass uses examples of such language, some of it heartless, to illustrate the pluses and minuses of becoming a doctor. The essay first appeared as a "Hers" column in the New York Times.

"Mrs. Tolstoy is your basic LOL in NAD, admitted for a soft rule- 1 out MI," the intern announces. I scribble that on my patient list. In other words Mrs. Tolstoy is a Little Old Lady in No Apparent Distress who is in the hospital to make sure she hasn't had a heart attack (rule out a myocardial infarction). And we think it's unlikely that she has had a heart attack (a *soft* rule-out).

If I learned nothing else during my first three months of work- 2 ing in the hospital as a medical student, I learned endless jargon and abbreviations. I started out in a state of primeval innocence, in which I didn't even know that "s̄ CP, SOB, N/V" meant "without chest pain, shortness of breath, or nausea and vomiting." By the end I took the abbreviations so for granted that I would complain to my mother the English professor, "And can you believe I had to put down *three* NG tubes last night?"

"You'll have to tell me what an NG tube is if you want me to 3 sympathize properly," my mother said. NG, nasogastric—isn't it obvious?

I picked up not only the specific expressions but also the pat- 4 terns of speech and the grammatical conventions; for example, you never say that a patient's blood pressure fell or that his car-diac enzymes rose. Instead, the patient is always the subject of the verb: "He dropped his pressure." "He bumped his enzymes." This sort of construction probably reflects that profound irrita-tion of the intern when the nurses come in the middle of the night to say that Mr. Dickinson has disturbingly low blood pressure. "Oh, he's gonna hurt me bad tonight," the intern may say, inevita-bly angry at Mr. Dickinson for dropping his pressure and creating a problem.

When chemotherapy fails to cure Mrs. Bacon's cancer, what 5 we say is, "Mrs. Bacon failed chemotherapy."

"Well, we've already had one hit today, and we're up next, 6 but at least we've got mostly stable players on our team." This means that our team (group of doctors and medical students) has already gotten one new admission today, and it is our turn again, so we'll get whoever is next admitted in emergency, but at least most of the patients we already have are fairly stable, that is, unlikely to drop their pressures or in any other way get suddenly sicker and hurt us bad. Baseball metaphor is pervasive: a no-hit-ter is a night without any new admissions. A player is always a patient—a nitrate player is a patient on nitrates, a unit player is a patient in the intensive-care unit, and so on, until you reach the terminal player.

It is interesting to consider what it means to be winning, 7 or doing well, in this perennial baseball game. When the intern hangs up the phone and announces, "I got a hit," that is not cause for congratulations. The team is not scoring points; rather, it is getting hit, being bombarded with new patients. The object of the game from the point of view of the doctors, considering the players for whom they are already responsible, is to get as few new hits as possible.

These special languages contribute to a sense of closeness 8 and professional spirit among people who are under a great deal of stress. As a medical student, it was exciting for me to discover that I'd finally cracked the code, that I could understand what doctors said and wrote and could use the same formulations myself. Some people seem to become enamored of the jargon for its own sake, perhaps because they are so deeply thrilled with the idea of medicine, with the idea of themselves as doctors.

I knew a medical student who was referred to by the interns on 9 the team as Mr. Eponym because he was so infatuated with epon-ymous terminology,[1] the more obscure the better. He never said "capillary pulsation" if he could say "Quincke's pulses." He would lovingly tell over the multinamed syndromes—Wolff-Parkinson-White, Lown-Ganong-Levine, Henoch-Schonlein—until the temp-tation to suggest Schleswig-Holstein or Stevenson-Kefauver or Baskin-Robbins became irresistible to his less reverent colleagues.

And there is the jargon that you don't ever want to hear your- 10 self using. You know that your training is changing you, but there are certain changes you think would be going a little too far.

The resident was describing a man with devastating terminal 11 pancreatic cancer. "Basically he's CTD," the resident concluded. I reminded myself that I had resolved not to be shy about asking when I didn't understand things. "CTD?" I asked timidly.

The resident smirked at me. "Circling The Drain."   12

The images are vivid and terrible. "What happened to Mrs. 13 Melville?"

"Oh, she boxed last night." To box is to die, of course.   14

Then there are the more pompous locutions that can make 15 the beginning medical student nervous about the effects of medical training. A friend of mine was told by his resident, "A pregnant woman with sickle-cell represents a failure of genetic counseling."

Mr. Eponym, who tried hard to talk like the doctors, once 16 explained to me, "An infant is basically a brainstem preparation."

---

[1]*Eponymous* means "named after"—in this case, medical terminology is named after researchers. [Editors' note.]

A brainstem preparation, as used in neurological research, is an animal whose higher brain functions have been destroyed so that only the most primitive reflexes remain, like the sucking reflex, the startle reflex, and the rooting reflex.

    The more extreme forms aside, one most important function 17 of medical jargon is to help doctors maintain some distance from their patients. By reformulating a patient's pain and problems into a language that the patient doesn't even speak, I suppose we are in some sense taking those pains and problems under our jurisdiction and also reducing their emotional impact. This linguistic separation between doctors and patients allows conversations to go on at the bedside that are unintelligible to the patient. "Naturally, we're worried about adreno-CA," the intern can say to the medical student, and lung cancer need never be mentioned.

    I learned a new language this past summer. At times it thrills 18 me to hear myself using it. It enables me to understand my colleagues, to communicate effectively in the hospital. Yet I am uncomfortably aware that I will never again notice the peculiarities and even atrocities of medical language as keenly as I did this summer. There may be specific expressions I manage to avoid, but even as I remark them, promising myself I will never use them, I find that this language is becoming my professional speech. It no longer sounds strange in my ears — or coming from my mouth. And I am afraid that as with any new language, to use it properly you must absorb not only the vocabulary but also the structure, the logic, the attitudes. At first you may notice these new alien assumptions every time you put together a sentence, but with time and increased fluency you stop being aware of them at all. And as you lose that awareness, for better or for worse, you move closer and closer to being a doctor instead of just talking like one.

Meaning

1. What point does Klass make about medical jargon in this essay? Where does she reveal her main point explicitly?

2. What useful purposes does medical jargon serve, according to Klass? Do the examples in paragraphs 9–16 serve these purposes? Why, or why not?

Purpose and Audience

1. What does Klass imply when she states that she began her work in the hospital "in a state of primeval innocence" (paragraph 2)? What does this phrase suggest about her purpose in writing the essay?

2. From what perspective does Klass write this essay: that of a medical professional? someone outside the profession? a patient? someone else? To what extent does she expect her readers to share her perspective? What evidence in the essay supports your answer?

3. Given that she is writing for a general audience, does Klass take adequate care to define medical terms? Support your answer with examples from the essay.

Method and Structure

1. Why does Klass begin the essay with an example rather than a statement of her main idea? What effect does this example produce? How does this effect support her purpose in writing the essay?

2. Although Klass uses many examples of medical jargon, she avoids the dull effect of a list by periodically stepping back to make a general statement about her experience or the jargon—for instance, "I picked up not only the specific expressions but also the patterns of speech and the grammatical conventions" (paragraph 4). Locate other places—not necessarily at the beginnings of paragraphs—where Klass breaks up her examples with more general statements.

3. OTHER METHODS   Klass uses several other methods besides example, among them classification, definition, and cause-and-effect analysis. What effects—positive and negative—does medical jargon have on Klass, other students, and doctors who use it?

Language

1. What is the tone of this essay? Is Klass trying to be humorous or tongue-in-cheek about the jargon of the profession, or is she serious? Where in the essay is the author's attitude toward her subject the most obvious? (If necessary, see the Glossary for an explanation of *tone*.)

2. Klass refers to the users of medical jargon as both *we/us* (paragraphs 1, 5, 6, 17) and *they/them* (7), and sometimes she shifts from *I* to *you* within a paragraph (4, 18). Do you think these shifts are effective or distracting? Why? Do the shifts serve any function?

3. Klass obviously experienced both positive and negative feelings about mastering medical jargon. Which words and phrases in the last paragraph reflect positive feelings, and which negative?

Writing Topics

1. Klass likens her experience learning medical jargon to that of learning a new language (paragraph 18). If you are studying or have learned a second language, write an essay in which you explain the "new alien assumptions" you must make "every time you put together a sentence." Draw your examples not just from the new language's grammar and vocabulary but from its underlying logic and attitudes. For instance, does one speak to older people differently in the new language? make requests differently? describe love or art differently?

2. Klass's essay explores the "separation between doctors and patients" (paragraph 17). Has this separation affected you as a patient or as the relative or friend of a patient? If so, write an essay about your experiences. Did the medical professionals rely heavily on jargon? Was their language comforting, frightening, irritating? Based on your experience and on Klass's essay, do you believe that the separation between doctors and patients is desirable? Why, or why not?

3. Most groups focused on a common interest have their own jargon. If you belong to such a group—for example, runners, football fans, food servers, engineering students—spend a few days listening to yourself and others use this language and thinking about the purposes it serves. Which aspects of this language seem intended to make users feel like insiders? Which seem to serve some other purpose, and what is it? In an essay, explain what this jargon reveals about the group and its common interest, using as many specific examples as you can.

ANNA QUINDLEN

Winner of the Pulitzer Prize for commentary in 1992, Anna Quindlen writes sharp, candid columns on subjects ranging from family life to social issues to international politics. She was born in 1953 in Philadelphia, where she grew up, as she puts it, "an antsy kid with a fresh mouth." *After graduating from Barnard College, Quindlen began writing for the* New York Post *and then joined the* New York Times, *where she worked her way up from a city hall reporter to a regular columnist. Quindlen left the* Times *in 1995, and from 1999 to 2010 she wrote columns and articles for* Newsweek *magazine. Her columns have been collected in* Living Out Loud *(1988),* Thinking Out Loud *(1993), and* Loud and Clear *(2004). Quindlen is also the author of the novels* Object Lessons *(1991),* One True Thing *(1994),* Black and Blue *(1998),* Blessings *(2002),* Rise and Shine *(2006), and* Every Last One *(2010); the nonfiction books* How Reading Changed My Life *(1998),* A Short Guide to a Happy Life *(2000), and* Being Perfect *(2005); and the memoirs* Good Dog. Stay. *(2007) and* Lots of Candles, Plenty of Cake *(2012).*

Homeless

In this essay, Quindlen uses examples to explore the importance of having a place to call "home." The selection is from her collection Living Out Loud.

Her name was Ann, and we met in the Port Authority Bus Termi- 1
nal several Januarys ago. I was doing a story on homeless people. She said I was wasting my time talking to her; she was just
passing through, although she'd been passing through for more
than two weeks. To prove to me that this was true, she rummaged
through a tote bag and a manila envelope and finally unfolded a
sheet of typing paper and brought out her photographs.

They were not pictures of family, or friends, or even a dog or 2
cat, its eyes brown-red in the flashbulb's light. They were pictures

of a house. It was like a thousand houses in a hundred towns, not suburb, not city, but somewhere in between, with aluminum siding and a chain-link fence, a narrow driveway running up to a one-car garage and a patch of backyard. The house was yellow. I looked on the back for a date or a name, but neither was there. There was no need for discussion. I knew what she was trying to tell me, for it was something I had often felt. She was not adrift, alone, anonymous, although her bags and her raincoat with the grime shadowing its creases had made me believe she was. She had a house, or at least once upon a time had had one. Inside were curtains, a couch, a stove, potholders. You are where you live. She was somebody.

I've never been very good at looking at the big picture, taking 3 the global view, and I've always been a person with an overactive sense of place, the legacy of an Irish grandfather. So it is natural that the thing that seems most wrong with the world to me right now is that there are so many people with no homes. I'm not simply talking about shelter from the elements, or three square meals a day or a mailing address to which the welfare people can send the check—although I know that all these are important for survival. I'm talking about a home, about precisely those kinds of feelings that have wound up in cross-stitch and French knots on samplers over the years.

Home is where the heart is. There's no place like it. I love my 4 home with a ferocity totally out of proportion to its appearance or location. I love dumb things about it: the hot-water heater, the plastic rack you drain dishes in, the roof over my head, which occasionally leaks. And yet it is precisely those dumb things that make it what it is—a place of certainty, stability, predictability, privacy, for me and for my family. It is where I live. What more can you say about a place than that? That is everything.

Yet it is something that we have been edging away from 5 gradually during my lifetime and the lifetimes of my parents and grandparents. There was a time when where you lived often was where you worked and where you grew the food you ate and even where you were buried. When that era passed, where you lived at least was where your parents had lived and where you would live with your children when you became enfeebled. Then, suddenly where you lived was where you lived for three years, until you could move on to something else and something else again.

And so we have come to something else again, to children who 6
do not understand what it means to go to their rooms because they
have never had a room, to men and women whose fantasy is a
wall they can paint a color of their own choosing, to old people
reduced to sitting on molded plastic chairs, their skin blue-white in
the lights of a bus station, who pull pictures of houses out of their
bags. Homes have stopped being homes. Now they are real estate.

People find it curious that those without homes would rather 7
sleep sitting up on benches or huddled in doorways than go to shelters. Certainly some prefer to do so because they are emotionally
ill, because they have been locked in before and they are damned if
they will be locked in again. Others are afraid of the violence and
trouble they may find there. But some seem to want something
that is not available in shelters, and they will not compromise, not
for a cot, or oatmeal, or a shower with special soap that kills the
bugs. "One room," a woman with a baby who was sleeping on her
sister's floor, once told me, "painted blue." That was the crux of it;
not size or location, but pride of ownership. Painted blue.

This is a difficult problem, and some wise and compassion- 8
ate people are working hard at it. But in the main I think we
work around it, just as we walk around it when it is lying on
the sidewalk or sitting in the bus terminal—the problem, that is.
It has been customary to take people's pain and lessen our own
participation in it by turning it into an issue, not a collection of
human beings. We turn an adjective into a noun: the poor, not
poor people; the homeless, not Ann or the man who lives in the
box or the woman who sleeps on the subway grate.

Sometimes I think we would be better off if we forgot about 9
the broad strokes and concentrated on the details. Here is a
woman without a bureau. There is a man with no mirror, no wall
to hang it on. They are not the homeless. They are people who
have no homes. No drawer that holds the spoons. No window to
look out upon the world. My God. That is everything.

Meaning

1. What is Quindlen's thesis?
2. What distinction is Quindlen making in her last paragraph when
   she says, "They are not the homeless. They are people who have no
   homes"?

Purpose and Audience

1. What do you think is Quindlen's purpose in writing this essay? Why does she believe that having a home is important?
2. What key assumptions does the author make about her audience? Are the assumptions reasonable? Where does she specifically address an assumption that might undermine her view?

Method and Structure

1. Why do you think Quindlen begins with the story of Ann? How else might Quindlen have begun her essay?
2. What is the effect of Quindlen's examples of her own home?
3. OTHER METHODS   Quindlen uses examples to support an argument. What position does she want readers to recognize and accept?

Language

1. What is the effect of "My God" in the last paragraph?
2. How might Quindlen be said to give new meaning to the old cliché "Home is where the heart is" (paragraph 4)? (See the Glossary for a definition of *cliché*.)
3. What is meant by "crux" (paragraph 7)? Where does the word come from?

Writing Topics

1. Write an essay that gives a detailed definition of *home* by using your own home(s), hometown(s), or experiences with home(s) as supporting examples. (See Chapter 8 if you need help with definition.)
2. Have you ever moved from one place to another? What sort of experience was it? Write an essay about leaving an old home and moving to a new one. Was there an activity, an experience, or an object that helped ease the transition?
3. Address Quindlen's contention that turning homelessness into an issue avoids the problem, that we might "be better off if we forgot about the broad strokes and concentrated on the details" (paragraph 9).
4. Write a brief essay in which you agree or disagree with Quindlen's assertion that a home is "everything." Can a person be fulfilled without a permanent home? In your answer, take into account the values and associations that might underlie an attachment to a place; Quindlen mentions "certainty, stability, predictability, privacy" (paragraph 4), but there are others, including some (such as resistance to change and budget limitations) that are less positive.

BRENT STAPLES

Brent Staples was born in 1951 in Chester, Pennsylvania. After receiving a BA from Widener University and a PhD in psychology from the University of Chicago, he began writing on culture and politics for the New York Times *in 1985. Since 1990 he has been a member of the* Times *editorial board and a contributor to publications including* Ms., Harper's Magazine, Slate, *and the* New York Times Magazine. *Staples has also published two books:* Parallel Time: Growing Up in Black and White *(1994), a memoir; and* An American Love Story *(1999), a companion book to the PBS documentary about an interracial family.*

Black Men and Public Space

First published in Harper's Magazine, *this selection relates the prejudice Staples has faced as a black man walking city streets after dark. The essay also appeared in a slightly different form in* Parallel Time.

My first victim was a woman—white, well dressed, probably in 1 her late twenties. I came upon her late one evening on a deserted street in Hyde Park, a relatively affluent neighborhood in an otherwise mean, impoverished section of Chicago. As I swung onto the avenue behind her, there seemed to be a discreet, uninflammatory distance between us. Not so. She cast back a worried glance. To her, the youngish black man—a broad six feet two inches with a beard and billowing hair, both hands shoved into the pockets of a bulky military jacket—seemed menacingly close. After a few more quick glimpses, she picked up her pace and was soon running in earnest. Within seconds she disappeared into a cross street.

That was more than a decade ago. I was twenty-two years 2 old, a graduate student newly arrived at the University of Chicago. It was in the echo of that terrified woman's footfalls that I first began to know the unwieldy inheritance I'd come into—the ability to alter public space in ugly ways. It was clear that she thought herself the quarry of a mugger, a rapist, or worse. Suffering a bout of insomnia, however, I was stalking sleep, not defenseless wayfarers. As a softy who is scarcely able to take a knife to a raw chicken—let alone hold one to a person's throat—I was surprised, embarrassed, and dismayed all at once. Her flight made me feel like an accomplice in tyranny. It also made it clear that I was indistinguishable from the muggers who occasionally seeped into the area from the surrounding ghetto. That first encounter, and those that followed, signified that a vast, unnerving gulf lay between nighttime pedestrians—particularly women—and me. And I soon gathered that being perceived as dangerous is a hazard in itself. I only needed to turn a corner into a dicey situation, or crowd some frightened, armed person in a foyer somewhere, or make an errant move after being pulled over by a policeman. Where fear and weapons meet—and they often do in urban America—there is always the possibility of death.

In that first year, my first away from my hometown, I was to 3 become thoroughly familiar with the language of fear. At dark, shadowy intersections, I could cross in front of a car stopped at a traffic light and elicit the *thunk, thunk, thunk, thunk* of the driver—black, white, male, or female—hammering down the door locks. On less traveled streets after dark, I grew accustomed to but never comfortable with people crossing to the other side of the street rather than pass me. Then there were the standard unpleasantries with policemen, doormen, bouncers, cabdrivers, and others whose business it is to screen out troublesome individuals *before* there is any nastiness.

I moved to New York nearly two years ago and I have remained 4 an avid night walker. In central Manhattan, the near-constant crowd cover minimizes tense one-on-one street encounters. Elsewhere—in SoHo, for example, where sidewalks are narrow and tightly spaced buildings shut out the sky—things can get very taut indeed.

After dark, on the warrenlike streets of Brooklyn where I live, 5 I often see women who fear the worst from me. They seem to have set their faces on neutral, and with their purse straps strung across their chests bandolier-style, they forge ahead as though bracing themselves against being tackled. I understand, of course, that the danger they perceive is not a hallucination. Women are particularly vulnerable to street violence, and young black males are drastically overrepresented among the perpetrators of that violence. Yet these truths are no solace against the kind of alienation that comes of being ever the suspect, a fearsome entity with whom pedestrians avoid making eye contact.

It is not altogether clear to me how I reached the ripe old age 6 of twenty-two without being conscious of the lethality nighttime pedestrians attributed to me. Perhaps it was because in Chester, Pennsylvania, the small, angry industrial town where I came of age in the 1960s, I was scarcely noticeable against a backdrop of gang warfare, street knifings, and murders. I grew up one of the good boys, had perhaps a half-dozen fistfights. In retrospect, my shyness of combat has clear sources.

As a boy, I saw countless tough guys locked away; I have 7 since buried several, too. They were babies, really—a teenage cousin, a brother of twenty-two, a childhood friend in his mid-twenties—all gone down in episodes of bravado played out in the streets. I came to doubt the virtues of intimidation early on. I chose, perhaps unconsciously, to remain a shadow—timid, but a survivor.

The fearsomeness mistakenly attributed to me in public places 8 often has a perilous flavor. The most frightening of these confusions occurred in the late 1970s and early 1980s, when I worked as a journalist in Chicago. One day, rushing into the office of a magazine I was writing for with a deadline story in hand, I was mistaken for a burglar. The office manager called security and, with an ad hoc posse, pursued me through the labyrinthine halls, nearly to my editor's door. I had no way of proving who I was. I could only move briskly toward the company of someone who knew me.

Another time I was on assignment for a local paper and kill- 9 ing time before an interview. I entered a jewelry store on the city's affluent Near North Side. The proprietor excused herself and returned with an enormous red Doberman pinscher straining at the end of a leash. She stood, the dog extended toward me, silent to my questions, her eyes bulging nearly out of her head. I took a cursory look around, nodded, and bade her good night.

Relatively speaking, however, I never fared as badly as 10 another black male journalist. He went to nearby Waukegan, Illinois, a couple of summers ago to work on a story about a murderer who was born there. Mistaking the reporter for the killer, police officers hauled him from his car at gunpoint and but for his press credentials would probably have tried to book him. Such episodes are not uncommon. Black men trade tales like this all the time.

Over the years, I learned to smother the rage I felt at so often 11 being taken for a criminal. Not to do so would surely have led to madness. I now take precautions to make myself less threatening. I move about with care, particularly late in the evening. I give a wide berth to nervous people on subway platforms during the wee hours, particularly when I have exchanged business clothes for jeans. If I happen to be entering a building behind some people who appear skittish, I may walk by, letting them clear the lobby before I return, so as not to seem to be following them. I have been calm and extremely congenial on those rare occasions when I've been pulled over by the police.

And on late-evening constitutionals I employ what has proved 12 to be an excellent tension-reducing measure: I whistle melodies from Beethoven and Vivaldi and the more popular classical composers. Even steely New Yorkers hunching toward nighttime destinations seem to relax, and occasionally they even join in the tune. Virtually everybody seems to sense that a mugger wouldn't be warbling bright, sunny selections from Vivaldi's *Four Seasons*. It is my equivalent of the cowbell that hikers wear when they know they are in bear country.

Meaning

1. In paragraph 5 Staples says he understands that the danger women fear when they see him "is not a hallucination." Do you take this to mean that Staples perceives himself to be dangerous? Explain.
2. Staples says, "I chose, perhaps unconsciously, to remain a shadow—timid, but a survivor" (paragraph 7). What are the usual connotations of the word *survivor*? Is "timid" one of them? How can you explain this apparent discrepancy? (For the definition of *connotation*, see the Glossary.)

Purpose and Audience

1. What is the purpose of this essay? Do you think Staples believes that he (or other African American men) will cease "to alter public space in ugly ways" (paragraph 5) in the near future? Does he suggest any

long-term solution for "the kind of alienation that comes of being ever the suspect" (5)?

2. The concept of altering public space is relatively abstract. How does Staples convince you that this phenomenon really takes place?

Method and Structure

1. The author employs a large number of examples in a fairly small space. He cites three specific instances that involved him, several general situations, and one incident involving another African American man. How does Staples avoid having the piece sound like a list? How does he establish coherence among all these examples? Look, for example, at details and transitions. (See the Glossary for explanations of *coherence* and *transitions*.)

2. OTHER METHODS Many of Staples's examples are actually anecdotes—brief narratives. The opening paragraph is especially notable. Why is it so effective?

Language

1. What does the author accomplish by using the word *victim* in the essay's first paragraph? Is the word used literally? What tone does it set for the essay? (If necessary, see the Glossary under *tone*.)

2. The word *dicey* (paragraph 2) comes from British slang. Without looking it up in your dictionary, can you figure out its meaning from the context in which it appears?

Writing Topics

1. Write an essay narrating either an experience of altering public space yourself or an experience of being a witness when someone else altered public space. What changes did you observe in the behavior of the people around you? Was your behavior similarly affected? In retrospect, do you think your reactions were justified?

2. Write an essay using examples to show how a trait of your own or of someone you know well always seems to affect people, positively or negatively.

3. Consider, more broadly than Staples does, what it means to alter public space. Staples would rather not have the power to do so, but it *is* a power, and it could perhaps be positive in some circumstances (wielded by a street performer, for instance, or the architect of a beautiful new building on campus). Write an essay expanding on Staples's essay in which you examine the pros and cons of altering public space. Use specific examples as your evidence.

FRANCINE PROSE

An acclaimed woman of letters, Francine Prose has written nearly forty books of fiction, essays, analysis, and young adult literature, most recently the critical literary history Anne Frank: The Book, the Life, the Afterlife *(2009) and the novel* My New American Life *(2011). She is a contributing editor for* Harper's Magazine *and regularly publishes essays and articles in a wide range of newspapers and magazines, including the* Wall Street Journal, *the* New York Times, Glamour, Mademoiselle, *the* Atlantic, *and* Art News. *She has also translated three works of holocaust fiction from Polish to English. Born in Brooklyn, New York, Prose graduated from Radcliffe College in 1968 and teaches at Bard College, where she is the current Distinguished Writer in Residence.*

Which Came First?

Which came first, the chicken or the egg? Prose takes off from that age-old conundrum to ponder the functions of unanswerable questions. She wrote this essay in 2011 for an egg-themed issue of Spirit, *the in-flight magazine for Southwest Airlines.*

Everyone's heard the question. But few of us can remember when 1 or where we heard it first, or even when we first realized that such inexplicable questions existed.

I'm pretty certain that I was a child, and that I heard the rid- 2 dle (I assumed it was a riddle) from one of those smarty-pants kid comedians with a repertoire of bad jokes. Why did the chicken cross the road? To get to the other side. I also have a vague memory of hearing it from one of those grade-school show-offs who liked stumping the younger kids with the Big Metaphysical Questions: Where do we go after we die? What's on the other side of the sky? How do you know your parents are really your parents?

Later, I suppose, I included it in the category of dizzying Zen 3 questions designed to send the brain spinning in ways that are supposed to lead, counterintuitively, to tranquility and enlightenment. What is the sound of a tree falling in the forest when no one's around? What is the sound of one hand clapping? When I thought about these questions, I got the dizziness without the bliss. The chicken and egg, the tree falling in the forest, where the universe ends—I'd get a slightly sickened feeling. It was the cerebral equivalent of a fun-house ride, like tumbling down the rabbit hole that takes Alice to Wonderland.

Unlike questions that are designed to have no logical solu-   4
tion and subvert the reasoning mind, the chicken–egg dilemma usefully describes any number of very real situations—circumstances in which it's hard or impossible to decide what came first, what is cause, and what is effect. Which came first, the cheerful disposition or the happy marriage? The popularity or the confidence? The economic downturn or the decline in consumer spending? Every one of these is an invitation to stretch our minds, to consider how complex life is, from emotions to economics.

For those who want solutions, answers do exist. The Book of   5
Genesis[1] is unequivocal about the fact that God created birds on the fourth day—so the egg must have come after that. According to Darwin, the chicken and egg evolved simultaneously from earlier creatures that were like chickens but were not chickens and did not lay eggs.[2]

But, of course, neither explanation has been enough for scien-   6
tists, with their driving curiosity about how exactly the processes of life occur, about the chain of events and the chain of command that make one thing follow the next. They, along with the rest of us, will be interested and pleased to find out that researchers have finally solved the mystery of the chicken and the egg.

Not being a scientific person myself, I will try to explain, as   7
simply as possible, the results of their research, at least as I read about it on the Internet.

In an article with the deceptively dry title of "Structural Con-   8
trol of Crystal Nuclei by an Eggshell Protein," scientists from the universities of Sheffield and Warwick in Great Britain used a super-computer to find a protein that is required for the development of

[1]The first part of the Bible. [Editors' note.]
[2]English naturalist Charles Darwin (1809–1882) outlined his theory of evolution in *Origin of Species* (1859). [Editors' note.]

the shell. This protein, ovocledidin-17 (OC-17), is found in the ovaries of chickens. No shell can be made without the ovaries, no egg without the chicken, and so we arrive at the solution to our mystery: The chicken came before the egg. Even I can understand this.

So where did the chicken come from? The brain starts spinning again. 9

Because the funny thing is, the mystery of which came first 10 was never about the answer. Let's say it was the chicken. Let's say it was the egg. What difference does knowing make?

The endurance of that question, and of our fascination with 11 it, is about a kind of experience we human beings seem to want: an experience of the insoluble, of the mysterious and confounding. It's less of a medical mystery or riddle with a solution than an invitation to watch our reflection getting smaller in an infinity of mirrors. Thinking about the question, especially for a child, is the low-tech, homey version of going outside on a clear night and contemplating the immensity of the starry sky. What's beyond the universe? Which came first, the egg or the chicken?

Meaning

1. "Everyone's heard the question," Prose says in her opening statement (paragraph 1). To what question is she referring? Why doesn't she ask it outright?

2. According to the author, which came first, the chicken or the egg? How does she know? Put her explanation into your own words.

Purpose and Audience

1. Is the author's main purpose to answer the question posed in her title, to report the findings of scientists, to wax philosophical, to inform and persuade, or something else entirely? What details in the essay support your conclusion?

2. Prose's essay is notable for combining the perspectives of children, philosophers, and scientists. Which perspective, if any, does the writer ultimately favor, and why?

Method and Structure

1. The main idea of this essay is stated toward its end. What is Prose's point? Why does she withhold her thesis until the conclusion?

2. Although filled with abstract concepts, Prose's essay does not lack for examples. Study the questions in paragraphs 2 to 4 and explain how they do and don't work the way examples should: to bring generalizations down to earth.

3. OTHER METHODS Explain how Prose uses the method of classification to organize her examples. Into which category of questions does the chicken-and-egg dilemma fall?

Language

1. Why do you suppose the author uses capital letters for "Big Metaphysical Questions" (paragraph 2)? What is the effect of capitalizing this phrase?

2. Prose asks several questions in this essay, but answers only one. Why? Do you find the unanswered questions effective or disconcerting?

Writing Topics

1. Think of a time when you felt "an experience of the insoluble, of the mysterious and confounding" (paragraph 11). In an essay, relate both the circumstances leading to this experience and your sense of it. How did encountering something unknowable make you feel: awed? humbled? frightened? frustrated? something else? Do you agree that this is "a kind of experience we human beings seem to want" (11)? Why, or why not?

2. Regarding questions of cause and effect, Prose asks, "Which came first, the cheerful disposition or the happy marriage? The popularity or the confidence? The economic downturn or the decline in consumer spending?" (paragraph 4). Drawing on examples from your own experience, choose one of these questions—or another question they suggest to you—and explore the possibility of an answer in a short essay.

3. In comparing answers from the Book of Genesis and Charles Darwin (paragraph 5), Prose glosses over an enduring controversy. Or does she? Write an essay that analyzes "Which Came First?" as an argument for or against either (or both) of the competing theories of creation and evolution.

Writing with the Method

EXAMPLE

Select one of the following statements, or any other statement they suggest, and agree or disagree with it in an essay developed by example. Be sure to choose a topic you care about so that the example or examples are a means of communicating an idea, not an end in themselves.

Family

1. In happy families, talk is the main activity.
2. Grandparents relate more closely to their grandchildren than to their children.
3. Sooner or later, children take on the personalities of their parents.

Behavior and Personality

4. Rudeness is on the rise.
5. Facial expressions often communicate what words cannot say.
6. New technologies are making us stupid and lazy.

Education

7. The best college courses are the difficult ones.
8. Education is an easy way to get ahead in life.
9. Social activities are essential to a well-rounded education.

Politics and Social Issues

10. Talk radio can influence public policy.
11. Drug or alcohol addiction does not happen just to "bad" people.
12. Unemployment is hardest on those over fifty years old.
13. The best musicians treat social and political issues in their songs.

Rules for Living

14. Murphy's Law: If anything can go wrong, it will go wrong, and at the worst possible moment.
15. Lying may be justified by the circumstances.
16. A good friend offers help and support without being asked.

Chapter 4

DIVISION OR ANALYSIS

USING THE METHOD

Division and **analysis** are interchangeable terms for the same method. *Division* comes from a Latin word meaning "to force asunder or separate." *Analysis* comes from a Greek word meaning "to undo." Using this method, we separate a whole into its elements, examine the relations of the elements to one another and to the whole, and reassemble the elements into a new whole informed by the examination. The method is essential to understanding and evaluating objects, works, and ideas.

Analysis (as we will call it) is the foundation of **critical thinking**, the ability to see beneath the surface of things, images, events, and ideas; to uncover and test assumptions; to see the importance of context; and to draw and support independent conclusions. The method is a daily occurrence in our lives, whether we ponder our relationships with others, decide whether a certain movie was worthwhile, or try to understand a politician's campaign promises. It is also essential to college learning, whether in discussing a work of writing, reviewing a psychology experiment, or interpreting a business case. Analysis is the basic operation in at least four other methods discussed in this book: classification (Chapter 5), process analysis (Chapter 6), comparison and contrast (Chapter 7), and cause-and-effect analysis (Chapter 9).

At its most helpful, analysis peers inside an object, institution, work of art, policy, or any other whole. It identifies the parts, examines how the parts relate, and leads to a conclusion about the meaning, significance, or value of the whole. The subject of any analysis is usually singular—a freestanding, coherent unit, such as a bicycle or a poem, with its own unique constitution of elements. (In contrast, classification, the subject of the next chapter, usually starts with a plural subject, such as bicycles or the poems of the Civil War, and groups them according to their shared features.) You choose the subject and with it a **principle of analysis**, a framework that determines how you divide the subject and thus what elements are relevant to the discussion.

Sometimes the principle of analysis will be self-evident, especially when the subject is an object, such as a car or a camera, that can be picked apart in only a limited number of ways. Most of the time, however, the principle you choose will depend on your view of the whole. In academic disciplines, businesses, and the professions, distinctive principles are part of what the field is about and are often the subject of debate within the field. In art, for instance, some critics see a painting primarily as a visual object and concentrate on its composition, color, line, and other formal qualities; other critics see a painting primarily as a social object and concentrate on its content and context (cultural, economic, political, and so on). Both groups use a principle of analysis that is a well-established way of looking at painting, yet each group finds different elements and thus meaning in a work.

Writers have a great deal of flexibility in choosing a principle of analysis, but the principle also must meet certain requirements: it should be appropriate for the subject and the field or discipline; it should be significant; and it should be applied thoroughly and consistently. Analysis is not done for its own sake but for a larger goal of illuminating the subject, perhaps concluding something about it, perhaps evaluating it. But even when the method culminates in evaluation—in the writer's judgment of the subject's value—the analysis should represent the subject as it actually is, in all its fullness and complexity. In analyzing a movie, for instance, a writer may emphasize one element, such as setting, and even omit some elements, such as costumes; but the characterization of the whole must still apply to *all* the elements. If it does not, readers can be counted on to notice; so the writer must single out any wayward element(s) and explain why they do not substantially undermine the framework and thus weaken the opinion.

DEVELOPING AN ESSAY BY DIVISION OR ANALYSIS

Getting Started

Analysis is one of the most readily available methods for developing a subject: almost anything whole can be separated into its elements, from a piece of fruit to a play by Shakespeare to an economic theory. In college and at work, many writing assignments will demand analysis with a verb such as *analyze, criticize, discuss, evaluate, interpret,* or *review.* If you need to develop your own subject for analysis, think of something whose meaning or significance puzzles or intrigues you and whose parts you can distinguish and relate to the whole—for instance, an object such as a machine, an artwork such as a poem, a media product such as a news broadcast, an institution such as a hospital, a relationship such as stepparenting, or a social issue such as sheltering the homeless.

Dissect your subject, looking at the actual physical thing when possible, imagining it in your mind if necessary. Make detailed notes of all the elements you see, their distinguishing features, and how those features work together. In analyzing someone's creation, tease out the creator's influences, assumptions, intentions, conclusions, and evidence. You may have to go outside the work for some of this information—researching an author's background, for instance, to uncover the biases that may underlie his or her opinions. Even if you do not use all this information in your final draft, it will help you identify the elements and help keep your analysis true to the subject.

If you begin by seeking meaning or significance, you will be more likely to find a workable principle of analysis and less likely to waste time on a hollow exercise. Each question below suggests a distinct approach to the subject's elements—a distinct principle of analysis—that makes it easier to isolate the elements and to see their connections.

> To what extent is an enormously complex hospital a community in itself?
>
> What is the function of the front-page headlines in the local tabloid newspaper?
>
> Why did a certain movie have such a powerful effect on you and your friends?

Forming a Thesis

A clear, informative thesis sentence (or sentences) is crucial in division or analysis because readers need to know the purpose and structure of your analysis in order to follow your points. If your exploratory question proves helpful as you gather ideas, you can also use it to draft a thesis sentence: answer it in such a way that you state your opinion about your subject and reveal your principle of analysis.

QUESTION To what extent is an enormously complex hospital a community in itself?

THESIS SENTENCE The hospital encompasses such a wide range of personnel and services that it resembles a good-sized town.

QUESTION What is the function of the front-page headlines in the local tabloid newspaper?

THESIS SENTENCE The newspaper's front page routinely appeals to readers' fear of crime, anger at criminals, and sympathy for victims.

QUESTION Why did a certain movie have such a powerful effect on you and your friends?

THESIS SENTENCE The film is a unique and important statement of the private terrors of adolescence.

Note that all three thesis sentences imply an explanatory purpose—an effort to understand something and share that understanding with the reader. The third thesis sentence, however, conveys a persuasive purpose as well: the writer hopes that readers will accept her evaluation of the film.

A well-focused thesis sentence benefits not only your readers but also you as a writer, because it gives you a yardstick to judge the completeness, consistency, and supportiveness of your analysis. Don't be discouraged, though, if your thesis sentence doesn't come to you until *after* you've written a first draft and had a chance to discover your interest. Writing about your subject may be the best way for you to find its meaning and significance.

Organizing

In the introduction to your essay, let readers know why you are bothering to analyze your subject: Why is the subject significant? How might the essay relate to the experiences of readers or be useful to them? A subject unfamiliar to readers might be summarized or described, or part of it (an anecdote or quotation, say) might be used to tantalize readers. A familiar subject might be introduced with a surprising fact or an unusual perspective. An evaluative analysis might open with an opposing viewpoint.

In the body of the essay you'll need to explain your principle of analysis according to the preceding guidelines. The arrangement of elements and analysis should suit your subject and purpose: you can describe the elements and then offer your analysis, or you can introduce and analyze elements one by one. You can arrange the elements from least to most important, least to most complex, most to least familiar, spatially, or chronologically. Devote as much space to each element as it demands: there is no requirement that all elements be given equal space and emphasis if their complexity or your framework dictates otherwise.

Most analysis essays need a conclusion that assembles the elements, returning readers to a sense of the whole subject. The conclusion can restate the thesis, summarize what the essay has contributed, consider the influence of the subject or its place in a larger picture, or (especially in an evaluation) assess the effectiveness or worth of the subject.

Drafting

If your subject or your view of it is complex, you may need at least two rough drafts of an analysis essay—one to discover what you think and one to clarify your principle, cover each element, and support your points with concrete details and vivid examples (including quotations if the subject is a written work). Plan on two drafts if you're uncertain of your thesis when you begin: you'll probably save time in the long run by attending to one goal at a time. Especially because the analysis essay says something about the subject by explaining its structure, you need to have a clear picture of the whole and relate each part to it.

As you draft, be sure to consider your readers' needs as well as the needs of your subject and your own framework:

- *If the subject is unfamiliar to your readers,* you'll need to carefully explain your principle of analysis, define all specialized terms, distinguish parts from one another, and provide ample illustrations.

- *If the subject is familiar to readers,* your principle of analysis may not require much justification (as long as it's clear), but your details and examples must be vivid and convincing.

- *If readers may dispute your way of looking at your subject,* be careful to justify as well as to explain your principle of analysis.

Whether readers are familiar with your subject or not, always account for any evidence that may seem not to support your opinion—either by showing how, in fact, the evidence is supportive or explaining why it is unimportant. (If contrary evidence refuses to be dispensed with, you may have to rethink your approach.)

Revising and Editing

When you revise and edit your essay, use the following questions to uncover any weaknesses remaining in your analysis.

- *Is your principle of analysis clear?* The significance of your analysis and your view of the subject should be apparent throughout your essay.

- *Is your analysis complete?* Have you identified all elements according to your principle of analysis and determined their relationships to one another and to the whole? If you have omitted some elements from your discussion, will the reason for their omission be clear to readers?

- *Is your analysis consistent?* Is your principle of analysis applied consistently to the entire subject (including any elements you have omitted)? Do all elements reflect the same principle, and are they clearly separate rather than overlapping? You may find it helpful to check your draft against your list of elements or your outline, or to outline the draft itself.

- *Is your analysis well supported?* Is the thesis supported by clear assertions about parts of the subject, and are the assertions supported by concrete, specific evidence (sensory details, facts, quotations, and so on)? Do not rely on your readers to prove your thesis.
- *Is your analysis true to the subject?* Is your thesis unforced, your analysis fair? Is the reassembly of elements into a new whole faithful to the original? Be wary of leaping to a conclusion that distorts the subject.

MARGARET VISSER

Born in 1940 in South Africa, folklorist Margaret Visser was raised in Zambia and lived in England, France, Iraq, and the United States before settling in Toronto, Ontario. (She is a naturalized citizen of Canada.) Visser was educated at the University of Toronto, where she earned a BA and a PhD in classics. She taught at York University in Toronto and has published articles in scholarly and popular periodicals. Visser also appears on television and radio, discussing her discoveries about the history and social mythology of daily life. "The extent to which we take everyday objects for granted," she says, "is the precise extent to which they govern and inform our lives." Five books illuminate this important territory: Much Depends on Dinner *(1986),* The Rituals of Dinner *(1991),* The Way We Are *(1994),* The Geometry of Love *(2000), and* The Gift of Thanks *(2008).*

The Ritual of Fast Food

In this excerpt from The Rituals of Dinner, *an investigation of table manners, Visser analyzes the fast-food restaurant. What do we seek when we visit such a place? How does the management oblige us? Success hinges on predictability.*

An early precursor of the restaurant meal was dinner served to the public at fixed times and prices at an eating house or tavern. Such a meal was called, because of its predetermined aspects, an "ordinary," and the place where it was eaten came to be called an "ordinary," too. When a huge modern business conglomerate offers fast food to travelers on the highway, it knows that its customers are likely to desire No Surprises. They are hungry, tired, and not in a celebratory mood; they are happy to pay—provided that the price looks easily manageable—for the safely predictable, the convenient, the fast and ordinary.

Ornamental formalities are pruned away (tables and chairs 2 are bolted to the floor, for instance, and "cutlery" is either nonexistent or not worth stealing); but rituals, in the sense of behavior and expectations that conform to preordained rules, still inform the proceedings. People who stop for a hamburger—at a Wendy's, a Harvey's, a McDonald's, or a Burger King—know exactly what the building that houses the establishment should look like; architectural variations merely ring changes on rigidly imposed themes. People want, perhaps even need, to *recognize* their chain store, to feel that they know it and its food in advance. Such an outlet is designed to be a "home away from home," on the highway, or anywhere in the city, or for Americans abroad.

Words and actions are officially laid down, learned by the 3 staff from handbooks and teaching sessions, and then picked up by customers in the course of regular visits. Things have to be called by their correct names ("Big Mac," "large fries"); the McDonald's rubric in 1978 required servers to ask "Will that be with cheese, sir?" "Will there be any fries today, sir?" and to close the transaction with "Have a nice day." The staff wear distinctive garments; menus are always the same, and even placed in the same spot in every outlet in the chain; prices are low and predictable; and the theme of cleanliness is proclaimed and tirelessly reiterated. The company attempts also to play the role of a lovable host, kind and concerned, even parental: it knows that blunt and direct confrontation with a huge faceless corporation makes us suspicious, and even badly behaved. So it stresses its love of children, its nostalgia for cozy warmth and for the past (cottage roofs, warm earth tones), or its clean, brisk modernity (glass walls, smooth surfaces, red trim). It responds to social concerns—when they are insistent enough, sufficiently widely held, and therefore "correct." McDonald's for example, is at present busy showing how much it cares about the environment.

Fast-food chains know that they are ordinary. They *want* to 4 be ordinary, and for people to think of them as almost inseparable from the idea of everyday food consumed outside the home. They are happy to allow their customers time off for feasts— on Thanksgiving, Christmas, and so on—to which they do not cater. Even those comparatively rare holiday times, however, are turned to a profit, because the companies know that their favorite customers—law-abiding families—are at home together then, watching television, where carefully placed commercials will spread the word concerning new fast-food products, and re-imprint the image of the various chain stores for later, when the long stretches of ordinary times return.

Families are the customers the fast-food chains want: solid 5 citizens in groups of several at a time, the adults hovering over their children, teaching them the goodness of hamburgers, anxious to bring them up to behave typically and correctly. Cus-tomers usually maintain a clean, restrained, considerate, and competent demeanor as they swiftly, gratefully, and informally eat. Fast-food operators have recently faced the alarming realiza-tion that crack addicts, craving salt and fat, have spread the word among their number that French fries deliver these substances easily, ubiquitously, cheaply, and at all hours. Dope addicts at family "ordinaries"! The unacceptability of such a thought was neatly captured by a news story in the *Economist* (1990) that spelled out the words a fast-food proprietor can least afford to hear from his faithful customers, the participants in his polite and practiced rituals: the title of the story was "Come on Mabel, let's leave." The plan to counter this threat included increasing the intensity of the lighting in fast-food establishments—drug addicts, apparently, prefer to eat in the dark.

The formality of eating at a restaurant belonging to a fast-food 6 chain depends upon the fierce regularity of its product, its simple but carefully observed rituals, and its environment. Supplying a hamburger that adheres to perfect standards of shape, weight, temperature, and consistency, together with selections from a pre-set list of trimmings, to a customer with fiendishly precise expec-tations is an enormously complex feat. The technology involved in performing it has been learned through the expenditure of huge sums on research, and after decades of experience—not to mention the vast political and economic ramifications involved in maintaining the supplies of cheap beef and cheap buns. But these costs and complexities are, with tremendous care, hidden from view. We know of course that, say, a Big Mac is a cultural con-struct: the careful control expended upon it is one of the things we are buying. But McDonald's manages—it must do so if it is to suc-ceed in being ordinary—to provide a "casual" eating experience. Convenient, innocent simplicity is what the technology, the ruth-less politics, and the elaborate organization serve to the customer.

Meaning

1. In paragraph 6 Visser writes, "Supplying a hamburger that adheres to perfect standards of shape, weight, temperature, and consistency . . . to a customer with fiendishly precise expectations is an enormously complex feat." How does this statement illustrate Visser's main idea?
2. What do you think Visser means by the statement that "a Big Mac is a cultural construct" (paragraph 6)?

Purpose and Audience

1. What is Visser's purpose in writing this essay: to propose more interesting surroundings and menus at fast-food restaurants? to argue that the patrons of these establishments are too demanding? to explain how these chains manage to satisfy so many customers? something else?
2. Whom does Visser seem to imagine as her audience? Is she writing for sociologists? for managers at corporations such as McDonald's and Burger King? for diners who patronize fast-food restaurants? What evidence in the essay supports your answer?

Method and Structure

1. How does Visser's analysis, breaking the fast-food experience down into its elements, help her achieve her purpose?
2. Into what elements does Visser divide the fast-food restaurant? Be specific, supporting your answer with examples from the text.
3. OTHER METHODS   In paragraph 5 Visser uses cause-and-effect analysis to explain both why crack addicts began to frequent chain restaurants and why these restaurants couldn't risk including addicts among their clientele. What does this cause-and-effect analysis add to the analysis of fast-food restaurants? How would addicts, whose money is presumably as good as anyone else's, interfere with the operation of these restaurants?

Language

1. What is Visser's tone? How seriously does she take her subject? (See the Glossary for a discussion of *tone*.)
2. Visser writes that McDonald's used to require its servers to ask patrons, depending on their order, "Will that be with cheese, sir?" or "Will there be any fries today, sir?" (paragraph 3). What would be the purpose of such questions? How would you characterize this use of language?

3. According to Visser, people who patronize fast-food restaurants "want, perhaps even need, to *recognize* their chain store" (paragraph 2); they are looking for "the safely predictable, the convenient, the fast and ordinary" (1). Find other instances in the essay where Visser describes the people who eat in these restaurants. What portrait emerges of these customers? How does this portrait contribute to Visser's overall message?

Writing Topics

1. What kinds of junk food do you regularly consume? Think about when and where and why you eat it, and then write an essay in which you analyze your behavior as a consumer of junk food. Make a list of all the elements that constitute this activity and the setting in which it occurs. In your essay, examine each element to show what it contributes to the whole. Be sure your principle of analysis is clear to readers.

2. In her last paragraph, Visser writes that the "costs and complexities" of providing "a 'casual' eating experience" in a fast-food restaurant are "hidden from view." Does this seem appropriate to you, or would you rather know what the corporation feeding you puts into its operation, such as the "economic ramifications involved in maintaining the supplies of cheap beef and cheap buns"? Write an essay exploring the issues this question raises for you.

3. All of us have probably experienced a particular moment (or perhaps many moments) when we were willing to dine out on anything *but* fast food. What do you think we are seeking at such times? Following Visser's example, write an essay analyzing the "culture" of a particular *non*chain restaurant. How does the management deliver what the customer wants?

THOMAS DE ZENGOTITA

A contributing editor for Harper's Magazine, *Thomas de Zengotita (born 1943) earned a PhD in anthropology from Columbia University in 1985 and teaches at both the Dalton School (a private preparatory school in Manhattan) and New York University's graduate school. His essays have appeared in the* Nation, Shout, *the scholarly journal* Cultural Anthropology, *and the* Huffington Post. *De Zengotita's interest in the influences of mass media led him to develop the analytic concept of* mediation, *which theorizes that every aspect of our consciousness is filtered through what we see and hear in popular culture. He elaborates on this central idea of his critical work in* Mediated: How the Media Shapes Your World and the Way You Live in It *(2005), his widely acclaimed first book.*

American Idol Worship

A major tenet of de Zengotita's theory of mediation is that the media flatter audiences by suggesting that popular culture is ultimately about the people who consume it. (As he explains it, contemporary media offer "a place where everything is addressed to us, everything is for us, and nothing is beyond us anymore.") In this essay, written in 2006 and published in both the Los Angeles Times *and the* Christian Science Monitor, *de Zengotita examines how this flattery works in one of the most popular media productions going—the television show* American Idol.

When the ratings numbers came in after last week's Grammy 1 Awards, the news wasn't good for the professionals. A show that features amateurs had attracted a far bigger audience than had one with the likes of Madonna, Coldplay, and U2. . . . *American Idol* drew almost twice as many viewers as the awards show. What's going on here? Why does this reality show consistently attract the weekly attention of close to 35 million viewers?

It's a nexus of factors shaping the "virtual revolution" unfold- 2
ing all around us, on so many fronts. Think chat rooms, *Myspace*
.com, blogs, life journals illustrated with photos snapped by cell
phones, flash-mobbing, marathon running, focus groups, talk
radio, e-mails to news shows, camcorders, sponsored sports teams
for tots—and every garage band in town with its own CD. What
do all these platforms have in common? They are all devoted to
otherwise anonymous people who don't want to be mere spectators. In this virtual revolution, it's not workers against capital-
ists—that's so nineteenth century. In our mediated world, it's
spectators against celebrities, with spectators demanding a share
of the last scarce resource in the overdeveloped world—attention. The *American Idol* format combines essential elements of
this revolution.

Have you followed the ruckus over why people don't have 3
heroes anymore—in the old-fashioned statesman, warrior, genius,
artist kind of way? People concerned with education are especially alarmed. They invest a lot of energy in trying to rekindle an
aura of greatness around the Founding Fathers. But it's hopeless.
Ask natural-born citizens of the mediated world who their heroes
are, and their answers fall into one of two categories: somebody
in their personal lives or performers—above all, pop music
performers.

The "everyday hero" answer reflects the virtual revolution, 4
but what about performers? Why are they so important to their
fans? Because, in concert especially, these new kinds of heroes
create an experience of belonging that their fans would otherwise never know, living as they do in a marketplace of lifestyles
that can make one's existence feel optional. That's why there's
a religious quality to a concert when the star meets the audience's awesome expectations and creates, in song and persona,
a moment in which each individual feels personally understood
and, at the same time, fused with other fans in a larger common
identity. "Performer heroes" are, in the end, all about us. They
don't summon us to serve a cause—other than the one of being
who we are. So, naturally, they have been leaders of the virtual
revolution. From their perch on high, they make us the focus of
attention.

American Idol takes the next step. It unites both aspects of 5
the relationship—in the climactic final rounds, a fan becomes an

idol; the ultimate dream of our age comes true before our eyes
and in our hearts.

That's mediational magic.   6

And don't forget the power of music. *American Idol* wouldn't 7
be what it is if, say, amateur actors were auditioning. You can
disagree with someone about movie stars and TV shows and still
be friends. But you can't be friends with someone who loves the
latest boy band, in a totally unironic way, if you are into Gillian
Welch. That's because tastes in pop music go right to the core
of who you are, with a depth and immediacy no other art form
can match. Music takes hold of you on levels deeper than articu-
lated meaning. That's why words, sustained by music, have such
power. There is nothing like a song for expressing who we are.

That brings us to the early rounds of *American Idol*, in which 8
contestants are chosen for the final competition in Hollywood.
The conventional wisdom is that they're an exercise in public
humiliation, long a staple of reality TV. That's not wrong, as far
as it goes, but it isn't just any old humiliation exercise—it is the
most excruciating form of voluntary personal humiliation the
human condition allows for because it involves the most revealing kind of performance there is, this side of pornography. During
this phase of the show, the audience, knowing it will eventually
fuse in a positive way with a finalist idol, gets to be in the most
popular clique on the planet, rendering snarky judgments on one
of the most embarrassing pools of losers ever assembled.

American Idol gives you so many ways to feel good about 9
yourself.

No wonder it's a hit.   10

Meaning

1. What is de Zengotita's thesis? Where does he state it explicitly? Try
to summarize the central meaning of de Zengotita's analysis in a
sentence or two of your own.

2. According to de Zengotita, what elements define the "virtual revolution" (paragraph 2)? How does *American Idol* bring together these
elements to create an irresistible media experience?

3. What do you think de Zengotita means when he writes, "*American
Idol* . . . unites both aspects of the relationship—in the climactic
final rounds, a fan becomes an idol; the ultimate dream of our age
comes true before our eyes and in our hearts. . . . That's mediational

magic" (paragraphs 5 and 6)? According to de Zengotita, how does *American Idol* transform both the contestants and the audience?

Purpose and Audience

1. What do you think was de Zengotita's purpose in writing this essay? Does he want to shock, inform, persuade, or entertain his readers? Something else? What evidence from the text supports your viewpoint?
2. What assumptions does de Zengotita make about his audience? Does he assume that his readers are familiar with *American Idol*? with his theory of *mediation*? How familiar with the show (or the author's theory) would readers have to be in order to understand de Zengotita's analysis?

Method and Structure

1. De Zengotita's immediate subject of analysis is *American Idol*, but he's also using the show to examine a wider phenomenon. What is that wider phenomenon? How does the author's analysis of *American Idol* explain it?
2. What is de Zengotita's principle of analysis, and what elements of *American Idol* does he analyze? How does he reassemble these elements into a new whole? Support your answer with evidence from the essay.
3. De Zengotita begins his essay by contrasting *American Idol*'s ratings with those for the Grammy Awards. How does beginning with this comparison foreshadow the conclusions he draws about the implications of the "virtual revolution" in popular culture?
4. OTHER METHODS   In addition to division, de Zengotita examines causes and effects to show how *American Idol*'s individual elements explain its popularity. What does this cause-and-effect analysis add to the analysis of *American Idol*? What would be lost without it?

Language

1. This essay combines loose, informal language—"What's going on here?" (paragraph 1) and "that's so nineteenth century" (2)—with scholarly vocabulary to explore a complex idea. What do you suppose is the author's purpose in employing these different levels of diction? What is the effect on you as a reader? (If necessary, see *diction* in the Glossary.)
2. Throughout his essay, de Zengotita shifts back and forth between first person (*we, us, our*), second person (*you*), and third person

(*they*/*them*). Can you find an underlying purpose for the different uses? Do the shifts add to or detract from the essay's overall effect? Why?

Writing Topics

1. Write an essay in which you describe your favorite TV show or Webcast and explain what makes it so enjoyable for you. Just as de Zengotita took *American Idol* apart to understand its popularity, explain what elements contribute to the appeal of the program you selected. Does its appeal rest mostly on the actors involved, the places depicted, the story line, or other features? Does it make you think about who you are as a person or change your view of the world? If it is merely good "entertainment," describe what makes it so.

2. Although the idea of *mediation* may seem complicated, it boils down to a relatively simple concept: de Zengotita believes that popular culture influences the way we perceive the world and ourselves. What do you think of this notion? Do the media control how you think, or can you pick and choose among its offerings without being affected in any meaningful way? Write an essay that uses the concept of mediation to explore your relationship with an aspect of popular culture of your choosing (for example, you might examine how a fashion or "lifestyle" magazine has changed the way you look at yourself, or describe how a song changed your attitude toward a problem you were facing). Or, if you don't accept the concept of mediation, write an essay that uses examples from your own experience to explain why you disagree with de Zengotita.

3. American television programs are watched all over the world: *Baywatch*, for example, is one of the most popular shows in Germany, and *Desperate Housewives* is popular in China. Many global viewers say they watch the programming to improve their English language skills or to learn about American culture. But what are they learning? Write an essay that focuses on a particular type of show—network news, for example, or medical dramas—and explores how a non-American viewer might interpret it. Does the program provide an accurate depiction of life in the United States, or does it distort reality?

SCOTT RUSSELL SANDERS

Scott Russell Sanders was born in Memphis, Tennessee, in 1945. After attending Brown University and Cambridge University, he went on to teach English at Indiana University in Bloomington. Throughout his career, he has published novels, collections of short stories, and children's books, but he is best known for his essay collections, including Secrets of the Universe: Essays on Family, Community, Spirit, and Place *(1991),* Staying Put: Making a Home in a Restless World *(1993),* Writing from the Center *(1995),* Hunting for Hope: A Father's Journeys *(1998),* The Country of Language *(1999), and* The Force of Spirit *(2000). His most recent book,* A Conservationist Manifesto *(2009), contemplates the conflicts between consumer culture and environmental stewardship.*

The Men We Carry in Our Minds

"The Men We Carry in Our Minds" first appeared in Milkweed Chronicle *in 1984. Looking back at the men he knew as a child, Sanders compellingly analyzes his own mixed feelings toward feminism.*

"This must be a hard time for women," I say to my friend Anneke. 1
"They have so many paths to choose from, and so many voices calling them."

"I think it's a lot harder for men," she replies. 2

"How do you figure that?" 3

"The women I know feel excited, innocent, like crusaders in a 4
just cause. The men I know are eaten up with guilt."

We are sitting at the kitchen table drinking sassafras tea, our 5
hands wrapped around the mugs because this April morning is cool and drizzly. "Like a Dutch morning," Anneke told me earlier.
She is Dutch herself, a writer and midwife and peacemaker, with the round face and sad eyes of a woman in a Vermeer[1] painting

---

[1]The Dutch painter Jan Vermeer (1632–1675) is best known for his realistic portrayals of quiet domestic scenes. [Editors' note.]

who might be waiting for the rain to stop, for a door to open. She leans over to sniff a sprig of lilac, pale lavender, that rises from a vase of cobalt blue.

"Women feel such pressure to be everything, do everything," 6 I say. "Career, kids, art, politics. Have their babies and get back to the office a week later. It's as if they're trying to overcome a million years' worth of evolution in one lifetime."

"But we help one another. We don't try to lumber on alone, 7 like so many wounded grizzly bears, the way men do." Anneke sips her tea. I gave her the mug with owls on it, for wisdom. "And we have this deep-down sense that we're in the *right*—we've been held back, passed over, used—while men feel they're in the wrong. Men are the ones who've been discredited, who have to search their souls."

I search my soul. I discover guilty feelings aplenty—toward 8 the poor, the Vietnamese, Native Americans, the whales, an endless list of debts—a guilt in each case that is as bright and unambiguous as a neon sign. But toward women I feel something more confused, a snarl of shame, envy, wary tenderness, and amazement. This muddle troubles me. To hide my unease I say, "You're right, it's tough being a man these days."

"Don't laugh." Anneke frowns at me, mournful-eyed, through 9 the sassafras steam. "I wouldn't be a man for anything. It's much easier being the victim. All the victim has to do is break free. The persecutor has to live with his past."

How deep is this past? I find myself wondering after Anneke 10 has left. How much of an inheritance do I have to throw off? Is it just the beliefs I breathed in as a child? Do I have to scour memory back through father and grandfather? Through St. Paul? Beyond Stonehenge and into the twilit caves? I'm convinced the past we must contend with is deeper even than speech. When I think back on my childhood, on how I learned to see men and women, I have a sense of ancient, dizzying depths. The back roads of Tennessee and Ohio where I grew up were probably closer, in their sexual patterns, to the campsites of Stone Age hunters than to the genderless cities of the future into which we are rushing.

The first men, besides my father, I remember seeing were 11 black convicts and white guards, in the cottonfield across the road from our farm on the outskirts of Memphis. I must have been three or four. The prisoners wore dingy gray-and-black zebra suits, heavy as canvas, sodden with sweat. Hatless, stooped, they chopped weeds in the fierce heat, row after row, breathing the acrid dust of boll-weevil poison. The overseers wore dazzling white shirts and broad shadowy hats. The oiled barrels of their shotguns flashed in the sunlight. Their faces in memory are utterly blank. Of course those men, white and black, have become for me an emblem of racial hatred. But they have also come to stand for the twin poles of my early vision of manhood—the brute toiling animal and the boss.

When I was a boy, the men I knew labored with their bodies. 12 They were marginal farmers, just scraping by, or welders, steel-workers, carpenters; they swept floors, dug ditches, mined coal, or drove trucks, their forearms ropy with muscle; they trained horses, stoked furnaces, built tires, stood on assembly lines wrestling parts onto cars and refrigerators. They got up before light, worked all day long whatever the weather, and when they came home at night they looked as though somebody had been whipping them. In the evenings and on weekends they worked on their own places, tilling gardens that were lumpy with clay, fixing broken-down cars, hammering on houses that were always too drafty, too leaky, too small.

The bodies of the men I knew were twisted and maimed in 13 ways visible and invisible. The nails of their hands were black and split, the hands tattooed with scars. Some had lost fingers. Heavy lifting had given many of them finicky backs and guts weak from hernias. Racing against conveyor belts had given them ulcers. Their ankles and knees ached from years of standing on concrete. Anyone who had worked for long around machines was hard of hearing. They squinted, and the skin of their faces was creased like the leather of old work gloves. There were times, studying them, when I dreaded growing up. Most of them coughed, from dust or cigarettes, and most of them drank cheap wine or whiskey, so their eyes looked bloodshot and bruised. The fathers of my friends always seemed older than the mothers. Men wore out sooner. Only women lived into old age.

As a boy I also knew another sort of men, who did not sweat 14 and break down like mules. They were soldiers, and so far as I could tell they scarcely worked at all. During my early school years we lived on a military base, an arsenal in Ohio, and every day I saw GIs in the guardshacks, on the stoops of barracks, at the wheels of olive drab Chevrolets. The chief fact of their lives was boredom. Long after I left the arsenal I came to recognize the sour smell the soldiers gave off as that of souls in limbo. They were all waiting—for wars, for transfers, for leaves, for promotions, for the end of their hitch—like so many braves waiting for the hunt to begin. Unlike the warriors of older tribes, however, they would have no say about when the battle would start or how it would be waged. Their waiting was broken only when they practiced for war. They fired guns at targets, drove tanks across the churned-up fields of the military reservation, set off bombs in the wrecks of old fighter planes. I knew this was all play. But I also felt certain that when the hour for killing arrived, they would kill. When the real shooting started, many of them would die. This was what soldiers were *for*, just as a hammer was for driving nails.

Warriors and toilers: those seemed, in my boyhood vision, to 15 be the chief destinies for men. They weren't the only destinies, as I learned from having a few male teachers, from reading books, and from watching television. But the men on television—the politicians, the astronauts, the generals, the savvy lawyers, the philosophical doctors, the bosses who gave orders to both sol- diers and laborers—seemed as remote and unreal to me as the figures in tapestries. I could no more imagine growing up to become one of these cool, potent creatures than I could imagine becoming a prince.

A nearer and more hopeful example was that of my father, 16 who had escaped from a red-dirt farm to a tire factory, and from the assembly line to the front office. Eventually he dressed in a white shirt and tie. He carried himself as if he had been born to work with his mind. But his body, remembering the early years of slogging work, began to give out on him in his fifties, and it quit on him entirely before he turned sixty-five. Even such a partial escape from man's fate as he had accomplished did not seem pos- sible for most of the boys I knew. They joined the army, stood in line for jobs in the smoky plants, helped build highways. They were bound to work as their fathers had worked, killing them- selves or preparing to kill others.

A scholarship enabled me not only to attend college, a rare 17 enough feat in my circle, but even to study in a university meant for children of the rich. Here I met for the first time young men who had assumed from birth that they would lead lives of comfort and power. And for the first time I met women who told me that men were guilty of having kept all the joys and privileges of the earth for themselves. I was baffled. What privileges? What joys? I thought about the maimed dismal lives of most of the men back home. What had they stolen from their wives and daughters? The right to go five days a week, twelve months a year, for thirty or forty years to a steel mill or a coal mine? The right to drop bombs and die in war? The right to feel every leak in the roof, every gap in the fence, every cough in the engine, as a wound they must mend? The right to feel, when the lay-off comes or the plant shuts down, not only afraid but ashamed?

I was slow to understand the deep grievances of women. This 18 was because, as a boy, I had envied them. Before college, the only people I had ever known who were interested in art or music or literature, the only ones who read books, the only ones who ever seemed to enjoy a sense of ease and grace were the mothers and daughters. Like the menfolk, they fretted about money, they scrimped and made-do. But, when the pay stopped coming in, they were not the ones who had failed. Nor did they have to go to war, and that seemed to me a blessed fact. By comparison with the narrow, ironclad days of fathers, there was an expansiveness, I thought, in the days of mothers. They went to see neighbors, to shop in town, to run errands at school, at the library, at church. No doubt, had I looked harder at their lives, I would have envied them less. It was not my fate to become a woman, so it was easier for me to see the graces. Few of them held jobs outside the home, and those who did filled thankless roles as clerks and waitresses. I didn't see, then, what a prison a house could be, since houses seemed to me brighter, handsomer places than any factory. I did not realize—because such things were never spoken of—how often women suffered from men's bullying. I did learn about the wretchedness of abandoned wives, single mothers, widows; but I also learned about the wretchedness of lone men. Even then I could see how exhausting it was for a mother to cater all day to the needs of young children. But if I had been asked, as a boy, to choose between tending a baby and tending a machine, I think I would have chosen the baby. (Having now tended both, I know I would choose the baby.)

So I was baffled when the women at college accused me and 19 my sex of having cornered the world's pleasure. I think something like my bafflement has been felt by other boys (and by girls as well) who grew up in dirt-poor farm country, in mining country, in black ghettos, in Hispanic barrios,[2] in the shadows of factories, in third world nations—any place where the fate of men is as grim and bleak as the fate of women. Toilers and warriors. I realize now how ancient these identities are, how deep the tug they exert on men, the undertow of a thousand generations. The miseries I saw, as a boy, in the lives of nearly all men I continue to see in the lives of many—the body-breaking toil, the tedium, the call to be tough, the humiliating powerlessness, the battle for a living and for territory.

When the women I met at college thought about the joys and 20 privileges of men, they did not carry in their minds the sort of men I had known in my childhood. They thought of their fathers, who were bankers, physicians, architects, stockbrokers, the big wheels of the big cities. These fathers rode the train to work or drove cars that cost more than any of my childhood houses. They were attended from morning to night by female helpers, wives and nurses and secretaries. They were never laid off, never short of cash at month's end, never lined up for welfare. These fathers made decisions that mattered. They ran the world.

The daughters of such men wanted to share in this power, 21 this glory. So did I. They yearned for a say over their future, for jobs worthy of their abilities, for the right to live at peace, unmolested, whole. Yes, I thought, yes yes. The difference between me and these daughters was that they saw me, because of my sex, as destined from birth to become like their fathers, and therefore an enemy to their desires. But I knew better. I wasn't an enemy, in fact or in feeling. I was an ally. If I had known, then, how to tell them so, would they have believed me? Would they now?

Meaning

1. Sanders's opening (paragraphs 1–10) relates a conversation he had with a female friend about the relative positions of men and women in the early 1980s when the essay was written. How did Sanders's opinion differ from his friend's? How do Sanders's thoughts here illustrate the main idea of the essay? How is this central idea reinforced by the essay's two concluding paragraphs?

[2]A Spanish-speaking community. [Editors' note.]

2. What employment options does Sanders say were available to the men he knew when he was growing up? What other responsibilities made the lives of such men difficult?

3. When he went to college in the mid-1960s, Sanders was "baffled" that women there believed "men were guilty of having kept all the joys and privileges of the earth for themselves" (paragraph 17). Why was he so baffled? How did his image of women from his childhood contribute to his lack of understanding?

Purpose and Audience

1. What would you say is Sanders's purpose in this essay? Is he simply sharing his own experiences, trying to change readers' minds about the status of men and women in contemporary society, or attempting something else? Why do you think so?

2. Sanders ends his essay with two questions. What do these questions suggest to you about his imagined audience?

Method and Structure

1. What are the elements of Sanders's childhood vision of manhood? What does his analysis reveal about his feelings toward feminism?

2. In terms of subject and focus, this essay can be divided into three main sections. What are these sections, and what is each section's primary focus?

3. OTHER METHODS   Sanders relies on comparison and contrast throughout this essay. Note some specific instances of comparison and contrast, and explain what these contribute to Sanders's larger point.

Language

1. Analyze paragraph 12 to consider Sanders's use of verbs (such as *swept* and *dug*) and verb forms (such as *tilling* and *fixing*). What is the effect of the verbs and verb forms in this passage?

2. What might be the significance of Sanders's use of the verb *carry* in the title of the essay? How would the effect differ if Sanders had titled the essay "The Men We Remember"?

Writing Topics

1. In his essay Sanders focuses on the two main social classes he recognized as a child: the laboring class that included "warriors and

toilers" (paragraph 15) and the professional class that represented "power" and "glory" (21). Many would argue, though, that class distinctions in the United States are more complex than this, consisting of various hierarchies of social class. Develop an essay that analyzes your own views on social class in the United States today, describing clearly and fully the characteristics of each class you distinguish. Take a humorous approach to the subject if you wish.

2. Write an essay focusing on the images of men that you carry in your mind, beginning with your childhood observations. Be sure that, like Sanders, you support your analysis with specific examples. Alternatively, you could write an essay focusing on the women you carry in your mind.

3. Writing in the mid-1980s, Sanders refers to the "genderless cities of the future into which we are rushing" (paragraph 10). To what extent have the distinctions between women and men decreased over the past thirty years? To what extent have they stayed the same—or even increased? In an essay, consider the current state of women and men in relation to each other and to society.

DIVISION OR ANALYSIS

Select one of the following topics, or any other topic they suggest, for an essay developed by analysis. Be sure to choose a topic you care about so that analysis is a means of communicating an idea, not an end in itself.

People, Animals, Objects

1. The personality of a friend or relative
2. The personality of a politician, teacher, or other professional
3. An animal such as a cat, dog, horse, cow, spider, or bat
4. A machine or appliance such as a car engine, harvesting combine, laptop computer, hair dryer, toaster, or sewing machine
5. A nonmotorized vehicle such as a skateboard, in-line skate, bicycle, or snowboard
6. A building such as a hospital, theater, or sports arena

Ideas

7. The perfect city
8. The perfect crime
9. A theory or concept in a field such as psychology, sociology, economics, biology, physics, engineering, or astronomy
10. The evidence in a political argument (written, spoken, or reported in the news)

Aspects of Culture

11. A stereotype
12. A typical hero or villain in science fiction, romance novels, war movies, or movies or novels about adolescents
13. A popular Web site or Internet trend
14. A literary work: short story, novel, poem, essay, screenplay
15. A visual work: painting, sculpture, building
16. A musical work: song, concerto, symphony, opera
17. A performance: sports, acting, dance, music, speech
18. The slang of a particular group or occupation

Chapter 5

CLASSIFICATION

USING THE METHOD

We **classify** when we sort things into groups: kinds of cars, styles of writing, types of customers. Because it creates order, classification helps us make sense of our experiences and our surroundings. With it, we see the correspondences among like things and distinguish them from unlike things, similarities and distinctions that can be especially helpful when making a decision or encouraging others to see things from a new perspective. Because classification helps us name things, remember them, and discuss them with others, it is also a useful method for developing and sharing ideas in writing.

Writers classify primarily to explain a pattern in a subject that might not have been noticed before: a sportswriter, for instance, might observe that basketball players tend to fall into one of three groups based on the aggressiveness of their play. Sometimes writers also classify to persuade readers that one group is superior: the sportswriter might argue that one style of basketball play is more effective than the other two.

Classification involves a three-step process:

1. Separate things into their elements, using the method of division or analysis (previous chapter).
2. Isolate the similarities among the elements.
3. Group or classify the things based on those similarities, matching like with like.

The following diagram illustrates a classification essay that appears later in this chapter, "Show Me the Money" by Walter Mosley (p. 173). Mosley's subject is Americans, and he sees four distinct kinds:

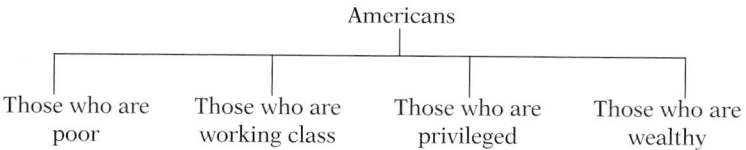

All the members of Mosley's overall group share at least one characteristic: they are Americans. The members of each subgroup also share at least one characteristic: they are poor, for instance, or privileged. The members of each subgroup exist independently of each other, and none of them is essential to the existence of the subgroup: the working class would continue to exist even if some workers were without jobs.

The number of groups in a classification scheme depends entirely on the basis for establishing the classes in the first place. There are two systems:

- In a **complex classification** like Mosley's, each individual fits firmly into one class because of at least one distinguishing feature shared with all members of that class but not with any members of any other classes. All the wealthy have more money than they think they need, but none of the poor, working class, or privileged people do.

- In a **binary or two-part classification**, two classes are in opposition to each other. Often, one group has a certain characteristic that the other group lacks. For instance, poor people could be classified into those who have homes and those who don't. A binary scheme is useful to emphasize the possession of a particular characteristic, but it is limited if it specifies nothing about the members of the "other" class except that they lack the trait. (An old joke claims that there are two kinds of people in the world—those who classify, and all others.)

Sorting items demands a **principle of classification** that determines the groups by distinguishing them. For instance, Mosley's principle in identifying four groups of Americans is their access to money. Principles for sorting a year's movies might be genre (action-adventures, comedies, dramas); place of origin (domestic, foreign); or cost of production (low-budget, medium-budget, high-budget). Your choice of a principle depends on your interest.

Although you may emphasize one class over the others, the classification itself must be complete and consistent. A classification of movies by genre would be incomplete if it omitted comedies. It would be inconsistent if it included action-adventures, comedies, dramas, low-budget films, and foreign films: such a system mixes *three* principles (genre, cost, origin); it omits whole classes (what of high-budget domestic dramas?); and it overlaps other classes (a low-budget foreign action-adventure would fit in three different groups).

DEVELOPING AN ESSAY BY CLASSIFICATION

Getting Started

Classification essays are often assigned in college: you might be asked to identify three major schools of therapy for a psychology class, for instance, or to categorize difficult personality types for a business communication course. When you need to develop your own subject for a classification essay, think of one large class of things whose members you've noticed fall into subclasses, such as study habits, midnight grocery shoppers, or political fund-raising appeals. Be sure that your general subject forms a class in its own right—that all its members share at least one important quality. Then look for your principle of classification, the quality or qualities that distinguish some members from others, providing poles for the members to group themselves around. One such principle for political fund-raising appeals might be the different methods of delivery, such as direct marketing, media advertising, meetings, or the Internet.

While generating ideas for your classification, keep track of them in a list, diagram, or outline to ensure that your principle is applied thoroughly (all classes) and consistently (each class relating to the principle). Fill in the list, diagram, or outline with the distinguishing features of each class and with examples that will clarify your scheme.

Forming a Thesis

You will want to state your principle of classification in a thesis sentence so that you know where you're going and your readers know where you're taking them. Be sure the sentence also conveys a *reason* for the classification so that the essay does not become a dull list of categories. The following tentative thesis statement is mechanical; the revision is more interesting.

> TENTATIVE THESIS SENTENCE Political fund-raising appeals are delivered in any of six ways.
>
> REVISED THESIS SENTENCE Of the six ways to deliver political fund-raising appeals, the three that rely on personal contact are generally the most effective.

(Note that the revised thesis sentence implies a further classification based on whether the appeals involve personal contact or not.)

Organizing

The introduction to a classification essay should make clear why the classification is worthwhile: What situation prompted the essay? What do readers already know about the subject? What use might they make of the information you will provide? Unless your principle of classification is self-evident, you may want to explain it briefly — though save extensive explanation for the body of the essay.

In the body of the essay the classes may be arranged in order of decreasing familiarity or increasing importance or size — whatever pattern provides the emphasis you want and clarifies your scheme for readers. You should at least mention each class, but some classes may demand considerable space and detail.

A classification essay often ends with a conclusion that restores the wholeness of the subject. Among other uses, the conclusion might summarize the classes, comment on the significance of one particular class in relation to the whole, or point out a new understanding of the whole subject gained from the classification.

Drafting

For the first draft of your classification, your main goal will be to establish your scheme: spelling out the purpose and principle of classification and defining the groups so that they are complete and consistent, covering the subject without mixing principles or overlapping. The more you've planned your scheme, the less difficult the draft will be. If you can also fill in the examples and other details needed to develop the groups, do so.

Be sure to consider your readers' needs as you draft. For a subject familiar to readers, such as study habits, you probably wouldn't need to justify your principle of classification, but you would need to enliven the classes themselves with vivid examples. For an unfamiliar subject, in contrast, you might need to take considerable care in explaining the principle of classification as well as in detailing the classes.

Revising and Editing

The following questions can help you revise and edit your classification.

- *Will readers see the purpose of your classification?* Let readers know early why you are taking the trouble to classify your subject, and keep this purpose evident throughout the essay.
- *Is your classification complete?* Your principle of classification should create categories that encompass every representative of the general subject. If some representatives will not fit the scheme, you may have to create a new category or revise the existing categories to include them.
- *Is your classification consistent?* Consistency is essential to save readers from confusion or irritation. Make sure all the classes reflect the same principle and that they do not overlap. Remedy flaws by adjusting the classes or creating new ones.

DEBORAH TANNEN

Well known for her books on how people communicate, Deborah Tannen is a linguist with a knack for popular writing. She was born in 1945 in Brooklyn, New York, and attended Hunter College High School in Manhattan. She received a BA from Harpur College (now part of Binghamton University), an MA from Wayne State University, and a PhD from the University of California at Berkeley. Tannen attributes her interest in linguistics partly to a childhood hearing impairment that she says schooled her in "tone of voice, attitude, and all the other conversational signals" in addition to the words themselves. She has been teaching linguistics since 1979 at Georgetown University, publishes extensively in scholarly and popular periodicals, and lectures widely. Her best-selling books, all concerning communication breakdowns and how to repair them, include That's Not What I Meant! *(1986),* You Just Don't Understand *(1990),* The Argument Culture *(1998),* I Only Say This Because I Love You *(2001),* You're Wearing That? *(2006), and* You Were Always Mom's Favorite! *(2009).*

But What Do You Mean?

Tannen's most popular books examine differences in the ways men and women talk to each other. In this essay, excerpted in Redbook *magazine from Tannen's book* Talking from 9 to 5 *(1994), she examines seven areas of miscommunication between genders.*

Conversation is a ritual. We say things that seem obviously the thing to say, without thinking of the literal meaning of our words, any more than we expect the question "How are you?" to call forth a detailed account of aches and pains. 1

Unfortunately, women and men often have different ideas about what's appropriate, different ways of speaking. Many of the conversational rituals common among women are designed to take the other person's feelings into account, while many of 2 the conversational rituals common among men are designed to maintain the one-up position, or at least avoid appearing one-down. As a result, when men and women interact—especially at work—it's often women who are at the disadvantage. Because women are not trying to avoid the one-down position, that is unfortunately where they may end up.

Here, the biggest areas of miscommunication.   3

1. Apologies

Women are often told they apologize too much. The reason 4 they're told to stop doing it is that, to many men, apologizing seems synonymous with putting oneself down. But there are many times when "I'm sorry" isn't self-deprecating, or even an apology; it's an automatic way of keeping both speakers on an equal footing. For example, a well-known columnist once interviewed me and gave me her phone number in case I needed to call her back. I misplaced the number and had to go through the newspaper's main switchboard. When our conversation was winding down and we'd both made ending-type remarks, I added, "Oh, I almost forgot—I lost your direct number, can I get it again?" "Oh, I'm sorry," she came back instantly, even though she had done nothing wrong and *I* was the one who'd lost the number. But I understood she wasn't really apologizing; she was just automatically reassuring me she had no intention of denying me her number.

Even when "I'm sorry" *is* an apology, women often assume it 5 will be the first step in a two-step ritual: I say "I'm sorry" and take half the blame, then you take the other half. At work, it might go something like this:

A: When you typed this letter, you missed this phrase I inserted.
B: Oh, I'm sorry. I'll fix it.
A: Well, I wrote it so small it was easy to miss.

When both parties share blame, it's a mutual face-saving 6 device. But if one person, usually the woman, utters frequent apologies and the other doesn't, she ends up looking as if she's taking the blame for mishaps that aren't her fault. When she's only partially to blame, she looks entirely in the wrong.

I recently sat in on a meeting at an insurance company where 7
the sole woman, Helen, said "I'm sorry" or "I apologize" repeatedly. At one point she said, "I'm thinking out loud. I apologize."
Yet the meeting was intended to be an informal brainstorming
session, and *everyone* was thinking out loud.

The reason Helen's apologies stood out was that she was 8
the only person in the room making so many. And the reason
I was concerned was that Helen felt the annual bonus she had
received was unfair. When I interviewed her colleagues, they said
that Helen was one of the best and most productive workers—yet
she got one of the smallest bonuses. Although the problem might
have been outright sexism, I suspect her speech style, which differs from that of her male colleagues, masks her competence.

Unfortunately, not apologizing can have its price too. Since 9
so many women use ritual apologies, those who don't may be
seen as hard-edged. What's important is to be aware of how often
you say you're sorry (and why), and to monitor your speech based
on the reaction you get.

2. Criticism

A woman who cowrote a report with a male colleague was hurt 10
when she read a rough draft to him and he leapt into a critical
response—"Oh, that's too dry! You have to make it snappier!" She
herself would have been more likely to say, "That's a really good start.
Of course, you'll want to make it a little snappier when you revise."

Whether criticism is given straight or softened is often a 11
matter of convention. In general, women use more softeners. I
noticed this difference when talking to an editor about an essay
I'd written. While going over changes she wanted to make, she
said, "There's one more thing. I know you may not agree with
me. The reason I noticed the problem is that your other points
are so lucid and elegant." She went on hedging for several more
sentences until I put her out of her misery: "Do you want to cut
that part?" I asked—and of course she did. But I appreciated her
tentativeness. In contrast, another editor (a man) I once called
summarily rejected my idea for an article by barking, "Call me
when you have something new to say."

Those who are used to ways of talking that soften the impact of 12
criticism may find it hard to deal with the right-between-the-eyes

style. It has its own logic, however, and neither style is intrinsically better. People who prefer criticism given straight are operating on an assumption that feelings aren't involved: "Here's the dope. I know you're good; you can take it."

3. Thank-Yous

A woman manager I know starts meetings by thanking everyone 13 for coming, even though it's clearly their job to do so. Her "thank-you" is simply a ritual.

A novelist received a fax from an assistant in her publish- 14 er's office; it contained suggested catalog copy for her book. She immediately faxed him her suggested changes and said, "Thanks for running this by me," even though her contract gave her the right to approve all copy. When she thanked the assistant, she fully expected him to reciprocate: "Thanks for giving me such a quick response." Instead, he said, "You're welcome." Suddenly, rather than an equal exchange of pleasantries, she found herself positioned as the recipient of a favor. This made her feel like responding, "Thanks for nothing!"

Many women use "thanks" as an automatic conversation starter 15 and closer; there's nothing literally to say thank you for. Like many rituals typical of women's conversation, it depends on the goodwill of the other to restore the balance. When the other speaker doesn't reciprocate, a woman may feel like someone on a seesaw whose partner abandoned his end. Instead of balancing in the air, she has plopped to the ground, wondering how she got there.

4. Fighting

Many men expect the discussion of ideas to be a ritual fight— 16 explored through verbal opposition. They state their ideas in the strongest possible terms, thinking that if there are weaknesses someone will point them out, and by trying to argue against those objections, they will see how well their ideas hold up.

Those who expect their own ideas to be challenged will 17 respond to another's ideas by trying to poke holes and find weak links—as a way of *helping*. The logic is that when you are challenged you will rise to the occasion: Adrenaline makes your mind sharper; you get ideas and insights you would not have thought of without the spur of battle.

But many women take this approach as a personal attack. 18 Worse, they find it impossible to do their best work in such a contentious environment. If you're not used to ritual fighting, you begin to hear criticism of your ideas as soon as they are formed. Rather than making you think more clearly, it makes you doubt what you know. When you state your ideas, you hedge in order to fend off potential attacks. Ironically, this is more likely to *invite* attack because it makes you look weak.

Although you may never enjoy verbal sparring, some women 19 find it helpful to learn how to do it. An engineer who was the only woman among four men in a small company found that as soon as she learned to argue she was accepted and taken seriously. A doctor attending a hospital staff meeting made a similar discovery. She was becoming more and more angry with a male colleague who'd loudly disagreed with a point she'd made. Her better judgment told her to hold her tongue, to avoid making an enemy of this powerful senior colleague. But finally she couldn't hold it in any longer, and she rose to her feet and delivered an impassioned attack on his position. She sat down in a panic, certain she had permanently damaged her relationship with him. To her amazement, he came up to her afterward and said, "That was a great rebuttal. I'm really impressed. Let's go out for a beer after work and hash out our approaches to this problem."

5. Praise

A manager I'll call Lester had been on his new job six months 20 when he heard that the women reporting to him were deeply dissatisfied. When he talked to them about it, their feelings erupted; two said they were on the verge of quitting because he didn't appreciate their work, and they didn't want to wait to be fired. Lester was dumbfounded: He believed they were doing a fine job. Surely, he thought, he had said nothing to give them the impression he didn't like their work. And indeed he hadn't. That was the problem. He had said *nothing*—and the women assumed he was following the adage "If you can't say something nice, don't say anything." He thought he was showing confidence in them by leaving them alone.

Men and women have different habits in regard to giving 21 praise. For example, Deirdre and her colleague William both gave presentations at a conference. Afterward, Deirdre told William, "That was a great talk!" He thanked her. Then she asked, "What did you think of mine?" and he gave her a lengthy and detailed critique. She found it uncomfortable to listen to his comments. But she assured herself that he meant well, and that his honesty was a signal that she, too, should be honest when he asked for a critique of his performance. As a matter of fact, she had noticed quite a few ways in which he could have improved his presentation. But she never got a chance to tell him because he never asked—and she felt put down. The worst part was that it seemed she had only herself to blame, since she *had* asked what he thought of her talk.

But had she really asked for his critique? The truth is, when 22 she asked for his opinion, she was expecting a compliment, which she felt was more or less required following anyone's talk. When he responded with criticism, she figured, "Oh, he's playing 'Let's critique each other'"—not a game she'd initiated, but one which she was willing to play. Had she realized he was going to criticize her and not ask her to reciprocate, she would never have asked in the first place.

It would be easy to assume that Deirdre was insecure, whether 23 she was fishing for a compliment or soliciting a critique. But she was simply talking automatically, performing one of the many conversational rituals that allow us to get through the day. William may have sincerely misunderstood Deirdre's intention—or may have been unable to pass up a chance to one-up her when given the opportunity.

6. Complaints

"Troubles talk" can be a way to establish rapport with a colleague. 24 You complain about a problem (which shows that you are just folks) and the other person responds with a similar problem (which puts you on equal footing). But while such commiserating is common among women, men are likely to hear it as a request to *solve* the problem.

One woman told me she would frequently initiate what she 25 thought would be pleasant complaint-airing sessions at work. She'd talk about situations that bothered her just to talk about them, maybe to understand them better. But her male office mate would quickly tell her how she could improve the situation. This left her feeling condescended to and frustrated. She was delighted to see this very impasse in a section in my book *You Just Don't Understand*, and showed it to him. "Oh," he said, "I see the problem. How can we solve it?" Then they both laughed, because it had happened again: He short-circuited the detailed discussion she'd hoped for and cut to the chase of finding a solution.

Sometimes the consequences of complaining are more seri-   26 ous: A man might take a woman's lighthearted griping literally, and she can get a reputation as a chronic malcontent. Furthermore, she may be seen as not up to solving the problems that arise on the job.

7. Jokes

I heard a man call in to a talk show and say, "I've worked for   27 two women and neither one had a sense of humor. You know, when you work with men, there's a lot of joking and teasing." The show's host and the guest (both women) took his comment at face value and assumed the women this man worked for were humorless. The guest said, "Isn't it sad that women don't feel comfortable enough with authority to see the humor?" The host said, "Maybe when more women are in authority roles, they'll be more comfortable with power." But although the women this man worked for *may* have taken themselves too seriously, it's just as likely that they each had a terrific sense of humor, but maybe the humor wasn't the type he was used to. They may have been like the woman who wrote to me: "When I'm with men, my wit or cleverness seems inappropriate (or lost!) so I don't bother. When I'm with my women friends, however, there's no hold on puns or cracks and my humor is fully appreciated."

The types of humor women and men tend to prefer dif-   28 fer. Research has shown that the most common form of humor among men is razzing, teasing, and mock-hostile attacks, while among women it's self-mocking. Women often mistake men's teasing as genuinely hostile. Men often mistake women's mock self-deprecation as truly putting themselves down.

Women have told me they were taken more seriously when   29 they learned to joke the way the guys did. For example, a teacher who went to a national conference with seven other teachers (mostly women) and a group of administrators (mostly men) was annoyed that the administrators always found reasons to leave boring seminars, while the teachers felt they had to stay and take notes. One evening, when the group met at a bar in the hotel, the principal asked her how one such seminar had turned out. She retorted, "As soon as you left, it got much better." He laughed out loud at her response. The playful insult appealed to the men—but there was a trade-off. The women seemed to back off from her after this. (Perhaps they were put off by her using joking to align herself with the bosses.)

There is no "right" way to talk. When problems arise, the cul- 30 prit may be style differences—and *all* styles will at times fail with others who don't share or understand them, just as English won't do you much good if you try to speak to someone who knows only French. If you want to get your message across, it's not a question of being "right"; it's a question of using language that's shared—or at least understood.

Meaning

1. What does Tannen mean when she writes, "Conversation is a ritual" (paragraph 1)?
2. What does Tannen see as the fundamental difference between men's and women's conversational strategies?
3. Why is "You're welcome" not always an appropriate response to "Thank you"?

Purpose and Audience

1. What is Tannen's purpose in writing this essay? What does she hope it will accomplish?
2. Whom does Tannen see as her primary audience? Analyze her use of the pronoun *you* in paragraphs 9 and 19. Whom does she seem to be addressing here? Why?

Method and Structure

1. This essay has a large cast of characters: twenty-three to be exact. What function do these characters serve? How does Tannen introduce them to the reader? Does she describe them in sufficient detail?
2. How does Tannen's description of a columnist as "well-known" (paragraph 4) contribute to the effectiveness of her example?

3. OTHER METHODS For each of her seven areas of miscommunication, Tannen compares and contrasts male and female communication styles and strategies. Summarize the main source of misunderstanding in each area.

Language

1. What is the effect of "I put her out of her misery" (paragraph 11)? What does this phrase usually mean?
2. What does Tannen mean by a "right-between-the-eyes style" (paragraph 12)? What is the figure of speech involved here? (See the Glossary under *figures of speech*.)
3. What is the effect of Tannen's use of figurative verbs, such as "barking" (paragraph 11) and "erupted" (20)? Find at least one other example of the use of a verb in a nonliteral sense.

Writing Topics

1. Write an essay classifying unconscious patterns of speech into categories of your own devising. For example, when someone says "Have a good trip," do you answer "You too," even if the other person isn't going anywhere? Do you find yourself overusing certain words or phrases such as "like" or "you know"? You might sort out the examples by context ("phone blunders," "faulty farewells"), by purpose ("nervous tics," "space fillers"), or by some other principle of classification. Given your subject matter, you might want to adopt a humorous tone.
2. How well does your style of communication conform to that of your gender as described by Tannen? Write a short essay about a specific communication problem or misunderstanding you have had with someone of the opposite sex (sibling, friend, parent, significant other). How well does Tannen's differentiation of male and female communication styles account for your particular problem?
3. How true do you find Tannen's assessment of miscommunication between the sexes? Consider the conflicts you have observed between your parents, among fellow students or coworkers, in fictional portrayals in books and movies. Are Tannen's conclusions confirmed or called into question by your own observations and experiences? Write an essay confirming or questioning Tannen's generalizations, using your own examples.

STEPHANIE ERICSSON

Stephanie Ericsson was born in Dallas, Texas, in 1953 and grew up in San Francisco, California. Much of her writing draws on personal experience and reflection to examine love, loss, and grief. Her first book, Companion Through the Darkness: Inner Dialogues on Grief *(1993) began as a series of journal entries she wrote following the unexpected death of her husband. She followed it with* Companion into the Dawn: Inner Dialogues on Loving *(1997). A freelance writer, Ericsson has worked in television, film, and advertising. She lives in St. Paul, Minnesota.*

The Ways We Lie

"The Ways We Lie," which Ericsson wrote from her notes for Companion into the Dawn, *first appeared in the* Utne Reader. *The essay examines the destructive potential of various types of lies, including those that seem necessary and even beneficial.*

The bank called today and I told them my deposit was in the mail, 1 even though I hadn't written a check yet. It'd been a rough day. The baby I'm pregnant with decided to do aerobics on my lungs for two hours, our three-year-old daughter painted the living-room couch with lipstick, the IRS put me on hold for an hour, and I was late to a business meeting because I was tired.

I told my client that traffic had been bad. When my partner 2 came home, his haggard face told me his day hadn't gone any better than mine, so when he asked, "How was your day?" I said, "Oh, fine," knowing that one more straw might break his back. A friend called and wanted to take me to lunch. I said I was busy. Four lies in the course of a day, none of which I felt the least bit guilty about.

We lie. We all do. We exaggerate, we minimize, we avoid 3 confrontation, we spare people's feelings, we conveniently forget, we keep secrets, we justify lying to the big-guy institutions.

Like most people, I indulge in small falsehoods and still think of myself as an honest person. Sure I lie, but it doesn't hurt anything. Or does it?

I once tried going a whole week without telling a lie, and 4 it was paralyzing. I discovered that telling the truth all the time is nearly impossible. It means living with some serious consequences: The bank charges me $60 in overdraft fees, my partner keels over when I tell him about my travails, my client fires me for telling her I didn't feel like being on time, and my friend takes it personally when I say I'm not hungry. There must be some merit to lying.

But if I justify lying, what makes me any different from slick 5 politicians or the corporate robbers who raided the S&L industry? Saying it's okay to lie one way and not another is hedging. I cannot seem to escape the voice deep inside me that tells me: When someone lies, someone loses.

What far-reaching consequences will I, or others, pay as a 6 result of my lie? Will someone's trust be destroyed? Will someone else pay *my* penance because I ducked out? We must consider the *meaning of our actions*. Deception, lies, capital crimes, and misdemeanors all carry meanings. *Webster's* definition of *lie* is specific:

> 1: a false statement or action especially made with the intent to deceive;
>
> 2: anything that gives or is meant to give a false impression.

A definition like this implies that there are many, many ways 7 to tell a lie. Here are just a few.

The White Lie

> *A man who won't lie to a woman has very little consideration for her feelings.* — BERGEN EVANS

The white lie assumes that the truth will cause more damage than 8 a simple, harmless untruth. Telling a friend he looks great when he looks like hell can be based on a decision that the friend needs a compliment more than a frank opinion. But, in effect, it is the liar deciding what is best for the lied to. Ultimately, it is a vote of no confidence. It is an act of subtle arrogance for anyone to decide what is best for someone else.

Yet not all circumstances are quite so cut-and-dried. Take, for 9
instance, the sergeant in Vietnam who knew one of his men was
killed in action but listed him as missing so that the man's family
would receive indefinite compensation instead of the lump-sum
pittance the military gives widows and children. His intent was
honorable. Yet for twenty years this family kept their hopes alive,
unable to move on to a new life.

Façades

Et tu, Brute? — CAESAR

We all put up façades to one degree or another. When I put on a 10
suit to go to see a client, I feel as though I am putting on another
face, obeying the expectation that serious businesspeople wear
suits rather than sweatpants. But I'm a writer. Normally, I get up,
get the kid off to school, and sit at my computer in my pajamas
until four in the afternoon. When I answer the phone, the caller
thinks I'm wearing a suit (though the UPS man knows better).

But façades can be destructive because they are used to seduce 11
others into an illusion. For instance, I recently realized that a former friend was a liar. He presented himself with all the right looks
and the right words and offered lots of new consciousness theories, fabulous books to read, and fascinating insights. Then I did
some business with him, and the time came for him to pay me.
He turned out to be all talk and no walk. I heard a plethora of reasonable excuses, including in-depth descriptions of the big break
around the corner. In six months of work, I saw less than a hundred bucks. When I confronted him, he raised both eyebrows and
tried to convince me that I'd heard him wrong, that he'd made no
commitment to me. A simple investigation into his past revealed a
crowded graveyard of disenchanted former friends.

Ignoring the Plain Facts

Well, you must understand that Father Porter is only human.
— A MASSACHUSETTS PRIEST

In the '60s, the Catholic Church in Massachusetts began hear- 12
ing complaints that Father James Porter was sexually molesting
children. Rather than relieving him of his duties, the ecclesiastical

authorities simply moved him from one parish to another between 1960 and 1967, actually providing him with a fresh supply of unsuspecting families and innocent children to abuse. After treatment in 1967 for pedophilia, he went back to work, this time in Minnesota. The new diocese was aware of Father Porter's obsession with children, but they needed priests and recklessly believed treatment had cured him. More children were abused until he was relieved of his duties a year later. By his own admission, Porter may have abused as many as a hundred children.

Ignoring the facts may not in and of itself be a form of lying, but consider the context of this situation. If a lie is *a false action done with the intent to deceive*, then the Catholic Church's conscious covering for Porter created irreparable consequences. The church became a co-perpetrator with Porter. 13

Deflecting

When you have no basis for an argument, abuse the plaintiff.
—CICERO

I've discovered that I can keep anyone from seeing the true me by being selectively blatant. I set a precedent of being up-front about intimate issues, but I never bring up the things I truly want to hide; I just let people assume I'm revealing everything. It's an effective way of hiding. 14

Any good liar knows that the way to perpetuate an untruth is to deflect attention from it. When Clarence Thomas exploded with accusations that the Senate hearings were a "high-tech lynching," he simply switched the focus from a highly charged subject to a radioactive subject.[1] Rather than defending himself, he took the offensive and accused the country of racism. It was a brilliant maneuver. Racism is now politically incorrect in official circles—unlike sexual harassment, which still rewards those who can get away with it. 15

Some of the most skilled deflectors are passive-aggressive people who, when accused of inappropriate behavior, refuse to respond to the accusations. This you-don't-exist stance infuriates the accuser, who, understandably, screams something obscene 16

---

[1]Ericsson is referring to the 1991 hearings to confirm Thomas for the Supreme Court, at which Anita Hill accused Thomas of sexual harassment. [Editors' note.]

out of frustration. The trap is sprung and the act of deflection successful, because now the passive-aggressive person can indignantly say, "Who can talk to someone as unreasonable as you?" The real issue is forgotten and the sins of the original victim become the focus. Feeling guilty of name-calling, the victim is fully tamed and crawls into a hole, ashamed. I have watched this fighting technique work thousands of times in disputes between men and women, and what I've learned is that the real culprit is not necessarily the one who swears the loudest.

Omission

The cruelest lies are often told in silence. —R. L. STEVENSON

Omission involves telling most of the truth minus one or two key 17 facts whose absence changes the story completely. You break a pair of glasses that are guaranteed under normal use and get a new pair, without mentioning that the first pair broke during a rowdy game of basketball. Who hasn't tried something like that? But what about omission of information that could make a difference in how a person lives his or her life?

For instance, one day I found out that rabbinical legends tell of 18 another woman in the Garden of Eden before Eve. I was stunned. The omission of the Sumerian goddess Lilith from Genesis—as well as her demonization by ancient misogynists as an embodiment of female evil—felt like spiritual robbery. I felt like I'd just found out my mother was really my stepmother. To take seriously the tradition that Adam was created out of the same mud as his equal counterpart, Lilith, redefines all of Judeo-Christian history.

Some renegade Catholic feminists introduced me to a view of 19 Lilith that had been suppressed during the many centuries when this strong goddess was seen only as a spirit of evil. Lilith was a proud goddess who defied Adam's need to control her, attempted negotiations, and when this failed, said adios and left the Garden of Eden.

This omission of Lilith from the Bible was a patriarchal strat- 20 egy to keep women weak. Omitting the strong-woman archetype of Lilith from Western religions and starting the story with Eve the Rib has helped keep Christian and Jewish women believing they were the lesser sex for thousands of years.

Stereotypes and Clichés

*Where opinion does not exist, the status quo becomes stereotyped
and all originality is discouraged.* —BERTRAND RUSSELL

Stereotype and cliché serve a purpose as a form of shorthand.   21
Our need for vast amounts of information in nanoseconds has
made the stereotype vital to modern communication. Unfortunately, it often shuts down original thinking, giving those hungry
for the truth a candy bar of misinformation instead of a balanced
meal. The stereotype explains a situation with just enough truth
to seem unquestionable.

All the "isms"—racism, sexism, ageism, et al.—are founded   22
on and fueled by the stereotype and the cliché, which are lies of
exaggeration, omission, and ignorance. They are always dangerous. They take a single tree and make it a landscape. They destroy
curiosity. They close minds and separate people. The single mother
on welfare is assumed to be cheating. Any black male could tell you
how much of his identity is obliterated daily by stereotypes. Fat
people, ugly people, beautiful people, old people, large-breasted
women, short men, the mentally ill, and the homeless all could
tell you how much more they are like us than we want to think. I
once admitted to a group of people that I had a mouth like a truck
driver. Much to my surprise, a man stood up and said, "I'm a truck
driver, and I never cuss." Needless to say, I was humbled.

Groupthink

*Who is more foolish, the child afraid of the dark, or the man
afraid of the light?* —MAURICE FREEHILL

Irving Janis, in *Victims of Group Think*, defines this sort of lie   23
as a psychological phenomenon within decision-making groups
in which loyalty to the group has become more important than
any other value, with the result that dissent and the appraisal of
alternatives are suppressed. If you've ever worked on a committee
or in a corporation, you've encountered groupthink. It requires
a combination of other forms of lying—ignoring facts, selective
memory, omission, and denial, to name a few.

The textbook example of groupthink came on December 7, 24
1941. From as early as the fall of 1941, the warnings came in, one
after another, that Japan was preparing for a massive military
operation. The navy command in Hawaii assumed Pearl Harbor
was invulnerable — the Japanese weren't stupid enough to attack
the United States' most important base. On the other hand, racist stereotypes said the Japanese weren't smart enough to invent
a torpedo effective in less than 60 feet of water (the fleet was
docked in 30 feet); after all, US technology hadn't been able to
do it.

On Friday, December 5, normal weekend leave was granted 25
to all the commanders at Pearl Harbor, even though the Japanese consulate in Hawaii was busy burning papers. Within the
tight, good-ole-boy cohesiveness of the US command in Hawaii,
the myth of invulnerability stayed well entrenched. No one in the
group considered the alternatives. The rest is history.

Out-and-Out Lies

*The only form of lying that is beyond reproach is lying for its
own sake.* — OSCAR WILDE

Of all the ways to lie, I like this one the best, probably because I 26
get tired of trying to figure out the real meanings behind things.
At least I can trust the bald-faced lie. I once asked my five-year-
old nephew, "Who broke the fence?" (I had seen him do it.) He
answered, "The murderers." Who could argue?

At least when this sort of lie is told it can be easily confronted. 27
As the person who is lied to, I know where I stand. The bald-
faced lie doesn't toy with my perceptions—it argues with them.
It doesn't try to refashion reality, it tries to refute it. *Read my lips.*
. . . No sleight of hand. No guessing. If this were the only form
of lying, there would be no such things as floating anxiety or the
adult-children-of-alcoholics movement.

Dismissal

*Pay no attention to that man behind the curtain! I am the
Great Oz!* — THE WIZARD OF OZ

Dismissal is perhaps the slipperiest of all lies. Dismissing feel- 28
ings, perceptions, or even the raw facts of a situation ranks as a
kind of lie that can do as much damage to a person as any other
kind of lie.

The roots of many mental disorders can be traced back to 29
the dismissal of reality. Imagine that a person is told from the
time she is a tot that her perceptions are inaccurate. *"Mommy,
I'm scared."* "No you're not, darling." *"I don't like that man next
door, he makes me feel icky."* "Johnny, that's a terrible thing to say,
of course you like him. You go over there right now and be nice
to him."

I've often mused over the idea that madness is actually a sane 30
reaction to an insane world. Psychologist R. D. Laing supports
this hypothesis in *Sanity, Madness and the Family*, an account of
his investigation into the families of schizophrenics. The common thread that ran through all of the families he studied was a
deliberate, staunch dismissal of the patient's perceptions from a
very early age. Each of the patients started out with an accurate
grasp of reality, which, through meticulous and methodical dismissal, was demolished until the only reality the patient could
trust was catatonia.

Dismissal runs the gamut. Mild dismissal can be quite handy 31
for forgiving the foibles of others in our day-to-day lives. Tod-
dlers who have just learned to manipulate their parents' attention
sometimes are dismissed out of necessity. Absolute attention from
the parents would require so much energy that no one would get
to eat dinner. But we must be careful and attentive about how far
we take our "necessary" dismissals. Dismissal is a dangerous tool,
because it's nothing less than a lie.

Delusion

We lie loudest when we lie to ourselves.   —ERIC HOFFER

I could write the book on this one. Delusion, a cousin of dis- 32
missal, is the tendency to see excuses as facts. It's a powerful lying
tool because it filters out information that contradicts what we
want to believe. Alcoholics who believe that the problems in their
lives are legitimate reasons for drinking rather than results of the

drinking offer the classic example of deluded thinking. Delusion uses the mind's ability to see things in myriad ways to support what it wants to be the truth.

But delusion is also a survival mechanism we all use. If we were to fully contemplate the consequences of our stockpiles of nuclear weapons or global warming, we could hardly function on a day-to-day level. We don't want to incorporate that much reality into our lives because to do so would be paralyzing. 33

Delusion acts as an adhesive to keep the status quo intact. It shamelessly employs dismissal, omission, and amnesia, among other sorts of lies. Its most cunning defense is that it cannot see itself. 34

• • •

The liar's punishment . . . is that he cannot believe anyone else. —GEORGE BERNARD SHAW

These are only a few of the ways we lie. Or are lied to. As I said earlier, it's not easy to entirely eliminate lies from our lives. No matter how pious we may try to be, we will still embellish, hedge, and omit to lubricate the daily machinery of living. But there is a world of difference between telling functional lies and living a lie. Martin Buber once said, "The lie is the spirit committing treason against itself." Our acceptance of lies becomes a cultural cancer that eventually shrouds and reorders reality until moral garbage becomes as invisible to us as water is to a fish. 35

How much do we tolerate before we become sick and tired of being sick and tired? When will we stand up and declare our *right* to trust? When do we stop accepting that the real truth is in the fine print? Whose lips do we read this year when we vote for president? When will we stop being so reticent about making judgments? When do we stop turning over our personal power and responsibility to liars? 36

Maybe if I don't tell the bank the check's in the mail I'll be less tolerant of the lies told me every day. A country song I once heard said it all for me: "You've got to stand for something or you'll fall for anything." 37

Meaning

1. What is Ericsson's thesis?
2. Does Ericsson think it's possible to eliminate lies from our lives? What evidence does she offer?
3. If it were possible to eliminate lies from our lives, why would that be desirable?

Purpose and Audience

1. What is this essay's purpose?
2. Identify instances where Ericsson directly addresses her audience. What does she accomplish by using the pronoun *we* throughout the essay?

Method and Structure

1. Ericsson starts out by recounting her own four-lie day (paragraphs 1–2). What is the effect of this introduction?
2. At the beginning of each kind of lie, Ericsson provides an epigraph, a short quotation that forecasts a theme. Which of these epigraphs work best, do you think? What are your criteria for judgment?
3. What is the message of Ericsson's conclusion? Does the conclusion work well? Why, or why not?
4. OTHER METHODS   Examine the way Ericsson uses definition and example to support her classification. Which definitions are clearest? Which examples are the most effective? Why?

Language

1. In paragraph 35 Ericsson writes, "Our acceptance of lies becomes a cultural cancer that eventually shrouds and reorders reality until moral garbage becomes as invisible to us as water is to a fish." How do the two figures of speech in this sentence—cancer and garbage—relate to each other? (See *figures of speech* in the Glossary.)
2. Occasionally Ericsson's anger shows through, as in paragraphs 12–13 and 18–20. Is the tone appropriate in these cases? Why, or why not?

Writing Topics

1. Consider some lies that you have told, whether large or seemingly harmless. Develop one or more of these lies into an essay. You may

choose to elaborate on your lies by classifying according to some principle or by narrating the story of a particular lie and its outcome. Try to give your reader a sense of your motivation for lying in the first place.

2. Ericsson writes, "All the 'isms'—racism, sexism, ageism, et al.—are founded on and fueled by the stereotype and the cliché, which are lies of exaggeration, omission, and ignorance. They are always dangerous. They take a single tree and make it a landscape" (paragraph 22). Write an essay discussing stereotypes and how they work to encourage prejudice. Use Ericsson's definition as a base, and expand it to include stereotypes you find particularly injurious. How do these stereotypes oversimplify? How are they "dangerous"?

3. Evaluate the success of Ericsson's essay, considering especially how effectively her evidence supports her generalizations. Are there important categories she overlooks, exceptions she neglects to account for, gaps in definitions or examples? Offer specific evidence for your own view, whether positive or negative.

Resources for Teaching

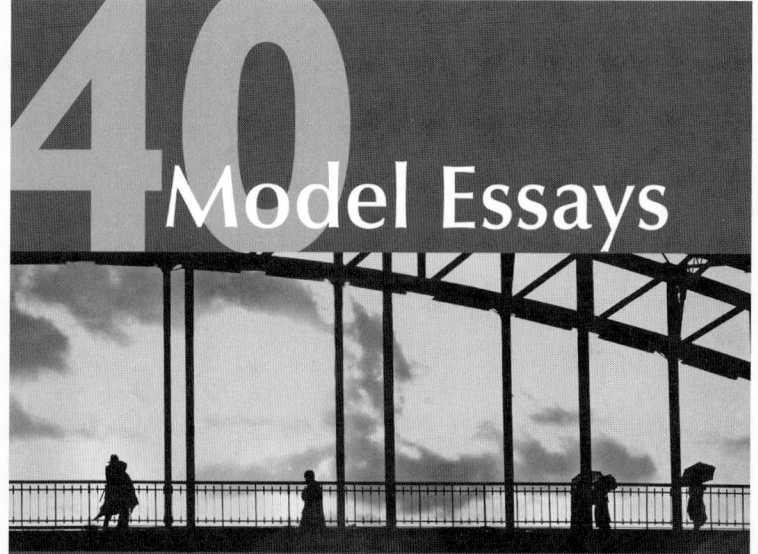

40 Model Essays

A PORTABLE ANTHOLOGY

SECOND EDITION

Jane E. Aaron • Ellen Kuhl Repetto

Resources for Teaching

40 Model Essays

A Portable Anthology
Second Edition

JANE E. AARON

ELLEN KUHL REPETTO

Bedford/St. Martin's   BOSTON ◆ NEW YORK

Manufactured in the United States of America.

7 6 5 4 3 2
f   e   d c   b   a

For information, write: Bedford/St. Martin's, 75 Arlington Street, Boston, MA 02116   (617-399-4000)

ISBN 978-1-4576-3786-5

Contents

I
USING *40 MODEL ESSAYS*

The structure of *40 Model Essays* is uncomplicated: an introduction coaches students on reading and writing, and ten chapters explain and illustrate ten rhetorical methods of development.

INTRODUCTION TO READING AND WRITING

You may wish to discuss the introduction explicitly in class, adapting all or parts of it to your syllabus; or you may find the introduction self-explanatory enough simply to ask students to read it on their own. Either way, the introduction lays useful groundwork for a reading and writing course. It explains and illustrates how critical reading is linked to good writing, how to read a text critically, how to work productively through the initial stages of writing, and how to revise and edit one's own drafts.

A highlight of the introduction is the discussion of Edward P. Jones's essay "Shacks," showing how a critical reader might approach an essay and what conclusions might result. This discussion is organized around generalized versions of the questions that appear after each essay in Chapters 1–10. These questions — divided into the four categories of meaning, purpose and audience, method and structure, and language — invite students to consider the elements an author calls on in constructing an essay. By observing how a critical reader might answer these questions for Jones's essay, students have an opportunity to see what kinds of answers they might provide to the questions following the other essays in the book — and, more significant, to begin honing their own skills as critical readers.

Jones's essay combines many of the methods of development (definition, example, description, etc.), thus providing an overview of the methods treated separately in the subsequent chapters. At

1

the same time, the discussion of Jones's essay introduces a point assumed throughout *40 Model Essays*: writers rarely use a single method alone but gain shape, texture, and clarity for their writing by applying whatever method is best suited to a particular point or purpose.

To engage students actively in writing during the first or second class period, you might ask them to do some prewriting as preparation for reading the Jones essay. Here are possible questions: What about the first months of college makes you feel homesick or lonely? How do you stay connected with family and friends from home? Or, to move in another direction, you might ask these questions: What special talent(s) do you have? How do you feel about your abilities as a writer? Do you think you can improve with practice? After reading Jones's essay, students could compare their responses with his and with one another's. They may see Jones's as more complete and insightful than their own, noting that he presents his experience and feelings vividly; but that may prompt some students to recall similar lessons from their own experience and help them see how they might enrich their own writing.

The rest of the introduction provides an overview of the writing process, detailing the basic concepts, terms, and stages that are then used in the introductions to the rhetorical methods. This section includes a discussion of revising and editing. Two bulleted lists of revision and editing questions guide students through rethinking and correcting their own work. Then, in the introduction to each rhetorical method, a more specific revision and editing checklist appears with questions especially relevant to the method.

TEN CHAPTERS ON THE METHODS OF DEVELOPMENT

Chapter Introductions

The introductions to Chapters 1–10 all proceed in the same way. The opening section, "Using the Method," discusses the purposes for which the method is suited and provides essential concepts and definitions. The next section, "Developing a _____ Essay," suggests strategies for starting, focusing, organizing, drafting, and revising and editing an essay using the method.

The Essays

The selections in *40 Model Essays* satisfy several criteria. Most important, they plainly illustrate the rhetorical methods, and they are interesting. The essays vary in length and complexity, so a student will find many of them imitable; yet they are substantial enough for sharpening reading skills and encouraging lively discussion. Longer essays provide transition to more challenging academic work.

Biographical and Essay Headnotes

These prefaces to the essays establish a context for each essay, offering background on the writer's interests and expertise in his or her subject and providing information about his or her intended audience. Students are often inclined to skip sections like these, so it may be worthwhile to point out how helpful the headnotes can be for analyzing the essays along with the discussion questions.

Discussion Questions

The questions following each essay help students analyze and evaluate the essay, either on their own or in class discussions. The questions are organized in four groups — meaning, purpose and audience, method and structure, and language — that lead students to examine the essay with an increasingly sharp focus. As mentioned earlier, the four groups of questions correspond to those following Jones's essay in the general introduction. Possible answers to the questions are provided in this manual.

Writing Topics

At least three writing topics follow each essay. Some relate to the essay's content; some suggest a subject compatible with the method introduced in the chapter; several ask students to research a subject raised by the essay.

In addition to the topics following each essay, every chapter ends with a set of supplementary writing suggestions. Titled "Writing with the Method," these suggestions include many possibilities for applying the chapter's method of development.

II

COMBINING *40 MODEL ESSAYS* WITH OTHER MATERIALS

Because of its brevity, *40 Model Essays* can be easily combined with other classroom materials and approaches, including other textbooks, library research, current newspaper and magazine articles, and the writing of your own students.

OTHER TEXTBOOKS

Though brief, *40 Model Essays* anticipates many student questions about the use of the methods of development; hence you can ask students to read the chapter introductions independently, reserving class time to discuss the chapter's theme or the application of the writing principles.

Given its coverage of the writing process, *40 Model Essays* can complement a handbook or a rhetoric. It can inspire writing assignments and guide students through the stages of drafting, revising, and editing. For more detailed discussion of specific problems—such as paragraph coherence, clear sentences, or word choice—and for help with grammar and punctuation, students can consult the other textbook. A class that meets three days a week could spend one day discussing an essay from the reader, one day discussing and planning the students' own essays, and one day covering sentence-level issues.

Or you may want to pair *40 Model Essays* with a literature anthology, using the chapter introductions and the essay models to guide students as they construct their own essays in response to literature. The discussions of description (Chapter 1) and narration (Chapter 2) may help students analyze the descriptive and narrative passages they encounter in short stories or novels; and you may want to discuss the similarities and differences between fictional and nonfictional description and narration. Using these methods, students could experiment with either fiction or nonfiction (or both, contrasting in a class discussion the problems they encountered with each). You can also emphasize that much writing about literature relies heavily on example (Chapter 3), comparison and contrast (Chapter 7), cause-and-effect analysis (Chapter 9), and argument and persuasion (Chapter 10); and you can tailor assignments in which students use these methods to explain, analyze, or evaluate the readings in the literature anthology.

RESEARCH TOOLS

You may wish to help prepare students for academic writing by asking them to use outside sources in at least some of their writing. Many of the essays and themes in *40 Model Essays* invite further investigation—in particular, the readings on the environment in Chapter 10. Occasional suggestions for research writing ask students to consult a dictionary, an encyclopedia, the *New York Times Index*, or a book or an article found through the library catalog, a periodicals database, or the Internet. The assignments are specific and limited so that students can quickly find and read the other sources, using most of their time to construct their essays.

If you incorporate research into the course, you may wish to spend a class period or two introducing students to the library and its basic reference tools. You may also teach formats for documentation of sources, such as those in the *MLA Handbook for Writers of Research Papers* or almost any handbook on writing.

READING FROM CURRENT SOURCES

One advantage of a brief collection like *40 Model Essays* is that you can supplement the essays with topical articles on the book's themes or examples of the methods of development or both. Op-ed pieces, essays in *Time* and *Newsweek* or *Slate* and *Salon*, articles in the school or local newspaper, letters to the editor—all of these are good sources. Students are often surprised to see how the "textbook" methods abound in current periodicals, and they often respond well to the immediacy of last week's or yesterday's news items. In small groups or in the class as a whole, students can analyze the structure of these samples using questions like those first presented in the introduction to reading and writing. Outside readings can also serve as the basis for in-class writing topics.

You can also encourage students to look for thematic connections or applications of the methods of development and bring them into class. For instance, students may watch for ways they use the methods in their own lives: comparing and contrasting in order to buy a car; analyzing causes and effects in order to uncover the reasons for an unexpectedly high or low grade. Or students may examine television programs, films, magazines, and other sources for ideas to support the essays' or the class's approach to a topic such as using language or defining gender roles. And, of course, students can watch for the methods in the readings, lectures, and exams of their other courses: the descriptive lab report in chemistry, the cause-and-effect analysis in history, and so on.

STUDENT WRITING

Like many instructors, you may rely on students' own writing to provide the substance of some class discussion. Given drafts of student papers to read, students may work in small groups or in pairs, using the method of careful reading and analysis recommended in the introduction to reading and writing. Then students can evaluate their peers' writing, making specific recommendations for improving each draft. When the paper employs a particular method of development, students may tailor their recommendations by referring to the chapter introduction to that method. To instruct students in this kind of peer-editing procedure—or instead of the small-group work—you may want to go over a sample student essay with the whole class.

In addition to responding to the essays in the reader, students may respond, in writing, to one another's essays. Especially for topics in argument and persuasion (Chapter 10), you can circulate one or two provocative student essays and ask the class to write arguments countering (or reinforcing) points made in those essays. Or students can exchange their own argumentative essays blindly and then write an essay in response to the one they receive. Knowing that someone will be responding to their essays invites students to formulate their arguments specifically and persuasively—perhaps more so than if they were writing just for you.

III

TEACHING THE READINGS IN
40 MODEL ESSAYS

Chapter 1

DESCRIPTION

E. B. WHITE

Once More to the Lake *(p. 28)*

Like much of White's writing, this essay illustrates the power of description to evoke both physical sensations and emotions. The details and rituals of White's summer place often evoke similar memories in students of all ages. But younger students may have difficulty appreciating White's chilling recognition of mortality (last paragraph), and a few of them may at first dismiss the essay as little more than an adult's version of "What I Did Last Summer." Question 2 under "Purpose and Audience" provides an opportunity to uncover and discuss these attitudes. And the first writing topic encourages students to appreciate White's deeper meaning by recalling a time when they relived a childhood experience through someone younger.

Meaning

1. The main idea of the essay is that even as we relive cherished experiences of childhood and see our behavior and feelings repeated in the next generation, we cannot stop or reverse time to escape death.

White's identification with his son is so complete that he can feel the clammy bathing suit. But for White the unpleasant sensation is suddenly ghastly—a physical reminder of his own mortality.

2. As pleasant as White finds the illusion of time standing still, he is also disturbed by it. The dizzy, creepy sensation seems to forbode the "chill of death" at the end.

3. The change from three tracks to two represents one of the obvious small changes at the lake, from horse-drawn to motorized vehicles. But the narrowed choices in tracks seem to represent a more subtle change for White—the narrowing of a person's choices with increasing age.

Purpose and Audience

1. White seems to explain that even as mortality closes in on it, each generation is immortalized in the behavior, feeling, and memory of the next generation.

2. The answers to this question will vary, of course. Class discussion of specific passages that engage students, or fail to engage them, should increase everyone's appreciation for the detail in White's writing and for his ideas.

3. White seems to be lost in his reverie about the old boats. The complexity of his memory conveys not only how much has stayed with him but also how significant every operation was to him. Learning to handle the boat was a rite of passage—and like all such rites it held mysteries and set the learner apart from the uninitiated. Hence the undefined boating terms: we see the complexity and importance, but we are not meant to understand. Boat handling is a rite of passage for White's son as well, yet the new outboards are the most disturbing change at the lake.

Method and Structure

1. White seems to want to express his feelings about the trip to the lake and to make a point about mortality in general (see question 1 under "Purpose and Audience"). To re-create his state of mind, he uses subjective description: his choice of details conveys the feelings of "peace and goodness and jollity" that the trip evokes (paragraph 10), as well as the "creepy sensation" (4) that time seems to be standing still.

2. Flashbacks occur in paragraphs 2–3, 9, and 10–11. Past and present are indistinct in paragraphs 5, 6, 8, and 12, reflecting and intensifying White's illusion that the present and the past are the same.

3. In paragraph 12, White uses narration to recount a thunderstorm, a memorable event from his trip to the lake. Comparison and

contrast allows him to show that the main events of a storm at the lake—the dramatic climax, the calm aftermath, and the reactions of the campers—have not changed much since he was a boy. White's use of these methods conveys his point about the inextricable link between generations.

Language

1. White's tone is dreamy and reverent. The adjectives invest the description with feeling, leading readers to see the lake filtered through White's experience of it.

2. Repetitions and restatements of time illusion in paragraphs 4–11: "the illusion that he was I . . . that I was my father," "dual existence" (4); "everything was as it always had been, . . . the years were a mirage," "the same . . . the same . . . the same" (5); "There had been no years" (6); "there having been no passage of time, only the illusion of it as in a dropped curtain" (7); "fadeproof," "unshatterable," "forever and ever, summer without end" (8); "the same place," "just as it always had been," "I had trouble making out which was I, the one walking at my side, the one walking in my pants" (11).

    In describing the oncoming storm (12), White repeats the time illusion five times in five sentences: "an old melodrama that I had seen long ago," "had not changed in any important respect," "still the big scene," "The whole thing was so familiar," "it was all the same." Starting with "In midafternoon," all the sentences in the paragraph lack predicates, and without verbs the details of the storm are literally timeless.

    Paragraph 12's extended metaphor, which compares the storm with a melodrama featuring dramatic music and hungry, even sadistic gods ("grinning and licking their chops"), introduces an ominous note into the essay. "Deathless," compared with the earlier "indelible" and "fadeproof" (8), is also ominous.

WILLIAM LEAST HEAT-MOON
Dance of the Hobs *(p. 37)*

Students should enjoy Heat-Moon's entertaining and engagingly descriptive tale of his encounter with a mysterious, luminous apparition in the Ozarks. Structured as a ghost story (see Writing Topic 3), "Dance of the Hobs" reads like something Edgar Allan

Poe might have written—if he had had a contemporary sense of humor and an ear for southwestern backcountry dialect.

A good way to begin discussion is to focus on the first writing topic. What similar tales have students heard in their hometowns or at school? Campus folklore can be especially evocative: if a popular legend or rumor circulates at your school, encourage students to investigate it, perhaps visiting the site involved or searching the campus newspaper's archives for details, and then report on what they learn.

Readers especially taken by Heat-Moon's essay will also enjoy the *Weird US* book series. An outgrowth of a self-published New Jersey 'zine (*Weird NJ*), the books are edited by self-taught folklorists Mark Sceurman and Mark Moran and share readers' experiences with urban legends and quirky sites in at least twenty states and several regions. Visit *weirdus.com* for more information.

Meaning

1. Heat-Moon is drawn to the Quapaw Light and the stories surrounding it because the apparition is a mystery, "an authentic optical phenomenon reportedly unexplained by science" (paragraph 18). For Heat-Moon, observing the light is a mystical, almost religious, experience, "like stepping back into the Dark Ages . . . , when mysteries overwhelmed explications and ignorance transcended illumination, a time when superstition could extinguish enlightenment, when priestly obfuscations manipulated folk into blind faiths" (18).

2. Heat-Moon didn't expect to see a ghost, but rather something ghostlike. "Manifestation of a spectrum" is a play on words: The word *spectrum* suggests specter, or ghost, but in physics it refers to radiating energy forms, specifically light.

3. Heat-Moon's straightforward thesis appears in his last paragraph: "The Quapaw Ghost Light is remarkable but not incredible, modest but worth its myth, possessed of the power of the peculiar." His point is simply that mysteries are fun.

Purpose and Audience

1. The writer means to entertain. As Writing Topic 3 suggests, Heat-Moon is essentially telling a ghost story, engaging his readers' imaginations yet emphasizing that the spook in question is harmless, if it is even real.

2. Heat-Moon is both puzzled and delighted by the light, which he describes as a small, flickering white ball that sometimes fades into red and then back into white while darting through the air. The dominant impression is that of a sprightly, playful, and mischievous living thing.

3. Heat-Moon expects that his readers will be as skeptical as he was, but he also recognizes that most people enjoy a good ghost story. He repeatedly stresses that the light is a mystery, that several people in the area (whom he quotes) have seen it, that even those who have seen it aren't sure what to make of it. He softens his readers' doubts by acknowledging the validity of "the sanity question" (paragraph 3) and insisting that he was driven mostly by curiosity, not by a real expectation of seeing anything. He also offers several possible rational explanations for the phenomenon (in paragraph 7 especially) to assure readers that he doesn't necessarily accept that the light is a specter of some sort; there may indeed be some physical cause. (Readers interested in Heat-Moon's analysis of that cause might find a copy of *Roads to Quoz* and read Chapter 10.)

Method and Structure

1. Although Heat-Moon assumes the persona of an impersonal "observer," his description is subjective, invested with emotions. Throughout, the description conveys both his doubt and his delight over what he anticipates as well as what he sees.

2. The majority of Heat-Moon's details take the form of figures of speech, and most of them are delightful. Especially fun are the metaphors in "[m]elodious calls of toads roused the darkness" (paragraph 5) and "a white-hot poker thrust through a black tent" (11); the similes in "I began walking as if I were wading the night" (6) and "like an animal moving its head side to side as it fixes on its quarry" (11); the hyperbole of "it upended astrophysics in its shifting from a red dwarf to a white giant" (16); and the personification of the light itself, most notable in the name "Spooky" (16) and comments like "She's a homebody" (4).

3. Heat-Moon refers back to the librarian's line—simply a colorful way of describing a fright-induced heart attack—in paragraph 12 to stress how jittery he was. The repetition is funny for its regional twang and sense of irony, but it also effectively circles back to an earlier point and validates what others have said to the author. Some readers might notice that Heat-Moon uses the same device when he repeats, in paragraph 10, the words "Spoof Light," originally uttered by the man who asks "How does a sane person see what isn't there?" (paragraph 2).

4. The dialogue builds suspense and previews what's to come. By quoting locals, Heat-Moon also invokes the rumored, whispery nature of much folklore. And the exchange between Heat-Moon and his wife creates a sense of immediacy, encouraging readers to imagine themselves there with the couple as they witness the light's movements.

Language

1. Heat-Moon combines formal, academic vocabulary with an abundance of regional dialect and colloquialisms. The mixture of objective, almost scientific language—such as "[b]ased on no physical evidence except declarations written and spoken" (paragraph 3)—with colorful phrases and exclamations (especially the nonsensical "Nodgort" and the exuberant "Holy Willie!" [12]) underscores the conflict between the writer's desire to be rational and his love of the weird.

2. The capital letters impart a comic sense of formality and ironic distance between Heat-Moon and his subject (which many readers might dismiss as silly).

3. "The thing glimmered and shimmered, twinkled and blinked, flickered and fluttered, glistened and winked" reads like a nursery rhyme and perfectly captures Heat-Moon's unrestrained childish glee.

JOAN DIDION

The Santa Ana (p. 44)

Joan Didion's piece is an excellent example of descriptive writing. Her colorful yet unsettling images appeal to the senses—sight, sound, taste, and touch. Didion's precision permits the reader to share her sensual impressions of and experiences with the "persistent [and] malevolent" (paragraph 3) Santa Ana wind. Perhaps the most interesting question to begin discussion with your students is whether Didion admires the destructive force she writes about. Because it may remind students of one phenomenon that drives them crazy where they live, Didion's essay could start a discussion about such phenomena, leading into questions 1 and 2 under "Writing Topics."

Meaning

1. Didion's statement of thesis is found in paragraph 6: "[T]he violence and the unpredictability of the Santa Ana affect the entire quality of life in Los Angeles, accentuate its impermanence, its unreliability. The wind shows us how close to the edge we are."

2. The wind leaves the city dry, hot, and still. It makes people a little crazy, "drying the hills and the nerves to the flash point" (paragraph 1). "The baby frets. The maid sulks" (1). It makes Didion testy and argumentative, causing her to "rekindle a waning argument with the telephone company" (1). Indians used to throw themselves into the sea when the Santa Ana came. Didion's neighbor holes up inside, and the neighbor's husband runs around with a machete. People go to their doctors complaining of "headaches and nausea and allergies, about 'nervousness,' about 'depression'" (3). Schoolchildren become unmanageable. People have even committed murder.

3. A mechanistic view holds that human behavior is entirely controlled by outside forces (in this case, a force of nature). The opposite view would be that humans act of their own accord, that they have free will.

4. The last sentence could be read both literally (Los Angeles is on the edge of the continent) and figuratively (life in Los Angeles pushes residents to the edge of sanity).

Purpose and Audience

1. The essay uses the Santa Ana to make a larger point about the craziness of life in Los Angeles. Didion seems to be responding to the problem she states in paragraph 6: "It is hard for people who have not lived in Los Angeles to realize how radically the Santa Ana figures in the local imagination." The essay also has a self-expressive element: such a potent force begs to be written about and affords Didion the opportunity to explore its dramatic effects on herself and her surroundings.

2. Didion is writing for the outsider as well: "It is hard for people who have not lived in Los Angeles to realize how radically the Santa Ana figures in the local imagination" (paragraph 6). We know she is from the city because the essay is written from a personal, insider's point of view and she uses the first person: "when I first moved to Los Angeles" (2); "just as we had always known it would be in the end" (6).

Method and Structure

1. Because the wind itself is intangible, Didion is limited to describing its physical and psychological effects: on nature (the Pacific, peacocks, the sky in paragraph 2), on property (the fires and property damage

described in paragraph 4), and on people (see the second question under "Meaning"). By describing these effects so vividly and thoroughly, she brings to life a phenomenon that people who have not lived in Los Angeles would otherwise have trouble understanding.

2. Paragraphs 1 and 2 are mostly subjective: Didion describes the first signs of a Santa Ana coming on as she is writing, then goes on to describe its effects on herself and on her neighbors. Paragraphs 3–5 are mostly objective, based on literary and journalistic sources: Didion situates the Santa Ana in the context of other malevolent winds throughout the world, attempts a scientific explanation for its effects, discusses the two violent seasons in Los Angeles, and recounts a particularly devastating Santa Ana in 1957. Paragraph 6 returns to a subjective point of view: Didion suggests that the Santa Ana is emblematic of life in southern California.

3. The quotation helps move the essay from examples based on Didion's personal experience to examples she has heard or read about.

4. Didion's description relies on concrete examples because her subject is intangible. Her examples are colorful and memorable and paint a vivid portrait for the outsider of what it's like to live with such a malign phenomenon.

Language

1. Use of the first person makes the description more personal and intimate, helping us feel the effects of the Santa Ana as though we are there. The present tense gives a sense of immediacy to the essay, creating the impression that Didion is spontaneously recording her thoughts.

2. The colorful images (the glossy ocean, screaming peacocks in trees, the yellow sky) bring the effects of the Santa Ana to life and make them memorable. The imagery is surreal because it's jarring, otherworldly.

JUDITH ORTIZ COFER
Silent Dancing (p. 50)

Judith Ortiz Cofer's essay navigates complicated terrain, memory shaped by dreams, old film, dialogue with parents, and details accumulated as a child. Together, these elements work to provide a rich portrait of Cofer's singular experience and also of a larger experience, that of Puerto Ricans who came to the United States in the 1950s and 1960s.

Ask students to work together in small groups to arrive at an understanding of how the essay's interlocking pieces fit together. The second question under "Method and Structure" can help because it points to Cofer's use of italics and small print to distinguish the films and the dreams.

Students who are intrigued by Cofer's Latina perspective may want to read more of Cofer's writing, such as the book *Silent Dancing*, or one of the following: *Reclaiming Medusa: Short Stories by Contemporary Puerto Rican Women*, edited by Diana Velez (1988); Julia Alvarez's *How the Garcia Girls Lost Their Accents* (1991); or Laura Esquivel's *Like Water for Chocolate* (1992). A film based on Esquivel's book was released in 1993 and is available on DVD.

Meaning

1. Cofer's father's experience with racist landlords (paragraphs 5–8) and his insistence on assimilating as quickly as possible (12–14) suggest that he longed to be accepted into mainstream America. The fact that Cofer's mother could not read English (13) and the comfort "El building" offered her (12) demonstrate her fear that living outside the Puerto Rican community would be lonely and difficult.

2. Cofer says in paragraph 24 that the speeches are from her dreams, but she has tuned her remembered dreams to a very likely representation of the speech of these relatives. When the *tiá política* recalls "the comment your mother made to a neighbor" about a baby flushed down the toilet (paragraph 27), the details resonate as genuine.

Purpose and Audience

1. Cofer wants readers to understand the cultural shifts that accompanied Puerto Ricans' immigration to the United States and especially the way she as a girl experienced them.

2. The essay was first published in the *Georgia Review*, so readers may or may not have been familiar with Puerto Rican culture. Cofer's detailed descriptions of the home movie as well as the quoted speeches in paragraphs 25–29 vividly convey the customs of her Puerto Rican family, enabling readers to understand their experiences adjusting to the mainland United States. Although Cofer uses a few Spanish words, their meaning is usually discernible from context clues. In some cases—*la mancha* (paragraph 11), *día*

de Reyes (14), *gandules* (21), and *pasteles* (22), for example—she offers explicit definitions to ensure that readers understand her meaning.

Method and Structure

1. Cofer was obviously sensitive and observant. She was also curious, as evidenced by her banging on shared pipes (paragraph 4).

2. Passages in italics describe the film, placing the reader in a darkened room where the focus is not on the full sweep of Cofer's past but on a specific night and the importance of the film that resulted. The smaller type presents imagined speeches reconstructed from Cofer's dreams. Separating these passages from the regular text distinguishes Cofer's own memories from the other kinds of recollection. By highlighting them, Cofer heightens their importance in her story.

3. Perhaps along with "nostalgic," "comical and sad" seems a fair description of the essay's dominant impression and its overall tone.

4. The three women represent the transition from Puerto Rican to American, from the newly arrived girlfriend through the more adapted mother to the eagerly Americanized cousin.

Language

1. Like the silent dancing Cofer watches onscreen, memory can be both dreamlike and incomplete.

2. The simile illustrates the importance and value of music to the people Cofer remembers from childhood.

Chapter 2

NARRATION

LANGSTON HUGHES
Salvation *(p. 69)*

Students usually understand and identify with Hughes's childhood
emotions, for nearly everyone can recall an early experience of
disappointed expectations. That point of connection can provide
a starting place for discussion of the essay.

Though Hughes does provide informative details on the revival, students who are unfamiliar with the ideas of sin, salvation,
and the like may participate in discussion more actively if they are
given some brief background information. In contrast, students
whose own religious experiences parallel those of Hughes's aunt,
rather than of Hughes himself, may bring to the essay their own
strong convictions and may therefore have difficulty understanding (and accepting, even as a different opinion) Hughes's point.

Meaning

1. Hughes's point seems to be that his faith was shattered because he
   was not saved and because his lie passed for salvation. Whereas at
   first he is naively faithful, in the end he feels shameful and betrayed.
2. Hughes decides to get up because of the pressure he feels and because Westley has lied without suffering for it. Afterward, however,
   he feels betrayed that Jesus did not save him from the pressure or
   from lying.
3. Hughes plays on the word *salvation*. In saying that he "was saved
   from sin. . . . But not really saved" (first two sentences), he means
   that he performed the ritual convincingly yet felt no spiritual
   change. He pretended to be saved and in doing so lost his faith. For

Hughes, at least, salvation seems a sham. (It is also possible that the adult Hughes felt he *had* in a sense been saved—from hypocrisy.)

Purpose and Audience

1. Clearly, the experience was a significant one for Hughes (paragraph 15), and that fact alone could explain his including the essay in his autobiography. He does not seem critical of his aunt and the other adults in the congregation; as an adult he seems to understand that they would "see" Jesus in other than the literal way he expected to "see" (15). But this play on *see* itself may point out another purpose of the essay: to underscore the literal-mindedness of children, their inability to comprehend the abstractions by which adults live. Hughes may also have wanted to illustrate the point at which a child learns to rely on himself or herself, not on others, for truth.

2. Hughes does not assume that his readers are familiar with the kind of service he describes. Particularly in paragraphs 1, 3, 4, 11, 13, and 14, he provides details that clarify the procedure, such as the purpose and activity of a revival (1), the appeals made to the children (3, 4), and the blessing of the children (14).

3. The dialogue, lines from hymns, and descriptions of the noise level in the church (e.g., paragraphs 3 and 7) re-create the pressure Hughes felt in a way that simple assertions such as "Everyone was after me to get up" could not possibly do. Besides sound, the details contributing to the sense of pressure include heat (6), loneliness (6, 11), time (6, 11), the aunt's presence (7), and Westley's proud grin (11).

Method and Structure

1. The autobiographical narrative form makes this more personal, and probably more memorable, than an argumentative essay would be. A title of an argumentative essay on the same subject might be "Hypocrisy in Organized Religion." Such an essay also would probably be more objective, presenting both sides of the subject, and possibly more objectionable to those who disagreed with the author's opinion.

2. Examples of explanation in Hughes's narrative: what he expected salvation to be like (paragraph 2); who Westley is (6). Examples of compression of time: several weeks of the revival retold in just a few sentences (1); the procession of children to the altar (6). Example of omitted events: the gap between the end of the meeting (14) and Hughes in bed that night (15). Example of expanded time: the moments before Hughes decides to be saved (7–12).

   By condensing or omitting some events, Hughes keeps the narrative moving and emphasizes the crucial moments of pressure leading to his decision. These moments are drawn out in a way that makes us sympathize with Hughes's predicament, understand his reason for lying, and share his sense of shame and betrayal.

3. Examples of transitions: "then" (paragraph 3); "still" (5); "finally," "now" (6); "then," "while" (7); "now" (11); "suddenly" (13); "when," "then" (14); "that night," "now," "anymore" (15).

4. The process analysis is important because many readers will not have been to a revival meeting or will not understand how one works. It also puts us inside the process, allowing us to see it through Hughes's eyes.

Language

1. Hughes as an adult seems both amused and sorrowful. His use of "young sinners" (paragraph 1) is ironic, and a similar wryness runs through his descriptions of Westley (6, 11) and even of his predicament (7, 11). But there is no amusement in the last paragraph, where Hughes conveys his pain and a sense of loss. Here the juxtaposition of Hughes's wish not to cry (because it is childish and he does not want his aunt to hear) with his inability to keep from crying (some form of *cry* appears four times) intensifies the sense of sorrow.

2. Hughes achieves the breathless pattern of a child reporting an overwhelming experience, thus leading us to see the experience from a child's view rather than an adult's.

3. The young Hughes seems to expect a literal physical experience (paragraphs 5, 7, 15); he will "see" something that "comes to" him from the outside. Hughes's aunt, in contrast, believes that one can "see" Jesus in one's soul (2); the seeing is not literal but spiritual. Hughes's understanding of *see* makes his disappointment and sense of betrayal inevitable.

ANNIE DILLARD

The Chase (p. 74)

Students should enjoy Dillard's dramatic rendering of a childhood thrill, which is likely to inspire them to write their own tales of glories past. Dillard is at her narrative and descriptive best here, capturing the feeling of childhood and the rhythm of the chase. Vivid, convincing detail is, of course, the key to making a story compelling, and only through careful word choice will students be able to re-create their excitement as effectively as Dillard does hers. The narrative provides rich opportunity to discuss how such description operates: see question 4 under "Method and Structure" and question 3 under "Language."

Meaning

1. "[T]hat you have to fling yourself at what you're doing, you have to point yourself, forget yourself, aim, dive" (paragraph 13); that the unbridled, unfettered enthusiasm of childhood comes from whole-hearted concentration on whatever you're doing; that the courage to do it is simultaneously the catalyst for and reward of childhood enthusiasms, enthusiasms most adults (though not the driver of the Buick) abandon.

2. Getting in trouble is not per se a means to happiness—total concentration and courage and commitment, to the point of forgetting yourself, is. Being open to this kind of abandon may well get you into trouble, but it's the *abandon* rather than the trouble that leads to happiness.

Purpose and Audience

1. To recapture the glories of childhood, to re-create its adrenaline rush, and possibly to remind adults what they are missing—getting the most out of life.

2. Dillard's shift to *you* moves the spotlight from herself, the narrator, to the reader. The reader becomes an active participant in the football plays described, thus increasing the immediacy and intensity of the scene Dillard is trying to create.

Method and Structure

1. Dillard could have chosen to illustrate the enthusiasm of youth and its loss in adulthood through example, which would have brought concreteness to a general observation (much as the narration, a kind of extended example, does here), or comparison and contrast, which would have placed the change at the center of the essay. But the vivid narration brings with it an immediacy and a memorableness that might be hard to achieve through these other methods.

2. The elaborate detail in paragraph 12—including specific homes, a woodpile, and an intersection—gives a feel for the intricacy and length of the chase. But to go on in this way, mentioning every feature of the landscape, would probably try readers' patience. Thus in

succeeding paragraphs Dillard summarizes: the chase runs "block after block" (13, 14).

3. This sentence entices readers to read on and also lets readers know that whatever "trouble" Dillard got into was not serious. Hence, readers can relax, become fully engaged in the story, and vicariously enjoy the chase.

4. Description contributes specific concrete details that bring the scene to life. Some are "up to our boot tops in snow" (paragraph 3), "tire chains come clanking from afar" (7), "a smashed star with a hump in the middle" (8), "every breath tore my throat" (14), "there was a prow of snow beneath [the man's cuffs] on his shoes and socks" (16).

Language

1. Dillard seamlessly interweaves a child's straightforward, declarative language and limited experience ("Some boys taught me to play football" [paragraph 1]; "we all popped it one" [5]; "this time, the only time in all of life" [9]) with an adult's greater powers of observation and more sophisticated perspective ("complex trail of beige chunks like crenellated castle walls" [5]; "we reverted to the natural solitude of children" [5]).

2. Dillard feels admiration and approval because the man throws himself into the chase with the same verve she and her friends do. Some evidence: "a man got out of it [the car], running. He didn't even close the car door" (9); "incredibly, he was still after us" (10); "Any normal adult would have quit. . . . He was a thin man, all action. All of a sudden, we were running for our lives" (10); all of paragraph 13; "He impelled us forward" (14); "he would never give up, this man" (14); "The point was that he had chased us passionately without giving up, and so he had caught us" (19).

3. Both images suggest presents, gifts, magic, enchantment, a childhood fantasy world.

JENNIFER FINNEY BOYLAN
In the Early Morning Rain *(p. 80)*

The problems faced by LGBT youth have been very much in the news lately, raising grave concerns about their psychological well-being as well as spurring efforts to stop bullying and intolerance. Boylan's earnest tale of suicidal thoughts and ultimate self-acceptance is one of many that have been told, but it loses none of its power for feeling somewhat familiar.

Unfortunately some students are likely to feel hostility toward Boylan precisely because of her transgender status. To lessen resistance, you might begin by asking what they know of the *It Gets Better* project for which she wrote. You could break the class into groups of three or four and have them research what it means in the early twenty-first century for a young person to be lesbian, gay, bisexual, or transgendered. Come up with a few contextual categories: gender identity, attitudes toward homosexuality, bullying, suicides, or other firsthand reminiscences of coming out (especially the videos posted at *itgetsbetter.org*). Each group could then present its findings for five to ten minutes, ending with a class discussion of Boylan's story. (Note: If this sort of background research is something you'd like to have students do fairly regularly, you might consider rotating the responsibility so that just one group works and reports on any given essay.)

Meaning

1. Boylan emphatically states her main point for readers three times in paragraphs 18 and 22: *"You're going to be all right."* The message is a variation on the project title *It Gets Better*.

2. As a young man, Boylan's strongest desire was to live as a woman. He believed that if he did so, however, more traditional dreams (romance, family, acceptance) would have to be sacrificed because social conventions would not allow such things for a transgendered person. That the belief turned out to be wrong is significant to the adult Boylan's story.

Purpose and Audience

1. The somewhat jarring shift to *you* at the end of the narrative reveals that Boylan is writing directly to young people who are struggling with gender and sexuality issues (and quite possibly contemplating suicide). Her purpose is to reassure them that like her, they'll be okay.

2. In describing with compassion her own feelings of denial (paragraph 1), sadness (4), isolation (5–7), confusion (8), and despair (10–16), Boylan seems to assume that readers will recognize some aspects of themselves in her story. She neither defends her choices nor elaborates on her emotional states, suggesting that she believes her experience will be familiar to her audience.

Method and Structure

1. The passage describes Boylan's half-hearted, almost passive attempt at suicide. It is more detailed than other parts of the essay because of its central importance to the story and because the sense of supernatural intervention marks a turning point in the author's life.

2. Here, as everywhere, dialogue lends immediacy to any scene an author creates. In Boylan's case, it also creates a sense of intimacy with readers.

3. Some students may struggle to understand the meaning of *transgender*, which shifts subtly through the essay. Technically a condition in which a person born into one gender identifies psychologically with the other, *transgender*, as Boylan defines it early on, is a shameful secret and a source of deep-seated confusion and despair (paragraphs 1–2); she then refines its meaning to explain that as a biological male she "was female in spirit" and so felt conflicted and broken (7). By the end of the essay, however, Boylan defines being transgendered as her "greatest gift" (20) and, in a metaphorical sense, her "home" (23).

Language

1. Students who sense the irony will probably express it in any of several ways. Boylan's joke is that nationality is more obvious and less immutable than gender, although she may not have seen her situation that way at the time. At the same time, she manages to get a chuckle by exposing the contrasts between outward appearance and inward reality, something she also does with the description of the "Maryland spring, with its cherry blossoms and its bursting tulips and all its bullshit" in paragraph 2 and of the "moth-eaten rabbit" posing for souvenir photos in paragraph 4.

2. Boylan is insistent that she heard a voice, even suggesting that it spoke out loud; but she leaves open the possibility that the sound was only in her head when she asks if "it really change[s] things all that much, to give a name to the spirits that are watching out for us" (paragraph 19) and concludes that the spiritual reassurance came from her "future self" (20). Some students might also note that Boylan presents herself as a very real voice of reassurance for readers, emphasizing that she hopes they will hear as clearly as she did.

GEORGE ORWELL
Shooting an Elephant *(p. 85)*

Orwell's gripping narrative, told with vivid detail and an appealing self-effacement, tends to stick in the memory of anyone who studies it. Orwell's elegant prose may at first put some students off, but even they will soon enough be caught up in the narrator's tale.

Indelible as it is, the essay may strike students as remote from their concerns because it takes place in a country and a time far from their own. If you find this response, point out that the essay tells of doing what seems necessary, even what's wrong, to save face. Governments and their representatives everywhere, including our own, commit dubious actions for just this reason. The second writing suggestion can help students discover the relation between Orwell's experience and their own: ask students to scour newspapers and TV news programs for examples of contemporary face-saving among public officials. In small groups, each student could present one such example for discussion of the perpetrator's likely motives and the effects of such behavior.

Meaning

1. The answer is twofold. He had to save face—that was the more important reason. But, as he mentions in paragraph 9, his being a bad shot also influenced his behavior by injecting an element of fear.

2. He expresses the epiphany most clearly and vehemently in paragraph 7: "I perceived in this moment that when the white man turns tyrant it is his own freedom that he destroys"—and so on to the end of the paragraph.

3. The coolie's death put the young Orwell "legally in the right." By the time he wrote "Shooting an Elephant," though, Orwell was no longer motivated by any need to save face. He had the courage to tell his story truthfully and unsparingly, awful as it was. It seems clear that the mature Orwell did not share his younger self's view of the coolie's death.

Purpose and Audience

1. Orwell's purpose is clearly to show, through his experience of shooting the elephant, how the need to save face motivates—indeed,

compels—the actions of himself and every other imperialist. He seems to want to convince readers that this motivation is dangerous and fuels the oppression of imperialism.

2. With hindsight, Orwell has a broader and deeper perspective on the events. At the time, he was bitter, embarrassed, and a little afraid. In retrospect, he can see his foolishness and the tyranny he helped to further.

Method and Structure

1. These paragraphs, because they reveal so much about the author's feelings toward his job and toward the Burmese who made it difficult, shed light on the complex motives that resulted in the unnecessary shooting. They also, perhaps, somewhat justify the author's behavior—to himself and to us.

2. He explains the circumstances best in his opening paragraphs. He had come to hate imperialism and all that it stood for. Still, because it was his job, he had to do "the dirty work of Empire." Adding to his misery was the abuse he and his English compatriots had to endure from the Burmese.

3. The Burmese are portrayed as both detestable (spitting on European women, yelling "with hideous laughter," "sneering") and pitiable ("wretched prisoners huddling in the stinking cages," "gray, cowed faces," "scarred buttocks"). The contradiction makes Orwell's position "perplexing and upsetting."

Language

1. The term refers to the annual period when a male elephant is most sexually aroused and is often violent.

2. The adjectives in paragraphs 11 and 12 reveal Orwell's guilt over transforming a noble "great beast" into a powerless, suffering animal. These adjectives include "stricken," "shrunken, shrunken, immensely old," "rattling," "tortured," "dreadful," and "powerless."

Chapter 3

EXAMPLE

PERRI KLASS

She's Your Basic LOL in NAD *(p. 102)*

Klass's subject is inherently interesting to students: even if they don't hope or plan to go to medical school, they are at least intrigued by doctors. This essay addresses the issue of how language establishes the boundaries of groups. As such, it could initiate a discussion of special languages—in particular, technical terminology, jargon, and slang. Before or after reading the essay, students could discuss (in class or in writing) the purposes and effects of special language—is it alienating? mysterious? authoritative? Other sources of jargon worth examining include a sports broadcast, a conversation between computer specialists, or the writing class itself (for example, what effects do expressions like *comma splice* and *relative clause* have on students?). The goal of any of these discussions is to arrive at an understanding of when jargon is useful, necessary, and effective and when it is superfluous, distracting, or downright harmful.

Klass's essay beautifully surmounts a central difficulty in essays developed by example: how to weave together many examples without sounding monotonous. She avoids tedium through sentence variety and also by varying the way she presents her examples: she explains some medical terms in parenthetical comments, others by anecdote; she treats some briefly, lingers over others; she groups those having to do with baseball into a separate class. Students often overlook the importance of variety—or, if they are aware that their writing lacks it, don't quite know how to remedy the problem. Klass's essay provides a useful model.

(Question 2 under "Method and Structure" focuses their attention on this point.)

Meaning

1. Klass's point is that learning medical jargon marks a rite of passage into doctorhood, a passage mitigated by her realization that the "new alien assumptions" (paragraph 18) of the language are not wholly positive or for the better. She reveals her full point in the final paragraph.

2. To Klass, medical jargon serves two useful purposes: the language builds "closeness and professional spirit" (8), and it creates distance between doctors and patients (17). Given Klass's evident distaste for the disrespectful and even inhumane jargon illustrated in paragraphs 10–16, those particular expressions seem unlikely to build her professional spirit. They certainly do create distance between doctor and patient.

Purpose and Audience

1. Klass implies that she lost something by becoming a doctor, that she sees something idyllic about the lack of knowledge she had before and something corrupted about her now-complex life. The phrase suggests that she wants to explain a process that medical students must go through and also *why* they must go through it—in part, why the corrupted state is necessary for doctors.

2. Klass is halfway between a nondoctor and a doctor; she's looking ahead, gaining knowledge, but still clearly remembers that state of "primeval innocence" (paragraph 2). She expects her readers not to know about the doctor side, which she is at pains to explain for them in paragraphs 1, 2, 4, and many others, but she expects readers to identify with the nondoctor side: see, for example, "endless jargon and abbreviations" (2), terms that go "a little too far" (10), "I had resolved not to be shy" (11), and jargon that makes "the beginning medical student nervous about the effects of medical training" (15).

3. Answers will vary. Klass does not define every term (for example, "nasogastric," [paragraph 3]; "cardiac enzymes," [4]; "sickle-cell," [15]). But in most if not all cases her meaning is clear without definitions: we don't need to know exactly what's wrong with the patient to see the point being made about jargon.

Method and Structure

1. Klass begins with an example for the sake of interest—and to create a sense of mystery: What are these terms? Will they be defined? She

immediately makes her audience feel befuddled, thus putting them in the position she was in when she started working in the hospital—and in the position of a patient. The opening example in effect gives readers a capsule version of Klass's experience, which is what she wants to explain.

2. Other examples: "This sort of construction probably reflects . . . profound irritation" (paragraph 4); "Baseball metaphor is pervasive" (6); "Some people seem to become enamored of the jargon for its own sake" (8); "Then there are the more pompous locutions" (15).

3. Effects: camaraderie (paragraph 8), excitement (8, 18), arrogance and pomposity (8–15), discomfort (15, 18), distance (17).

Language

1. Klass is deeply concerned about the desensitizing effects that medical jargon has had on her and her colleagues. This seriousness toward her subject is most evident in the last paragraph: the tone becomes graver as Klass makes her concerns explicit. The essay's black humor is cautionary, serving to expose a troubling phenomenon.

2. Answers will vary. The shifts between *we/us* and *they/them* may be seen as emphasizing that Klass's own role is shifting: she doesn't identify fully with the doctors. The shifts between *I* and *you* are more difficult to justify thematically, though Klass evidently uses you—especially in paragraph 18—to extend her conclusions beyond herself.

3. Positive: "thrills," "communicate effectively," "professional speech," "closer and closer to being a doctor." Negative: "uncomfortably," "peculiarities and even atrocities," "avoid," "strange," "afraid," "alien."

ANNA QUINDLEN

Homeless (p. 108)

In this direct, personal essay, Quindlen uses detailed examples to explore what it is to be without a home. The essay provides a likely occasion for class discussion of the importance of a home and what a home *is*.

You might also use the essay as a springboard for discussing practical measures to help solve the problem of homelessness.

Working in groups of three or four, students could discuss the practicalities of Quindlen's claim that nothing but a home will solve the problems of the homeless: with this as a premise, what can be done to achieve this goal? Fifteen minutes of collaborative brainstorming on this question should give students enough time to prepare for a class discussion of the issues Quindlen raises.

Meaning

1. Quindlen's thesis (in paragraphs 8–9) is that abstraction from particular human beings to "issues" may distance us from problems and impede their solution—in this case, solving homelessness with homes.

2. The key is in paragraph 8: "The homeless" distances us from the problem suffered by particular people with particular needs.

Purpose and Audience

1. Quindlen shows the importance of having a place to live—it makes you "somebody" (paragraph 2), provides "certainty, stability, predictability, privacy" (4), and "pride of ownership" (7). She seems to make this point for a larger purpose—to argue that by turning homelessness into a "big picture" issue (3), we overlook the pain of real people who live without homes: "Ann or the man who lives in the box or the woman who sleeps on the subway grate" (8).

2. The author assumes that the reader has a home and feels strongly about it. Some students may not feel as strongly about having a home as Quindlen does. In paragraph 7, she addresses readers' likely assumption that shelters are better than the streets.

Method and Structure

1. Quindlen might have begun with a statement of her opinion (among other options), but the story of Ann draws the reader in and illustrates Quindlen's point. It also, perhaps even more important, reinforces Quindlen's argument that we should focus more on particular people with particular problems.

2. The examples bring Quindlen to earth and magnify the loss suffered by the homeless.

3. She wants readers to agree that nothing short of homes will solve the problems of homeless people.

Language

1. It invests her opinion with passion and urgency.
2. Not only do our hearts reside in and take nourishment from our homes, but we can also show heart by providing homes for those who lack them.
3. *Crux* is a Latin word meaning "cross." In English it is a critical point or essential feature.

BRENT STAPLES

Black Men and Public Space (p. 112)

As Brent Staples demonstrates, the most gripping and convincing examples are often brief anecdotes. In this essay, examples of Staples's discovery—of the "alienation that comes of being ever the suspect"—take up most of the room. In addition, Staples gives examples of "tough guys" who died in street violence (paragraph 7) and precautions he takes to appear less threatening (11–12). His vivid opening paragraph, with its opening sentence pretending that he is a killer, deserves special scrutiny.

For collaborative work on this essay, you might focus on just what public space is and what happens to us when we enter it. Students might try to define *public space* by coming up with examples and discovering what the examples have in common. How do they feel different in private versus public space? Once they have their examples and definitions, the groups could reassemble as a class to arrive at a generally accepted definition.

As an alternative, you could encourage students to explore their own feelings about public space, either in discussion or in their journals. Do they feel more or less welcome, safe, or at home? They might also find it helpful to create a list of generalizations in small groups. What does it mean to be a student, a woman, a man, a member of a particular religious or ethnic group, and so on in American public spaces? Working in small groups, students will probably feel freer to discuss their experiences; you might even consider dividing the groups along gender lines for those women and men who might be reluctant to speak up.

Meaning

1. If we keep on reading, we find Staples acknowledging that women are often the victims of street violence, some of it perpetrated by young African American males. He believes, though, that reports have been exaggerated. He takes pains to make clear that he isn't dangerous. He considers himself not a tough guy but a "softy" who hates to cut up a raw chicken (paragraph 2); he has shrunk from street fights (6); his own brother and others have been killed in "episodes of bravado" (7).

2. By using *survivor* in this context, Staples gives the word fresh connotations. Usually it suggests rugged strength, ability to endure, and so on, but here Staples helps us to understand that, in an area of gang warfare, knifings, and murders, timidity is a form of self-preservation.

Purpose and Audience

1. Students will state the author's purpose variously. Staples writes to communicate his experience as a black man of whom others are needlessly frightened. He writes to explain his discovery that, when mistaken for a criminal, it is wiser not to react with rage but to take precautions to appear less threatening. However the writer's purpose is put, this is a piece of personal experience and observation; we do not see Staples trying to predict the future or proposing any long-term solutions.

2. Staples convinces by giving examples: anecdotes from his own experience (paragraphs 1, 5, 8, 9) and that of another African American male (10).

Method and Structure

1. The examples are set forth in detail too rich to seem a mere bare-bones list. The similar nature of all the examples lends the essay coherence and, to give it even more, Staples uses transitions skillfully. In nearly every paragraph, the opening sentence is transitional, and transitional phrases indicate time: "One day," "Another time," "a couple of summers ago."

2. Beginning with the scene of a near-empty street at night and a frightened woman fleeing him, Staples dramatizes his thesis and immediately sets forth a typical, recurrent situation.

Language

1. As we have seen, Staples's essay uses a narrative hook at the start, and, to make the hook grab hard, the writer deliberately misleads

us. The word *victim* leads us to take him for a self-confessed criminal. By the end of the paragraph, we doubt our impression, and in
his second paragraph, Staples explains that he is harmless, can
hardly take a knife to a chicken. If we look back on the opening
paragraph, we see the discrepancy between the word *victim* and
reality. In truth, the fleeing woman is mistaken and fearful, a person on whom the innocent narrator has no designs. This discrepancy makes clear the writer's ironic attitude. As the essay proceeds,
he expresses a mingling of anger, humor, and resignation.

2. Students will have fun defining *dicey* ("risky, unpredictable"), recalling that shooting dice is, of course, a game of chance.

FRANCINE PROSE

Which Came First? *(p. 117)*

With this brief essay, Francine Prose gives students what many assume will be a central feature of their time in college: a heady con-
templation of the meaning of life. She also slips them a question any
student should ask at some point: What is the purpose and value of
knowledge? A danger in teaching this essay, perhaps, is that students
without Prose's skill may be inspired to emulate her lazy philoso-
phizing without quite achieving the desired effect. Some students,
though, just might surprise you with the delightful thinking and
writing they can produce when they ponder impossible questions.

Small groups can be useful for helping students through the
brainstorming part of writing an essay. Students might appreciate
having time to talk about the examples they have listed in preparing to write an essay for either of the first two writing topics. Group
members can help each other expand their lists and find the details that will bring their experiences to life.

Meaning

1. "Which came first? The chicken or the egg?" Prose starts the question
in her title and alludes to the rest of it in paragraphs 3 and 4. She
withholds the full question until the very end of the essay because, as
she says, "Everyone's heard [it]" (paragraph 1): She assumes readers
will automatically fill in the second half upon reading the first.

2. Prose cites a research study published by English scientists to assert that the chicken came first (paragraph 8). As she summarizes the study, eggs cannot form shells without a specific protein provided by a chicken's ovaries; therefore the chicken must precede the egg.

Purpose and Audience

1. Prose writes to indulge an opportunity to wax philosophical, to ponder "the Big Metaphysical Questions" (paragraph 2). As she explains her thinking, "the mystery of which came first was never about the answer" (10). Instead, impossible questions, such as the one she explores in the essay, encourage people to look beyond themselves and embrace the unknown—that is, to have "an experience of the insoluble, of the mysterious and confounding" (11).

2. Prose favors the childlike sense of wonder and disorientation that she opens with, and to which she returns in the last paragraph. She prefers that perspective because it's both humbling and exhilarating.

Method and Structure

1. The author's thesis is that the answers to questions like "Which came first?" are unsatisfying and unimportant. One does far better, she says, to seek mysteries rather than solutions. By withholding her point Prose is able to demonstrate it first, encouraging readers to reach her conclusion on their own.

2. The examples of "inexplicable questions" seem to do the opposite of what examples should do: They cloud readers' minds with abstractions (in this case, that's exactly what the author wants to accomplish). But they also make very clear to readers what the author means by each generalization of their types (see the next question).

3. Prose uses classification to sort her examples of unanswerable questions into four categories: riddles (paragraph 2), "Big Metaphysical Questions" (2), "dizzying Zen questions" (3), and difficult cause-and-effect relationships (4). She puts the chicken-and-egg dilemma into each group in turn, finally concluding that it concerns a universal experience.

Language

1. The capitalization of "Big Metaphysical Questions" emphasizes the supposed importance of such questions while at the same time subtly mocking the sense of gravity with which people tend to approach them.

2. Prose loads the essay with unanswered questions to support her point that they stretch the mind. She wants readers to feel as disconcerted by the questions as she does.

Chapter 4

DIVISION OR ANALYSIS

MARGARET VISSER
The Ritual of Fast Food *(p. 129)*

Visser's essay focuses on an experience many students probably take for granted: eating at a fast-food restaurant. Students may wonder, Why *not* take fast-food meals for granted? Visser suggests some reasons in her last paragraph. Questions 2 and 3 under "Language" are intended to help students begin thinking about this issue, as is the second writing topic.

Meaning

1. This sentence provides a good illustration of Visser's main idea: that the apparently informal, comfortable, and predictable fast-food restaurant is actually the result of a tremendous amount of money, research, time, effort, and ingenuity. In short, it is not really quick or easy at all; it only appears that way to the patron.

2. A "cultural construct" is a concept created from elements of the culture. A Big Mac is not just a hamburger; when you buy one, you are also buying a whole set of cultural expectations about its appearance, size, shape, temperature, texture, taste, and how quickly it will be served. These expectations are unconscious and pervasive.

Purpose and Audience

1. Visser's purpose is explanatory.

2. Visser seems to imagine a general audience rather than a professional one. Her essay includes little, if any, sociological terminology,

and the people who run McDonald's chains already know the information Visser presents. (Since Visser mentions their handbooks and teaching sessions in paragraph 3, she has apparently had access to their inside information.) Visser assumes that her readers take fast-food establishments for granted, that they are oblivious to the "costs and complexities" (paragraph 6) of the fast-food experience, which is of course precisely what the restaurants themselves want of their customers.

Method and Structure

1. Division allows Visser to reveal how chains and their customers thrive by following certain common rituals—rituals the chains are probably more aware of than their customers are. In paragraph 2 Visser writes that these rituals "inform the proceedings"; she then goes on to analyze the rituals in paragraphs 2–5.

2. Visser divides the restaurant into four elements: the environment, its rituals, its customers, and its products. The environment encompasses the restaurant's architecture (customers "know exactly what the building that houses the establishment should look like," [paragraph 2]); interior decor ("cottage roofs, warm earth tones" or "glass walls, smooth surfaces, red trim," [3]); and a predictable ambience ("distinctive garments" and menus "in the same spot" and featuring the same content "in every outlet," [3]). Rituals include the employees' use of standard language and the "time off for [holiday] feasts" (4). The restaurant's ideal customers are families who "maintain a clean, restrained, considerate, and competent demeanor" (5). Finally, the restaurant's product must adhere to standards of "fierce regularity" (6).

3. Although it is not, of course, true that all crack addicts necessarily look different from everyone else in a fast-food establishment, the restaurants can't afford to be tolerant. Filthy or crazy or violent crack addicts would violate the code of the "clean, restrained, considerate, and competent demeanor" (paragraph 5) expected of restaurant patrons. This, in turn, would drive "desirable" customers out the door.

Language

1. Visser seems to take her subject quite seriously. She writes with the formality and detached objectivity of the anthropologist: "rituals, in the sense of behavior and expectations that conform to preordained rules, still inform the proceedings" (paragraph 2); "architectural variations merely ring changes on rigidly imposed themes"

(2); "The staff wear distinctive garments" (3); "in groups of several at a time, the adults hovering over their children" (5). Nevertheless, she is writing for a general audience, and her language is not stuffy or academic.

2. The ostensible purpose of such questions is to be helpful—to remind customers of something they simply forgot to order. The real purpose, of course, is to get customers to buy something they had not originally intended to buy. Student responses to the last part of the question will vary. Some people regard these questions as harmless, but others resent their intrusion and manipulation.

3. Other instances: the company "knows that blunt and direct confrontation with a huge faceless corporation makes us suspicious, and even badly behaved" (paragraph 3); customers are "watching television, where carefully placed commercials will . . . re-imprint the image of the various chain stores for later" (4); "adults hovering over their children, teaching them the goodness of hamburgers, anxious to bring them up to behave typically and correctly. Customers usually maintain a clean, restrained, considerate, and competent demeanor" (5).

   The portrait that emerges is not flattering. Customers come off as childlike, susceptible, passive, and malleable. This picture is an integral part of the "casual" eating experience Visser describes: if the customers did not play these roles (which most do not realize they're playing), the whole system would collapse.

THOMAS DE ZENGOTITA
American Idol Worship *(p. 134)*

De Zengotita's essay focuses on a popular culture phenomenon that many students enjoy but probably have not thought about critically: the reality show *American Idol*. Although most fans never stop to think about why the show is so popular, de Zengotita suggests some reasons for giving the question serious academic attention in his second and third paragraphs: the "virtual revolution" epitomized by *American Idol* affects our perceptions not only of the world around us but of ourselves as well. Questions 1 and 3 under "Meaning" and question 1 under "Purpose and Audience" are intended to help students begin to think about this question, as are the second and fourth writing topics.

The concept of "mediation" may prove challenging to some of your students, but most of them, having grown up thoroughly immersed in popular culture and implicitly trained to question its messages, will probably grasp the idea intuitively right away. Try not to let them get caught up in the jargon of de Zengotita's scholarly theorizing: the complexities of mediational theory are not essential to understanding his analysis of *American Idol*. If students are interested, however, the author's book *Mediated: How the Media Shapes Your World and the Way You Live in It* (2005) is a relatively accessible and consistently fascinating read. The introductory chapter, in particular, does a good job of explaining the basics of the author's conceptual framework.

Meaning

1. De Zengotita's thesis can be found in the first and last lines of paragraph 2. The reasons behind *American Idol*'s popularity, he asserts, lie in "a nexus of factors shaping the 'virtual revolution' unfolding all around us. . . . The *American Idol* format combines essential elements of this revolution." He repeats his thesis in the last two one-sentence paragraphs: "*American Idol* gives you so many ways to feel good about yourself. No wonder it's a hit."

2. For de Zengotita, the "virtual revolution" is marked by the audience's unwillingness to be "mere spectators" (paragraph 2) of the media. Recent technologies—notably, Internet file-sharing venues and the accessibility of digital photography and recording—make it easy for regular people to create and distribute their own media productions. *American Idol* takes the demographic impulse of the virtual revolution and repackages it for audience members, who in turn get to feel as if they had a hand in creating not only the show but also the individual "idols" themselves.

3. Students may struggle with this concept at first, but it's actually pretty simple. The central conceit of *American Idol* is that it turns everyday people—the fans—into musical heroes. The people watching the show are encouraged to imagine themselves as contestants, and they are given the voting power to decide which contestants will win, so they form a double identity in which they have the ability to transform themselves into superstars. Stardom is the ultimate fantasy for people immersed in a popular culture that repeatedly tells them they're the center of the media universe, hence the "magic" of the show.

Purpose and Audience

1. De Zengotita sets out to explain why *American Idol* is popular. His primary purpose is, therefore, explanatory. But in encouraging his readers to examine the show closely, he's also trying to persuade them to develop a critical understanding of their own relationships with the "mediated word," as he describes it. By breaking a popular reality show down into its component parts, he forces us to look more closely at why it appeals to us. And by taking a critical rather than a personal stance toward his subject, the author attempts to exempt himself from the mediating influences he analyzes. How successful he is in that effort is open to debate.

2. De Zengotita assumes that he is addressing people who have seen *American Idol* and enjoyed it, but who have not thought fully about the show's implications. At the same time, the author is careful to describe individual elements of the show in enough detail so that the rare reader who has not seen it would probably have no trouble following his analysis.

   The question of being well versed in de Zengotita's *mediation* theory is a little trickier. Certainly if readers are well versed in the concept of *mediation* as he defines it, it will help them follow his analysis of *American Idol*. All the same, perceptive readers should be able to grasp the basic idea—that popular culture influences how we perceive ourselves—from the context of the essay. Even if *mediation* means nothing to readers, however, de Zengotita's analysis of *American Idol* is developed thoroughly enough to make sense on its own merit and to open a few eyes to a new way of looking at the show.

Method and Structure

1. In de Zengotita's assessment, the unprecedented popularity of *American Idol* epitomizes the implications of the "virtual revolution" for consumers and producers of media products. Any of the examples the author cites in paragraph 2—chat rooms, live journals, etc.— could serve to illustrate his point that new technologies and platforms are profoundly transforming the ways we interact with the media. But *American Idol* is so popular, and its influence is so wide-reaching, that it's an ideal subject for his analysis of this phenomenon.

2. De Zengotita is interested in the elements of *American Idol* that draw on the "'virtual revolution' unfolding all around us" (paragraph 2). Those elements, as he sees them, are the show's appeal to the "everyday hero" (3), its creation of "performer heroes" (4), the "power of music" in general (7), and the program's infamous exploitation of the

contestants' "voluntary personal humiliation" (8). All of these elements combine to make "you . . . feel good about yourself" (9).

3. De Zengotita finds it striking that "a show that features amateurs" (paragraph 1) is more popular than one that features professional musicians, but younger readers in particular won't be surprised by the discrepancy. And that is the essence of the author's point: just as the Grammy Awards and *American Idol* compete for viewership, the current media landscape as a whole pits "spectators and celebrities" (2) in a bid for attention. The spectators are winning, de Zengotita argues, because the deck is stacked in their favor. If the major function of popular culture is to make the spectator feel good, as the author believes, any program that directly involves the spectator in the spectacle is going to win.

4. The cause-and-effect component allows de Zengotita to anticipate and answer the question so often raised by division or analysis: so what? The author could have analyzed the elements of the show without examining the reasons for (and the implications of) its popularity, but the exercise would have seemed empty to most readers. Certainly it wouldn't have satisfied de Zengotita, whose long-abiding interest in the media's effect on individual consciousness was his reason for examining the show in the first place.

Language

1. Your students may be relieved to know that several reviewers of *Mediated* complained about de Zengotita's predilection for mixing colloquial and scholarly language. He attempts to make complex ideas more accessible and "hip" by speaking the language of his high school students—hoping both to draw in readers who would normally avoid academic or philosophical subjects and to present himself as a savvy participant in media culture (rather than as an objective or disconnected academic observer). The effect depends on each reader's attitude. Some readers find it jarring and distracting to the point of invalidating de Zengotita's authority as a writer; others find it a reassuring source of the kind of performer-audience fusion that de Zengotita writes about.

2. The different points of view are part of de Zengotita's effort to form a common bond with his readers. Astute readers might suggest that the author uses first person when he wants to count himself among the audience of a particular form of entertainment, third person when he's trying to appear objective, and second person only at the end. Unfortunately, however, there appears to be no discernible pattern of his usage, probably a consequence of his original writing situation. (The essay originated as a newspaper column, so presumably

it was written quickly.) As an exercise, you might try asking your students to revise the essay (or parts of it) to use a consistent point of view. Then ask them how the changes affect the piece's readability.

SCOTT RUSSELL SANDERS

The Men We Carry in Our Minds *(p. 139)*

This thematically complex essay begins with a conversation between Sanders and a feminist friend who sees gender—at least in the past—in terms of women as victims and men as persecutors. To Sanders, the issue is not nearly so clear cut. The men Sanders knew growing up were anything but powerful, and the women seemed to enjoy more privileges. Sanders shared in none of the privileges afforded to the fathers of the feminists he met in college, and he fears that women such as his friend will never understand this.

It is important for students to recognize that Sanders wrote this essay in the 1980s—a time when the feminist movement's struggles were beginning to pay off. This is the context of Sanders's opening conversation with his friend about whether it is more difficult to be a man or a woman. You might begin class discussion by asking whether this question can be answered definitively thirty years later—or whether it is still even worth asking.

Meaning

1. Sanders feels that it must be a difficult time for women; they "have so many paths to choose from, and so many voices calling them" (paragraph 1). His friend, in contrast, finds these new paths exciting. It is a more difficult time to be a man, she claims, since "'the persecutor has to live with his past'" (9). Paragraphs 8 and 10 introduce Sanders's main idea that, in his experience, the relative privileges of men and women are not exactly as his friend claims. In the two concluding paragraphs, Sanders makes it explicit that growing up among the working poor, he did not share the privileges

of supposedly "male" power; the men of his class, he feels, were more oppressed than the women.

2. Men from Sanders's background worked as laborers or soldiers — occupations that required either backbreaking exertion or the threat of going to war. After work and on weekends, these men further labored at home "tilling gardens that were lumpy with clay, fixing broken-down cars, hammering on houses that were always too drafty, too leaky, too small" (paragraph 12).

3. Sanders knew men of privilege and power only through images on television, so to him they were "remote and unreal" (paragraph 15). The men of his experience shared none of the "privileges of the earth," so he had difficulty understanding the grievances of feminists. As a child, he envied women; they were "the only ones who ever seemed to enjoy a sense of ease and grace" (18).

Purpose and Audience

1. Students may have different thoughts about Sanders's purpose. Certainly, he seems to want to explain and justify his view of feminism, but he might also want readers to reconsider the commonly held image of men as oppressors and women as victims.

2. While Sanders is obviously not writing to women alone, the final two questions do suggest that he is especially interested in appealing to a female readership. He explicitly wonders here whether he can change women's views of himself as oppressor.

Method and Structure

1. Sanders examines the following elements of his childhood vision of manhood: "the body-breaking toil, the tedium, the call to be tough, the humiliating powerlessness, the battle for a living and for territory" (paragraph 19). His analysis reveals that he is an "ally" (21) of the feminist cause; he identified with the women in college who "yearned for a say over their future, for jobs worthy of their abilities, for the right to live at peace, unmolested, whole" (21).

2. The first section (paragraphs 1–10) relates his conversation with a friend about men and women. The second section (11–16) describes the men Sanders grew up with. Finally, the third section (17–21) explores Sanders's difficulty understanding the feminist conception of male "joys and privileges" (20).

3. Paragraph 11 contrasts a group of convicts and their guards. Paragraphs 12 and 13 compare and contrast laborers and soldiers. The end of paragraph 17 and paragraph 18 compare and contrast the men

and women Sanders grew up with. And in paragraph 21 Sanders compares himself to the women he met at college. In each case, this method reinforces Sanders's theme of the relationships among power, gender, and class.

Language

1. The numerous strong, active verbs in this paragraph convey the extent of the hard labor that eventually broke the men Sanders knew as a boy.
2. The verb *carry* in the title implies a burden. Sanders doesn't recall these men with particular fondness, although he sympathizes with their plight. They weigh heavily on his mind. Sanders implies that we are all burdened with long-standing images of class and gender.

Chapter 5

CLASSIFICATION

DEBORAH TANNEN
But What Do You Mean? *(p. 153)*

The linguist Deborah Tannen came into national prominence with *You Just Don't Understand*, a book about misunderstandings between men and women in conversation. Since then, she has continued to disseminate much of her research through the mass media, trying to help people solve the communication problems of daily life. Oliver Sacks, another intellectual who often addresses a general audience, wrote of *You Just Don't Understand*: "Deborah Tannen combines a novelist's ear for the way people speak with a rare power of original analysis. It is this that makes her an extraordinary sociolinguist, and it is this that makes her book such a fascinating look at that crucial social cement, conversation."

This is one essay that students should be able to apply easily to their own lives, although the men in your class may be more resistant than the women. The essay will certainly evoke a wide range of student response, which should lead to lively class discussion.

Here is an in-class exercise to test Tannen's theories: Ask students to bring in dialogues that illustrate conflict from novels, plays, or movie scripts, deleting characters' names and direct references to gender. Have students read the dialogues out loud and try to guess characters' genders, justifying their choices. Encourage students to look for instances of Tannen's seven categories of miscommunication in the dialogues. (A variation is to cross-cast the dialogues, with women reading men's lines and vice versa, and see if they are still believable.)

Meaning

1. Much of what we say is based on pure protocol, which serves as a kind of social cement. We're not so much communicating facts as establishing a rapport with the other person. This way of speaking is often so automatic and predictable that we aren't even aware of what we're saying. (See also the first writing suggestion.)

2. "Many of the conversational rituals common among women are designed to take the other person's feelings into account, while many of the conversational rituals common among men are designed to maintain the one-up position, or at least avoid appearing one-down" (paragraph 2).

3. "Thank you" is not always used as an expression of gratitude, but is simply a ritual, "an automatic conversation starter and closer" (paragraph 15). An answer of "You're welcome" results in an imbalance between the speakers.

Purpose and Audience

1. Tannen is pointing out the areas of communication with the most frequent misunderstandings between the sexes. She seems to hope that a better understanding of how men's and women's communication styles differ will help eliminate such misunderstandings. A secondary purpose is to show women how their problems in the workplace may be linked to their style of communication.

2. This essay originally appeared in slightly different form in *Talking from 9 to 5*, a book intended for a male and female audience. Because this version of the essay appeared in *Redbook*, a women's magazine, here Tannen uses *you* to address women readers: "What's important is to be aware of how often you say you're sorry (and why), and to monitor your speech based on the reaction you get" (paragraph 9); "Although you may never enjoy verbal sparring, some women find it helpful to learn how to do it" (19).

Method and Structure

1. Tannen uses these characters as examples of her points. She adds variety to the essay by referring to people alternately by their first names (real or fictitious) or by their functions ("a well-known columnist," paragraph 4; "a woman manager I know," 13). As characters in the service of Tannen's argument, they do not need to be described in detail. Tannen reveals only what is relevant to her point. (See also the next question.)

2. That the columnist is well known makes her apology all the more unexpected, less likely to be chalked up to insecurity.

3. (1) Apologies: Women apologize more than men. They see apology as a way of keeping both speakers on an equal footing, of sharing responsibility. Men take apologies at face value, seeing them as self-deprecating. (2) Criticism: Women tend to soften criticism more than men. Men prefer "straight answers." (3) Thank-yous: Women say "thank you" more often, as a ritual. Men take "thank you," like "I'm sorry," more literally. (4) Fighting: Men see conversation as a battleground, stating their ideas and criticizing those of others in the strongest possible terms. Women often perceive this approach as a personal attack. (5) Praise: Women often assume that the absence of praise is the equivalent of criticism. For men, in contrast, praise is often implied when no criticism is given. Women who ask for criticism may really be asking for praise, but men will give them what they ask for. (6) Complaints: Women complain as a way of bonding with others. Men see these complaints as a call for a solution. (7) Jokes: "[T]he most common form of humor among men is razzing, teasing, and mock-hostile attacks, while among women it's self-mocking. Women often mistake men's teasing as genuinely hostile. Men often mistake women's mock self-deprecation as truly putting themselves down" (paragraph 28).

Language

1. The humor here relies on exaggeration. It usually refers to finishing off a suffering animal.
2. Tannen uses the metaphor of a gun: criticism as shooting.
3. These verbs liven up the essay and inspire a strong visual or auditory impression. Other examples are "leapt into a critical response" (paragraph 10) and "poke holes" (17).

STEPHANIE ERICSSON

The Ways We Lie *(p. 162)*

Lying and being lied to are universal human experiences. This selection offers a thoughtful look at lying that should inspire lively class discussion. One way to begin work on the essay is to ask students to give their definitions of *lying*. Write the responses on the board, and invite students to challenge each other's definitions. What consensus does the class reach? What are the points of contention?

Ericsson admits that sometimes we lie for reasons that seem almost virtuous — to protect someone else's feelings, for example. How justifiable are the various kinds of lies she lists? Divide the class into five groups and have each group look closely at two sections of the essay, two kinds of lies. From what perspectives are these examples of unexcusable lies? Who would assert that they were necessary, valid, or reasonable manipulations of the truth? Once these viewpoints are established, ask each group to give a comprehensive definition of a *lie*. How do the groups' definitions differ, considering which sections the students examined?

Meaning

1. Ericsson's thesis is that the lies we tell in everyday life, however seemingly unimportant and even necessary, cause us to lose our sensitivity to larger, more damaging lies.

2. No, it would not be possible to eliminate lies completely. Ericsson's experience (paragraph 4) supports this, as do the benefits of different lies, such as the sergeant's lie to help a soldier's family (9), the dismissal to help ration a parent's energy (31), and the delusion to help us function despite the possibility of global disaster (33).

3. Eliminating lies might help ourselves and others to perceive reality clearly; it would be more just; and it would sharpen our awareness of the lies we are told.

Purpose and Audience

1. The purpose is to examine the roles that lying plays in our lives and its effect of dulling our insistence on the truth.

2. Ericsson addresses her audience throughout, but particularly in the opening and closing paragraphs. This strategy helps her draw readers into the essay, encouraging them to recognize that we all lie and are lied to and that we often think of these lies as harmless. By using the pronoun *we*, she shows that she is not free from blame, either. By addressing her audience at the end of the essay, she strengthens her call to action, encouraging readers to do their best to live more honest lives.

Method and Structure

1. She's not casting blame, since she's as much a liar as any of her readers. She puts herself eye-to-eye with her readers.

2. Answers will vary. The epigraphs could be judged on pithiness, wit, relation to the category following, and other criteria. Some favorites

are Cicero before paragraph 14, Freehill before 23, Wilde before 26, Hoffer before 32, and Shaw before 35.

3. Ericsson's message is that as much as possible, tell yourself the truth and insist on it in others or the "moral garbage" will become "invisible." Her conclusion is very effective—it clearly shows the relation of the everyday lie to the Big Lie and urges that honesty begin where she has been showing lies begin, with each of us individually.

4. Answers will vary. Some of Ericsson's most pointed definitions are those of the white lie ("a vote of no confidence," paragraph 8), the stereotype ("a candy bar of misinformation instead of a balanced meal," 21), and delusion ("an adhesive to keep the status quo intact," 34). Some highly effective examples are the illustrations of group-think with Pearl Harbor (24–25), out-and-out lies with her nephew's assertion that "murderers" broke the fence (26), and delusion with alcoholics (32).

Language

1. The internal disease of cancer (the lies we tell ourselves and others) affects our perception of the external garbage we're floating in (the lies told to us).

2. The tone seems more appropriate in the first passage than in the second. It may be strong to say that the Catholic Church was a "co-perpetrator" with Porter (paragraph 13), but its actions were deceitful and harmful. Ericsson's feelings about the "omission of Lilith from the Bible" (20) are a little harder to credit. The events she mentions are the subject of extensive scholarly inquiry and far from proved, and imputing contemporary motives to ancient people is ahistorical. (Still, the issue is a live one: just in recent years, the church has condemned the elevation of the goddess by some of its members.)

WALTER MOSLEY
Show Me the Money (p. 173)

Mosley's essay is more challenging than the other essays in the chapter, but it should capture students' interest because it touches on a subject that affects everyone: money. Whether students approach his classification from the belief that America is a classless society or from a conviction that class is endemic, Mosley's categorizations of wealth are likely to come as a surprise—especially to those who define themselves as middle-class.

Some students will surely be put off by Mosley's strong language, while others may embrace the writer's socialist perspective. Such political divisions could lead to compelling (if contentious) classroom debate, provided you set some ground rules for mutual respect and thoughtful deliberation. Alternatively you might focus on how Mosley structures his argument, noting how a third of the essay sets up his reasons for categorizing Americans by class (paragraphs 1–9) and another third explains the implications of his system (17–21). Mosley uses classification, which comprises the middle of the essay (10–16), to advance a serious (and controversial) argument, not as an end in itself.

Meaning

1. Mosley's thesis, which he uses as a transition between his classification system and his assessment of its implications, appears in the middle of his essay. "Most Americans," he says, "are working-class wage-slaves, arguing that they're better off. This fantasy, more than any other confusion, hobbles us. Because we fear to see how delicate our economic state is, we cannot motivate ourselves to demand change" (paragraph 16).

2. Even though he's a successful writer with a large list of best-selling novels to his credit, Mosley counts himself among the majority: he considers himself working class. This group, he says, is by far the predominant class in America, even if most people think of themselves as middle class.

3. The statement is an effective summary of the Marxist critique of capitalism. Mosley's point is that the rich don't earn their wealth. Rather, he argues, the money enjoyed by the upper classes is derived from the hard work of the working class. In other words, the rich exploit the labors of the poor for their own benefit.

Purpose and Audience

1. Mosley's essay is a call to arms intended to inspire readers to fight the system. He may indeed mean to offer some consolation to those of us who are struggling under the financial structure of American society, but more than that, he wants to "motivate [readers] to demand change" (paragraph 16).

2. Mosley wrote this for the *Nation*, a progressive magazine with a strong political focus and a well-educated, high-income subscriber base. According to the magazine's own demographic profiles, more than three-quarters of its readers hold a college degree, more than half hold a graduate degree, nearly half earn $75,000 or more a year, and the vast majority are employed in a professional or managerial position. Mosley knows this about his readers, but despite their relative affluence, he tries to shake them out of their belief that they are middle class or better, at least partly by his continual use of the first person plural (*we, us*) to refer to the working class.

3. Mosley's categories are surprising if nothing else. He strengthens his unconventional classification by offering his own definition of terms. In Mosley's system, most of us are working class not because we hold blue-collar jobs or struggle financially, but because he defines the working class as those who depend on a regular paycheck to stay afloat—regardless of the size of the paycheck.

Method and Structure

1. Classification is the perfect method for Mosley's purpose, which is to change his readers' conception of how the American class system is structured and where they fit into that system. Re-sorting the classes according to his own principle of analysis is a very effective way to get his readers to rethink their positions. Classification lets him redraw the lines around poor, middle class, and rich and to position his readers in a class to which they would never have assigned themselves.

2. Mosley groups Americans into three major classes: rich, poor, and middle class, the last of which he further subdivides into the "working class" and "the class of limited privilege" (paragraph 12). His principle of classification is outlined in paragraphs 10 and 11: he defines class not by the conventional markers of bank balance or job description, but by people's "ability to cover the basic necessities in their lives" and the options they have available to them. He makes these distinctions because although most of his readers think of themselves as middle class and comfortable, he wants to show that they're closer to the working class than they are to the wealthy. By changing his readers' perceptions of their own financial status, he hopes to realign their political allegiances and redirect their goals.

3. The heart of Mosley's classification appears in paragraphs 10–16, and it shouldn't be surprising that he devotes most of that space to explaining what he means by the "working class." He needs to briefly explain what he means by "poverty" (10) and "wealth" (11), but to truly convince his readers that they are actually working class, he needs to define that category with the most detail.

4. Definition is essential to Mosley's purpose because he is proposing new understandings of terms that most people interpret far differently than he wants them to. If he didn't clarify his use of the terms "poverty," "wealth," "middle class," "working class," and "class of limited privilege," readers would assume these terms' traditional meanings, which would cause them to misunderstand Mosley's classification entirely.

Language

1. Mosley's tone is ponderous and highly polemical. He is quite serious, verging on angry, and certainly determined. Whether that strengthens or weakens the effectiveness of his argument depends on each reader's preference. Many readers will be put off by his tone; others will find that it aligns with their own views.

2. Mosley's diction suggests that his audience is educated (as the readers of the *Nation* tend to be), which further implies that they also earn above-average salaries (also true of *Nation* readers). By using the first person to address this audience, he emphasizes their (and his own) position among the working class, which is the primary subject of his essay.

3. Mosley's position is undoubtedly that of a Marxist, as his explicit reference to Marxism makes clear. Additional examples of overtly Marxist language include "the sweat, the sacrifice and ultimately the blood of working men and women" (paragraph 3); "citizens" (5); "relationship to your labor" (6); "capitalism, the accrual of wealth from labor" (17); and "we are not partners in the corporation of America" (19).

Chapter 6

PROCESS ANALYSIS

FIROOZEH DUMAS
Sweet, Sour, and Resentful *(p. 186)*

Popular humorist Firoozeh Dumas has made it her mission to humanize Iranian people in the American consciousness, a mission that seems especially important in the context of political unrest and wars in the Middle East, nuclear proliferation, and terrorism.

Younger students may not be familiar with the Iranian revolution to which Dumas refers or with the ensuing exodus of Iranian families to America and Americans' distrust of them in the 1970s and 1980s. You may want to flesh out the basic outline provided in the footnote on page 187: In the late 1970s, fundamentalist Muslims fostered political and religious unrest in the country, culminating in a coup and the exile of American-backed Shah Reza Pahlavi. In his place, revolutionaries installed Ayatollah Ruhollah Khomeini, who was determined to jettison Western influence and restructure Iranian culture and politics around strict interpretation of Islamic religious rule. In 1979, Khomeini supporters captured fifty-three Americans at the US embassy in Tehran, precipitating a hostage crisis that lasted 444 days and ended in a botched rescue attempt and embarrassment for the Carter administration; the hostages were released upon Ronald Reagan's inauguration in 1981. (During the same period, Iran was attacked by Iraq, leading to a brutal war that lasted until 1988.) Backlash against Iranians in the United States—the vast majority of whom had fled the violence and repression in their country—was severe and included general hostility, physical attacks, and demands for universal deportation.

Meaning

1. The dinners provided an opportunity to orient recent Iranian immigrants to life in California; they also allowed the hosts to share "the hospitality that Iranians so cherish" (paragraph 3) as well as to stay connected to their roots. For both the hosts and the guests, the elaborate and traditional Persian meals helped to maintain a sense of community; they also served as a bittersweet "reminder of the life [they] had left behind" (10).

2. "As I watched my mother experience the same draining routine week after week, I decided that tradition is good only if it brings joy to all involved. . . . Sometimes, even our most cherished beliefs must evolve" (paragraph 12).

3. Dumas suggests potluck, or requiring guests to contribute to the meals by bringing food with them. Based on the way Dumas characterizes her (traditional, diplomatic, judgmental of inadequate or lazy cooks, perfectionist, and controlling), it seems unlikely that her mother would have relinquished the role of hostess, no matter how much it strained her. However, Dumas does relate the process in the past tense, so it's possible that her mother did, indeed, scale back her efforts—or that the number of guests dwindled after the first wave of Iranian immigration in the late 1970s and early 1980s.

Purpose and Audience

1. Dumas wants to share a belief that she developed as a witness to her mother's exhaustion and resentment—the importance of adapting tradition and beliefs when circumstances demand it. To some extent, she is also relating the impetus behind her own assimilation to American culture.

2. "Sweet, Sour, and Resentful" was, as the introduction to the essay indicates, first published in the now-defunct *Gourmet*, an upscale magazine for "foodies" (paragraph 5) that often featured complicated recipes and travel essays. Dumas could reasonably assume, then, that her readers held a strong interest in food and culture. Most readers of the magazine would have had some experience preparing elaborate dishes, hunting down elusive ingredients, and hosting large gatherings themselves, so it's likely they could empathize with the difficulties and stresses the author's mother endured—if not her resentment.

Method and Structure

1. The introductory paragraphs establish the context behind the elaborate weekly meals: the guests who came to the author's parents' condo

every weekend were reluctant immigrants, possibly even refugees, displaced from their "real home" (paragraph 1) by war. At the same time, the introduction indicates the parallels between Iranian culture and American culture to help make Iranians seem less "foreign" to readers — one of Dumas's overriding goals as a writer.

2. Although Dumas identifies "the first step" as "preparing the herbs" (paragraph 6), the process actually began with her father taking phone calls and extending invitations to near strangers. Next came menu planning (on Mondays) and softening the neighbors with gifts of food (paragraph 4), followed by Tuesday shopping trips that usually ended in frustration. With all ingredients corralled, by midweek the author's parents began the simultaneous tasks of chopping by hand and frying herbs and onions (6); mixing, cooking, and rolling the contents of stuffed grape leaves (7); and preparing homemade yogurt and other side dishes (8). The guests would arrive on the weekends, at which time Dumas's mother cooked and drained the rice. The meals would then be served "buffet-style" (10) and consumed in a matter of minutes (11). The final step was "fielding thank-you phone calls from . . . guests" (12) and extending more invitations. With several overlapping stages occurring over the course of a week, Dumas ensures coherence by providing clear time markers and transitions throughout her analysis, then circling back to the first stage in her conclusion, implying that the process never ended.

3. By comparing bucolic local market days in Abadan with frustrating car-dependent shopping trips in California, Dumas harkens back to her introduction and underscores her point that adjusting to life in the United States was challenging and unpleasant for Iranian immigrants. At the same time, she emphasizes how much additional trouble her mother went to in order to give her guests a taste of home.

Language

1. Dumas's ironic tone in this essay borders on sarcasm but is nonetheless good-natured and appreciative. She tempers the implied criticism of her parents' and guests' behavior with several self-deprecating remarks, which is where most of her humor lies. You might ask students how the writer's attitude toward her parents would have come across without the mocking comments about her own abilities.

2. Dumas provides the Persian names for most of the dishes her mother prepared and served to guests every week. In doing so, she emphasizes the sense of home those meals provided for both her family and their guests. She ensures that American readers will understand the meaning by renaming each dish in an appositive phrase, such as "*fesenjan*, pomegranate stew with ground walnuts" (paragraph 4) or "*qormeh sabzi*, herb stew" (6).

3. In its literal sense, a "litmus test" is a chemical process that measures the pH level of a substance to determine where it falls within a range of base to acid; colloquially, the phrase refers to a basis for making a judgment. Dumas uses the term in its colloquial meaning, but notice the echo of "sweet" (base) and "sour" (acidic) with the title and the concept's effectiveness in evoking her mother's bitterness about performing her tasks.

LARS EIGHNER
Dumpster Diving *(p. 192)*

Eighner's essay is a wonderful model of a process analysis written for a larger purpose. While he does want to explain to his readers what it's like to be a scavenger, he is equally interested in sharing the lessons he has learned from scavenging and challenging the stereotypes of scavengers. You might begin discussion of this essay by asking students to jot down all the words and phrases they would have used to describe scavengers *before* they read this essay. After they read "Dumpster Diving," which words and phrases would they drop? Would they add any?

Meaning

1. Eighner is sorry for "the rat-race millions who have confounded their selves with the objects they grasp and who nightly scavenge the cable channels for they know not what" (paragraph 16)—in other words, for all who are preoccupied with material goods and wealth because they believe these things will make them happy. Dumpster diving has taught him the true value of material goods and how misguided is our culture's emphasis on them as a means to happiness.

2. Eighner keeps only "items of relatively immediate utility" (paragraph 7). An item's value rests entirely on whether or not he can use it or easily make it useful (see paragraph 13).

Purpose and Audience

1. Eighner's phrase "I prefer" clearly asserts that he has the ability to exercise choice, both over his vocabulary and over his life. His focus on fine points of meaning reveal him as intelligent and articulate, while his reference to foraging shows he is resourceful and capable.

Many of us have preconceived notions of scavengers as helpless, pathetic, desperate, perhaps even crazy. But Eighner presents himself in such a way that this is clearly not the case.

2. Eighner assumes that most of his readers don't know how much perfectly good food is thrown away; listing what he finds brings this point home. Eighner also assumes that his audience perceives scavengers as dirty and indiscriminate, so he takes a great deal of care to present the process of scavenging for food as one guided by common sense and hygienic concerns.

Method and Structure

1. During the first stage, the scavenger "is ashamed of being seen" (paragraph 5). During the second stage, the scavenger begins to find things that "look and smell brand-new" or are in "perfect working order"; he "begins to understand" that people throw away "a lot of perfectly good stuff" (6). He enters the third stage when he learns to restrict himself to "items of relatively immediate utility" (7). Some scavengers never make it that far, however. Once they realize how much is there for the taking, they "may become lost and never recover . . . trying to acquire everything they touch" (7). The implication is that they become obsessed with collecting things and unable to pursue other aims, while scavengers who *don't* get stuck can use scavenging as a means, not an end.

2. Eighner reserves the word *foraging* for foods that grow naturally and that he can collect when they are in season. *Scavenging* refers specifically to living off the refuse of others. This definition establishes that Eighner is intelligent, articulate, and forthright and therefore gives him both credibility and authority with his readers.

Language

1. Eighner's tone is simultaneously matter-of-fact and proud. His matter-of-fact, realistic attitude shows up in other statements: "I like the frankness of the word *scavenging*" (paragraph 3), and "I do not want to paint too romantic a picture. Dumpster diving has serious drawbacks as a way of life" (12). But he is also proud that he's good at what he does, which is revealed in "I think it a sound and honorable niche" (3) and in the fact that he considers himself a professional (9).

2. This formal style may be startling at first, since many of us do not expect street people to be educated, much less dignified. Eighner's dignity, however, is precisely what this language expresses. Some other examples: "I find from the experience of scavenging two rather deep lessons" (paragraph 13); "however fine or rare it may be" (13); "the transience of material being" (14); "desire to grab for the gaudy bauble has been largely sated" (16).

JESSICA MITFORD

Embalming Mr. Jones *(p. 197)*

Mitford's essay shows students that process analysis need not be a dull series of directions and demonstrates how the method can be used to explain and support a strongly held belief. But her sardonic view of funeral customs may shock some students. Discussing the underlying seriousness of the essay and Mitford's probable reasons for choosing such an approach helps answer those concerns. As an alternative, you may want to elicit defenses of funeral directors, their profession, and American funeral customs.

Meaning

1. Embalming and restoration make the corpse suitable for viewing by using costly measures to erase all traces of the cause of death. They are performed, Mitford seems to believe, because people are ignorant of the procedures (paragraphs 4, 5).

2. Americans know as little as they do because no effort is made to erase their ignorance. Mitford aims most of her attack at the funeral industry, which, she says, perpetuates the practices without any clearly defined legal rights and seems deliberately to keep relatives and the general public in the dark.

Purpose and Audience

1. Mitford analyzes the processes of embalming and restoration in the hope and expectation that readers will then question the practices themselves.

2. Mitford assumes that her audience is completely ignorant about the process of embalming—what is done, how it is done, why it is done, even what it costs.

3. Students will find their own examples of humor. Mitford uses humor to show how ludicrous funeral customs are when they are examined objectively, rather than under the emotional stress of bereavement. Humor also mitigates some of the gruesomeness of the process.

Method and Structure

1. Process analysis helps Mitford expose her view of the embalming custom as a morbid and absurd practice and allows her to present

the process in all its unsettling detail. She hopes to convince readers to reexamine their tacit approval of the practice by exposing the ugly secrets that lie behind a beautiful corpse. The unusual process analysis allows her to shock and amuse her audience simultaneously.

2. Mitford explains the process quite clearly. The main steps are removing the blood and replacing it with embalming fluid (paragraphs 9–11); removing entrails and replacing them with cavity fluid (13); replacing missing parts and repairing defects (15–16); "lip closure" (17); applying cosmetics, washing hair, manicuring, and so on (18–19); and "casketing" (20).

3. In paragraph 8 Mitford describes the undertaker's tools. In paragraph 10 she explains the "time element" in the process (while also illustrating the rudimentary quality of information on embalming). And in paragraph 14 she explains the objective of the restoration process.

4. The contrast suggests that we, unlike our ancestors, are fearful and shy about death and the dead and thus acquiesce in the funeral industry's wish to keep us ignorant of its practices.

Language

1. Mitford's tone is bitingly sarcastic, overlaid with a good dollop of black humor. Some examples: the brand names of the "aids" she mentions, such as "Throop Foot Positioner" (paragraph 8); sentences such as "Head off?" (15); words such as "jabbed" (13) and "routinely handled" (15).

2. Mitford's irony contributes substantially to her sarcastic tone and to the humor of the piece. Other examples of irony: "Beautiful Memory Picture" (paragraph 2), when the trussing, trimming, and slicing earlier in the sentence would produce quite the opposite effect; "For those who feel that there is something a little rudimentary, not to say haphazard, about this advice, a comforting thought is offered" (10); "The funeral industry is equal to the challenge" (14).

3. The contrast of informal style and formal textbook style underlines the discrepancy Mitford sees between the outward dignity and solemnity of funeral practices and their actual grotesqueness and humorousness. Other examples of informal style: "Just how soon should one get going on embalming?" (paragraph 10); "jabbed into the abdomen, poked around the entrails" (13). Other examples of textbook style: "any of the better funeral establishments" (8); "the embalmer has at hand a variety of restorative waxes" (15).

Chapter 7

COMPARISON AND CONTRAST

NANCY MAIRS
Disability *(p. 216)*

This essay may stimulate intense discussion as students reexamine their own attitudes toward people with disabilities. How true do students find Mairs's assessment of the "invisibility" of people with disabilities in our culture? Ask students to keep a log for one day, noting any references to or images of people with disabilities that they encounter. Have them share their findings in small groups. This activity should help them warm up for a full class discussion that seeks to understand the effects of "invisibility" on everyone, both the "temporarily abled" and people with disabilities.

Your campus may have an office or department devoted to the concerns of students and staff with disabilities. It could be productive to invite someone from that office to give a brief talk to your class about the experiences of the physically challenged at your institution.

Meaning

1. It shows the woman as one-dimensional, dominated by the fit male doctor and confined by her illness.
2. "Ms. Great American Consumer" is the advertiser's dream—someone who loves to buy things and would listen attentively to sales pitches.
3. Images of people with disabilities would help the nondisabled realize their connection to the disabled, would be fair, would bolster the self-esteem of people with disabilities, and might actually help sell things.

Purpose and Audience

1. Mairs's purpose is to bring an injustice to the reader's attention, showing how people with disabilities are erased from public awareness.

2. People with disabilities have probably noted the absence of disability in the media. The essay, however, might give them new insight into reasons for and consequences of that absence. "Temporarily Abled Persons" (paragraph 7) may view media depictions of disability in a new light, and many will likely agree with Mairs's call for more positive representation.

Method and Structure

1. Mairs compares herself with a disabled woman in a TV drama (paragraphs 2–4) and compares the effects on the disabled and the nondisabled people of not showing people with disabilities in the media (6–7). The comparisons clarify that people with disabilities are otherwise "normal" and doubly reinforce Mairs's thesis.

2. Generalizations: "I haven't noticed any woman like me on television" (paragraph 1); "physical disability . . . doesn't devour one wholly" (4); if disability "is effaced completely," the viewer "won't feel threatened" (5); "This kind of effacement or isolation has painful, even dangerous consequences" (6). Students are likely to find Mairs's generalizations valid: her assessment of television images would dovetail with theirs, and her authority as one who knows what it is to have a disability is unassailable.

3. Mairs defines her own characteristics (paragraph 1), then states that she cannot find them on TV. By using the word "Actually" (2), Mairs juxtaposes her generalization with one possible exception—which proves not to be one after all.

4. Mairs gives examples of television shows that depict people with disabilities as powerless (paragraphs 2–3); of the products she uses (tampons, mouthwash, lotions, bleach [4]); of ads in which the disabled could appear (5). The examples are ordinary, everyday ones. Their effect is to show how people with disabilities could be made part of the television world.

Language

1. Mairs's tone is partly humorous: "I'm easy to spot even in a crowd" (paragraph 1), "sucking breath mints and splashing on cologne and swigging wine coolers" (6). But it is also serious: "effacement or isolation has painful, even dangerous consequences" (6). Mairs's humor

makes her essay more accessible; her seriousness underscores the gravity of her topic.

2. Mairs's irony exposes the ridiculousness of the attitudes she opposes. Another example is "an illness-of-the-week like the daily special at your local diner" (paragraph 2).

3. The connotations are negative. Mairs is forestalling any nervous, evasive, or hostile reactions from her readers.

CHERYL PECK

Fatso *(p. 221)*

Peck's essay, both ironic and angry, addresses a heated topic: obesity. Though not specifically about the public health and political issues that comprise the current obesity debate, the essay does succeed in raising many issues and attitudes involved in it. As a large woman herself, Peck identifies several types of hostility and discrimination that overweight people face every day. She directly compares others' perceptions of her with her own perception of herself, finding disturbing similarities in the negative attitudes about "people of substance" on both sides. At the same time, she obliquely compares sizism with racism, a connection that some readers will appreciate and others will reject outright. Currently or formerly overweight students are sure to see themselves in some of her examples, but so might those who are "normal" weight or underweight; most readers will find her essay quite moving, regardless of where they fit on the spectrum.

Students who connect with Peck's writing will undoubtedly enjoy her essay collections *Fat Girls and Lawn Chairs* (2004) and *Revenge of the Paste Eaters* (2005). Both books are filled with personal reflections and very funny stories that resonate with readers, regardless of their backgrounds. It's worth reminding students that although Peck has published two books, she is not a professional writer. She worked full-time in a welfare office until her retirement and writes primarily for her own satisfaction. Yet she has developed both a strong style and a wide audience, a source of inspiration for other aspiring writers.

Meaning

1. Peck does not mean any of her "I have never" statements literally. Each example is drawn from her personal experience, as her references to specific incidents—such as the shoe store clerk's rude joke (paragraph 5), the grade school nicknames (5), or the hurtful letter she read in a magazine (6)—make clear. She is being bitterly ironic to underscore the difference between what people assume about her and what is actually true.

2. She is angry—an emotion Peck (again, ironically) denies in her last paragraph—not only because others have treated her badly but also because she has internalized many of the negative stereotypes applied to obese people and often treats herself as poorly as others do.

3. Although "person of substance" is a politically correct euphemism for an overweight person, the connotations of the word *substance* also suggest that these people are important and that there is more to them than their size alone.

Purpose and Audience

1. Peck is writing primarily to judgmental thin people—specifically she is responding to the person who made the hurtful comment to her friend at a fair and to the people who have told her that because she is a "middle-class white person" she has "no idea what it is like to be discriminated against" (paragraph 3). At the same time, however, because Peck is very forthright in counting herself among those who stereotype overweight people, we can also conclude that she is writing a cautionary tale for others who have internalized society's negative assessments of fat people.

2. Peck is trying to teach her readers not to discriminate against people of size by revealing the pain caused by snap judgments and insensitive comments. She underscores the importance of her message by implicitly comparing sizism to racism early in her essay (paragraph 3): both forms of discrimination, she insists, are equally hurtful. Peck acknowledges, however, that her lesson is a difficult one to learn. At three hundred pounds, she has caught herself making negative assumptions about other overweight people.

Method and Structure

1. This essay is based primarily on a point-by-point contrast between Peck's life as it is and her life as she imagines it would be if she were smaller. At the same time, she compares what others assume about her with how she sees herself. Her major points of comparison include

interpersonal relationships (paragraphs 5, 9, 11), media representations (6), and self-esteem (7, 8, 10). Peck also suggests an implicit comparison between racism and sizism (3), but she uses that to bolster her main point, not as the focus of the essay itself.

2. The comparison begins in Peck's discussion of racial discrimination in the third paragraph, but she deliberately waits until the fourth paragraph to make it clear that she is writing a comparison and contrast essay. On the first reading of paragraph 3, most readers will assume that she is writing from a somewhat detached point of view, interpreting her "I have never" statements literally. When Peck shifts to an obviously personal example of discrimination in paragraph 4 ("My feelings were not hurt"), however, she makes it clear that the types of racial discrimination outlined in the previous paragraph are actually meant to serve as examples of the discrimination she has experienced as a large woman.

3. Although she is writing about sizism in general, Peck uses profoundly personal examples to make her point. Some of the more notable examples include her humiliation in the shoe store (paragraph 4), her sexual awkwardness (8), and her encounter with the woman who suggested a weight-loss program (9). Obesity is a charged topic in contemporary America. By exposing her vulnerabilities in such a raw manner, Peck makes the subject personal and tries to form a bond with her readers, which increases her chances of success in making readers sympathetic to the difficulties and social stigmas that overweight people face.

Language

1. The title serves a couple of functions. It has a shock value that draws readers in more effectively than, say, "Obesity" would. At the same time, it recalls the name-calling that Peck experienced as a child and predicts the self-loathing that is a major theme of her essay. It could also serve as a verbalization of the prejudice that she describes in her introduction and responds to in the body of her comparison.

2. Peck's repeated invocation of the phrase "I have never" (as well as its variations) gives the essay coherence as well as a rhythm that is difficult to resist. At the same time, the parallelism created by her usage emphasizes that each incident she describes is equally important and on a par with the racial discrimination she discusses in paragraph 3. Some readers may also find in the phrase an echo of the exclamation "Well, I never!"—often uttered to express exasperation at an insult.

3. Peck is unmistakably sarcastic, bitter, and angry. Her tone will likely put some readers on the defensive despite her efforts to form a bond with them (see question 3, under "Method and Structure"). Other readers, particularly those who have had experiences similar to the

author's, may feel that the tone strengthens the essay and gives it a punch it might not otherwise have.

DAVID SEDARIS

Remembering My Childhood on the Continent of Africa *(p. 226)*

This essay is humorist David Sedaris's account of the exotic childhood and adolescent experiences of his partner Hugh—who grew up in various African outposts as the son of a US diplomat—as contrasted with Sedaris's far more mundane youth in suburban North Carolina. Students may initially have some trouble with Sedaris's subtle irony. You could begin discussion by asking class members whether they think Sedaris truly wishes he could have traded places with Hugh, whose youth, while "fascinating" in retrospect (paragraph 13), was in fact marked by some pretty gruesome and dangerous events. Sedaris admits that he can't acknowledge this fact because it means "I should have been happy with what I had" (21). Instead he retreats into fantasy, safely appropriating the stories he has heard from Hugh as memories of his own.

To pursue this question further, you could divide the class into small groups and have each group analyze the essay for evidence of Sedaris's clear awareness that Hugh's childhood "was not as glamorous as it sounds" (12). In reporting back their findings to the class, each group could consider what Sedaris seems to be suggesting about his own personality.

Sedaris's reading of *Me Talk Pretty One Day*, from which this essay comes, is available on audiotape and CD. Students may enjoy his distinctive delivery, familiar to anyone who has heard him on National Public Radio.

Meaning

1. Sedaris contrasts his own "unspeakably dull" middle-class American childhood (paragraph 8) with the much more exotic and eventful childhood of his friend Hugh, who, as the son of a diplomat, grew up in various countries in Africa.

2. Sedaris's envy is essentially ironic because many of Hugh's child-hood experiences seem pretty lonely and harrowing, beginning with the field trip to the slaughterhouse. This is true even when Sedaris writes of something that one might indeed be envious of: for example, Hugh's family had servants, but they included guards with machetes (paragraph 11), suggesting that the family was always in danger. In paragraph 21 Sedaris notes that while he was longing for more exotic adventures as a child, Hugh ("[s]omeone unknown to me" at the time) was probably longing for something more normal.

Purpose and Audience

1. Sedaris's purpose might seem to be to explain that his life was dull compared to Hugh's (paragraph 8) or that he makes up for his dull life by appropriating Hugh's (21). But hovering over all, just hinted, is the larger purpose of showing that Hugh's childhood, while much more exciting than Sedaris's and food for resentment and imagination, had terrible costs that Sedaris would not have wanted to pay.

2. Sedaris seems to assume that his audience is more familiar with the kind of experiences from his "unspeakably dull" childhood and will, like him, find Hugh's experiences more fascinating (though often gruesome). He spends more time describing incidents from Hugh's life than from his own. He spends several paragraphs, for example, describing many of Hugh's field trips (paragraphs 1–6) but only discusses a single field trip from his own childhood (7).

Method and Structure

1. Sedaris's point-by-point organization can be outlined as follows: comparison of field trips (paragraphs 1–7); of daily life (8); of access to popular culture, specifically movies and the circumstances of viewing them (9–10); of servants and security (11); of dangerous experiences (12–13); of meeting a celebrity (14); of Sedaris's ten-day visit with his senile grandmother and Hugh's two years living with strangers (15–19); and of vacations (20–21).

2. The opening conversation establishes the relationship between Sedaris and Hugh, particularly the fact that Hugh seems unfazed by his odd experiences. This opening also makes clear that Sedaris bases his knowledge of Hugh's experiences on such conversations.

3. Sedaris narrates stories from his own life and from Hugh's to point out how different their experiences have been. He arranges his comparison and contrast point by point, contrasting examples from various areas of his life and Hugh's (see the answer to question 1 above).

Language

1. The second and third, fourth and fifth, and sixth and seventh sentences in the paragraph are parallel in structure, which highlights the contrast that concludes each sentence. As Sedaris wittily puts it, "The verbs are the same, but [Hugh] definitely wins the prize when it comes to nouns and objects."

2. The term "petty thief" emphasizes the self-deprecating portrait that Sedaris has presented throughout. His use of Hugh's memories represents no "spiritual symbiosis" but is merely a way for Sedaris to live vicariously through the other man's experiences.

3. Almost any paragraph will provide examples of specific, concrete language. In paragraph 6 examples include "low-ceilinged concrete building," "small white piglet," "its dainty hooves clicking against the concrete floor," "class gathered in a circle," "turned from face to face," "drew a pistol from his back pocket, held it against the animal's temple, and shot the piglet, execution-style," and "Blood-spattered, frightened children wept."

RICHARD RODRIGUEZ

Private Language, Public Language (p. 234)

Rodriguez's reflections and anecdotes about his bilingual childhood exemplify fluid comparison and contrast. The central distinction between public alienation and private intimacy and security—between the "world" and the family—is one many students may relate to, whether or not they are bilingual. In addition, almost everyone has had difficulty with some form of language—first or second language, speech or writing. Both these topics (introduced in the first and third writing topics) could generate class discussion.

Bilingualism is a controversial topic, especially in states with large immigrant populations. The second writing topic invites students to explore and write about the issues.

Meaning

1. The main idea is suggested in paragraphs 5 and 18–19; in a more intense version of something experienced by all children (bilingual

or not), the bilingual child experiences a gulf between private intimacy within the family and public alienation outside the family.

2. Spanish represented "home," comfort, familiarity; English represented "the world," discomfort, unfamiliarity. The sounds of Spanish were quick and easy (paragraph 8), light, free, celebratory, expressive (22). Among his family, Rodriguez felt pleased, soothed, consoled (8), "joyful" (15); embraced (16); welcomed (19); secure (21); happy, intimate (22). The sounds of English, in contrast, were "exotic," "loud, booming with confidence," "firm" (10); "high nasal tones" (11); "noisy," "chirping chatter" (12); "hard" (21). Among *los gringos*, Rodriguez felt displeased (12), troubled (13), uneasy and embarrassed (14), frightened (18), wary and nervous (19), threatened (21).

3. Rodriguez's explanation in paragraphs 18–19 focuses on his sensitivity to sounds. Since he characterizes himself in paragraph 10 as "a listening child," his slow transition may have been caused by his sensitivity as well as by his bilingual environment.

Purpose and Audience

1. Although Rodriguez clearly expresses his memories, he seems to do so to explain a childhood experience that was more intense for him than for many children. Though his book *Hunger of Memory* does argue against bilingual education, this excerpt from the beginning of the book mentions the subject once (paragraph 5) and then drops it.

2. The Spanish words convey some of the sounds of the language and suggest the intensity of Rodriguez's memories.

Method and Structure

1. The smaller comparisons show the degree to which Rodriguez's experiences were shared by others (English-speaking children, barrio children), the discomfort he felt on his father's behalf (or because of his father) among *los gringos*, and the extent to which he outgrew the conflict between the two worlds.

2. The shift occurs at paragraph 15. Treating private language second intensifies the contrast: after the discomforting jangle of English, the happy comfort of Spanish is more appreciable.

3. The narratives illustrate discomfort in school (paragraphs 3–4), fear of strangers in authority (10), embarrassment for parents (14), and comfort among family (22). Such feelings are, of course, experienced by monolingual children, too. But for Rodriguez, a language barrier compounded the conflict. Rodriguez makes this point explicit in paragraph 3.

Language

1. The phonetic spelling of the American pronunciation of his name emphasizes its strangeness and harshness. The contrast between this form and the Spanish form—and the latter's placement in a paragraph by itself—stresses the different sounds of the two languages.

2. Examples of the two sets of words are given in the answer to question 2 under "Meaning." Among *los gringos*, the young Rodriguez was frightened and embarrassed. Among his family, he was comfortable, confident, and happy.

3. All of Rodriguez's figures of speech make his feelings as a boy more concrete and immediate for the reader. Other examples: "I turned to see my mother's face dissolve in a watery blur" (paragraph 4); "exotic polysyllabic sounds would bloom in the midst of their sentences" (10); "The air stirred with sound" (11); "sounds as confused as the threads of blue and green oil in the puddle" (14); "I would feel embraced by the sounds" (16); "I lingered too long, poised at the edge of language" (18); "I remained cloistered by sounds," "that military drum roll, the twirling roar of the Spanish *r*" (22).

Chapter 8

DEFINITION

JUDY BRADY

I Want a Wife *(p. 251)*

Brady's definition uses carefully selected examples to present an angry statement about the wife's place in the home and in society. Some students may initially misunderstand the essay and think Brady really does want a slave of her own. Other students may see the essay as excessively hostile toward wives, husbands, and marriage. And still other students may find Brady's sense of oppression somewhat passé, not as much an issue now as it was in the less liberated early 1970s. Class discussion may be guided by questions 1–3 under "Purpose and Audience" and by 2 and 3 under "Writing Topics."

Meaning

1. A wife is a person whose entire function is the selfless serving of others, especially the husband.

2. The wife's chief responsibilities are to work when doing so is beneficial to the spouse, to care for the children, to care for the house and to cook, to meet the spouse's physical and emotional needs, and to arrange and run social events. The wife's behavior should be entirely selfless. The spouse's responsibilities are to attend school and study and eventually to support dependents "if need be" (paragraph 3)—but nothing is required or contributed at home. The spouse's behavior may be entirely selfish.

Purpose and Audience

1. Brady's purpose is to attack society's—and men's—attitudes toward the role of a wife. She presents a deliberately one-sided definition, exaggerating to achieve this purpose.

68

2. Brady seems to assume that her readers are mostly women who will understand and appreciate her anger. Her perspective seems to be that of a middle-class woman in her twenties or early thirties: the wife works to put the spouse through school; the children are relatively young; the family lives in a house; and the couple has an active social life.

3. Answers will vary widely.

Method and Structure

1. Readers may take the role of a wife for granted—or may have in 1971—but Brady sees a need to show how the wife is taken advantage of. By presenting a slanted definition, she encourages readers to see things her way.

2. The definition is highly specific and clearly distinguishes the role of a wife from, say, the role of a housekeeper or a lover. It is also thorough in that it covers a wide range of responsibilities and behaviors. But some readers may think that the omission of any positive elements in the relationship between wife and spouse—what keeps the wife at the job: love? security?—makes the definition less than complete.

3. Paragraph 1 suggests the author is defined by society according to her role as a wife. Paragraph 2 presents a man who seems to view a wife's role just as Brady goes on to define it: he is divorced; he has left his child to his wife; and he wants "a wife"—as if anyone might do. The question at the end of the introduction leads into the definition; once the earlier question is answered, the final rhetorical question opens up the divorced man's wish and Brady's wish to everyone.

4. With classification, Brady makes the definition more manageable. She classifies the wife's responsibilities into financial support and child care (paragraph 3), housekeeping and cooking (4), emotional support (5), social organization (6), and sexual fulfillment (7). The categories are increasingly personal and intrusive, thus emphasizing the exploitation of women in marriage.

Language

1. Brady's tone is angry and contemptuous, and it is achieved largely through irony: for example, "It may mean a small cut in my wife's income . . . , but I guess I can tolerate that" (paragraph 3); "I want a wife who will not bother me with rambling complaints about a wife's duties" but "will listen to me when I feel the need to explain a rather difficult point I have come across in my course of studies" (5).

2. The repetition portrays the spouse as childish, demanding, and selfish.

3. Use of the phrase *my wife* emphasizes the spouse's depersonalization and possession of the wife. The phrase also allows Brady to avoid expressing a wish for another woman, which might be more distracting than the occasionally awkward sentences now in the essay.

4. Such expressions underline the irony.

GLORIA NAYLOR
The Meanings of a Word (p. 256)

Some students may approach this essay with apprehension. The word *nigger* is so highly charged that it's difficult for many people to utter, even when discussing it objectively. To ease students into the subject, you might ask them to do some journal writing as preparation for discussion of the essay. Possible questions: What does the word *nigger* mean to you? Who uses it? What effect does it have? Students can then compare their responses with one another's and with Naylor's. (Small groups might alleviate some students' discomfort with the topic.)

Meaning

1. Words don't mean anything in themselves; they only take on meaning within a specific social context. *Nigger* meant one thing among black people and another when used by white people.

2. Naylor states her main idea in the last sentence of paragraph 2: the power of a word derives from a consensus about its meaning among the people who use the word.

3. Naylor says that by reaching their own consensus about the meanings of *nigger*, African Americans have developed a powerful word for their own uses and simultaneously rendered the word powerless when spoken by whites. Responses to the last part of the question will vary.

Purpose and Audience

1. Naylor seems to have written her essay for at least two interlocking reasons: to express some childhood memories and through them to explain how words acquire meaning and power. A third purpose may

be revealed in paragraph 14: in disputing the view that the use of *nigger* among African Americans was an "internalization of racism," Naylor seems to want to convince readers that the African American use of *nigger* was instead a "head-on" confrontation with racism.

2. Naylor's careful picture of life in Harlem (paragraphs 4–5), as well as her precise explanation of the terms *nigger* and *girl*, indicates that she's writing to a primarily white audience. Presumably many African American readers would already be familiar with this information. In addition, Naylor takes pains to dispel any sense her readers may have that she and her family were victims. She presents her young self as somewhat bratty, given to lording it over a classmate (3), and she presents her extended family as a warm and lively group of hard workers (4–5) who had struggled against and survived "hard times, unemployment, the occasional bout of depression" (10).

Method and Structure

1. Naylor's point is that words always need to be placed in context, no matter how well we think we know what they mean.

2. When the white boy "spit[s] out" (paragraph 3) the word, Naylor knows it's something nasty, even without fully understanding the meaning. (This is confirmed by the teacher's scolding him.) Later, we hear that the word's meaning depends on who says it, whether it's singular or plural, and who is being described. In Naylor's community, the singular *nigger* is a term of approval or endearment — approval when spoken by acquaintances, endearment when spoken by a spouse or girlfriend. The plural term changes from being a positive to a negative term and reflects lack of self-respect. *Girl* is the feminine equivalent: when spoken directly to a woman and drawn out, it signifies worth; when used in the third person and shortened, it signifies disapproval.

3. In the two introductory paragraphs, Naylor establishes the importance of the spoken word (paragraph 1) and states her main idea (2). In paragraphs 3–5, she sets the scene for discussions of particular words by stepping back to recall a childhood incident (3) and to recreate the experience of being among her family (4–5). In the body of the essay, she clarifies the varied meanings of the terms *nigger* and *girl* and comments on why blacks adopted *nigger* (14). The final paragraph returns us to the childhood experience and its connection to a cultural problem.

4. The childhood incident is recounted in paragraphs 3 and 15. The narrative is important because Naylor is talking about the emotional content of words, the attitudes they convey, and the feelings they engender in different contexts. Without the narrative, the discussion

would be one-sided (only the positive uses of *nigger*), and the hurtful power of words would not be explicit.

Language

1. Naylor's tone is matter-of-fact and imperturbable ("I consider the written word inferior to the spoken," [paragraph 1]; "I will simply take the position . . ." [2]; "she took me in her lap and explained," [15]). From the first, aphoristic sentence, her style tends toward the academic ("nonsensical arrangement of sounds or letters without a consensus that assigns 'meaning,'" [2]; "In the singular," [6]; "When used with a possessive adjective," [9]; "In the plural," [10]; "used in third-person reference," [13]; "social stratum," "internalization of racism," [14]). Some students will appreciate the tempered, anthropological way she treats a sensitive subject; others may wish the essay were more contentious.

2. After hearing what the boy says, Naylor, the child, tattles to the teacher "in a loud voice" (paragraph 3). And in 4–11 she reinforces the sense of a child growing aware of her world by separating herself from the adults in her family: the people speaking are *they*, not *we* (4–6, 9–10). Also, the use of passive verbs such as *was used* (5), *was applied* (6), and *was drawn out* (11) further emphasizes that Naylor was listening in on adult conversations. That she chooses to convey this information from the child's perspective heightens the effect of her message: the words we hear as children influence the way we look at ourselves and those around us, and the context when we hear those words can make all the difference. By placing herself and her readers directly in those contexts, Naylor demonstrates the power of words.

3. Examples include the following: In the apartment the "clamor" was often "punctuated by the sound of a baby's crying somewhere in the back rooms or out on the street" (paragraph 5). Naylor's "countless aunts, uncles, and cousins" and their "assorted friends" came to the apartment "to let down their hair and put up their feet after a week of labor in the factories, laundries, and shipyards of New York" (4). They experienced "triumphs and disappointments in the various workings of their lives" (5) and admired men of "strength, intelligence, or drive" (6) and women of "wit, nerve, or daring" (11). They savored "their past history of struggle and present survival against the odds" (9) and despised the "lack of self-respect" of those "who neglected their children, . . . fought in public," and otherwise "overstepped the bounds of decency" (10). This language brings the community to life. Readers are not expected to take Naylor's word for it; they see the variety and complexity of these people.

AMY TAN

Mother Tongue *(p. 262)*

Tan writes lovingly and with humor about the "broken" English of her Chinese immigrant mother. Once a source of embarrassment to Tan, her mother's English is now the language of family intimacy. Tan concludes by reflecting on how the English she grew up with at home almost kept her from becoming a writer because, like many other Asian American students, she did better on standardized math and science tests than on standardized English tests.

To begin class discussion, you might ask students how they responded to Tan's portrait of her mother. What words would they use to describe the mother? Do they find her sympathetic? How do they feel about her "limited" English?

Meaning

1. Tan shows that her "mother tongue"—her mother's English—is "the language that helped shape the way I saw things, expressed things, made sense of the world" (paragraph 7). This language binds her to her mother and influences her as a writer (21).

2. Because of her limited English, people outside the Chinese American community often think Tan's mother is of limited intelligence. She receives poor service or is ignored altogether in commercial establishments (paragraph 9). Her broker did not respond to her as he would have to other clients (10–13), and even hospital personnel didn't treat her case seriously (14).

3. Because her SAT scores and grades were higher in math and science than in English, Tan was discouraged from pursuing an English degree in college (paragraph 15). But her rebellious streak led her to become an English major, a freelance business writer, and later a celebrated novelist (19–20).

Purpose and Audience

1. Her secondary purpose seems to be to suggest that it is unfair for writing teachers to dissuade Asian American students from an interest in writing.

2. If Tan were writing primarily to Asian Americans, she would probably assume a more shared understanding of what it means to grow up with parents or grandparents whose first language is not English; the tone would likely be more commiserative—"Haven't we all been through this?"—and she might even use the pronouns *we* and *you*.

Method and Structure

1. Tan develops her definition primarily through example—in paragraphs 4, 5–6, 11 and 13. She also makes clear in paragraphs 4, 7–9, and 21 her more personal definition of her "mother tongue."

2. The first section introduces the concept of "mother tongue" and what it means to Tan. The second defines Tan's mother's English in detail; here Tan suggests several consequences of growing up with her mother's broken English. The third section mentions the occasion that sparked the essay (being questioned about why few Asian Americans join creative writing programs) and reinforces Tan's point that her mother's English significantly influenced her as a writer. The first section is introductory, concluding with her central point. The second takes readers into Tan's past, and the third brings them back to the present. Tan uses the fact that she's been thinking about the subject as transition from each section to the next.

3. She uses a formal English "filled with carefully wrought grammatical phrases" (paragraph 3) and the "simple" English she spoke with her mother. She also uses her mother's "broken" English, a "watered down" translation of her mother's Chinese, and her translation of her own Chinese.

Language

1. Such labels suggest that her mother's language is in some way damaged or less than whole or that her mother is actually limited in her thinking. Tan hears her mother's language as "vivid, direct, full of observation and imagery" (paragraph 7).

2. Based on her examples, it seems Tan's English was not bound by conventional strictures. She could make imaginative leaps of language not limited, for example, to the grammatical structure "even though." And when faced with analogies, the vivid images the words brought to mind kept her from seeing the more mundane comparisons the test makers provided.

DAGOBERTO GILB
Pride *(p. 271)*

In this lyrical essay, Gilb defines the concept of pride by focusing specifically on the experiences of Mexican Americans—"good people who are too poor but don't notice" (paragraph 6). Based almost wholly on examples, the definition is beautifully developed in language that is poetic and highly concrete. The language is also deceptively simple: Gilb creates striking effects using words that will be familiar to students (with the possible exception of the Spanish words, which are defined in the editors' footnotes). He provides an excellent example for students to see that effective definition and description do not require sophisticated words—just specific, fresh language.

If you enjoy reading aloud, you might read the final paragraph to your students. Carefully wrought, it builds to a wonderfully satisfying conclusion.

Meaning

1. Here is a possible summary: *Pride* means hard work, achievement, love of family, respect for landscape and history, fearlessness—all despite poverty.

2. Paragraphs 8–10 expand the definition outside particular lives to the landscape and heritage of Mexican Americans.

3. Gilb's final paragraph offers a panoply of images of Mexican Americans: war heroes, factory workers, homemakers—human beings with the same feelings and needs as anyone else—all of whom feel a pride in who they are. The very color of their skin ("Beautiful brown") is a source of pride.

Purpose and Audience

1. Gilb's purpose here goes well beyond defining *pride*. The essay is a hymn to the lives, history, and culture of Mexican Americans. Gilb wants to share his vision with readers from all kinds of backgrounds.

2. Because he wrote the essay for visitors to an exhibit focused on Texas artifacts, Gilb can assume that his readers are familiar with

the region he invokes, so he doesn't need to describe the general landscape in much detail. (Notice, for example, that he rattles off the names of neighborhoods, landmarks, desert plants, and geographical features without bothering to explain what they are.) Instead, he focuses on the details his readers may not know: the specific clothing worn by the young woman, the little boy, and the boy's proud father, for instance. Because the exhibit took place in a history museum, Gilb can also assume that his readers will be well versed in the cultural and political tensions surrounding immigrant communities in Texas. He doesn't feel a need to make his argument explicit because he can count on readers to supply the background without much effort. For readers unfamiliar with Texas and its history, of course, this assumption could pose problems.

Method and Structure

1. Gilb's opening establishes diversity—an older man in a "starched and ironed uniform" (paragraph 2) hard at work, a boy in an oversized T-shirt hard at play, and a young woman in a wreck of a car dressed for a party—and it conveys camaraderie among these three people, together in a lighted parking lot surrounded by the deepest darkness.

2. Gilb may have varied his strategy because in the first instance, the sources of pride are not immediately obvious and he wants to make them clear. In the second instance, the source of pride goes without saying and he can move on.

3. The development of paragraph 7 is sophisticated. It begins with the image of the son sitting "a long time . . . on the front porch" (we don't know why until later). Then we see the boy in a brief flashback as a youngster with his dog ("both puppies then"). His exuberance leads him to the park, where his response to an insect bite shows how he has matured into a proud young man. Back home, he puts on the clothes he "wanted to iron himself," another sign of his pride. We don't know until two sentences later that these clothes are for his high school graduation. Now the focus shifts to the father (whose "eel-skin boots" are an especially vivid detail), embarrassed by the emotion he feels because of his pride in his son. Finally, the son accepts his diploma to the cheers of classmates and families, who could be calling "any name . . . any son's or daughter's," an image of their communal pride.

4. Gilb works for a specific mood in the opening, as discussed in the answer to question 1. He wants readers to *see* these people and the landscape they inhabit.

Language

1. The description is a good example of showing, not telling. Gilb doesn't just say the car is a big wreck. No, it is a "fatso American car" with "cross-eyed" headlights, a misfiring muffler, and "dry springs squeaking."

2. While the subject of the sentences in paragraph 8 is pride, an abstract concept, Gilb uses verbs referring to the senses: "hears," "sees," "listens," "smells," "eats." He personifies pride.

3. Students should see that the repetition of "the ones who" keeps this long sentence under control. They may also note that when he needs to, Gilb varies this phrase.

Chapter 9

CAUSE-AND-EFFECT ANALYSIS

MALCOLM GLADWELL

The Tipping Point *(p. 286)*

An excellent example of cause-and-effect analysis, this essay explores the causes of the dramatic reduction in New York City's crime rate during the 1990s. Gladwell begins by describing the specific effects he wishes to examine (paragraph 1), then moves on to analyze the causes that led to these effects.

You might begin class discussion by asking students how they would differentiate "quality-of-life" crimes from more serious crimes. Why might enforcement of laws against quality-of-life crimes often be relatively lax?

Meaning

1. The Broken Windows theory holds that "crime is the inevitable result of disorder" (paragraph 2). An unrepaired broken window on a street gives the impression that no one is in charge, leading to more broken windows and eventually to public disorder and crime. If, for example, a neighborhood doesn't police aggressive panhandling, then a potential thief might assume that theft wouldn't be policed either.

2. Gunn cracked down on subway graffiti because it symbolized "a collapse in the system" (paragraph 3). He felt that other improvements were not possible if subway cars continued to be vandalized. As a result of the crackdown, vandals realized their work would not last overnight and significantly reduced their graffiti painting.

3. Bratton first got officers to arrest fare beaters at subway stations and insisted that they run checks on all those arrested. Later, as chief of

police, he cracked down on quality-of-life crimes—"the above-ground equivalents of turnstile-jumping and graffiti" (paragraph 8). These measures led to a dramatic decrease first in subway crime and later in crime in general. The lesson: "Minor, seemingly insignificant quality-of-life crimes" lead to violent crime (8).

Purpose and Audience

1. Most students probably will agree that Gladwell successfully explains how the Tipping Point concept applies to crime reduction in New York City. Clearly, reducing minor crime significantly affected violent crime rates as well.

2. By quoting the officials who initiated the procedures responsible for reducing crime in New York City, Gladwell brings to his readers direct authority for his points. He likely hopes this authority will help convince readers that his explanation is sound. (In addition, the quotations from Bratton in paragraph 7 suggest his "colorful" personality.)

Method and Structure

1. Any attempt to explain *why* something happened (in this case, why crime rates in New York City declined so rapidly) will appropriately rely on cause-and-effect analysis.

2. The idea of the Tipping Point cannot be applied to national crime rates, which declined for a variety of reasons. Gladwell needs to establish from the outset that while some of these factors affected crime rates in New York City, other causes contributed to the rapidity and scale of the decline.

3. The early definition of the Broken Windows theory is important to Gladwell's development here, because the theory provided the basis for the policies instituted by Gunn and Bratton that led to the decrease in crime.

Language

1. Like a fashion trend, crime resembles a virus in that it spreads through a population from person to person. People are more likely to break laws if they perceive a lawless environment; they "catch" their behavior from others around them.

2. This shift in tone is likely meant to suggest what someone at the time might have said about Gunn's decision to focus on graffiti

when the New York subway system faced such enormous problems. Gladwell, in effect, *creates* a quotation that leads into Gunn's explanation and refutation.

STEVEN PINKER

Mind Over Mass Media *(p. 293)*

Readers may not recognize that Pinker's essay is largely a response to the publication of Nicholas Carr's *The Shallows: What the Internet Is Doing to Our Brains* (2010), a book-length expansion of the analysis he put forth in his widely read essay "Is Google Making Us Stupid?" In both works, Carr—a journalist—draws on neuroscience and psychology to warn that instant access to information is reshaping our brains and changing the way we think. Clearly Pinker thinks such concerns are pseudoscientific bunk.

Pinker makes no effort to hide his irritation with Carr and other media critics sounding similar alarms. Discussion could focus on when and why it is appropriate to reveal emotion in a piece of scientific writing and to what extent tone interferes with or contributes to reason. Alternatively, you might ask students to read Carr's essay (available at *theatlantic.com/magazine/archive/2008/07/is-google-making-us-stupid/6868/*) and compare the writers' arguments.

Meaning

1. Despite other writers' claims to the contrary, Pinker insists that new media, such as the Internet and computer software, do not diminish intelligence. Quite the opposite: He believes that electronic tools encourage more efficient processing of information and ideas. "Far from making us stupid," he says in his final statement, "these technologies are the only things that will keep us smart."

2. Neural plasticity refers to the idea, recently confirmed by scientists, that patterns of mental activity shape the paths used by electrical impulses to travel through the brain. Repeated activities strengthen related neural pathways, while neglected pathways tend to shrink. Some scientists and observers worry that the activities associated with using new media, such as instant gratification and

visual stimulation, "rewire" the brain and make it less capable of deep, protracted thinking. Although Pinker acknowledges that a new or repeated "experience can change the brain" (paragraph 5), he rejects concerns that those changes limit its functioning.

Purpose and Audience

1. Pinker writes both to dismiss concerns that electronic media diminish intelligence and to reassure people that technology will not harm them. But mostly, he seems to take great pleasure in entertaining readers by mocking ideas he finds ridiculous.

2. The first assumption Pinker makes is that his readers will be familiar with the arguments he takes issue with, especially those put forth by Nicholas Carr (this almost certainly will not hold true for students). Other assumptions include that readers are fairly well educated and value learning for its own sake, that they have a passing familiarity with recent cognitive research (the neural plasticity and multitasking studies he mentions were much discussed in news outlets at the time he wrote), and that they use the technologies he discusses. Students may also notice that he assumes a relatively affluent, adult readership.

Method and Structure

1. Throughout his essay, Pinker supplements his own observations with examples and references to studies published by other writers and scientists, sometimes identifying them by name, sometimes not. The unattributed evidence in particular might strike some students as anecdotal or unreliable; whereas most are likely to find the attributed works more convincing.

2. Pinker's analysis opens with a general overview of the history of new-media worries in paragraphs 1–3, offers a "reality check" to dismiss current worries in paragraph 4, then follows a point/counterpoint pattern in paragraphs 5–10. He summarizes the gist of a concern that has been expressed by media critics—that "experience can change the brain" (paragraph 5), that "the brain takes on the qualities of whatever it consumes" (8), that "the constant arrival of information packets can be distracting or addictive" (9)—then explains why such concerns are misguided or flat-out wrong. He concludes by reminding readers of the power of self-discipline and education to maintain intelligence.

3. The dual comparison—Pinker compares fears and realities as well as past and present media—serves to provide background for his analysis and to remind readers that worries over new genres are

nothing new. By intimating that "such panics" (paragraph 3) tend to be irrational and, ultimately, unfounded, he establishes the main point of his argument from the start.

Language

1. The tone is strikingly condescending and irritable. Pinker's irritation seems controlled, but often he expresses sarcasm or impatience — and outright mockery — as in his description of "cognitive neuroscientists [who] roll their eyes at such talk" (paragraph 5) and his portrayal of media critics as "primitive peoples" (8) with irrational beliefs. Some readers might be put off by the resulting sense of hostility, but Pinker's insults are clever enough (and vicious enough) to win over others, especially if they think of themselves as smarter than most.

2. Some metaphors: "skim on the surface of knowledge rather than dive to its depths" (paragraph 2); "does not mean the brain is a blob of clay pounded into shape by experience" (5); "information-processing capacities of the brain" (6). Some similes: "discoveries are multiplying like fruit flies" (4); "the informational equivalent of 'you are what you eat'" (8). Some hyperbole: "scientists . . . rarely touch paper and cannot lecture without *PowerPoint*" (4); "it's not as if information is stored in the pancreas" (5). Although a few of them seem to border on cliché, the figures of speech reinforce Pinker's ethos as a very smart person who knows his way around language.

BARBARA EHRENREICH
Cultural Baggage (p. 298)

In this essay, Ehrenreich explores what an ethnic background means to her. At first embarrassed not to have a noteworthy "cultural heritage," she suddenly realizes — in what she calls an epiphany — that "Think for yourself," her father's maxim, actually constituted the pivotal force of her ancestors' cultural traditions.

The informal, conversational tone of this piece might at first give students the mistaken impression that this is a lighthearted look at what can only be considered one of the most tangled issues in America. It may require several readings to investigate Ehrenreich's claims fully.

Meaning

1. The heritage Ehrenreich embraces is that of "skepticism, curiosity and wide-eyed ecumenical tolerance" (paragraph 12). She traces this heritage to her family: to her mother, who believed in trying new things (4) and adopting new practices (10); to her father, who told her "Think for yourself" and "Always ask why" (10); and to their parents and grandparents, "who [did] not carry on traditions, who [did] not do things just because someone [had] done them before" (9).

2. Ehrenreich questions here whether as a woman of white, Anglo-Saxon background she automatically sees herself as "normal" and sees people of other ethnic backgrounds as "different," as "other than normal." Such unconscious categorizing is often viewed as a subtle, but pervasive, form of ethnocentrism or racism.

3. As a girl, Ehrenreich played with the idea of embracing her Scots background but was ultimately put off by what she saw as its primitive traditions (paragraphs 5–6). Later, after marrying someone of Jewish ancestry, she tried to encourage Jewish traditions with her children, but they found her efforts somewhat hypocritical, given that she is an atheist and that not even their father's parents were practicing Jews (7–8).

Purpose and Audience

1. Ehrenreich's thesis is that, as much as a specific cultural identity, "skepticism, curiosity and wide-eyed ecumenical tolerance are also worthy elements of the human tradition" (paragraph 12); and, in a quotation from her children, "the world would be a better place" without ethnic or religious identity (13).

2. Ehrenreich's purpose seems somewhat complex, so answers may vary. Ultimately she doesn't seem to be defending her lack of ethnic identity, over which she feels she has no control. At least implicitly, she does seem to be trying to persuade some readers that more universal human traditions exist than those related to ethnic identity (paragraph 12), but her larger purpose is really to present for readers the evolution of her own sense of tradition and cultural identity — from her slight embarrassment at having "none" (2) through her childhood inventions (5–6) to her ultimate "epiphany" (9–10). Read in this light, her thesis (see question 1 here) is more a statement of personal belief than one of argument.

3. Ehrenreich seems to be writing for an audience made up of both groups. Nowhere does she make any sort of special appeal to readers who identify themselves ethnically or to those who do not. Writing for a fairly general audience, Ehrenreich apparently assumes that

readers are reasonably well educated (for example, some of her vo-cabulary is sophisticated), that they are primarily Americans (her focus is on American groups), and that they perhaps haven't given much thought to the kinds of nonethnic traditions she celebrates.

Method and Structure

1. Ehrenreich first considers why she feels no particular ethnic iden-tity (paragraphs 5–7), then writes about the family heritage that she realizes helped to shape her sense of identity and personal values (9–12). The focus of the essay is precisely this exploration of how she came to be who she is.

2. The question asked by her friend in the opening, which Ehrenreich found herself embarrassed trying to answer, is answered decisively by her children in the closing.

3. Ehrenreich asks the questions that guided her own search for an-swers about tradition and identity.

4. In paragraph 3 Ehrenreich contrasts the ethnic pride of those who were reclaiming their roots in the 1960s and 1970s with her own dis-comfort at not being able to share their experience. In paragraph 12 she sets religion and ethnic tradition against other "worthy elements of the human tradition" that she finds just as important, if not more so. The two paragraphs, coming at the start and the end of her essay, suggest the evolution of her understanding.

Language

1. The tone of this essay is measured, thoughtful, even formal at times. But the tone is occasionally lightened by humor ("I pretended to believe that the bagpipe was a musical instrument" [paragraph 5], "whose idea of cuisine was stuffed sheep gut washed down with whisky" [6], "tiny pagans" [8]) and by colloquial language ("bimbo" [6], "put the screws on me, ethnicity-wise" [7], "ahem" [13]).

2. Italicizing the phrase suggests that the speaker gave it special vocal emphasis. In a larger sense, though, doing the "same things now" that one's ancestors did 2,000 years ago is a value Ehrenreich comes to question and reject.

3. Purim is a traditional Jewish holiday. Kwanzaa is a seven-day Afri-can American celebration, first observed in 1965, that has ties to African traditions. And Solstice is an ancient pagan celebration prac-ticed by modern-day Wiccans and others. Ehrenreich's point here is to suggest that if the celebrants of these newer holidays find them re-ligiously or ethnically light, they could turn to "skepticism, curiosity and wide-eyed ecumenical tolerance."

4. She makes the point that she is among those who do not wish to identify (or be identified) with any particular race except perhaps the race of humankind.

STEPHEN JAY GOULD

Sex, Drugs, Disasters, and the Extinction of Dinosaurs (p. 304)

Why did the dinosaurs vanish? Students intrigued by this perennial puzzle will warm to this essay, where Gould sets forth much solid learning in a light-handed style. Gould tries to justify his flamboyant title in his third paragraph. Sex, drugs, and violence are "the primally fascinating themes of our culture," and for each a corresponding, widely held (or once widely held) hypothesis accounts for the dinosaurs' disappearance. Gould not only analyzes these three answers to the question but also dismisses two of them as "silly" and supports the third as the most probable.

What other kinds of unanswered (or unanswerable) questions might students explore in an essay modeled on Gould's? Have the class generate as many potential questions as they can and write them on the board. Working in groups of three or four, students should choose a question for a collaborative essay. As a group, they can generate as many hypotheses as possible to answer this question. Each group member can have the responsibility to research one possibility, and the whole group can come together to write the essay.

Meaning

1. A good scientific hypothesis is testable: It can generate both refuting and confirming evidence. It throws light on other subjects, even remote ones (paragraph 4). But useless speculation cannot be tested, nor can it be supported by evidence. It leads to no conclusions; it remains merely "an intriguing idea" (5).

2. On the whole, Gould's essay supports hypothesis number 3, "disasters," in paragraph 5. But Gould's thesis is larger: that one of the three hypotheses "represents science at its grandest and most useful."

3. Both the testicular theory and the overdose theory, according to Gould, qualify as "[u]seless speculation," or a theory that "generates

no testable hypothesis, and offers no way to obtain potentially refuting evidence"; at the same time, both ignore the "wider contexts and systems" of mass extinction (paragraph 5). He outlines how these flaws apply to the testicular theory in paragraph 18, how they apply to the overdose theory in paragraphs 19–20, and how they apply to both in paragraphs 23–24.

4. Nuclear holocaust is analogous to the asteroid or comet—"disaster"—theory, which is the only one of the three theories Gould examines that qualifies as a valid scientific hypothesis. Just as falling space debris may have led to the extinction of dinosaurs millions of years ago, a nuclear holocaust today could lead to the extinction of humanity.

Purpose and Audience

1. Most students will appreciate Gould's accessible style and clear, entertaining explanations. To help laypeople understand a complex subject, Gould defines specialized terms (for example, *angiosperms* in paragraph 2 and *marine plankton* in 6); clearly outlines the three hypotheses early in the essay (5); and offers concrete examples and clear explanations of scientific theories (Galileo's theory of the unequal scaling of surfaces and volumes, for example, in 9).

2. Why not read aloud "Do Not Go Gentle into That Good Night," from Dylan Thomas's *Collected Poems*, or in many anthologies? It's only nineteen lines long. Students don't have to know the poem, but if they do they'll better appreciate Gould's ironic humor. They'll need to be told that Thomas is addressing his dying father, urging the old man to resist death.

Method and Structure

1. A diagram of the causal chain (paragraphs 15–16) might look like this:

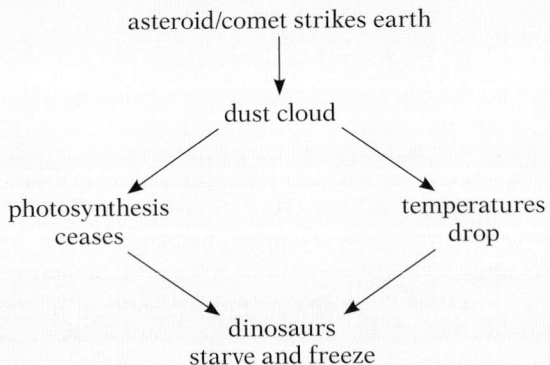

2. The process analyses explain how science works (paragraphs 4–5) and how each of the three theories explains the extinction of the dinosaurs (9–12, 14, 16). Without the first instance, we would not understand Gould's criteria for evaluating the three theories. Without the other instances, we would not understand the theories themselves.

Language

1. "Hit parade of primal fascination" (paragraph 17), Gould's allusion to the old radio show "Your Hit Parade" (or *Hit Parader*, a magazine of song lyrics), makes clear that he regards some theories as no more substantial than passing crazes in popular music. The phrase "testicular frying" (18)—suggesting a mess of "Texas strawberries" sautéed in butter or something—seems an archly comic dismissal of the theory. These phrases are ironic, practically sarcastic.

2. Separate from what? Separate from all else on earth at the time when the dinosaurs died. The problem, as Gould sees it, is not merely what happened to the dinosaurs, but what phenomenon could have occurred on earth at that moment about 65 million years ago.

Chapter 10

ARGUMENT AND PERSUASION

BILL McKIBBEN

Waste Not, Want Not *(p. 331)*

McKibben uses an arsenal of persuasive strategies in this essay, including ethical appeals, emotional appeals, and rational appeals such as statistics and examples, and a clear problem-solution organization. The "Purpose and Audience" questions will help students see that McKibben takes great care to bond with his audience, perhaps because his proposal may not be easy for even the most environmentally conscious readers to act on.

To introduce the essay, you could have the class as a whole compile a list of objections to reducing personal consumption for environmental reasons. After reading the essay, students can discuss whether—and how effectively—McKibben counters each objection. Then, when they've read Derrick Jensen's rebuttal of McKibben's proposal, they can compare the two essays for their strategies and effectiveness. See the discussion of Jensen's essay on p. 91 of this manual.

Meaning

1. Paragraphs 4–5 and 9–10 center on the environment, paragraphs 7 and 11–13 center on the economy, and paragraphs 6, 8, and 14–15 touch on both at the same time. According to McKibben, adopting a simpler lifestyle would improve the world in two ways: by protecting the planet from the devastation caused by waste, and by allowing people more time and money to pursue relationships, cultural enlightenment, and the common good.

2. McKibben blames the consumer economy, especially the actions of manufacturers and advertisers, but also individuals' desire for money and things. Among the examples of waste he cites are disposable water bottles (paragraph 3), manufacturing that favors cost savings over efficiencies (4–5, 8), junk mail (6), automotive torque (7), personal trash (9–10), education (11), military spending (13), soil (14), talent (14), executive excess (15), and large houses (17).

3. McKibben's proposed solution is to reduce personal consumption: "The economic mess now transfixing us will mean some kind of change. We can try to hang on to the status quo—living a Walmart life so we can buy cheaply enough to keep the stream of stuff coming. Or we can say uncle" (paragraph 18). He asks readers to embrace a lifestyle of thrift, returning to a time of "Yankee frugality" when we "couldn't imagine wasting money on ourselves, made do or did without" (16).

Purpose and Audience

1. McKibben seems to expect that many, if not most, readers will agree with his assessment of the problem but not necessarily his solution— a reasonable expectation, given that he's writing for *Mother Jones*, whose audience is mostly liberal and environmentally aware. In opening with a personal tale of the satisfaction of recycling, McKibben presents himself as someone who holds the same values his readers do, but then he attempts to jar them into deeper consciousness by stressing the quantity of "unnecessary" waste (3). Throughout his examples of shameful behavior in the rest of the essay, he addresses the perpetrators as *you* and *we*—implicating his readers in the wastefulness and unacceptable behavior he describes. By the time he reaches his proposal, the resulting sense of shared responsibility for the problem should, he seems to hope, soften readers' resistance to change and sacrifice.

2. No doubt, McKibben counts consumerism and politics as contributors to the problems he addresses. He chides government for supporting the nuclear industry (paragraph 8) and engaging in war (13), expresses dismay that college graduates seem more interested in money than culture (11), and faults both industry and government for placing financial concerns ahead of human ones (12). His solution, however, is entirely personal—at least for the purposes of this essay. McKibben would probably agree with Jensen that wholesale economic and political changes are necessary too, but his goal in this case is to persuade his readers to live less wastefully on an individual scale.

Method and Structure

1. Examples of *emotional appeals*: the mention of trees and time wasted
   by junk mail (6); the suggestion that fast acceleration "makes you
   look like an idiot, or a teenager" (7); the concern for workers and
   children (12); the examples of profligate CEOs (15). Examples of
   ethical appeals: McKibben's presentation of his community recycling
   experience (1–3); his admiration for learning (11); his use of *we*
   (throughout). Examples of *rational appeals*: statistical evidence (e.g.,
   7, 9); the structure of the argument, dealing with opponents' arguments (see "Method and Structure" question 3). Students' judgments
   of these appeals will of course vary widely depending on their knowledge and beliefs.

2. The syllogism:

   Major premise: All waste hurts the economy and the environment.

   Minor premise: Personal consumption produces waste.

   Conclusion: Personal consumption hurts the economy and the
   environment.

   Some students might point out, like Derrick Jensen does in "Forget
   Shorter Showers" (p. 339), that not all consumption is personal;
   others might reject the premise that waste is harmful: either com-
   plication could render the conclusion invalid.

3. McKibben addresses opposing viewpoints somewhat obliquely, usually making an attempt at common ground and then following it
   with his own assertion. He acknowledges the effectiveness of the
   Clean Air and Clean Water Acts in paragraph 4, for instance, and
   accepts that clean-burning engines reduce carbon emissions before
   asserting that such emissions still contribute to global warming (5).
   He accepts that some efforts are "maybe perhaps vaguely useful" before suggesting that other efforts could be "actually useful instead"
   (8). The closest he seems to come to a direct counterargument is in
   paragraph 9, where he establishes the volumes of waste produced
   by a large population before refuting the idea that "population is at
   the root of our troubles." Some students might feel that the author's
   attempts at counterargument are unfair or at the very least grudg-
   ing; others may not be able to identify them at all; still others might
   find them amusing.

4. McKibben identifies nine categories of waste in paragraphs 4–14:
   "old-fashioned waste, the dangerous, sooty kind" (4); "waste that
   comes from everything operating as it should, only too much so" (5);
   waste that comes from doing something that manifestly doesn't
   need doing" (6–7); "waste that comes with doing something maybe
   perhaps vaguely useful when you could be doing something actually

useful instead" (8); solid waste (9–10); wasted education (11); waste of human capital (12); government waste (13); and waste of natural resources (14). In each case, he offers examples of the kinds of waste he means and establishes their effects. The distinctions establish the scope of the problem and suggest that personal waste is not only significant but the only kind that readers have the power to reduce: "Our wasteful habits wouldn't matter much if there were just a few of us," McKibben says (9).

Language

1. McKibben counts himself among the people overwhelmed by waste. By peppering the essay with colloquialisms and attempts at humor, he lightens the mood and establishes a bond with readers. The tone also allows him to express frustration at the situation.

2. "Stuffporn" is jargon for advertising; "throughput" is jargon for production or output. Other examples of language borrowed from business and economics include "multiply it by proximity" (9), "inefficiencies" (12), "boondoggle" (12), "margin" (14), "open sourcing" (18), "hyperconsumerism" (19), and "stimulus" (19). McKibben uses most of these words ironically, highlighting the absurdity of business philosophies and practices.

DERRICK JENSEN
Forget Shorter Showers (p. 339)

Both Derrick Jensen and Bill McKibben are regular contributors to *Orion* magazine. Although McKibben's essay (p. 331) was published in *Mother Jones*, Jensen's essay, published a month later in *Orion*, seems a direct response to his colleague. Read together, these essays should help students recognize that ideas need not be dual opposites or rigid pro/con debates to merit argument. Jensen's strong reaction to McKibben's proposal (and others like it) also shows students how an intelligent and knowledgeable reader like Jensen can counter what may have seemed airtight arguments. Following Jensen's example, students may in turn question some of his arguments, evidence, or assumptions (the first writing topic suggests a specific approach).

Meaning

1. Jensen's thesis, stated in the first and last sentences of paragraph 8, is that simple living is "ineffective at causing the sorts of changes necessary to stop this culture from killing the planet." What Jensen wants instead is to "destroy the industrial economy that is destroying the real, physical world"—a revolution. His thesis refutes McKibben's claim that cutting back on personal consumption will help the environment.

2. Jensen agrees with McKibben on many points: Both believe the environment is in trouble, both place a great deal of the blame on consumer economy and inadequate government, and both see a desperate need for change. They disagree, however, on one key point: Whether consuming less as individuals will do any good. McKibben sees personal choice as the primary driver of consumer economy; therefore, reducing consumption will reduce the damage caused by industry. Jensen, on the other hand, sees industrial culture as the driver; therefore that culture must be rejected and replaced with a different system of values.

3. A double bind is an either-or situation in which both choices lead to bad results. Jensen believes that we've become trapped into seeing only two options: continue consuming and harming the planet at our current pace, or reduce consumption and harm the planet more slowly; both have the end result of "killing the planet" (paragraph 7). Jensen proposes a third option: dismantling the consumer economy altogether. (Although note that he doesn't specify what system he proposes in its stead.)

Purpose and Audience

1. By stating that he is a practitioner of simple living himself, Jensen attempts to build common ground with his opponents. He applauds the practice but wants readers to accept that they need to do more.

2. Jensen seems to address environmental activists (*Orion* magazine states that its mission is "to inform, inspire, and engage individuals and grassroots organizations in becoming a significant cultural force for healing nature and community"). He apparently hopes to jolt readers out of what he views as dangerous complacency and persuade them to take, or at least support, strong political action. Students' responses to Jensen, as to McKibben, will depend on their openness to his arguments.

3. Jensen's description is sparse; he tells us simply that each American resident produces 1,660 pounds of trash per year (paragraph 5) and offers three examples of items that might be kept out of landfills (shopping bags, toasters, and tennis shoes). McKibben refers to the

work of a photographer to paint an alarming image, with extensive examples and numbers, of "the volumes we manage" (9) to throw away. McKibben's details place readers more deeply at the root of the problem, whereas Jensen glosses over such details because he sees individuals' impact as negligible.

Method and Structure

1. *Rational appeals*: like McKibben, Jensen uses statistics and other evidence to support his argument (e.g., paragraphs 2, 3, 5), and he walks readers through his deductive reasoning (e.g., 7–11). *Ethical appeals*: as an environmental activist, Jensen portrays himself as someone who cares deeply about the environment; he also concedes that he practices simple living (6). *Emotional appeals*: questioning the sanity of simple living proponents (1), depictions of death and dying (3, 7–8, 11), multiple repetitions of the phrase "killing the planet" (7–8), the suggestion that humans can help the earth as well as harm it (8, 10, 12), absolving readers from blame (9), the assertion that simple living is an act of "suicide" (11).

2. The examples are shocking and grab readers' attention from the start. But Jensen has a stronger reason for invoking them: He sees the environmental crisis as being on par with the political crises he uses to frame the essay. Much as activists refused to work within the systems of Nazi Germany, antebellum America, Tsarist Russia, and gender and racial oppression—and instead revolted against them—Jensen believes that environmental activists today must reject the status quo and take decisive political action for radical change.

3. Jensen suggests from the beginning that simple-living advocates ignore the question and fail to see the real issue at hand. He accuses them of oversimplification in paragraphs 2–5 especially, portrays them as falling victim to either-or thinking in paragraph 7, and questions their deductions by claiming that simple living is "predicated on the flawed notion that humans inevitably harm their land-base" (8) and asserting that "the logic behind simple living as a political act is suicide" (11).

   Some students might see an element of ad hominem attack in Jensen's portrayal of simple-living advocates "dancing naked around a fire" (1). Those unconvinced of global warming or climate change might accuse Jensen of begging the question: because the planet is dying, we must do something radical to save it. Those who do worry about the environment, on the other hand, might consider Jensen's conclusion—the planet is in trouble, so we must abolish capitalism—a non sequitur, although he takes great pains to explain the connection.

4. The main point—that the current global economic system is destroying the planet—has more punch because Jensen enumerates specific

effects of consumer culture. McKibben claims one set of effects (waste), whereas Jensen asserts and analyzes others that are, in his judgment, worse.

Language

1. Of the given adjectives, *frustrated* and *militant* seem to be the most appropriate to describe Jensen's tone. At times the author sounds exasperated and condescending, as in "well, no" (paragraph 3) and "Uh, I've got some bad news" (5). At other times Jensen seems cautiously optimistic, especially when he reminds readers that there are positive actions they can take to help the planet (8, 10, 12). Overall, he takes a strong militant tone urging readers to revolution.

2. "Or let's talk water. . . . Or let's talk energy. . . . Or let's talk waste." Each of these deliberate sentence fragments follows the same grammatical pattern. The fragments and the parallelism together build a sense of urgency.

3. Jensen knows his proposal is radical and will come off as extreme. By quoting a respected environmental writer, he attempts to persuade readers that his ideas are both reasonable and shared by others.

VIRGINIA POSTREL
In Praise of Chain Stores *(p. 345)*

Given the state of the economy and recent declarations that small business is the foundation of future economic growth, students might be surprised by Postrel's argument in favor of big business. It may be worth noting that several of the retail outlets she mentions have failed in the years since this essay was published, leaving thousands of empty storefronts in their wake. Whether or not such failures affect the persuasiveness of her argument, Postrel's position should intrigue students who recognize themselves in her examples, especially if they're among those who have accepted the common assumption that chain stores are an unpleasant but necessary evil in modern American life.

One way to initiate discussion may be to ask students who Postrel's audience is and how she seems to perceive them (see question 1 under "Purpose and Audience"). Building on this question, have students discuss the various audiences they write to when they compose arguments. Their instructors? Their friends? Members of a particular group who have the power to act on their ideas? How do their strategies change according to their assumed readership?

Meaning

1. Postrel cites complaints, exemplified by statements made by Thomas Friedman and Rachel Dresbeck, that the ubiquity of chain stores drains cities and towns of local color, with the result that "everywhere looks like everywhere else" (paragraph 4). Although she agrees that "you do find the same chains everywhere" (1), she rejects the general complaint on two grounds. First, she argues, places do *not* all look the same: "[t]errain and weather and culture" are as varied and distinct as they've always been (4–5). And second, she points out, the criticisms she opposes tend to come from privileged travelers who have no right to complain: "this isn't tourism; it's life," she says (9). And for those who live in the places in question, chains provide multiple benefits that far outweigh any concerns about appearances.

2. Rejecting chain stores, Postrel argues in paragraphs 7–10, deprives local residents of amenities, slows development, and, most important, deadens cities by "driving business to the suburbs" (10).

Purpose and Audience

1. A *cosmopolite* is a sophisticated urban traveler. Synonyms in the essay include "urbanists" (paragraph 3), "journalists looking for obvious local color" (5), "frequent travelers" (7), and "tourists" (8). Postrel seems to imagine—justifiably—that readers of the *Atlantic* fit this description. She assumes that her audience consists of educated elites who share critics' disdain for national chains—a disdain, she implies, that is born of bias and privilege.

2. Her purpose is to persuade activists and local planning boards that their opposition to chain stores is not only misguided but destructive. She seems to expect readers to take positive action toward approving chain stores in local development.

Method and Structure

1. The introduction serves to establish the argument that Postrel will counter. By expressing the opposing viewpoint uncritically, she shows that she understands readers' concerns, then surprises them by rejecting such concerns as "obvious nonsense" (paragraph 4).

2. Postrel gives five specific reasons in paragraphs 7 and 8 to support her position that chain stores are good for America: they lower prices for consumers, they create efficiency for businesses, they provide variety for local residents, they facilitate the growth of emerging towns, and they offer consistency and familiarity for those who relocate. How persuasive students find these reasons will depend, of course, on their own perspectives and assumptions.

3. For Postrel, "character" (or "local color") (paragraph 5) is the sum of ineffable qualities that make a place unique—the distinct landscapes, weather patterns, and traditions that differentiate one place from another. She is careful to define the term because, in order to refute critics who argue that chains have resulted in a universal sameness across the country, she first has to establish that local character still exists, and that it has nothing to do with retail outlets: "Stores don't give places their character. Terrain and weather and culture do" (5).

Language

1. "Every well-traveled cosmopolite knows that America is mind-numbingly monotonous" (paragraph 1). "The suburbs are the worst" (2). "Chandler must be hell" (2). The irony in Postrel's introduction effectively sets up her point that her opponents' position is "obvious nonsense" (4), although it may confuse some readers initially.

2. In her introduction, Postrel quotes opposing views without comment so that she can establish the nature of the argument (and conventional wisdom) she will counter. Then, in the body of her essay, she quotes journalists and consumers who praise chain establishments to back up her assertion that regular people are grateful for such stores and restaurants. And in her conclusion, she quotes an expert to establish the validity of her most significant point: that opposition to chain stores is harmful to communities.

SHERRY TURKLE
Privacy Has a Politics (p. 352)

Turkle is both a renowned scholar and an engaging storyteller. In "Privacy Has a Politics" the author's narrative skill helps support her argument that by failing to protect their privacy, Americans risk losing civil liberties.

Of the people who relinquish their privacy online, Turkle is clearly most concerned for high school and college students. It seems equally clear that she doesn't imagine those students as part of her audience. Classroom discussion might begin with how accurate your students find the author's characterization of them and their peers (see question 3 under "Language"). How much information about themselves have they revealed online? Are they comfortable with such levels of self-exposure, or have they felt twinges of worry? Why? Do they think Turkle portrays their attitudes and actions fairly? And to what extent does their assessment of the author's assumptions affect their response to her argument?

Meaning

1. The author cites a combination of peer pressure (paragraphs 2, 5, 8), insecurity (6), and naiveté (2, 9) to explain why high school and college students so readily expose themselves through technology. She reminds readers of the potential for embarrassment (2) and asserts the possibility for government surveillance (3–6) and loss of civil liberties (7–9) in an effort to persuade them to hold their personal information private.

2. In paragraphs 3–5, Turkle blames an Internet version of Foucault's panopticon—a sense of surveillance and potential censure intensified by the lack of privacy online—for creating "a chilling effect on political speech" (1) and a fear of engaging in "political behavior that might get you into trouble" (2). She amplifies her concern in paragraph 7, when she cautions that "the Internet has fulfilled the dream of the panopticon."

3. Turkle warns that Americans' ability to protect their rights is threatened by the political apathy stemming from a feeling of helplessness (paragraph 6) inculcated by an online culture that asserts the best response to lack of privacy "is to just be good" (7). The less privacy we have as individuals, she argues, the more we resign ourselves to government abuse.

Purpose and Audience

1. Turkle's thesis is stated most fully in paragraph 9: "In democracy, perhaps we all need to begin with the assumption that everyone has something to hide, a zone of private action and reflection, one that must be protected no matter what our techno-enthusiasms." Her purpose is to make readers rethink their positions, of course, but more so to start "a conversation" (10) by questioning assumptions.

2. Turkle's audience, while nonspecialized, is apparently educated, for her essay contains several cultural and historical references (a wiretapping scandal, Foucault's panopticon, the McCarthy era, Luddites) that young students, in particular, might not be expected to recognize.

Method and Structure

1. By acknowledging the Web's political benefits before raising concerns about its political dangers, Turkle simultaneously addresses an opposing viewpoint and enhances her credibility by establishing herself as a reasonable observer.

2. Turkle's argument appeals to both reason and emotion. The closest reasoning appears in paragraphs 4–6, where the author seeks causes and forges a connection between acquiescence to expectations of self-surveillance and resignation in the face of "public exposure." She appeals to emotion throughout, but especially when discussing her teenaged informants—for instance, in paragraph 9: "I am haunted . . ."

3. Turkle says that she regards the mailbox episode as a "civics lesson." Certainly it offers a powerful reminder that the US government has been known to monitor and jail its citizens for highly questionable reasons, and could feasibly do so again. At the same time, the story allows her to reiterate her conviction that privacy is a fundamental American right and to explain how it protects civil liberty.

Language

1. In its literal sense, a panopticon is an architectural design that places an observation tower at the center of a round structure. In Foucault's metaphor, it is a cultural environment that fosters a paranoid sense of constant exposure, creating a dystopia in which citizens police themselves out of fear. What troubles Turkle is not just that Foucault's vision of imposed discipline seems to have become reality online, but also that some technology advocates have misinterpreted the concept, "with no apparent irony" (paragraph 7), as a justification for giving up privacy (3).

2. The allusion is to the early nineteenth-century political movement in which textile workers, led by Ned Ludd, protested the Industrial Revolution by smashing machinery. The term *Luddite* has come to carry a negative connotation, suggesting a stubborn resistance to technological change. Turkle is insisting that despite her concerns, she doesn't mean to be destructive.

3. Although Turkle exhibits a genuine concern for young people, some students might (reasonably) find her tone patronizing or condescending.

MARTIN LUTHER KING, JR.

I Have a Dream (p. 358)

King's inspirational speech offers an excellent opportunity to explore the use and effectiveness of emotional appeals (see questions 2 and 3 under "Purpose and Audience"). It also, of course, provides a context for discussing the improvements or lack of improvements in African American civil rights over the past four decades.

As effective as it is in print, the speech was even more effective in King's original delivery. A recording or film of his delivery—sonorous and movingly cadenced—can help students appreciate why the speech is so memorable. It can also encourage comparison between written and spoken persuasion: what are the strengths and weaknesses of each form?

Meaning

1. African Americans, along with white people who support them, must continue to strive nonviolently for freedom, justice, and equality.
2. The nation's African Americans are oppressed by segregation and discrimination—isolated in poverty, subject to police brutality and harassment, denied access to public places, denied the vote.
3. Violence would deprive the civil rights movement of "dignity and discipline," and it would lose supporters (paragraph 6). Those who have been jailed or beaten should view their suffering as "creative" and have "faith that unearned suffering is redemptive" (8).
4. King dreams of brotherhood, equality, freedom, justice, and peace. By alluding to the American dream, he reminds his audience that none of these components of the dream are a reality for African Americans.

Purpose and Audience

1. King wanted to inspire his listeners to continue their struggle nonviolently—while also sending a message to the nation about the movement's determination to achieve its goals. Thus he emphasizes why the struggle is important (paragraphs 1–4); warns of the movement's seriousness (5); urges nonviolence (6); urges struggle until the goals are won, whatever the hardships (7–9); and details a dream of a different America (10–23).

2. King is primarily addressing people who, like him, want equality for African Americans and are willing to work for it. He assumes that the audience agrees with him in paragraphs 1–5 and 10–23; but in paragraphs 6–9 he addresses listeners' impatience, frustration, fatigue, and fear.

3. King's listeners are already convinced of the need for change; they do not require a rational argument. Emotional appeals are particularly effective in inspiring an audience to act. King appeals to pride and dignity in paragraphs 6–9; to his listeners' religious beliefs in paragraphs 8, 18–19, and 23; and to their patriotism in paragraphs 1, 3, 11, and 20–22.

4. In paragraphs 5 and 7 King lets doubters and opponents know that the struggle will not stop until the goals of freedom, equality, and justice are fully achieved.

Method and Structure

1. King first establishes the common ground with his listeners (paragraphs 3–5); then urges them to continue struggling nonviolently, whatever the emotional or physical costs (6–9); and finally creates a picture of the better world they can help achieve with their action (10–23). Thus he builds to an inspirational crescendo.

2. As mentioned in the editors' headnote to the speech, King spoke from the steps of the Lincoln Memorial, and Lincoln's Emancipation Proclamation was, as King says, "a joyous daybreak to end the long night of captivity." In reminding listeners—both followers and opponents—of what had been promised one hundred years before, King sets up an effective contrast with what actually occurred and underlines the necessity and urgency of change.

3. The Declaration of Independence created a bank of justice with "vaults of opportunity" (paragraph 4) and issued a note to all Americans that promised "life, liberty, and the pursuit of happiness." But the check issued to African Americans bounced, despite the fact that the bank had ample funds of freedom and justice. Most students will presumably find the comparison both clever and effective: it presents the plight of African Americans in terms readily understandable to everyone, while suggesting that the nation's unshared wealth consists of freedom and justice as well as money.

Language

1. King's language does not convey bitterness or hatred. Only once does he refer to those responsible for oppression and segregation ("whose

governor's lips are presently dripping with the words of interposition and nullification," paragraph 16). Otherwise, he focuses on the condition of African Americans and the work they have to do, and his words convey compassion, fervor, resoluteness: "lonely island of poverty" (2); "dark and desolate valley of segregation" (4), "There will be neither rest nor tranquility" (5), "We can never be satisfied" (7), "battered by the storms of persecution" (8), "Mississippi, a desert state sweltering with the heat of injustice and oppression" (13).

2. Throughout the speech, King's metaphors depict oppression as low, hot, dry, and dark: "the flames of withering injustice," "the long night of captivity" (paragraph 1); "the dark and desolate valley of segregation" (4); "This sweltering summer of the Negro's legitimate discontent" (5); "a desert state sweltering with the heat of injustice and oppression" (13). In contrast, King depicts freedom and equality as elevated, cool, moist, and light: "a joyous daybreak" (1); "the sunlit path of racial justice" (4); "an invigorating autumn of freedom and equality," "the bright day of justice" (5); "justice rolls down like waters" (7); "an oasis of freedom and justice" (13); "from every mountainside, let freedom ring" (20–22).

JONATHAN SWIFT

A Modest Proposal *(p. 365)*

Given the wars, genocide, nuclear threat, and terrorism of the twentieth and early twenty-first centuries, it is perhaps not surprising that students sometimes fail to see the irony in Swift's proposal. The editors' headnote to the essay (p. 365) should help prevent this misunderstanding, but one or two students may still arrive in class expressing outrage at Swift's monstrous plan, only to be embarrassed or angered when they learn the truth. If such a response seems likely, you can avert it by opening the discussion with the question of where Swift's irony first becomes apparent in the essay (all three "Purpose and Audience" questions, especially the second, can help). This question leads easily into a discussion of irony and satire—what they are, how they are created, what they achieve that straightforward expression does not, and so on.

Throughout the essay, Swift assumes the character of an entirely reasonable, thoughtful man who genuinely sympathizes with the poor and wants to help them. That this character makes such monstrous recommendations contributes substantially to the irony, of course. The second question under "Method and Structure" leads students to analyze how Swift makes his character seem so reasonable.

Meaning

1. The proposal is to kill Irish infants at the age of one year and sell their flesh for meat to the wealthy. The main problem is that Irish peasants and laborers have no way to relieve their poverty, since they are oppressed by their landlords and have no reasonable source of income. Swift's proposal will provide peasants with a salable commodity while relieving them of the financial burden of raising their children.

2. The reasonable solutions are outlined in paragraph 29 (e.g., developing Irish industry, eliminating factions, improving the national character) but rejected because Swift has lost faith that "some hearty and sincere attempt to put them in practice" (30) will ever occur. He reveals his disillusionment with "sincere attempts" in paragraph 31: he has become "wearied out for many years with offering vain, idle, visionary thoughts, and at length utterly despairing of success."

Purpose and Audience

1. The *narrator's purpose* is to suggest a way of solving the persistent problem of Ireland's poor. *Swift's purpose* is to condemn the oppression and self-centeredness of the English and Irish that both create and perpetuate the condition of the poor. The purposes overlap in confronting the poverty and the inability or refusal of those responsible to do anything about it. They diverge in recommending solutions: Swift has none beyond the reasonable and despairs of their implementation; his narrator has a better idea.

2. Similar clues appear in paragraph 22 and then often in 29 and 31–32. Swift may have inserted them partly to prevent misreadings and partly to score some points more directly than irony would allow.

3. Answers will vary. Many students may see that Swift's pushing morality to its limits would awaken readers to Ireland's problems. Other students may not be able to move beyond their repulsion to appreciate Swift's point. Thus satire may be very effective at jarring readers into new ways of thinking, but it can also overshadow the point it is intended to make.

Method and Structure

1. Paragraphs 1–7 introduce the needs the proposal addresses and some calculations it is based on. (The long introduction is necessary to pave the way for the proposal.) Paragraphs 8–16 present the proposal, some more calculations to show its potential, and some ideas of how it would work. Paragraphs 17–18 present and reject a possible "refinement" of the proposal. Paragraph 19 dispenses with a possible remaining problem. Paragraphs 20–28 lay out the plan's many advantages. Paragraphs 29–33 anticipate objections and dispense with them.

2. The narrator repeatedly describes the time and care he has spent pondering this problem (paragraph 4, first sentence; the use of the first person with verbs of consideration in 6: "I calculate," "I subtract," "I apprehend," "I confess," etc.). He puts forth his proposal with modesty and humility (8, 10). His attitude is respectful throughout ("as I must confess," 15; "although I rather recommend," 16; "But with due deference," 17). He piously objects to cruelty (5, 17). He refers repeatedly to the good of the nation (2, 7, 19, 21, 23, 29, 33). This, together with the heavily ironic final paragraph, absolves him of any personal interest in the proposal.

3. *Process analysis examples*: the method of calculation (paragraph 6) and the workings of the proposal (10–15), both showing the proposal to be based on careful consideration. *Cause-and-effect analysis examples*: the advantages of the proposal (21–28), all positive ways the proposal will benefit both the poor (24, 26) and the rich (21–23, 25, 27–28).

Language

1. A few of the many examples of irony: "a fair, cheap, or easy method of making these children sound, useful members of the commonwealth" (paragraph 2); "we can neither employ them in handicraft or agriculture; we neither build houses . . . nor cultivate land" (6); "some scrupulous people might be apt to censure such a practice . . . as a little bordering upon cruelty" (17); "they are every day dying and rotting . . . as fast as can be reasonably expected. And as to the younger laborers, they are now in almost as hopeful a condition" (19).

2. The livestock expressions coolly dehumanize the Irish poor, making the narrator's proposal more palatable—and Swift's satire more horrifying. These expressions also reflect and thus satirize the attitudes of the English and the wealthy Irish toward the poor. Examples: "a child just dropped from its dam" (paragraph 4); "salable commodity" (7); "reserved for breed" (note also the comparison to "sheep, black cattle, or swine"), "one male will be sufficient to serve four females" (10); "Infant's flesh will be in season throughout the year" (13); "the

carcass of a good fat child, which . . . will make four dishes of excellent nutritive meat" (14); "dressing them hot from the knife as we do roasting pigs" (16); "their flesh was generally tough and lean," "they soon would become breeders themselves" (17); "procure the best receipts for dressing [the meat] to perfection" (25); "yearling child" (27).

3. Swift's style, of course, is both somewhat archaic ("increaseth," [paragraph 11]; "how well soever intended," [17]) and also quite formal, with long, complicated sentences, extensive subordination, learned words, and the like. For one example: "As to my own part, having turned my thoughts for many years upon this important subject, and maturely weighed the several schemes of other projectors, I have always found them grossly mistaken in their computation" (4). Undoubtedly, many students will find the style a stumbling block. Others, however, may recognize that it takes only a little patience to follow and becomes easier as they get used to it. They may also recognize that the formality of the style perfectly complements the narrator's stuffy self-presentation.

WALTER MOSLEY

A former computer programmer turned writer, Walter Mosley (born 1952) is best known for his critically acclaimed Easy Rawlins detective novels. Mosley grew up in the Watts section of Los Angeles, California, attended Goddard College, and received a BA in political science from Johnson State College. He worked for Mobil Oil for several years before pursuing a master's degree in writing from the City College of the City University of New York. In addition to the Easy Rawlins series, Mosley has published a number of mystery and science-fiction novels notable for examining issues of race and class—among them Blue Light *(1998),* Fearless Jones *(2001), and* The Last Days of Ptolemy Grey *(2010)—as well as several collections of short stories. An outspoken social critic and political activist, Mosley also writes provocative non-fiction, including regular essay contributions for the* New Yorker *and the* Nation; *as well as two books that analyze the failings of capitalism and American culture:* Workin' on the Chain Gang *(2000) and* Twelve Steps Toward Political Revelation *(2011). He lives in New York.*

Show Me the Money

In this essay Mosley proposes a new system for understanding class structure in the United States. A longer version first appeared in the Nation *as part of a cycle of essays Mosley wrote to start a dialogue about American cultural issues that have, as he put it, "weakened our spirits to the point of collapse."*

"The rich get richer . . ." This truism is irrefutable. ". . . and the 1
poor get poorer." We look away from ourselves, and our loved ones, when the latter phrase is used to complete the saying.

   Often only the first part of this age-old axiom is quoted. It's as 2
if we are silently saying, "There's no reason to talk about the poor, about poverty. Let's just accept the notion that money migrates toward money and leave it at that."

But where does this money, which moves so unerringly into 3 rich folks' pockets, come from? This is one of the most important questions in everyday working people's lives. Because the money that makes the rich richer comes out of the sweat, the sacrifice, and ultimately the blood of working men and women. . . .

Most people I know consider themselves middle-class work- 4 ers. They're making good money, they say, and have good credit at the bank. Their children will go to good colleges and get better jobs. They will retire in comfort and travel to Europe (or Africa) to see the genesis of their culture.

These self-proclaimed middle-class citizens feel a certain 5 private smugness about their proven ability to make it in this world while those in the working and lower classes—because of upbringing, lack of intelligence or will, or bad luck—are merely the fuel for the wealth of the nation.

But how do you know where you fit in the class system? Is it 6 a level of income? Is it defined by education or the kind of job you possess? Is class a function of your relationship to your labor? For instance, are you in the middle class because you own your own business? Or are we defined by our rung on the ladder? As long as we are not at the bottom (or the top), then we can say we are in the middle.

It's a difficult question because the economic state of every 7 one's life in this world is in perpetual flux. Depression, inflation, recession—all these and many other economic events continually change our finances and redefine our position in society. Our money grows in the bank, but at the same time it loses value. Our property increases in value, but taxes and expenses also rise. We say that we own the mortgage on our home, but more often than not the mortgage controls us. To buy a $10,000 home we pay $40,000 over thirty years. Where did that extra $30,000 go?

It seems to me that we need a rule-of-thumb definition of 8 class. We can't use the pristine forms of geometry to prove where we are and what we're worth. Mathematical sums don't define wealth; the ability to control your time and quality of life does.

I'd like to put forward a system of class definition that is 9 grounded in what I believe to be a common-sense approach to the issue.

Poverty is defined, in my system, by people not being able 10
to cover the basic necessities in their lives. Indispensable medical care, nutrition, a place to live: all these essentials, for poor
people, are often and chronically beyond reach. If a poor person
needs $10 a day to make ends meet, often he or she only makes
eight and a half.

Wealth, in my definition, is when money is no longer an issue 11
or a question. Wealthy people don't know how much money they
have or how much they make. Their worth is gauged in property,
natural resources and power, in doors they can go through and
the way the law works. Wealth moves like a shark over the rock-
bound crustaceans of the poor and working classes.

The middle classes, which logic would tell us occupy the 12
space between poverty and wealth, are made up of two very different subspecies. One is the working class; the other is the class
of limited privilege.

It is my proposition that the great majority of us fall into the 13
former group. The privileged middle class are people who have to
work for a living but who can buy almost anything they desire:
a summer cottage, a prestige car, berths at the finer schools for
their children. These people are lawyers, real estate developers,
the owners of small and successful businesses. If someone in the
class of privilege were to lose his job or experience reversals in his
business, he would have time (between nine and twelve months)
to consider his options before any part of his lifestyle would
necessitate change. His children could stay in private schools, he
could still go to fine restaurants and the opera on Friday nights,
and even donate to the same charities.

But if a person from the working class loses her job, she 14
would have to find an equivalent one within the month or it'll be
fast food and junior college for everyone in the family.

Working-class people are (excuse the Marxism) wage-slaves. 15
Those in the working class live on the edge of poverty, saying to
themselves that they are doing all right. They drink and watch far
too much TV. They buy Lotto tickets and live moderate lives that
are far beyond their means. The profit they generate flows to the
rich, and they borrow to fill out the coffers.

Most Americans are working-class wage-slaves, arguing that 16
they're better off. This fantasy, more than any other confusion,

hobbles us. Because we fear to see how delicate our economic state is, we cannot motivate ourselves to demand change.

Capitalism, the accrual of wealth from labor, is the religion 17 of America; poverty our cardinal sin. To recognize our position in relation to wealth would be perceived as a confession of wrong-doing, and so we stoically bear up, pretending we are doing all right. And because we don't see ourselves clearly, we have poor healthcare, no adequate insurance for old age, poisons in our water and our food and the continual nagging fear that things may at any moment fall apart.

Where is the money? It's not in our bank accounts or serving 18 our people. It's not in affordable housing, quality education or the development of sciences that would better the species and the planet. It's not being used for the purpose of global peace.

America is the wealthiest nation in the world, by far, but we 19 the American people are not wealthy. We, most of us, live on the border of poverty. In the distance are towering silvery skyscrap-ers housing our corporations and our billionaires. But do not be fooled. This skyline does not belong to us. We are not partners in the corporation of America. . . .

This knowledge, as depressing and oppressing as it is, is also 20 a harbinger of hope. Poverty is not our fault or our destiny. We, the poor and working class, have built this nation and it, along with all its fabulous wealth, belongs to us. From the Atlantic to the Pacific we, the workers, are the ones who hold sway. And every vault, every clinic, every drop of sweat fallen upon American soil is our democratic birthright. . . .

A man can be rich, but only a nation can be wealthy. And if 21 any person of any age suffers from poverty, then our whole coun-try bears the shame.

Meaning

1. What is the author's thesis? What reasons does he give for classifying?
2. In which category does Mosley place himself, and what does he say about this group in relation to the others?
3. In paragraph 3 Mosley writes, "The money that makes the rich rich-er comes out of the sweat, the sacrifice, and ultimately the blood of working men and women." What does he mean?

Purpose and Audience

1. What do you think Mosley's purpose is? Do you think his classification is really motivated by a desire to offer a "harbinger of hope" (paragraph 20)?

2. Who is Mosley's intended audience? What in the text supports your answer?

3. What do you think of Mosley's categories? Are they complete? convincing? If you know people in these categories, do they match Mosley's descriptions?

Method and Structure

1. How does or doesn't the method of classification lend itself to Mosley's purpose?

2. Summarize each of the groups Mosley identifies (even those he does not discuss in detail). What is Mosley's principle of classification? Why does he categorize the groups the way he does?

3. What do you notice about Mosley's organization and the space he devotes to each category? Why do you think he varies the amount of space he gives to the categories? Do some of the categories get shortchanged?

4. OTHER METHODS   In addition to classification, Mosley relies heavily on definition to advance his argument. Why do you think he defines each class so painstakingly? What would the essay lose if Mosley didn't define his terms?

Language

1. Examine Mosley's tone. How would you characterize his attitude toward his subject? Is he angry, resigned, hopeful, something else? Does his overall tone strengthen his argument or weaken it? Why? (If necessary, look up *tone* in the Glossary.)

2. Mosley uses a lot of "five-dollar words." He also injects the first person (*I*, *me*, *we*, and *our*) throughout his essay. How do his diction and point of view relate to his purpose and to his audience?

3. Mosley asks his readers to "excuse the Marxism" when he introduces the phrase "wage-slaves" in paragraph 15. Look up the term *Marxism* in a dictionary or encyclopedia and identify other economic terms in Mosley's essay that hold Marxist connotations. (See the Glossary for a definition of *connotation*.) What does his use of such politically charged language reveal about Mosley's relationship to his subject?

Writing Topics

1. Write a response to Mosley's essay. Does it anger you? irritate you? reassure you? inspire you? make you feel something else? Did it lead you to rethink your own class status? Do you find Mosley's categories, definitions, and conclusions to be fair? Why, or why not? Support your response with details from Mosley's essay and examples from your own experience.

2. Using Mosley's essay as a model, write an essay that proposes a new classification of a group of people (teachers, bosses, or salesclerks, for example) for the purpose of advancing an argument about a larger issue. Sort your subject into classes according to a consistent principle, and provide plenty of details to clarify the classes you decide on. In your essay, be sure to explain to your readers why the classification should persuade them to accept your argument.

3. Mosley's classification questions the foundations of the American dream, which holds that a person from even the most humble circumstances can achieve prosperity through determination and hard work. How realistic, or not, do you think the American dream is today? Write an essay answering this question. As evidence for your argument, you may want to discuss how, if at all, the American dream applies to you, given your social and economic background.

CLASSIFICATION

Select one of the following topics, or any other topic they suggest, for an essay developed by classification. Be sure to choose a topic you care about so that classification is a means of communicating an idea, not an end in itself.

People

1. Boring people
2. Laundromat users
3. Teachers or students
4. Parents or children

Psychology and Behavior

5. Ways of punishing misbehavior
6. Obsessions
7. Diets
8. Dreams

Things

9. Buildings on campus
10. Junk foods
11. Computer games
12. Cars or trucks

Sports and Performance

13. Styles of baseball pitching or another sports skill
14. Gym members
15. Styles of dance, guitar playing, acting, or another performance art

Communications Media

16. Talk-show hosts
17. Magazines or newspapers
18. Online discussion groups

Chapter 6

PROCESS ANALYSIS

USING THE METHOD

Game rules, repair manuals, cookbooks, science textbooks—these and many other familiar works are essentially process analyses. They explain how to do something (play Monopoly, patch a hole in the wall), how to make something (compost, bread), or how something happens (how hormones affect behavior, how a computer stores and retrieves data). That is, they explain a sequence of actions with a specified result (the **process**) by dividing it into its component steps (the **analysis**). Almost always, the purpose of process analysis is to explain, but sometimes a parallel purpose is to prove something about the process or to evaluate it: to show how easy it is to change a tire, for instance, or to urge aspiring marathon runners to follow a training regimen on the grounds of its safety and effectiveness.

Process analysis overlaps several other methods discussed in this book. The analysis is actually the method examined in Chapter 4—dividing a thing or concept into its elements. And we analyze a process much as we analyze causes and effects (Chapter 9), except that cause-and-effect analysis asks mainly *why* something happens or *why* it has certain results, whereas process analysis asks mainly *how*. Process analysis also overlaps narration (Chapter 2), for the steps involved are almost always presented in chronological sequence. But narration recounts a unique sequence of events with a unique result, whereas process analysis explains a series of steps with the same predictable result. You might narrate a particularly exciting baseball game, but you would analyze the process—the rules—of any baseball game.

Processes occur in several varieties, including mechanical (a car engine), natural (cell division), psychological (acquisition of sex roles), and political (the electoral process). Process analyses generally fall into one of two types:

- A **directive** process analysis tells you how to do or make something: bake a cake, tune a guitar, negotiate a deal, write a process analysis. You outline the steps in the process completely so that the reader who follows them can achieve the specified result. Generally you address the reader directly, using the second-person *you* ("You should think of negotiation as collaboration rather than competition") or the imperative (commanding) mood of verbs ("Add one egg yolk and stir vigorously").

- An **explanatory** process analysis provides the information necessary for readers to understand the process, but more to satisfy their curiosity than to teach them how to perform it. You may address the reader directly, but the third-person *he, she, it,* and *they* are more common.

Whether directive or explanatory, process analyses usually follow a chronological sequence. Most processes can be divided into phases or stages, and these in turn can be divided into steps. The stages of changing a tire, for instance, may be jacking up the car, removing the flat, putting on the spare, and lowering the car. The steps within, say, jacking up the car may be setting the emergency brake, blocking the other wheels, loosening the lug nuts, positioning the jack, and raising the car. Following a chronological order, you cover the stages in sequence and, within each stage, cover the steps in sequence.

To ensure that the reader can duplicate the process or understand how it unfolds, you must fully detail each step and specify the reasons for it. In addition, you must be sure that the reader grasps the sequence of steps, their duration, and where they occur. To this end, transitional expressions that signal time and place—such as *after five minutes, meanwhile, to the left,* and *below*—can be invaluable.

Though a chronological sequence is usual for process analysis, you may have to interrupt or modify it to suit your material.

You may need to pause in a sequence to provide definitions of specialized terms or to explain why a step is necessary or how it relates to the preceding and following steps. Instructions on how to change a tire, for instance, might stop you briefly to explain that the lug nuts should be slightly loosened *before* the car is jacked up in order to prevent the wheel from spinning afterward.

DEVELOPING AN ESSAY BY PROCESS ANALYSIS

Getting Started

You'll find yourself writing process analyses for your courses in school (for instance, explaining how a drug affects brain chemistry), in memos at work (recommending a new procedure for approving cost estimates), or in life outside work (giving written directions to a pet sitter). To find a subject when an assignment doesn't make one obvious, examine your interests or hobbies or think of something whose workings you'd like to research in order to understand them better. Explore the subject by listing chronologically all the necessary stages and steps.

Remember your readers while you are generating ideas. Consider how much background information they need, where specialized terms must be defined, and where examples must be given. Especially if you are providing instructions, consider what special equipment readers will need, what hitches they may encounter, and what the interim results should be. To build a table, for instance, what tools will readers need? What should they do if the table wobbles even after the corners are braced? What should the table feel like after the first sanding or the first varnishing?

Forming a Thesis

While you are exploring your subject, decide on the point of your analysis and express it in a thesis sentence that will guide your writing and tell your readers what to expect. The simplest thesis states what the process is and its basic stages. For instance:

> Building a table is a three-stage process of cutting, assembling, and finishing.

But you can increase your readers' interest in the process by also conveying your reason for writing about it. You might assert that a seemingly difficult process is actually quite simple, or vice versa:

> Changing a tire does not require a mechanic's skill or strength; on the contrary, a ten-year-old child can do it.

> Windsurfing may look easy, but it demands the knowledge of an experienced sailor and the balance of an acrobat.

You might show how the process demonstrates a more general principle:

> The process of getting a bill through Congress illustrates majority rule at work.

Or you might assert that a process is inefficient or unfair:

> The state's outdated registration procedure forces new car buyers to waste hours standing in line.

Regardless of how you structure your thesis sentence, try to make it clear that your process analysis has a point. Usually you will want to include a direct statement of your thesis in your introduction so that readers know what you're writing about and why the process should matter to them.

Organizing

Many successful process analyses begin with an overview of the process to which readers can relate each step. In such an introduction you can lead up to your thesis sentence by specifying when or where the process occurs, why it is useful or interesting or controversial, what its result is, and the like. Especially if you are providing instructions, you can also use the introduction (perhaps a separate paragraph) to provide essential background information, such as the materials readers will need.

After the introduction, you should present the stages, and the steps within each stage, distinctly and in chronological order, devoting perhaps one or two paragraphs to each stage. This ordered sequence helps readers see how a process unfolds or how to perform it. Try not to deviate from it unless you have good reason to—perhaps because your process requires grouping simultaneous steps, or your readers need definitions of terms, reasons for steps, connections between separated steps, and other explanations.

A process essay may end simply with the result. But you might conclude with a summary of the major stages, with a comment on the significance or usefulness of the process, or with a recommendation for changing a process you have criticized. For a directive process essay, you might state the standards by which readers can measure their success or give an idea of how much practice may be necessary to master the process.

Drafting

While drafting your process analysis, concentrate on getting in as many details as you can: every step, how each relates to the one before and after, how each contributes to the result. In revising you can always delete unnecessary details and connective tissue if they seem cumbersome, but in the first draft it's better to over-explain than underexplain.

Drafting a process analysis is a good occasion to practice a straightforward, concise writing style, because clarity is more important than originality of expression. Stick to plain language and uncomplicated sentences. If you want to dress up your style a bit, you can always do so after you have made yourself clear.

Revising and Editing

When you've finished your draft, ask a friend to read it. If you have explained a process, your friend should be able to understand it. If you have given instructions, your friend should be able to follow them, or imagine following them. Then examine the draft yourself against the following questions.

- *Have you adhered to a chronological sequence?* Unless there is a compelling and clear reason to use some other arrangement, the stages and steps of your analysis should proceed in chronological order. If you had to depart from that order—to define or explain or to sort out simultaneous steps—the reasons should be clear to your readers.

- *Have you included all necessary steps and omitted any unnecessary digressions?* The explanation should be as complete as possible but not cluttered with information, however interesting, that contributes nothing to the readers' understanding of the process.

- *Have you accurately gauged your readers' need for information?* You don't want to bore readers with explanations and details they don't need. But erring in the other direction is even worse, for your essay will achieve little if readers cannot understand it.

- *Have you shown readers how each step fits into the whole process and relates to the other steps?* If your analysis seems to break down into a multitude of isolated steps, you may need to organize them more clearly into stages.

- *Have you used plenty of informative transitions?* Transitions such as *at the same time* and *on the other side of the machine* indicate when steps start and stop, how long they last, and where they occur. (A list of such expressions appears in the Glossary under *transitions.*) The expressions should be as informative as possible; signals such as *first . . . second . . . third . . . fourteenth* and *next . . . next* do not help indicate movement in space or lapses in time, and they quickly grow tiresome.

FIROOZEH DUMAS

Born in 1966 in Abadan, Iran, and raised there until her family emigrated in 1972, Firoozeh Dumas has lived in northern California most of her life. After marrying a French immigrant she met while both were students at the University of California at Berkeley, Dumas took up writing about her unusual childhood and quirky family as a way to share stories with her children. The unanticipated result was a bestselling collection of essays: Funny in Farsi: A Memoir of Growing Up Iranian in America *(2003). Dumas decided to make a career of writing and has since published a second book,* Laughing Without an Accent: Adventures of an Iranian American, at Home and Abroad *(2008), as well as essays in the* New York Times Magazine, *the* Los Angeles Times, *the* Wall Street Journal, *the* San Francisco Chronicle, *and* Good Housekeeping. *She also lectures regularly and is an occasional guest on National Public Radio.*

Sweet, Sour, and Resentful

Dumas writes, she has said, partly to dispel American fears of Iranian people by revealing their "shared humanity." She does just that in this essay, written in 2009 for Gourmet *magazine, by taking a humorous look at the elaborate weekly dinner parties her family hosted when she was a child.*

My mother's main ingredient in cooking was resentment—not 1 that I can blame her. In 1979, my family was living temporarily in Newport Beach, California. Our real home was in Abadan, a city in the southwest of Iran. Despite its desert location and ubiquitous refineries, Abadan was the quintessential small town. Everybody's father (including my own) worked for the National

Iranian Oil Company, and almost all the moms stayed home. The employees' kids attended the same schools. No one locked their doors. Whenever I hear John Mellencamp's "Small Town," I think of Abadan, although I'm guessing John Mellencamp was thinking of somewhere else when he wrote that song.

By the time of the Iranian revolution,[1] we had adjusted to life 2 in California. We said "Hello" and "Have a nice day" to perfect strangers, wore flip-flops, and grilled cheeseburgers next to our kebabs. We never understood why Americans put ice in tea or bought shampoo that smelled like strawberries, but other than that, America felt like home.

When the revolution happened, thousands left Iran for 3 Southern California. Since we were one of the few Iranian families already there, our phone did not stop ringing. Relatives, friends, friends of relatives, friends of friends, and people whose connection we never quite figured out called us with questions about settling into this new land. Displaying the hospitality that Iranians so cherish, my father extended a dinner invitation to everyone who called. As a result, we found ourselves feeding dozens of people every weekend.

The marathon started on Monday, with my mother planning 4 the menu while letting us know that she was already tired. Fortunately, our rice dishes were made to be shared; our dilemma, however, was space. Our condo was small. Our guests squeezed onto the sofa, sat on the floor, or overflowed onto the patio. We eventually had to explain to our American neighbors why there were so many cars parked in front of our place every weekend. My mother, her diplomatic skills in full swing, had me deliver plates of Persian food, decorated with radish roses and mint sprigs, to them. In time, we learned not to share *fesenjan*, pomegranate stew with ground walnuts. "Yes, now that you mention it, it does look like mud, but it's really good," I'd explain, convincing no one.

Because my mother did not drive, my father took her to buy 5 ingredients every Tuesday after work. In Abadan, my mother and I had started most days in the market, going from vendor to vendor looking for herbs, vegetables, and fruits. The fish came from the

---

[1]In 1979 fundamentalist rebels led by Ayatollah Ruhollah Khomeini overthrew the Iranian monarchy and established the Islamic Republic of Iran, a theocratic dictatorship. [Editors' note.]

Karun and Arvand (Shatt al Arab) rivers, the *lavash* and the *sangak* breads were freshly baked, and the chickens were still alive. We were locavores by necessity and foodies without knowing it. In America, I learned that the time my parents spent shopping was in direct correlation to the degree of my mother's bad mood. An extra-long trip meant that my mother could not find everything she needed, a point she would make loud and clear when she got home: "Why don't they let fruit ripen here?" "Why are the chickens so huge and flavorless?" "I couldn't find fresh herbs." "My feet hurt." "How am I supposed to get everything done?"

The first step was preparing the herbs. My mother insisted 6 that the parsley, cilantro, and chives for *qormeh sabzi*, herb stew, had to be finely chopped by hand. The food processor, she explained, squished them. As she and my father sat across the table wielding huge knives, they argued incessantly. My father did his best to help her. It wasn't enough. As soon as the mountain of herbs was chopped, my mother started frying them. At any given time, my mother was also frying onions. Every few days, while my father was watching the six o'clock news, my mother would hand him a dozen onions, a cutting board, and a knife. No words were exchanged. Much to my father's relief, I once volunteered for this task, but apparently my slices were neither thin enough nor even. It took my father's precision as an engineer to slice correctly.

While all four burners were in use, my mother mixed the 7 ground beef, rice, split peas, scallions, and herbs for stuffed grape leaves. I chopped the stems of the grape leaves. I had tried stuffing them once, but my rolls, deemed not tight enough, were promptly unrolled and then rerolled by my mother.

In between cooking, my mother made yogurt—the thick, 8 sour variety that we couldn't find in America. She soaked walnuts and almonds in water to plump them up; fried eggplants for *kashk-e bademjan*, a popular appetizer with garlic, turmeric, mint, and whey; made *torshi-e limo*, a sour lemon condiment; and slivered orange peels. I had been fired from this task also, having left on far too much pith.

By the time our guests arrived, my mother was exhausted. 9 But the work was not finished. Rice, the foundation of the Persian meal, the litmus test of the cook's ability, cannot be prepared ahead of time. To wit, one day in Abadan, the phone rang when my mother was about to drain the rice. During the time it took her to answer the phone and tell her sister that she would call her back, the rice overcooked. Almost forty years later, I still remember my mother's disappointment and her explaining to my father that her sister had time to talk because my aunt's maid did all the cooking. My aunt did not even drain her own rice.

We certainly did not have a table big enough to set, so we simply stacked dishes and utensils, buffet-style. As the guest list grew, we added paper plates and plastic utensils. It was always my job to announce that dinner was ready. As people entered the dining room, they gasped at the sight of my mother's table. Her *zereshk polow*, barberry rice, made many emotional. There are no fresh barberries in America (my mother had brought dried berries from Iran in her suitcase), and the sight of that dish, with its distinct deep red hue, was a reminder of the life our guests had left behind.

Our dinners took days to cook and disappeared in twenty minutes. As our guests heaped their plates and looked for a place to sit, they lavished praise on my mother, who, according to tradition, deflected it all. "It's nothing," she said. "I wish I could've done more." When they told her how lucky she was to have me to help her, my mother politely nodded, while my father added, "Firoozeh's good at math."

On Sundays, my mother lay on the sofa, her swollen feet elevated, fielding thank-you phone calls from our guests. She had the same conversation a dozen times; each one ended with, "Of course you can give our name to your cousins." As I watched my mother experience the same draining routine week after week, I decided that tradition is good only if it brings joy to all involved. This includes the hostess. Sometimes, even our most cherished beliefs must evolve. Evolution, thy name is potluck.

Meaning

1. Why were weekend dinners so important to the author's parents and their guests? Consider not just the meals themselves but the larger context that prompted them.

2. In which sentence or sentences does Dumas state her thesis most directly?

3. What solution to her mother's exhausting role as hostess does Dumas propose in paragraph 12? Do you think her mother would have agreed to it? Why, or why not?

Purpose and Audience

1. What would you say is Dumas's purpose in this essay? Is it primarily to entertain readers by describing her family's weekly routine, or does she seem to have another purpose in mind?
2. How does Dumas seem to imagine her audience? To what extent could she assume that readers would appreciate her mother's situation?

Method and Structure

1. Why does Dumas begin her essay with an overview of life in Abadan and an allusion to the Iranian revolution (paragraphs 1–3)? What purpose does this opening serve?
2. What steps does Dumas identify in the process of hosting Iranian guests every weekend? How does she ensure that her analysis has coherence? (For a definition of *coherence*, see the Glossary.)
3. OTHER METHODS   What role does comparison and contrast play in paragraph 5?

Language

1. Explain how Dumas's tone contributes to the humor in her essay. (If necessary, look up *tone* in the Glossary.)
2. Where in the essay does Dumas use Persian words? What is their effect?
3. In paragraph 9, Dumas says that rice is "the litmus test" for Iranian cooks. What does she mean? What is a litmus test, and how does the phrase connect to the focus (and title) of Dumas's essay?

Writing Topics

1. Think of some rituals that are important to your family—for instance, a holiday celebration, a vacation activity, a way of decompressing after a stressful week. Choose one such ritual and write an essay that explains it to outsiders. Focus on the details and steps of the ritual itself as well as on the significance it has for you and for other members of your family.

2. What impression of herself does Dumas create in this essay? What adjectives would you use to describe the writer as she reveals herself on the page? Cite specific language from the essay to support your analysis.

3. Dumas writes about the struggle to adjust to mainstream American culture while maintaining ethnic ties. Based on "Sweet, Sour, and Resentful" and your own observations, write an essay that considers one aspect of the immigrant experience in the United States, such as the challenges of assimilation, the effects of prejudice, or the role of family ties and cultural loyalty.

LARS EIGHNER

*An essayist and fiction writer, Lars Eighner was born in 1948 in Texas
and attended the University of Texas at Austin. His novels and volumes of short fiction include* Bayou Boy and Other Stories *(1985),*
American Prelude *(1994),* Whispered in the Dark *(1995), and* Pawn
to Queen Four *(1995). He has also contributed essays and stories to*
Harper's Magazine, Advocate Men, *the* Guide, *and* Inches. *In 1988
Eighner became homeless after losing a job he had held for ten years
as an attendant in a mental hospital. His memoir about living on the
street,* Travels with Lizbeth *(1993), was critically acclaimed and sold
enough copies to get him back on his feet. Eighner now lives in a small
apartment in Austin.*

Dumpster Diving

This essay from the Utne Reader *was abridged from a prize-winning
piece first published in the* Threepenny Review *and later included in*
Travels with Lizbeth. *Eighner explains a process that you probably do
not want to learn: how to subsist on what you can scavenge from trash.
But, as Eighner observes, scavenging has lessons to teach about value.*

I began Dumpster diving about a year before I became homeless. 1

   I prefer the term *scavenging.* I have heard people, evidently 2
meaning to be polite, use the word *foraging,* but I prefer to reserve
that word for gathering nuts and berries and such, which I also
do, according to the season and opportunity.

   I like the frankness of the word *scavenging.* I live from the 3
refuse of others. I am a scavenger. I think it a sound and honorable
niche, although if I could I would naturally prefer to live the comfortable consumer life, perhaps—and only perhaps—as a slightly
less wasteful consumer owing to what I have learned as a scavenger.

   Except for jeans, all my clothes come from Dumpsters. Boom 4
boxes, candles, bedding, toilet paper, medicine, books, a typewriter,

a virgin male love doll, coins sometimes amounting to many dollars: all came from Dumpsters. And, yes, I eat from Dumpsters, too.

There is a predictable series of stages that a person goes 5 through in learning to scavenge. At first the new scavenger is filled with disgust and self-loathing. He is ashamed of being seen.

This stage passes with experience. The scavenger finds a pair 6 of running shoes that fit and look and smell brand-new. He finds a pocket calculator in perfect working order. He finds pristine ice cream, still frozen, more than he can eat or keep. He begins to understand: people do throw away perfectly good stuff, a lot of perfectly good stuff.

At this stage he may become lost and never recover. All the 7 Dumpster divers I have known come to the point of trying to acquire everything they touch. Why not take it, they reason, it is all free. This is of course, hopeless, and most divers come to realize that they must restrict themselves to items of relatively immediate utility.

The finding of objects is becoming something of an urban 8 art. Even respectable, employed people will sometimes find something tempting sticking out of a Dumpster or standing beside one. Quite a number of people, not all of them of the bohemian type, are willing to brag that they found this or that piece in the trash.

But eating from Dumpsters is the thing that separates the dil- 9 ettanti from the professionals. Eating safely involves three principles: using the senses and common sense to evaluate the condition of the found materials; knowing the Dumpsters of a given area and checking them regularly; and seeking always to answer the question "Why was this discarded?"

Yet perfectly good food can be found in Dumpsters. Canned 10 goods, for example, turn up fairly often in the Dumpsters I frequent. I also have few qualms about dry foods such as crackers, cookies, cereal, chips, and pasta if they are free of visible contaminants and still dry and crisp. Raw fruits and vegetables with intact skins seem perfectly safe to me, excluding, of course, the obviously rotten. Many are discarded for minor imperfections that can be pared away.

A typical discard is a half jar of peanut butter—though nonor- 11 ganic peanut butter does not require refrigeration and is unlikely to spoil in any reasonable time. One of my favorite finds is yogurt—often discarded, still sealed, when the expiration date has passed—because it will keep for several days, even in warm weather.

No matter how careful I am I still get dysentery at least once 12 a month, oftener in warm weather. I do not want to paint too romantic a picture. Dumpster diving has serious drawbacks as a way of life.

I find from the experience of scavenging two rather deep les- 13 sons. The first is to take what I can use and let the rest go. I have come to think that there is no value in the abstract. A thing I cannot use or make useful, perhaps by trading, has no value, however fine or rare it may be.

The second lesson is the transience of material being. I do not 14 suppose that ideas are immortal, but certainly they are longer-lived than material objects.

The things I find in Dumpsters, the love letters and rag dolls 15 of so many lives, remind me of this lesson. Now I hardly pick up a thing without envisioning the time I will cast it away. This, I think, is a healthy state of mind. Almost everything I have now has already been cast out at least once, proving that what I own is valueless to someone.

I find that my desire to grab for the gaudy bauble has been 16 largely sated. I think this is an attitude I share with the very wealthy—we both know there is plenty more where whatever we have came from. Between us are the rat-race millions who have confounded their selves with the objects they grasp and who nightly scavenge the cable channels for they know not what.

I am sorry for them.   17

Meaning

1. Eighner ends his essay with the statement "I am sorry for them." Whom is he sorry for, and why? How does this statement relate to the main point of Eighner's essay?
2. How does Eighner decide what to keep when he digs through Dumpsters? How does he decide a thing's value? What evidence in the essay supports your answer?

Purpose and Audience

1. How does paragraph 2 reveal that Eighner's purpose is not simply to explain how to scavenge but also to persuade his readers to examine any stereotypes they may hold about scavengers?

JESSICA MITFORD

Tough-minded, commonsensical, and witty, Jessica Mitford was described by Time *magazine as the "Queen of Muckrakers." She was born in England in 1917, the sixth of Lord and Lady Redesdale's seven children, and was educated entirely at home. Her highly eccentric family is the subject of novels by her sister Nancy Mitford and of her own autobiographical* Daughters and Rebels *(1960). In 1939, a few years after she left home, Mitford took up permanent residence in the United States, becoming a naturalized American citizen in 1944. Shortly afterward, moved by her long-standing antifascism and the promise of equality in a socialist society, she joined the American Communist party; her years as a "Red Menace" are recounted in* A Fine Old Conflict *(1977). In the late 1950s she turned to investigative journalism, researching and exposing numerous instances of deception, greed, and foolishness in American society. Her articles appeared in the* Nation, Esquire, *the* Atlantic, *and other magazines, and many of them are collected in* Poison Penmanship: The Gentle Art of Muckraking *(1979). Her book-length exposés include* The Trial of Dr. Spock *(1969),* Kind and Usual Punishment: The Prison Business *(1973), and* The American Way of Birth *(1992). Mitford died in 1996.*

Embalming Mr. Jones

In 1963 Mitford published The American Way of Death, *a daring and influential look at the standard practices of the American funeral industry. (*The American Way of Death Revisited, *nearly complete at Mitford's death, was published in 1998.) Mitford pegs the modern American funeral as "the most irrational and weirdest" custom of our affluent society, in which "the trappings of Gracious Living are transformed, as in a nightmare, into the trappings of Gracious Dying." This excerpt from the book, an analysis of the process of embalming a corpse and restoring it for viewing, demonstrates Mitford's sharp eye for detail, commanding style, and caustic wit.*

197

The drama begins to unfold with the arrival of the corpse at the   1
mortuary.

Alas, poor Yorick![1] How surprised he would be to see how his   2
counterpart of today is whisked off to a funeral parlor and is in
short order, sprayed, sliced, pierced, pickled, trussed, trimmed,
creamed, waxed, painted, rouged, and neatly dressed—transformed from a common corpse into a Beautiful Memory Picture.
This process is known in the trade as embalming and restorative
art, and is so universally employed in the United States and Canada that the funeral director does it routinely, without consulting
corpse or kin. He regards as eccentric those few who are hardy
enough to suggest that it might be dispensed with. Yet no law
requires embalming, no religious doctrine commends it, nor is
it dictated by considerations of health, sanitation, or even of personal daintiness. In no part of the world but in Northern America
is it widely used. The purpose of embalming is to make the corpse
presentable for viewing in a suitably costly container; and here
too the funeral director routinely, without first consulting the
family, prepares the body for public display.

Is all this legal? The processes to which a dead body may   3
be subjected are after all to some extent circumscribed by law.
In most states, for instance, the signature of next of kin must
be obtained before an autopsy may be performed, before the
deceased may be cremated, before the body may be turned over
to a medical school for research purposes; or such provision
must be made in the decedent's will. In the case of embalming,
no such permission is required nor is it ever sought.[2] A textbook,
The Principles and Practices of Embalming, comments on this:
"There is some question regarding the legality of much that is

---

[1]A line from Shakespeare's *Hamlet*, spoken by Hamlet in a graveyard as he
contemplates the skull of the former jester in his father's court. [Editors' note.]

[2]In 1982, nineteen years after this was written, the Federal Trade Commission
issued comprehensive regulations on the funeral industry, including the requirement that funeral providers prepare an itemized price list for their goods and
services. The list must include a notice that embalming is not required by law,
along with an indication of the charge for embalming and an explanation of the
alternatives. Consumers must give permission for embalming before they may
be charged for it. Shortly before her death, however, Mitford wrote that thirteen
years after the ruling the FTC had "watered down" the regulations and "routinely
ignored" consumer complaints against the funeral industry, enforcing the regulations only forty-two times. [Editors' note.]

done within the preparation room." The author points out that it would be most unusual for a responsible member of a bereaved family to instruct the mortician, in so many words, to "*embalm*" the body of a deceased relative. The very term *embalming* is so seldom used that the mortician must rely upon custom in the matter. The author concludes that unless the family specifies otherwise, the act of entrusting the body to the care of a funeral establishment carries with it an implied permission to go ahead and embalm.

Embalming is indeed a most extraordinary procedure, and 4 one must wonder at the docility of Americans who each year pay hundreds of millions of dollars for its perpetuation, blissfully ignorant of what it is all about, what is done, how it is done. Not one in ten thousand has any idea of what actually takes place. Books on the subject are extremely hard to come by. They are not to be found in most libraries or bookshops.

In an era when huge television audiences watch surgical 5 operations in the comfort of their living rooms, when, thanks to the animated cartoon, the geography of the digestive system has become familiar territory even to the nursery school set, in a land where the satisfaction of curiosity about all matters is a national pastime, the secrecy surrounding embalming can, surely, hardly be attributed to the inherent gruesomeness of the subject. Custom in this regard has within this century suffered a complete reversal. In the early days of American embalming, when it was performed in the home of the deceased, it was almost mandatory for some relative to stay by the embalmer's side and witness the procedure. Today, family members who might wish to be in attendance would certainly be dissuaded by the funeral director. All others, except apprentices, are excluded by law from the preparation room.

A close look at what does actually take place may explain in 6 large measure the undertaker's intractable reticence concerning a procedure that has become his major *raison d'être*.[3] Is it possible he fears that public information about embalming might lead patrons to wonder if they really want this service? If the funeral men are loath to discuss the subject outside the trade, the reader may, understandably, be equally loath to go on reading at this

[3]French, meaning "reason for being." [Editors' note.]

point. For those who have the stomach for it, let us part the for-maldehyde curtain. . . .

The body is first laid out in the undertaker's morgue—or 7 rather, Mr. Jones is reposing in the preparation room—to be readied to bid the world farewell.

The preparation room in any of the better funeral establish- 8 ments has the tiled and sterile look of a surgery, and indeed the embalmer–restorative artist who does his chores there is begin-ning to adopt the term "dermasurgeon" (appropriately corrupted by some mortician-writers as "demisurgeon") to describe his call-ing. His equipment, consisting of scalpels, scissors, augers, for-ceps, clamps, needles, pumps, tubes, bowls and basins, is crudely imitative of the surgeon's, as is his technique, acquired in a nine- or twelve-month post–high-school course in an embalming school. He is supplied by an advanced chemical industry with a bewildering array of fluids, sprays, pastes, oils, powders, creams, to fix or soften tissue, shrink or distend it as needed, dry it here, restore the moisture there. There are cosmetics, waxes, and paints to fill and cover features, even plaster of Paris to replace entire limbs. There are ingenious aids to prop and stabilize the cadaver: a Vari-Pose Head Rest, the Edwards Arm and Hand Positioner, the Repose Block (to support the shoulders during the embalm-ing), and the Throop Foot Positioner, which resembles an old-fashioned stocks.

Mr. John H. Eckels, president of the Eckels College of Mor- 9 tuary Science, thus describes the first part of the embalming procedure: "In the hands of a skilled practitioner, this work may be done in a comparatively short time and without mutilating the body other than by slight incision—so slight that it scarcely would cause serious inconvenience if made upon a living person. It is necessary to remove the blood, and doing this not only helps in the disinfecting, but removes the principal cause of disfigure-ments due to discoloration."

Another textbook discusses the all-important time element: 10 "The earlier this is done, the better, for every hour that elapses between death and embalming will add to the problems and com-plications encountered. . . ." Just how soon should one get going on the embalming? The author tells us, "On the basis of such scanty information made available to this profession through its rudimentary and haphazard system of technical research, we must conclude that the best results are to be obtained if the subject is embalmed before life is completely extinct—that is, before cellular death has occurred. In the average case, this would mean within an hour after somatic death." For those who feel that there is something a little rudimentary, not to say haphazard, about this advice, a comforting thought is offered by another writer. Speaking of fears entertained in early days of premature burial, he points out, "One of the effects of embalming by chemical injection, however, has been to dispel fears of live burial." How true; once the blood is removed, chances of live burial are indeed remote.

To return to Mr. Jones, the blood is drained out through the   11 veins and replaced by embalming fluid pumped in through the arteries. As noted in *The Principles and Practices of Embalming*, "every operator has a favorite injection and drainage point—a fact which becomes a handicap only if he fails or refuses to forsake his favorites when conditions demand it." Typical favorites are the carotid artery, femoral artery, jugular vein, subclavian vein. There are various choices of embalming fluid. If Flextone is used, it will produce a "mild, flexible rigidity. The skin retains a velvety softness, the tissues are rubbery and pliable. Ideal for women and children." It may be blended with B. and G. Products Company's Lyf-Lyk tint, which is guaranteed to reproduce "nature's own skin texture . . . the velvety appearance of living tissue." Suntone comes in three separate tints: Suntan; Special Cosmetic Tint, a pink shade "especially indicated for young female subjects"; and Regular Cosmetic Tint, moderately pink.

About three to six gallons of a dyed and perfumed solution   12 of formaldehyde, glycerin, borax, phenol, alcohol, and water is soon circulating through Mr. Jones, whose mouth has been sewn together with a "needle directed upward between the upper lip and gum and brought out through the left nostril," with the corners raised slightly "for a more pleasant expression." If he should be bucktoothed, his teeth are cleaned with Bon Ami and coated with colorless nail polish. His eyes, meanwhile, are closed with flesh-tinted eye caps and eye cement.

The next step is to have at Mr. Jones with a thing called a tro-   13 car. This is a long, hollow needle attached to a tube. It is jabbed into the abdomen, poked around the entrails and chest cavity, the contents of which are pumped out and replaced with "cavity fluid." This done, and the hole in the abdomen sewn up, Mr. Jones's face is heavily creamed (to protect the skin from burns which may be caused by leakage of the chemicals), and he is covered with a sheet and left unmolested for a while. But not for long—there is more, much more, in store for him. He has been embalmed, but not yet restored, and the best time to start the restorative work is eight to ten hours after embalming, when the tissues have become firm and dry.

The object of all this attention to the corpse, it must be 14 remembered, is to make it presentable for viewing in an attitude of healthy repose. "Our customs require the presentation of our dead in the semblance of normality . . . unmarred by the ravages of illness, disease or mutilation," says Mr. J. Sheridan Mayer in his *Restorative Art*. This is a rather large order since few people die in the full bloom of health, unravaged by illness and unmarked by some disfigurement. The funeral industry is equal to the challenge: "In some cases the gruesome appearance of a mutilated or disease-ridden subject may be quite discouraging. The task of restoration may seem impossible and shake the confidence of the embalmer. This is the time for intestinal fortitude and determination. Once the formative work is begun and affected tissues are cleaned or removed, all doubts of success vanish. It is surprising and gratifying to discover the results which may be obtained."

The embalmer, having allowed an appropriate interval to 15 elapse, returns to the attack, but now he brings into play the skill and equipment of sculptor and cosmetician. Is a hand missing? Casting one in plaster of Paris is a simple matter. "For replacement purposes, only a cast of the back of the hand is necessary; this is within the ability of the average operator and is quite adequate." If a lip or two, a nose or an ear should be missing, the embalmer has at hand a variety of restorative waxes with which to model replacements. Pores and skin texture are simulated by stippling with a little brush, and over this cosmetics are laid on. Head off? Decapitation cases are rather routinely handled. Ragged edges are trimmed, and head joined to torso with a series of splints, wires and sutures. It is a good idea to have a little something at the neck—a scarf or high collar—when time for viewing comes. Swollen mouth? Cut out tissue as needed from inside the lips. If too much is removed, the surface contour can easily be restored by padding with cotton. Swollen necks and cheeks are reduced by removing tissue through vertical incisions made down each side of the neck. "When the deceased is casketed, the pillow will hide the suture incisions . . . as an extra precaution against leakage, the suture may be painted with liquid sealer."

The opposite condition is more likely to present itself—that 16 of emaciation. His hypodermic syringe now loaded with massage cream, the embalmer seeks out and fills the hollowed and sunken areas by injection. In this procedure the backs of the hands and fingers and the under-chin area should not be neglected.

Positioning the lips is a problem that recurrently challenges 17 the ingenuity of the embalmer. Closed too tightly they tend to give a stern, even disapproving expression. Ideally, embalmers feel, the lips should give the impression of being ever so slightly parted, the upper lip protruding slightly for a more youthful appearance. This takes some engineering, however, as the lips tend to drift apart. Lip drift can sometimes be remedied by pushing one or two straight pins through the inner margin of the lower lip and then inserting them between the two upper front teeth. If Mr. Jones happens to have no teeth, the pins can just as easily be anchored in his Armstrong Face Former and Denture Replacer. Another method to maintain lip closure is to dislocate the lower jaw, which is then held in its new position by a wire run through holes which have been drilled through the upper and lower jaws at the midline. As the French are fond of saying, *il faut souffrir pour être belle*.[4]

If Mr. Jones has died of jaundice, the embalming fluid will 18 very likely turn him green. Does this deter the embalmer? Not if he has intestinal fortitude. Masking pastes and cosmetics are heavily laid on, burial garments and casket interiors are color-correlated with particular care, and Jones is displayed beneath rose-colored lights. Friends will say, "How *well* he looks." Death by carbon monoxide, on the other hand, can be rather a good thing from the embalmer's viewpoint: "One advantage is the fact that this type of discoloration is an exaggerated form of a natural pink coloration." This is nice because the healthy glow is already present and needs but little attention.

The patching and filling completed, Mr. Jones is now shaved, 19 washed, and dressed. Cream-based cosmetic, available in pink,

---

[4]French, meaning "It is necessary to suffer in order to be beautiful." [Editors' note.]

flesh, suntan, brunette, and blond, is applied to his hands and face, his hair is shampooed and combed (and, in the case of Mrs. Jones, set), his hands manicured. For the horny-handed son of toil special care must be taken; cream should be applied to remove ingrained grime, and the nails cleaned. "If he were not in the habit of having them manicured in life, trimming and shaping is advised for better appearance—never questioned by kin."

Jones is now ready for casketing (this is the present participle of the verb "to casket"). In this operation his right shoulder should be depressed slightly "to turn the body a bit to the right and soften the appearance of lying flat on the back." Positioning the hands is a matter of importance, and special rubber positioning blocks may be used. The hands should be cupped slightly for a more lifelike, relaxed appearance. Proper placement of the body requires a delicate sense of balance. It should lie as high as possible in the casket, yet not so high that the lid, when lowered, will hit the nose. On the other hand, we are cautioned, placing the body too low "creates the impression that the body is in a box." 20

Jones is next wheeled into the appointed slumber room where a few last touches may be added—his favorite pipe placed in his hand or, if he was a great reader, a book propped into position. (In the case of little Master Jones a Teddy bear may be clutched.) Here he will hold open house for a few days, visiting hours 10 a.m. to 9 p.m. 21

Meaning

1. According to Mitford, what is the purpose of embalming and restoration (see paragraphs 2 and 14)? If they are not required by law or religion or "considerations of health, sanitation, or even of personal daintiness" (2), why are they routinely performed?

2. Why do Americans know so little about embalming (paragraphs 3–6)? Does Mitford blame Americans themselves, the funeral industry, or both?

Purpose and Audience

1. What does Mitford reveal about her purpose when she questions whether the undertaker "fears that public information about embalming might lead patrons to wonder if they really want this service" (paragraph 6)?

2. Mitford's chief assumption about her readers is evident in paragraph 4. What is it?

3. Most readers find Mitford's essay humorous. Assuming you did, too, which details or comments struck you as especially amusing? How does Mitford use humor to achieve her purpose?

Method and Structure

1. Why do you think Mitford chose the method of process analysis to explore this particular social custom? What does the method allow her to convey about the custom? How does this information help her achieve her purpose?

2. Despite the fact that her purpose goes beyond mere explanation, does Mitford explain the process of embalming and restoration clearly enough for you to understand how it's done and what the reasons for each step are? Starting at paragraph 7, what are the main steps in the process?

3. Mitford interrupts the sequence of steps in the process several times. What information does she provide in paragraphs 8, 10, and 14 to make the interruptions worthwhile?

4. OTHER METHODS   Mitford occasionally uses other methods to develop her process analysis—for instance, in paragraph 8 she combines description and classification to present the embalmer's preparation room and tools; and in paragraph 5 she uses comparison and contrast to note changes in the family's knowledge of embalming. What does this contrast suggest about our current attitudes toward death and the dead?

Language

1. How would you characterize Mitford's tone? Support your answer with specific details, sentence structures, and words in the essay. (See the Glossary for a discussion of *tone*.)

2. Mitford is more than a little ironic—that is, she often says one thing when she means another or deliberately understates her meaning. Here are two examples from paragraph 10: "the all-important time element" in the embalming of a corpse; "How true; once the blood is removed, chances of live burial are indeed remote." What additional examples do you find? What does this persistent irony contribute to Mitford's tone? (For a fuller explanation of *irony*, consult the Glossary.)

3. Mitford's style in this essay is often informal, even conversational, as in "The next step is to have at Mr. Jones with a thing called a trocar" (paragraph 13). But equally often she seems to imitate the technical,

impersonal style of the embalming textbooks she quotes so extensively, as in "Another method to maintain lip closure is to dislocate the lower jaw" (17). What other examples of each style do you find? What does each style contribute to Mitford's purpose? Is the contrast effective, or would a consistent style, one way or the other, be more effective? Why?

Writing Topics

1. Think of a modern custom or practice that you find ridiculous, barbaric, tedious, or otherwise objectionable. Write an essay that analyzes the process by which your chosen custom or practice unfolds. Following Mitford's model, explain the process clearly while also conveying your attitude toward it.

2. Elsewhere in her book *The American Way of Death*, Mitford notes that the open casket at funerals, which creates the need for embalming and restoration, is "a custom unknown in other parts of the world. Foreigners are astonished by it." Write an essay in which you explore the possible reasons for the custom in the United States. Or, if you have strong feelings about closed or open caskets at funerals (derived from religious beliefs, family tradition, or some other source), write an essay agreeing or disagreeing with Mitford's treatment of embalming and restoration.

3. Read about funeral customs in another country. Write an essay in which you analyze the process covered in your sources and use it as the basis for agreeing or disagreeing with Mitford's opinion of embalming and restoration.

PROCESS ANALYSIS

Select one of the following topics, or any other topic they suggest, for an essay developed by process analysis. Be sure to choose a topic you care about so that process analysis is a means of communicating an idea, not an end in itself.

Technology and the Environment

1. How an engine or other machine works
2. How the Internet works
3. Setting up a recycling program in a home or an office
4. How solar energy can be converted into electricity

Education and Career

5. How children learn to dress themselves, play with others, read, or write
6. Interviewing for a job
7. Succeeding in a difficult course
8. Learning a foreign language
9. Coping with a bad boss

Entertainment and Hobbies

10. Performing a magic trick
11. Throwing a really *bad* party
12. Playing a sport or a musical instrument
13. Making great chili or some other dish

Health and Appearance

14. Getting physically fit
15. Climbing a mountain
16. Replacing a button on a shirt or a pair of pants
17. Cutting or coloring one's own hair

Family and Friends

18. Offering constructive criticism to a friend
19. Driving your parents, brother, sister, friend, or roommate crazy
20. Minimizing sibling rivalry
21. Making new friends in a new place

Chapter 7

COMPARISON AND CONTRAST

USING THE METHOD

An insomniac watching late-night television faces a choice between two zombie movies broadcasting at the same time. To make up her mind, she uses the dual method of comparison and contrast.

- **Comparison** shows the similarities between two or more subjects: the similar broadcast times and topics of the two movies force the insomniac to choose between them.
- **Contrast** shows the differences between subjects: the different actors, locations, and reputations of the two movies make it possible for the insomniac to choose one.

As in this example, comparison and contrast usually work together because any subjects that warrant side-by-side examination usually resemble each other in some respects and differ in other respects. (Since comparison and contrast are so closely related, the terms *comparison* and *compare* will be used from now on to designate both.)

You'll generally write a comparison for one of two purposes:

- To explain the similarities and differences between subjects so as to make either or both of them clear—an explanatory comparison.
- To evaluate subjects so as to establish their advantages and disadvantages, strengths and weaknesses—an evaluative comparison.

The explanatory comparison does not take a position on the relative merits of the subjects; the evaluative comparison does, and it usually concludes with a preference or a suggested course of action. In an explanatory comparison you might show how new income-tax laws differ from old laws. In an evaluative comparison on the same subject, you might argue that the old laws were more equitable than the new ones are.

Whether explanatory or evaluative, comparisons treat two or more subjects in the same general class or group: tax laws, religions, attitudes toward marriage, diseases, advertising strategies, diets, contact sports, friends, television shows. You may define the class to suit your interest—for instance, you might focus on crime dramas, on cable news programs, or on classic situation comedies. The class likeness ensures that the subjects share enough features to make comparison worthwhile. With subjects from different classes, such as an insect and a tree, the similarities are so few and differences so numerous—and both are so obvious—that explaining them would be pointless.

In writing a comparison, you select subjects from the same class and then, using division or analysis, identify the features shared by the subjects. These **points of comparison** are the attributes of the class and thus of the subjects within the class. For instance, the points of comparison for diets may be speed of weight loss, required self-discipline, and nutritional risk; for air pollutants they may be dangers to plants, animals, and humans. These points help you arrange similarities and differences between subjects, and, more important, they ensure direct comparison rather than a random listing of unrelated characteristics.

With two or more subjects, several points of comparison, and many similarities and differences, comparison clearly requires a firm organizational hand. You have two options for arranging a comparison:

- **Subject-by-subject**, in which the points of comparison are grouped under each subject so that the *subjects* are covered one at a time.
- **Point-by-point**, in which the subjects are grouped under each point of comparison so that the *points* are covered one at a time.

The following brief outlines illustrate the different arrangements as they might be applied to diets:

Subject-by-subject	Point-by-point
Harris's diet	Speed of weight loss
Speed of weight loss	Harris's diet
Required self-discipline	Marconi's diet
Nutritional risk	
	Required self-discipline
Marconi's diet	Harris's diet
Speed of weight loss	Marconi's diet
Required self-discipline	
Nutritional risk	Nutritional risk
	Harris's diet
	Marconi's diet

Since the subject-by-subject arrangement presents each subject as a coherent unit, it is particularly useful for comparing impressions of subjects: the dissimilar characters of two friends, for instance. However, covering the subjects one at a time can break an essay into discrete pieces and strain readers' memories, so this arrangement is usually confined to essays that are short or that compare several subjects briefly. For longer papers requiring precise treatment of the individual points of comparison—say, an evaluation of two proposals for a new student-aid policy—the point-by-point arrangement is more useful. Its chief disadvantage is that the reader can get lost in details and fail to see any subject as a whole. Because each arrangement has its strengths and weaknesses, you may sometimes combine the two in a single work, using the divided arrangement to introduce or summarize overall impressions of the subjects and using the alternating arrangement to deal specifically with the points of comparison.

DEVELOPING AN ESSAY BY COMPARISON AND CONTRAST

Getting Started

Whenever you observe similarities or differences between two or more members of the same general class—activities, people, ideas, things, places—you have a possible subject for comparison and contrast. Just be sure that the subjects are worth comparing and that you can do the job in the space and time allowed. For instance, if you have a week to complete a three-page paper, don't try to show all the similarities and differences between country music and rhythm and blues. The effort can only frustrate you and irritate your readers. Instead, limit the subjects to a manageable size—for instance, the lyrics of a representative song in each type of music—so that you can develop the comparisons completely and specifically.

To generate ideas for a comparison, explore each subject separately to pick out its characteristics, and then explore the subjects together to see what characteristics one suggests for the other. Look for points of comparison. Early on, you can use division or analysis (Chapter 4) to identify points of comparison by breaking the subjects' general class into its elements. A song lyric, for instance, could be divided into story line or plot, basic emotion, and special language such as dialect or slang. After you have explored your subjects fully, you can use classification (Chapter 5) to group your characteristics under the points of comparison. For instance, you might classify characteristics of two proposals for a new student-aid policy into qualifications for aid, minimum and maximum amounts to be made available, and repayment terms.

As you gain increasing control over your material, consider also the needs of your readers:

- Do they know your subjects well, or will you need to take special care to explain one or both of them?
- Will your readers be equally interested in similarities and differences, or will they find one more enlightening than the other?

Forming a Thesis

While you are shaping your ideas, you should begin formulating your controlling idea, your thesis. The first thing you should do is look over your points of comparison and determine whether they suggest an explanatory or evaluative approach.

The thesis of an evaluative comparison will generally emerge naturally because it coincides with the writer's purpose of supporting a preference for one subject over another:

THESIS SENTENCE (EVALUATION) The two diets result in similarly rapid weight loss, but Harris's requires much more self-discipline and is nutritionally much riskier than Marconi's.

In an explanatory comparison, however, your thesis will need to do more than merely reflect your general purpose in explaining. It should go beyond the obvious and begin to identify the points of comparison. For example:

TENTATIVE THESIS SENTENCE (EXPLANATION) Rugby and American football are the same in some respects and different in others.

REVISED THESIS SENTENCE (EXPLANATION) Though rugby requires less strength and more stamina than American football, the two games are very much alike in their rules and strategies.

These examples suggest other decisions you must make when formulating a thesis:

- Will you emphasize both subjects equally or stress one over the other?
- Will you emphasize differences, similarities, or both?

Keeping your readers in mind as you make these decisions will make it easier to use your thesis to shape the body of your essay. For instance, if you decide to write an evaluative comparison and your readers are likely to be biased against your preference or recommendation, you will need to support your case with plenty of specific reasons. If the subjects are equally familiar or important to your readers (as the diets are in the previous example), you'll want to give them equal emphasis, but if one subject is unfamiliar (as rugby is in this country), you will probably need to stress it over the other.

Knowing your audience will also help you decide whether to focus on similarities, differences, or both. Generally, you'll stress the differences between subjects your readers consider similar (such as diets) and the similarities between subjects they are likely to consider different (such as rugby and American football).

Organizing

Your readers' needs and expectations can also help you plan your essay's organization. An effective introduction to a comparison essay often provides some context for readers — the situation that prompts the comparison, for instance, or the need for the comparison. Placing your thesis sentence in the introduction also informs readers of your purpose and point, and it may help keep you focused while you write.

For the body of the essay, choose the arrangement that will present your material most clearly and effectively. Remember that the subject-by-subject arrangement suits brief essays that compare dominant impressions of the subjects, whereas the point-by-point arrangement suits longer essays that require emphasis on the individual points of comparison. If you are torn between the two—wanting both to sum up each subject and to show the two side by side—then a combined arrangement may be your wisest choice.

A rough outline like the models on page 210 can help you plan the basic arrangement of your essay and also the order of the subjects and points of comparison. If your subjects are equally familiar to your readers and equally important to you, then it may not matter which subject you treat first, even in a subject-by-subject arrangement. But if one subject is less familiar or if you favor one, then that subject should probably come second. You can also arrange the points themselves to reflect their importance and your readers' knowledge: from least to most significant or complex, from most to least familiar. Be sure to use the same order for both subjects.

Most readers know intuitively how a comparison works, so they will expect you to balance your comparison feature for feature as well. In other words, all the features mentioned for the first subject should be mentioned as well for the second, and any features not mentioned for the first subject should not suddenly materialize for the second.

The conclusion to a comparison essay can help readers see the whole picture: the chief similarities and differences between two subjects compared in a divided arrangement, or the chief characteristics of subjects compared in an alternating arrangement. In addition, you may want to comment on the significance of your comparison, advise readers on how they can use the information you have provided, or recommend a specific course of action for them to follow. As with all other methods of development, the choice of conclusion should reflect the impression you want to leave with readers.

Drafting

Drafting your essay gives you the chance to spell out your comparison so that it supports your thesis or, if your thesis is still tentative, to discover what you think by writing about your subject. You can use paragraphs to help manage the comparison as it unfolds:

- *In a subject-by-subject arrangement*, if you devote two paragraphs to the first subject, try to do the same for the second subject. For both subjects, try to cover the points of comparison in the same order and group the same ones in paragraphs.

- *In a point-by-point arrangement*, balance the paragraphs as you move back and forth between subjects. If you treat several points of comparison for the first subject in one paragraph, do the same for the second subject. If you apply a single point of comparison to both subjects in one paragraph, do the same for the next point of comparison.

This way of drafting will help you achieve balance in your comparison and see where you may need more information to flesh out your subjects and your points. If the finished draft seems to march too rigidly in its pattern, you can always loosen things up when revising.

Revising and Editing

When you are revising and editing your draft, use the following questions to be certain that your essay meets the principal requirements of the comparative method.

- *Are your subjects drawn from the same class?* The subjects must have notable differences *and* notable similarities to make comparison worthwhile — though, of course, you may stress one group over the other.

- *Does your essay have a clear purpose and say something significant about the subject?* Your purpose of explaining or evaluating and the point you are making should be evident in your thesis *and* throughout the essay. A vague, pointless comparison will quickly bore readers.

- *Do you apply all points of comparison to both subjects?* Even if you emphasize one subject, the two subjects must match feature for feature. An unmatched comparison may leave readers with unanswered questions or weaken their confidence in your authority.

- *Does the pattern of comparison suit readers' needs and the complexity of the material?* Although readers will appreciate a clear organization and roughly equal treatment of your subjects and points of comparison, they will also appreciate some variety in the way you move back and forth. You needn't devote a sentence to each point, first for one subject and then for the other, or alternate subjects sentence by sentence through several paragraphs. Instead you might write a single sentence on one point or subject but four sentences on the other—if that's what your information requires.

NANCY MAIRS

Nancy Mairs was born in 1943 in Long Beach, California, and grew up in the Boston area. After earning a BA from Wheaton College, she taught writing to high school and college students while working toward graduate degrees in creative writing and English literature from the University of Arizona. Due to multiple sclerosis, Mairs has used a wheelchair since 1993. Her essays, memoirs, and poetry candidly explore, as she has put it, "issues charged with personal significance," including death, disability, and feminism. Her essay collections include Plaintext *(1986),* Carnal Acts *(1990),* Waist-High in the World: A Life Among the Nondisabled *(1996),* A Troubled Guest *(2001), and, most recently,* A Dynamic God: Living an Unconventional Catholic Faith *(2007).*

Disability

In this essay, Mairs compares the media's depiction of disability with the reality that she experiences firsthand as a person afflicted with multiple sclerosis. "Disability" was first published in the New York Times *and later included in* Carnal Acts.

For months now I've been consciously searching for representa- 1
tion of myself in the media, especially television. I know I'd recognize this self because of certain distinctive, though not unique, features: I am a forty-three-year-old woman crippled with multiple sclerosis; although I can still totter short distances with the aid of a brace and a cane, more and more of the time I ride in a wheelchair. Because of these appliances and my peculiar gait, I'm easy to spot even in a crowd. So when I tell you I haven't noticed any women like me on television, you can believe me.

Actually, last summer I did see a woman with multiple sclero- 2
sis portrayed on one of those medical dramas that offer an illness-of-the-week like the daily special at your local diner. In fact, that

was the whole point of the show: that this poor young woman had MS. She was terribly upset (understandably, I assure you) by the diagnosis, and her response was to plan a trip to Kenya while she was still physically capable of making it, against the advice of the young, fit, handsome doctor who had fallen in love with her. And she almost did it. At least, she got as far as a taxi to the airport, hotly pursued by the doctor. But at the last she succumbed to his blandishments and fled the taxi into his manly protective embrace. No escape to Kenya for this cripple.

Capitulation into the arms of a man who uses his medical 3 powers to strip one of even the urge toward independence is hardly the sort of representation I had in mind. But even if the situation had been sensitively handled, according to the woman her right to her own adventures, it wouldn't have been what I'm looking for. Such a television show, as well as films like *Duet for One* and *Children of a Lesser God*, in taking disability as its major premise, excludes the complexities that round out a character and make her whole. It's not about a woman who happens to be physically disabled; it's about physical disability and the determining factor of a woman's existence.

Take it from me, physical disability looms pretty large in one's 4 life. But it doesn't devour one wholly. I'm not, for instance, Ms. MS, a walking, talking embodiment of a chronic incurable degenerative disease. In most ways I'm just like every other woman of my age, nationality, and socioeconomic background. I menstruate, so I have to buy tampons. I worry about smoker's breath, so I buy mouthwash. I smear my wrinkling skin with lotions. I put bleach in the washer so my family's undies won't be dingy. I drive a car, talk on the telephone, get runs in my pantyhose, eat pizza. In most ways, that is, I'm the advertisers' dream: Ms. Great American Consumer. And yet the advertisers, who determine nowadays who will get represented publicly and who will not, deny the existence of me and my kind absolutely.

I once asked a local advertiser why he didn't include disabled 5 people in his spots. His response seemed direct enough: "We don't want to give people the idea that our product is just for the handicapped." But tell me truly now: If you saw me pouring out puppy biscuits, would you think these kibbles were only for the puppies of the cripples? If you saw my blind niece ordering a Coke, would you switch to Pepsi lest you be struck sightless? No, I think the advertiser's excuse masked a deeper and more anxious rationale: To depict disabled people in the ordinary activities of daily life is to admit that there is something ordinary about disability itself, that it may enter anybody's life. If it is effaced completely, or at least isolated as a separate "problem," so that it remains at a safe distance from other human issues, then the viewer won't feel threatened by her or his own physical vulnerability.

This kind of effacement or isolation has painful, even dangerous consequences, however. For the disabled person, these include self-degradation and a subtle kind of self-alienation not unlike that experienced by other minorities. Socialized human beings love to conform, to study others and then mold themselves to the contours of those whose images, for good reasons or bad, they come to love. Imagine a life in which feasible others—others you can hope to be like—don't exist. At the least you might conclude that there is something queer about you, something ugly or foolish or shameful. In the extreme, you might feel as though you don't exist, in any meaningful social sense, at all. Everyone else is "there," sucking breath mints and splashing cologne and swigging wine coolers. You're "not there." And if not there, nowhere. 6

But this denial of disability imperils even you who are able-bodied, and not just by shrinking your insight into the physically and emotionally complex world you live in. Some disabled people call you TAPs, or Temporarily Abled Persons. The fact is that ours is the only minority you can join involuntarily, without warning, at any time. And if you live long enough, as you're increasingly likely to do, you may well join it. The transition will probably be difficult from a physical point of view no matter what. But it will be a good bit easier psychologically if you are accustomed to seeing disability as a normal characteristic, one that complicates but does not ruin human existence. Achieving this integration, for disabled and able-bodied people alike, requires that we insert disability daily into our field of vision: quietly, naturally, in the small and common scenes of our ordinary lives. 7

Meaning

1. Why does Mairs object to the TV show about the woman with multiple sclerosis (paragraphs 2–3)?

2. What does Mairs mean by the phrase "Ms. Great American Consumer" (paragraph 4)?

3. Why, according to Mairs, should there be images of people with disabilities on television?

4. What is Mairs's thesis? Restate it in your own words.

Purpose and Audience

1. What is this essay's purpose?

2. What lessons might both people with disabilities and people without disabilities take from this essay?

Method and Structure

1. What does Mairs compare and contrast in this essay? How does the comparison help her achieve her purpose?

2. What key generalizations does Mairs make to support her thesis? Do you find them valid? Why, or why not?

3. How does Mairs use her introduction to lay the groundwork for her essay? How does she make the transition from her introduction into the TV drama?

4. OTHER METHODS   Discuss how Mairs uses example to help build her case. What kinds of examples does she select? What are their effects?

Language

1. How would you characterize Mairs's tone in this essay? Point out specific sentences and words that establish it. What is the effect? (For an explanation of *tone*, see the Glossary.)

2. What is the function of irony in this essay (for example, in paragraph 5, "If you saw my blind niece ordering a Coke, would you switch to Pepsi lest you be struck sightless?")? (If necessary, consult the Glossary for the definition of *irony*.)

3. What are the connotations of the words "crippled," "totter," "appliances," and "peculiar gait" (paragraph 1)? What is the effect of these words in the essay's introduction? (For the definition of *connotation*, consult the Glossary.)

Writing Topics

1. Write an essay that explains how your own responses to people with disabilities might lead you to accept or dispute Mairs's call for depicting "disabled people in the ordinary activities of daily life."

2. Choose another group you think has been "effaced" in television advertising and programming—a racial, ethnic, or religious group, for instance. Write an essay detailing how and why that group is overlooked. How could representations of the group be incorporated into the media? What effects might such representation have?

3. Write an essay discussing how people with disabilities are treated in our society. You could narrate a day in the life of someone with a disability; you could compare and contrast the access and facilities your school provides for able-bodied students versus students with disabilities; you could classify social attitudes toward disabilities, with examples of each type.

4. Reread Mairs's essay carefully. Mairs tells us about herself through details and through tone (for example, through irony, intensity, and humor). Write an essay on how Mairs's self-revelations do or do not help further her thesis.

CHERYL PECK

Cheryl Peck (born 1951) has always lived in Michigan—first with her parents and four younger siblings on a nonworking farm; now in Three Rivers with her "Beloved," Nancy, and her cat, Babycakes. She attended the University of Michigan and worked in a welfare office for twenty-five years. After friends encouraged her to write down the personal stories she was always amusing them with, Peck started submitting humorous and poignant articles to a Kalamazoo lesbian newsletter and giving readings at a community church. Her self-published essay collection Fat Girls and Lawn Chairs *(2004) caught the attention of an editor at Warner Books, who brought the essays to a wider audience and cult favorite status. Peck followed it a year later with* Revenge of the Paste Eaters: Memoirs of a Misfit *(2005) and took an early retirement so she could devote her time to writing. She is currently working on a novel and a third collection of essays.*

Fatso

In most of her writing, Peck uses her ample size—"three hundred pounds (plus change)"—to fuel her self-deprecating brand of humor. This essay from Revenge of the Paste Eaters, *however, takes a decidedly different approach to the weight issues that have plagued the author all her life.*

My friend Annie and I were having lunch and we fell into a discussion of people of size. She told me she had gone to the fair with a friend of hers who is a young man of substance, and while he was standing in the midway, thinking about his elephant ear,[1] someone walked past him, said, "You don't need to eat that," and kept on walking away. Gone before he could register what had been said, much less formulate a stunning retort.

---

[1] Fried dough. [Editors' note.]

And that person was probably right: he did not need to eat 2
that elephant ear. Given what they are made of, the question then
becomes: Who *does* need to eat an elephant ear? And to what benefit? Are elephant ears inherently better for thin people than for
fat ones? Do we suppose that that one particular elephant ear will
somehow alter the course of this man's life in some way that all
of the elephant ears before it, or all of the elephant ears to follow,
might not? And last but not least, what qualifies any of us for the
mission of telling other people what they should or should not eat?

I have probably spent most of my life listening to other people 3
tell me that as a middle-class white person, I have no idea what it
is like to be discriminated against. I have never experienced the
look that tells me I am not welcome, I have never been treated
rudely on a bus, I have never been reminded to keep my place, I
have never been laughed at, ridiculed, threatened, snubbed, not
waited on, or received well-meaning service I would just as soon
have done without. I have never had to choose which streets I will
walk down and which streets I will avoid. I have never been told
that my needs cannot be met in this store. I have never experienced that lack of social status that can debilitate the soul.

My feelings were not hurt when I was twelve years old and 4
the shoe salesman measured my feet and said he had no women's
shoes large enough for me, but perhaps I could wear the boxes.

I have never been called crude names, like "fatso" or "lard- 5
bucket." . . . My nickname on the school bus was never "Bismarck,"
as in the famous battleship. No one ever assumed I was totally inept
in all sports except those that involved hitting things because—and
everyone knows—the more weight you can put behind it, the farther you can kick or bat or just bully the ball.

I have never picked up a magazine with the photograph of a 6
naked woman of substance on the cover, to read, in the following
issue, thirty letters to the editor addressing sizism, including one
that said, "She should be ashamed of herself. She should go on a
diet immediately and demonstrate some self-control. She is going
to develop diabetes, arthritis, hypertension, and stroke, she will
die an ugly death at an early age and she will take down the entire
American health system with her." And that would, of course, be
the only letter I remember. I would not need some other calm
voice to say, "You don't know that—and you don't know that the
same fate would not befall a thin woman."

No one has ever assumed I am lazy, undisciplined, prone to self-pity, and emotionally unstable purely based on my size. No one has ever told me all I need is a little self-discipline and I too could be thin, pretty—a knockout, probably, because I have a "pretty face"—probably very popular because I have a "good personality." My mother never told me boys would never pay any attention to me because I'm fat.

I have never assumed an admirer would never pay any attention to me because I'm fat. I have never mishandled a sexual situation because I have been trained to think of myself as asexual. Unattractive. Repugnant.

Total strangers have never walked up to me in the street and started to tell me about weight loss programs their second cousin in Tulsa tried with incredible results, nor would they ever do so with the manner and demeanor of someone doing me a nearly unparalleled favor. I have never walked across a parking lot to have a herd of young men break into song about loving women with big butts. When I walk down the street or ride my bicycle, no one has ever hung out the car window to yell crude insults. When I walk into the houses of friends I have never been directed to the "safe" chairs as if I just woke up this morning this size and am incapable of gauging for myself what will or will not hold me.

I have never internalized any of this nonexistent presumption of who I am or what I feel. I would never discriminate against another woman of substance. I would never look at a heavy person and think, "self-pitying, undisciplined tub of lard." I would never admit that while I admire beautiful bodies, I rarely give the inhabitants the same attention and respect I would a soul mate because I do not expect they would ever become a soul mate. I would never tell you that I was probably thirty years old before I realized you really *can* be too small or too thin, or that the condition causes real emotional pain.

I have never skipped a high school reunion until I "lose a few pounds." I have never hesitated to reconnect with an old friend. I will appear anywhere in a bathing suit. If my pants split, I assume—and I assume everyone assumes—it was caused by poor materials.

I have always understood why attractive women are offended when men whistle at them.

I have never felt self-conscious standing next to my male 13 friend who is five foot ten and weighs 145 pounds.

I am not angry about any of this. 14

Meaning

1. Throughout her essay Peck repeats that she has never experienced, done, or felt any of the things she describes. Is she telling the truth? How do you know? (Hint: look up *irony* in the Glossary.)

2. How does Peck feel about the discrimination she faces as an overweight woman? Why does she feel this way?

3. Several times in her essay, Peck refers to people "of substance" (paragraphs 1, 6, and 10). How might this phrase have a double meaning?

Purpose and Audience

1. For whom is Peck writing? Fat people? Thin people? Herself? What clues in the essay bring you to your conclusion?

2. What lesson might readers take from Peck's essay?

Method and Structure

1. What, precisely, is Peck comparing and contrasting in this essay? Identify a few of the points of comparison she uses to develop her main idea. Which of these points seem most important to her?

2. Where does Peck's comparison begin? How does she use a subtle shift in point of view to indicate that she does, indeed, know "what it is like to be discriminated against" (paragraph 3)? (If necessary, see *point of view* in the Glossary.)

3. OTHER METHODS Peck's comparison relies heavily on example, focusing on a series of incidents from her own life. Choose two examples, and consider what each contributes to Peck's point.

Language

1. Peck is cautious in the words she uses to refer to overweight people, preferring terms such as "woman of substance" (paragraphs 6 and 10) and "heavy person" (10) over the judgmental terms that some people have used to describe her (and that she has caught herself thinking about others). Why, then, does she use the obviously insulting "Fatso" as the title of her essay?

2. Peck uses the phrase "I have never" repeatedly (seventeen times, to be exact), as well as variations such as "I would never" and "I have not." What is the effect of this repetition?

3. How would you characterize the tone of this essay? How does it affect you as a reader?

Writing Topics

1. Peck's essay is in some respects an imagined response to the person who insulted her friend's friend. Think of a time when a stranger made an inappropriate or insensitive comment directed at you or someone close to you (or of a time when you overheard such a remark intended for someone else). Write an essay that responds to the person in question, explaining why his or her comment was offensive.

2. Write an essay expressing your opinion of Peck's essay. For instance, how would you respond to her complaint that people treat over-weight individuals unfairly? Does she overlook important considerations about health? Do you think she exaggerates any of her points? Agree or disagree with Peck, supporting your opinion with your own examples.

3. American society is famously obsessed with people's size. Media outlets have focused recently on what has been described as an "obesity epidemic," and weight loss is a multibillion-dollar industry in this country. But in many cultures (Samoan and Polynesian, for example), large bodies are prized over small ones. Identify one such culture, and find two or three brief sources that explain that culture's attitudes toward body shape (a librarian can help you). Write an essay that compares that culture's standards of physical beauty with America's. Which culture's ideals seem more reasonable to you? Express your preference in a clear thesis statement and support your evaluation with details.

DAVID SEDARIS

David Sedaris's hilarious yet often touching autobiographical essays have earned him both popular and critical acclaim; in 2001 he received the Thurber Prize for American Humor and was named Humorist of the Year by Time *magazine. Born in 1957, Sedaris grew up in North Carolina and attended the School of the Art Institute of Chicago, where he taught writing for several years before moving to New York City. Working odd jobs during the day and writing about them at night, Sedaris catapulted to near-overnight success in 1993 after reading on National Public Radio a piece about working as a department-store Christmas elf. Since then, he has been a frequent contributor to the* New Yorker, Esquire, *and public radio's* Morning Edition *and* This American Life. *In 1994 Sedaris published his first collection of essays,* Barrel Fever, *followed by* Naked *(1997),* Holidays on Ice *(1997),* Me Talk Pretty One Day *(2000),* Dress Your Family in Corduroy and Denim *(2004), and* When You Are Engulfed in Flames *(2008). His most recent book is* Squirrel Seeks Chipmunk *(2010), a collection of original fables about animals.*

Remembering My Childhood on the Continent of Africa

When considered alongside his partner Hugh's experiences growing up in Africa, Sedaris's basically normal North Carolina childhood seems rather mundane. In this essay from Me Talk Pretty One Day, *Sedaris uses multiple comparisons to comically highlight that normality.*

When Hugh was in the fifth grade, his class took a field trip to an Ethiopian slaughterhouse. He was living in Addis Ababa at the time, and the slaughterhouse was chosen because, he says, "it was convenient." 1

This was a school system in which the matter of proximity outweighed such petty concerns as what may or may not be 2 appropriate for a busload of eleven-year-olds. "What?" I asked. "Were there no autopsies scheduled at the local morgue? Was the federal prison just a bit too far out of the way?"

Hugh defends his former school, saying, "Well, isn't that the 3 whole point of a field trip? To see something new?"

"Technically yes, but . . ." 4

"All right then," he says. "So we saw some new things." 5

One of his field trips was literally a trip to a field where the 6 class watched a wrinkled man fill his mouth with rotten goat meat and feed it to a pack of waiting hyenas. On another occasion they were taken to examine the bloodied bedroom curtains hanging in the palace of the former dictator. There were tamer trips, to textile factories and sugar refineries, but my favorite is always the slaughterhouse. It wasn't a big company, just a small rural enterprise run by a couple of brothers operating out of a low-ceilinged concrete building. Following a brief lecture on the importance of proper sanitation, a small white piglet was herded into the room, its dainty hooves clicking against the concrete floor. The class gathered in a circle to get a better look at the animal, who seemed delighted with the attention he was getting. He turned from face to face and was looking up at Hugh when one of the brothers drew a pistol from his back pocket, held it against the animal's temple, and shot the piglet, execution-style. Blood spattered, frightened children wept, and the man with the gun offered the teacher and bus driver some meat from a freshly slaughtered goat.

When I'm told such stories, it's all I can do to hold back my 7 feelings of jealousy. An Ethiopian slaughterhouse. Some people have all the luck. When I was in elementary school, the best we ever got was a trip to Old Salem or Colonial Williamsburg, one of those preserved brick villages where time supposedly stands still and someone earns his living as a town crier. There was always a blacksmith, a group of wandering patriots, and a collection of bonneted women hawking corn bread or gingersnaps made "the ol'-fashioned way." Every now and then you might come across a doer of bad deeds serving time in the stocks, but that was generally as exciting as it got.

Certain events are parallel, but compared with Hugh's, my 8 childhood was unspeakably dull. When I was seven years old, my family moved to North Carolina. When he was seven years old,

Hugh's family moved to the Congo. We had a collie and a house cat. They had a monkey and two horses named Charlie Brown and Satan. I threw stones at stop signs. Hugh threw stones at crocodiles. The verbs are the same, but he definitely wins the prize when it comes to nouns and objects. An eventful day for my mother might have involved a trip to the dry cleaner or a conversation with the potato-chip deliveryman. Asked one ordinary Congo afternoon what she'd done with her day, Hugh's mother answered that she and a fellow member of the Ladies' Club had visited a leper colony on the outskirts of Kinshasa. No reason was given for the expedition, though chances are she was staking it out for a future field trip.

Due to his upbringing, Hugh sits through inane movies never 9 realizing that they're often based on inane television shows. There were no poker-faced sitcom martians in his part of Africa, no oil-rich hillbillies or aproned brides trying to wean themselves from the practice of witchcraft. From time to time a movie would arrive packed in a dented canister, the film scratched and faded from its slow trip around the world. The theater consisted of a few dozen folding chairs arranged before a bedsheet or the blank wall of a vacant hangar out near the airstrip. Occasionally a man would sell warm soft drinks out of a cardboard box, but that was it in terms of concessions.

When I was young, I went to the theater at the nearby shop- 10 ping center and watched a movie about a talking Volkswagen. I believe the little car had a taste for mischief but I can't be certain, as both the movie and the afternoon proved unremarkable and have faded from my memory. Hugh saw the same movie a few years after it was released. His family had left the Congo by this time and were living in Ethiopia. Like me, Hugh saw the movie by himself on a weekend afternoon. Unlike me, he left the theater two hours later, to find a dead man hanging from a telephone pole at the far end of the unpaved parking lot. None of the people who'd seen the movie seemed to care about the dead man. They stared at him for a moment or two and then headed home, saying they'd never seen anything as crazy as that talking Volkswagen. His father was late picking him up, so Hugh just stood there for an hour, watching the dead man dangle and turn in the breeze. The death was not reported in the newspaper, and when Hugh related the story to his friends, they said, "You saw the movie about the talking car?"

I could have done without the flies and the primitive the- 11
aters, but I wouldn't have minded growing up with a houseful of
servants. In North Carolina it wasn't unusual to have a once-a-
week maid, but Hugh's family had houseboys, a word that never
fails to charge my imagination. They had cooks and drivers, and
guards who occupied a gatehouse, armed with machetes. Seeing
as I had regularly petitioned my parents for an electric fence,
the business with the guards strikes me as the last word in quiet
sophistication. Having protection suggests that you are important. Having that protection paid for by the government is even
better, as it suggests your safety is of interest to someone other
than yourself.

Hugh's father was a career officer with the US State Depart- 12
ment, and every morning a black sedan carried him off to the
embassy. I'm told it's not as glamorous as it sounds, but in terms
of fun for the entire family, I'm fairly confident that it beats the
sack race at the annual IBM picnic. By the age of three, Hugh was
already carrying a diplomatic passport. The rules that applied
to others did not apply to him. No tickets, no arrests, no lug-
gage search: He was officially licensed to act like a brat. Being an
American, it was expected of him, and who was he to deny the
world an occasional tantrum?

They weren't rich, but what Hugh's family lacked finan- 13
cially they more than made up for with the sort of exoticism
that works wonders at cocktail parties, leading always to the
remark "That sounds fascinating." It's a compliment one rarely
receives when describing an adolescence spent drinking Icees
at the North Hills Mall. No fifteen-foot python ever wandered
onto my school's basketball court. I begged, I prayed nightly, but
it just never happened. Neither did I get to witness a military
coup in which forces sympathetic to the colonel arrived late at
night to assassinate my next-door neighbor. Hugh had been at
the Addis Ababa teen club when the electricity was cut off and
soldiers arrived to evacuate the building. He and his friends had
to hide in the back of a jeep and cover themselves with blankets
during the ride home. It's something that sticks in his mind for
one reason or another.

Among my personal highlights is the memory of having my 14
picture taken with Uncle Paul, the legally blind host of a Raleigh
children's television show. Among Hugh's is the memory of having

his picture taken with Buzz Aldrin on the last leg of the astronaut's world tour. The man who had walked on the moon placed his hand on Hugh's shoulder and offered to sign his autograph book. The man who led Wake County schoolchildren in afternoon song turned at the sound of my voice and asked, "So what's your name, princess?"

When I was fourteen years old, I was sent to spend ten days 15 with my maternal grandmother in western New York State. She was a small and private woman named Billie, and though she never came right out and asked, I had the distinct impression she had no idea who I was. It was the way she looked at me, squinting through her glasses while chewing on her lower lip. That, coupled with the fact that she never once called me by name. "Oh," she'd say, "are you still here?" She was just beginning her long struggle with Alzheimer's disease, and each time I entered the room, I felt the need to reintroduce myself and set her at ease. "Hi, it's me. Sharon's boy, David. I was just in the kitchen admiring your collection of ceramic toads." Aside from a few trips to summer camp, this was the longest I'd ever been away from home, and I like to think I was toughened by the experience.

About the same time I was frightening my grandmother, 16 Hugh and his family were packing their belongings for a move to Somalia. There were no English-speaking schools in Mogadishu, so, after a few months spent lying around the family compound with his pet monkey, Hugh was sent back to Ethiopia to live with a beer enthusiast his father had met at a cocktail party. Mr. Hoyt installed security systems in foreign embassies. He and his family gave Hugh a room. They invited him to join them at the table, but that was as far as they extended themselves. No one ever asked him when his birthday was, so when the day came, he kept it to himself. There was no telephone service between Ethiopia and Somalia, and letters to his parents were sent to Washington and then forwarded on to Mogadishu, meaning that his news was more than a month old by the time they got it. I suppose it wasn't much different than living as a foreign-exchange student. Young people do it all the time, but to me it sounds awful. The Hoyts had two sons about Hugh's age who were always saying things like "Hey that's *our* sofa you're sitting on" and "Hands off that ornamental stein. It doesn't belong to you."

He'd been living with these people for a year when he over- 17
heard Mr. Hoyt tell a friend that he and his family would soon be
moving to Munich, Germany, the beer capital of the world.

"And that worried me," Hugh said, "because it meant I'd have 18
to find some other place to live."

Where I come from, finding shelter is a problem the average 19
teenager might confidently leave to his parents. It was just something that came with having a mom and a dad. Worried that he
might be sent to live with his grandparents in Kentucky, Hugh
turned to the school's guidance counselor, who knew of a family
whose son had recently left for college. And so he spent another
year living with strangers and not mentioning his birthday. While
I wouldn't have wanted to do it myself, I can't help but envy the
sense of fortitude he gained from the experience. After graduating
from college, he moved to France knowing only the phrase "Do
you speak French?"—a question guaranteed to get you nowhere
unless you also speak the language.

While living in Africa, Hugh and his family took frequent vaca- 20
tions, often in the company of their monkey. The Nairobi Hilton,
some suite of high-ceilinged rooms in Cairo or Khartoum: These are
the places his people recall when gathered at a common table. "Was
that the summer we spent in Beirut or, no, I'm thinking of the time
we sailed from Cyprus and took the *Orient Express* to Istanbul."

Theirs was the life I dreamt about during my vacations in 21
eastern North Carolina. Hugh's family was hobnobbing with
chiefs and sultans while I ate hush puppies at the Sanitary Fish
Market in Morehead City, a beach towel wrapped like a hijab[1]
around my head. Someone unknown to me was very likely standing in a muddy ditch and dreaming of an evening spent sitting in
a clean family restaurant, drinking iced tea and working his way
through an extra-large seaman's platter, but that did not concern
me, as it meant I should have been happy with what I had. Rather
than surrender to my bitterness, I have learned to take satisfaction in the life that Hugh has led. His stories have, over time,
become my own. I say this with no trace of a kumbaya.[2] There is

[1]A headscarf worn by Muslim women. [Editors' note.]
[2]From the gospel-folk song with the line "Kumbaya, my Lord, kumbaya," meaning "Come by here." Probably because of its popularity in folk music, the word also
has negative connotations of passivity or touchy-feely spiritualism. [Editors' note.]

no spiritual symbiosis; I'm just a petty thief who lifts his memories the same way I'll take a handful of change left on his dresser. When my own experiences fall short of the mark, I just go out and spend some of his. It is with pleasure that I sometimes recall the dead man's purpled face or the report of the handgun ringing in my ears as I studied the blood pooling beneath the dead white piglet. On the way back from the slaughterhouse, we stopped for Cokes in the village of Mojo, where the gas-station owner had arranged a few tables and chairs beneath a dying canopy of vines. It was late afternoon by the time we returned to school, where a second bus carried me to the foot of Coffeeboard Road. Once there, I walked through a grove of eucalyptus trees and alongside a bald pasture of starving cattle, past the guard napping in his gatehouse, and into the waiting arms of my monkey.

Meaning

1. What is the subject of Sedaris's comparison and contrast in this essay?
2. There is a certain amount of irony in Sedaris's envy of Hugh's childhood. What is this irony? How does Sedaris make this irony explicit in paragraph 21? (If necessary, consult the Glossary under *irony*.)

Purpose and Audience

1. What do you think is the purpose of this essay? Take into account both Sedaris's obvious envy of Hugh's childhood and Sedaris's awareness that Hugh's life was often lonely and insecure. Is the thesis stated or only implied?
2. What assumptions does Sedaris make about his audience? Where in the essay do you see evidence of these assumptions?

Method and Structure

1. Does Sedaris develop his comparison and contrast subject by subject or point by point? Briefly outline the essay to explain your answer.
2. The first five paragraphs of the essay include a conversation between Sedaris and Hugh about Hugh's childhood. Why do you think the author opened the essay this way?
3. OTHER METHODS   How does Sedaris use narration to develop his essay? How does he use examples?

Language

1. How does Sedaris use parallelism in paragraph 8 to highlight the contrast between himself and Hugh? How does he then assess the point of this parallelism? (For the definition of *parallelism*, consult the Glossary.)
2. Sedaris offers the image of himself as a "petty thief" in paragraph 21. What is the effect of this image?
3. Sedaris's language in this essay is notably specific and concrete. Point to examples of such language just in paragraph 6. (If necessary, consult the Glossary under *specific words* and *concrete words*.)

Writing Topics

1. Write an essay in which you compare and contrast your own experiences with those of someone whose life you've envied. Have your feelings changed over time? Why, or why not?
2. Hugh's experiences living with strangers gave him a "sense of fortitude" (paragraph 19), according to Sedaris. When have you ever gone through a difficult experience that left you somehow stronger? Write an essay about such an experience that shows how you were different before and after.
3. How seriously does Sedaris want the readers of his essay to take him? Write an essay in which you analyze his tone, citing specific passages from the text to support your conclusions. (If necessary, consult the Glossary for the definition of *tone*.)

RICHARD RODRIGUEZ

Born in 1944 in San Francisco to Spanish-speaking Mexican immigrants, Richard Rodriguez entered school speaking essentially no English and left it with a PhD in English literature. In between, his increasing assimilation into the mainstream of American society meant increasing alienation from his parents and their culture—a simultaneous gain and loss that he often writes about. Rodriguez was educated in the Catholic schools of Sacramento, California; graduated from Stanford University; and earned a PhD from the University of California at Berkeley. A lecturer and writer, he is an editor at New American Media *and a contributing editor for* Harper's Magazine, US News & World Report, *and the* Los Angeles Times. *His books include* Days of Obligation: An Argument with My Mexican Father *(1992) and* Brown: The Last Discovery of America *(2002). Rodriguez's work frequently addresses the controversial programs of affirmative action and bilingual education, both of which his own experiences have led him to oppose. On bilingual education he says, "To me, public educators in a public schoolroom have an obligation to teach a public language. . . . The imperative is to get children away from those languages that increase their sense of alienation from the public society."*

Private Language, Public Language

In this excerpt from his memoir Hunger of Memory *(1982), Rodriguez tells of shuttling between the private language of family and the public language of society. His family spoke Spanish, his society English, but the distinction between an intimate private language and an alienating public language is experienced, he believes, by all children.*

I remember to start with that day in Sacramento—a California 1 now nearly thirty years past—when I first entered a classroom, able to understand some fifty stray English words.

The third of four children, I had been preceded to a neighbor- 2 hood Roman Catholic school by an older brother and sister. But neither of them had revealed very much about their classroom experiences. Each afternoon they returned, as they left in the morning, always together, speaking in Spanish as they climbed the five steps of the porch. And their mysterious books, wrapped in shopping-bag paper, remained on the table next to the door, closed firmly behind them.

An accident of geography sent me to a school where all my 3 classmates were white, many the children of doctors and lawyers and business executives. All my classmates certainly must have been uneasy on that first day of school—as most children are uneasy—to find themselves apart from their families in the first institution of their lives. But I was astonished.

The nun said, in a friendly but oddly impersonal voice, 4 "Boys and girls, this is Richard Rodriguez." (I heard her sound out: *Rich-heard Road-ree-guess*.) It was the first time I had heard anyone name me in English. "Richard," the nun repeated more slowly, writing my name down in her black leather book. Quickly I turned to see my mother's face dissolve in a watery blur behind the pebbled glass door.

Many years later there is something called bilingual educa- 5 tion—a scheme proposed in the late 1960s by Hispanic American social activists, later endorsed by a congressional vote. It is a program that seeks to permit non-English-speaking children, many from lower-class homes, to use their family language as the language of school. (Such is the goal its supporters announce.) I hear them and am forced to say no: it is not possible for a child—any child—ever to use his family's language in school. Not to understand this is to misunderstand the public uses of schooling and to trivialize the nature of intimate life—a family's "language."

Memory teaches me what I know of these matters; the boy 6 reminds the adult. I was a bilingual child, a certain kind—socially disadvantaged—the son of working-class parents, both Mexican immigrants.

In the early years of my boyhood, my parents coped very well 7 in America. My father had steady work. My mother managed at home. They were nobody's victims. Optimism and ambition led them to a house (our home) many blocks from the Mexican south

side of town. We lived among *gringos*[1] and only a block from the
biggest, whitest houses. It never occurred to my parents that they
couldn't live wherever they chose. Nor was the Sacramento of the
fifties bent on teaching them a contrary lesson. My mother and
father were more annoyed than intimidated by those two or three
neighbors who tried initially to make us unwelcome. ("Keep your
brats away from my sidewalk!") But despite all they achieved,
perhaps because they had so much to achieve, any deep feeling
of ease, the confidence of "belonging" in public was withheld
from them both. They regarded the people at work, the faces in
crowds, as very distant from us. They were the others, *los gringos*.
That term was interchangeable in their speech with another, even
more telling, *los americanos*. . . .

   In public, my father and mother spoke a hesitant, accented, 8
not always grammatical English. And they would have to
strain—their bodies tense—to catch the sense of what was rapidly said by *los gringos*. At home they spoke Spanish. The language of their Mexican past sounded in counterpoint to the English of public society. The words would come quickly, with ease.
Conveyed through those sounds was the pleasing, soothing, consoling reminder of being at home.

   During those years when I was first conscious of hearing, 9
my mother and father addressed me only in Spanish; in Spanish
I learned to reply. By contrast, English (*inglés*), rarely heard in
the house, was the language I came to associate with *gringos*. I
learned my first words of English overhearing my parents speak
to strangers. At five years of age, I knew just enough English for
my mother to trust me on errands to stores one block away. No
more.

   I was a listening child, careful to hear the very different 10
sounds of Spanish and English. Wide-eyed with learning, I'd listen to sounds more than words. First, there were English (*gringo*)
sounds. So many words were still unknown that when the butcher
or the lady at the drugstore said something to me, exotic polysyllabic sounds would bloom in the midst of their sentences. Often
the speech of people in public seemed to me very loud, booming
with confidence. The man behind the counter would literally ask,

[1]Spanish for "foreigners," especially Americans and the English. [Editors' note.]

"What can I do for you?" But by being so firm and so clear, the sound of his voice said that he was a *gringo*; he belonged in public society.

I would also hear then the high nasal tones of middle-class 11 American speech. The air stirred with sound. Sometimes, even now, when I have been traveling abroad for several weeks, I will hear what I heard as a boy. In hotel lobbies or airports, in Turkey or Brazil, some Americans will pass, and suddenly I will hear it again—the high sound of American voices. For a few seconds I will hear it with pleasure, for it is now the sound of my society—a reminder of home. But inevitably—already on the flight headed for home—the sound fades with repetition. I will be unable to hear it anymore.

When I was a boy, things were different. The accent of *los* 12 *gringos* was never pleasing nor was it hard to hear. Crowds at Safeway or at bus stops would be noisy with sound. And I would be forced to edge away from the chirping chatter above me.

I was unable to hear my own sounds, but I knew very well 13 that I spoke English poorly. My words could not stretch far enough to form complete thoughts. And the words I did speak I didn't know well enough to make into distinct sounds. (Listeners would usually lower their heads, better to hear what I was trying to say.) But it was one thing for *me* to speak English with difficulty. It was more troubling for me to hear my parents speak in public: their high-whining vowels and guttural consonants; their sentences that got stuck with "eh" and "ah" sounds; the confused syntax; the hesitant rhythm of sounds so different from the way *gringos* spoke. I'd notice, moreover, that my parents' voices were softer than those of *gringos* we'd meet. . . .

There were many times like the night at a brightly lit gasoline 14 station (a blaring white memory) when I stood uneasily, hearing my father. He was talking to a teenaged attendant. I do not recall what they were saying, but I cannot forget the sounds my father made as he spoke. At one point his words slid together to form one word—sounds as confused as the threads of blue and green oil in the puddle next to my shoes. His voice rushed through what he had left to say. And, toward the end, reached falsetto notes, appealing to his listener's understanding. I looked away to the lights of passing automobiles. I tried not to hear anymore. But I heard only too well the calm, easy tones in the attendant's reply.

Shortly afterward, walking toward home with my father, I shivered when he put his hand on my shoulder. The very first chance that I got, I evaded his grasp and ran on ahead into the dark, skipping with feigned boyish exuberance.

But then there was Spanish. *Español*: my family's language. 15 *Español*: the language that seemed to me a private language. I'd hear strangers on the radio and in the Mexican Catholic church across town speaking Spanish, but I couldn't really believe that Spanish was a public language, like English. Spanish speakers, rather, seemed related to me, for I sensed that we shared—through our language—the experience of feeling apart from *los gringos*. It was thus a ghetto Spanish that I heard and I spoke. Like those whose lives are bound by a barrio, I was reminded by Spanish of my separateness from *los otros*,[2] *los gringos* in power. But more intensely than for most barrio children—because I did not live in a barrio—Spanish seemed to me the language of home. (Most days it was only at home that I'd hear it.) It became the language of joyful return.

A family member would say something to me and I would 16 feel myself specially recognized. My parents would say something to me and I would feel embraced by the sounds of their words. Those sounds said: *I am speaking with ease in Spanish. I am addressing you in words I never use with* los gringos. *I recognize you as someone special, close, like no one outside. You belong with us. In the family.*

(*Ricardo.*)   17

At the age of five, six, well past the time when most other 18 children no longer easily notice the difference between sounds uttered at home and words spoken in public, I had a different experience. I lived in a world magically compounded of sounds. I remained a child longer than most; I lingered too long, poised at the edge of language—often frightened by the sounds of *los gringos*, delighted by the sounds of Spanish at home. I shared with my family a language that was startlingly different from that used in the great city around us.

For me there were none of the gradations between public and 19 private society so normal to a maturing child. Outside the house was public society; inside the house was private. Just opening

---

[2]Spanish: "the others." [Editors' note.]

or closing the screen door behind me was an important experience. I'd rarely leave home all alone or without reluctance. Walking down the sidewalk, under the canopy of tall trees, I'd warily notice the—suddenly—silent neighborhood kids who stood warily watching me. Nervously, I'd arrive at the grocery store to hear there the sounds of the *gringo*—foreign to me—reminding me that in this world so big, I was a foreigner. But then I'd return. Walking back toward our house, climbing the steps from the sidewalk, when the front door was open in summer, I'd hear voices beyond the screen door talking in Spanish. For a second or two, I'd stay, linger there, listening. Smiling, I'd hear my mother call out, saying in Spanish (words), "Is that you, Richard?" All the while her sounds would assure me: *You are home now; come closer; inside. With us.*

"*Sí,*" I'd reply.

Once more inside the house I would resume (assume) my place in the family. The sounds would dim, grow harder to hear. Once more at home, I would grow less aware of that fact. It required, however, no more than the blurt of the doorbell to alert me to listen to sounds all over again. The house would turn instantly still while my mother went to the door. I'd hear her hard English sounds. I'd wait to hear her voice return to soft-sounding Spanish, which assured me, as surely as did the clicking tongue of the lock of the door, that the stranger was gone.

Plainly, it is not healthy to hear such sounds so often. It is not healthy to distinguish public words from private sounds so easily. I remained cloistered by sounds, timid and shy in public, too dependent on voices at home. And yet it needs to be emphasized: I was an extremely happy child at home. I remember many nights when my father would come back from work, and I'd hear him call out to my mother in Spanish, sounding relieved. In Spanish, he'd sound light and free notes he never could manage in English. Some nights I'd jump up just at hearing his voice. With *mis hermanos*[3] I would come running into the room where he was with my mother. Our laughing (so deep was the pleasure!) became screaming. Like others who know the pain of public alienation, we transformed the knowledge of our public separateness and made it consoling—the reminder of intimacy. Excited, we joined

[3]Spanish: "my siblings." [Editors' note.]

our voices in a celebration of sounds. *We are speaking now the way we never speak out in public. We are alone—together,* voices sounded, surrounded to tell me. Some nights, no one seemed willing to loosen the hold sound had on us. At dinner, we invented new words. (Ours sounded Spanish, but made sense only to us.) We pieced together new words by taking, say, an English verb and giving it Spanish endings. My mother's instructions at bedtime would be lacquered with mock-urgent tones. Or a word like *sí* would become, in several notes, able to convey added measures of feeling. Tongues explored the edges of words, especially the fat vowels. And we happily sounded that military drum roll, the twirling roar of the Spanish *r*. Family language: my family's sounds. The voices of my parents and sisters and brothers. Their voices insisting: *You belong here. We are family members. Related. Special to one another. Listen!* Voices singing and sighing, rising, straining, then surging, teeming with pleasure that burst syllables into fragments of laughter. At times it seemed there was steady quiet only when, from another room, the rustling whispers of my parents faded and I moved closer to sleep.

Meaning

1. What is Rodriguez's main idea about public and private language?
2. What did language represent for the young Rodriguez? In answering, consider both his contrasting perceptions of the sounds of English and of Spanish and his contrasting feelings among *los gringos* and among his family.
3. What explanation does Rodriguez give for why his transition from private to public language took longer than most children's (paragraphs 18–19)? Given his characterization of himself as a child, especially in paragraph 10, does his slow transition seem attributable solely to his bilingual environment? Why?

Purpose and Audience

1. What seems to be Rodriguez's purpose in this piece? Is he primarily expressing his memories of childhood, explaining something about childhood in a bilingual environment and about childhood in general, or arguing against bilingual education? What passages support your answer?
2. Since he writes in English, Rodriguez is presumably addressing English-speaking readers. Why, then, does he occasionally use Span-

ish words (such as *gringos*, paragraph 7) without translating them? What do these words contribute to the essay?

Method and Structure

1. Rodriguez's comparison of private and public language includes smaller comparisons between himself and other children (paragraphs 3, 15, 18–19), himself as an adult and a child (11–12), and himself and his parents (13). What does each of these smaller comparisons contribute to Rodriguez's portrayal of himself and to his main idea?

2. Where does Rodriguez shift his focus from public language to private language? Why does he treat private language second? What effect does he achieve with the last paragraph?

3. OTHER METHODS   Rodriguez uses narration in paragraphs 3–4, 10, 14, and 22. Do you think the experiences and the feelings Rodriguez either expresses or implies are shared by children in one-language environments? What do these narratives contribute to Rodriguez's main idea?

Language

1. Why does Rodriguez spell out his name to reflect its pronunciation with an American accent (paragraph 4)? What does the contrast between this form of his name and the Spanish form (17) contribute to his comparison?

2. Compare the words Rodriguez uses to describe *los gringos* and their speech (paragraphs 4, 7, 10, 12, 14, 19) with those he uses to describe his family and their speech (paragraphs 7, 8, 13, 14, 16, 21, 22). What does his word choice tell you about his childhood attitudes toward each group of people?

3. Notice the figures of speech Rodriguez uses: for instance, "My words could not stretch far enough to form complete thoughts" (paragraph 13); "a blaring white memory" (14). What do these and other figures of speech convey about Rodriguez's feelings? (If necessary, consult the Glossary under *figures of speech*.)

Writing Topics

1. Rodriguez has said, "What I know about language—the movement between private and public society, the distance between sound and words—is a universal experience." Consider a "private" group you feel a part of—for instance, your family, friends, fellow athletes,

people who share the same hobby. How do the language, behaviors, and attitudes of the group distinguish it from "public" society? Write an essay in which you compare your perceptions of and feelings toward the two worlds.

2. Many books and articles have been written on the subject of bilingual education in American schools. Locate an article, book, or Web site that presents a variety of opinions on the issue. Or read what Rodriguez says about it in the rest of *Hunger of Memory*. Then write an essay in which you state and support your opinion on whether children whose first language is not English should be taught in English or in their native language.

3. Recall any difficulties you have had with language—learning English as a second language, learning any other second language, learning to read, overcoming a speech impediment, improving your writing in freshman composition. Write an essay in which you explain the circumstances and their significance for you.

Writing with the Method

COMPARISON AND CONTRAST

Select one of the following topics, or any other topic they suggest, for an essay developed by comparison and contrast. Be sure to choose a topic you care about so that the comparison and contrast is a means of communicating an idea, not an end in itself.

Experience

1. Two jobs you have held
2. Two experiences with discrimination
3. Your own version of an event you witnessed or participated in and someone else's view of the same event (perhaps a friend's or a reporter's)

People

4. Your relationships with two friends
5. Someone before and after marriage or the birth of a child
6. Two or more candidates for public office
7. Two relatives

Places and Things

8. A place as it is now and as it was years ago
9. Public and private transportation
10. Contact lenses and glasses
11. Two towns or cities

Art and Entertainment

12. The work of two artists or writers, or two works by the same person
13. Movies or television today and when you were a child
14. A high-school sports game and a professional game in the same sport
15. The advertisements on two very different Web sites

Education and Ideas

16. Talent and skill
17. Learning and teaching
18. Your study method and that of a classmate
19. A humanities course and a science or mathematics course

Chapter 8

DEFINITION

USING THE METHOD

Definition sets the boundaries of a thing, a concept, an emotion, or a value. In answering "What is it?" and also "What is it *not*?" definition specifies the main qualities of the subject and its essential nature. Since words are only symbols, pinning down their precise meanings is essential for us to understand ourselves and one another. Thus we use definition constantly, whether we are explaining a new word like *staycation* to someone who has never heard it or explaining what *culture* means on an essay examination.

There are several kinds of definition, each with different uses. One is the **formal definition**, a statement of the general class of things to which the word belongs, followed by the distinction(s) between it and other members of the class. For example:

	General Class	*Distinction(s)*
A submarine is	a seagoing vessel	that operates underwater.
A parable is	a brief, simple story	that illustrates a moral or religious principle.
Pressure is	the force	applied to a given surface.
Insanity is	a mental condition	in which a defendant does not know right from wrong.

A formal definition usually gives a standard dictionary meaning of the word (as in the first two examples) or a specialized meaning agreed to by the members of a profession or discipline (as in the last two examples, from physics and criminal law, respectively). It is most useful to explain the basic meaning of a term that readers need to know in order to understand the rest of a discussion. Occasionally you might also use a formal definition as a springboard to a more elaborate, detailed exploration of a word. For instance, you might define *pride* simply as "a sense of self-respect" before probing the varied meanings of the word as people actually understand it and then settling on a fuller and more precise meaning of your own devising.

This more detailed definition of *pride* could fall into one of two other types of definition: stipulative and extended. A **stipulative definition** clarifies the particular way you are using a word: you stipulate, or specify, a meaning to suit a larger purpose; the definition is part of a larger whole. For example, if you wanted to show how pride can destroy personal relationships, you might first stipulate a meaning of *pride* that ties in with that purpose. Though a stipulative definition may sometimes take the form of a brief formal definition, most require several sentences or even paragraphs. In a physics textbook, for instance, the physicist's definition of *pressure* quoted earlier probably would not suffice to give readers a good sense of the term or to eliminate all the other possible meanings they may have in mind.

While you use a formal or stipulative definition for some larger purpose, you write an **extended definition** for the sake of defining—that is, for the purpose of exploring a thing, quality, or idea in its full complexity and drawing boundaries around it until its meaning is complete and precise. Extended definitions usually treat subjects so complex, vague, or laden with emotions or values that people misunderstand or disagree over their meanings. The subject may be an abstract concept like *patriotism*, a controversial phrase like *beginnings of life*, a colloquial or slang expression like *hype*, a thing like *nanobot*, a scientific idea like *natural selection*, even an everyday expression like *nagging*. Besides defining, your purpose may be to persuade readers to accept a definition (for instance, that life begins at conception, or at birth), to explain (what is natural selection?), or to amuse (nagging as exemplified by notorious nags).

As the variety of possible subjects and purposes may suggest, an extended definition may draw on whatever methods will best accomplish the goal of specifying what the subject encompasses and distinguishing it from similar things, qualities, or concepts. Several strategies are unique to definition:

- **Synonyms**, or words of similar meaning, can convey the range of the word's meanings. For example, you could equate *misery* with *wretchedness* and *distress*.
- **Negation**, or saying what a word does not mean, can limit the meaning, particularly when you want to focus on only one sense of an abstract term, such as *pride*, that is open to diverse interpretations.
- The **etymology** of a word—its history—may illuminate its meaning, perhaps by showing the direction and extent of its change (*pride*, for instance, comes from a Latin word meaning "to be beneficial or useful") or by uncovering buried origins that remain implicit in the modern meaning (*patriotism* comes from the Greek word for "father"; *happy* comes from the Old Norse word for "good luck").

You may use these strategies of definition alone or together, and they may occupy whole paragraphs in an essay-length definition; but they rarely provide enough range to surround the subject completely. That's why most definition essays draw on at least some of the other methods discussed in this book. One or two methods may predominate: an essay on nagging, for instance, might be developed with brief narratives. Or several methods may be combined: a definition of *patriotism* could also compare it with *nationalism*, analyze its effects (such as the actions people take on its behalf), and give examples of patriotic individuals. The goal is not to employ every method in a sort of catalog of methods but to use those which best illuminate the subject. By drawing on the appropriate methods, you define and clarify your perspective on the subject so that the reader understands the meaning exactly.

DEVELOPING AN ESSAY BY DEFINITION

Getting Started

You'll sometimes be asked to write definition essays, as when a psychology exam asks for a discussion of *schizophrenia* or a political science assignment calls for an explanation of the term *totalitarianism.* To come up with a subject on your own, consider words that have complex meanings and are either unfamiliar to readers or open to varied interpretations. The subject should be something you know and care enough about to explore in great detail and surround completely. An idea for a subject may come from an overheard conversation (a reference to someone as "too patriotic"), a personal experience (a broken marriage you think attributable to one spouse's pride), or something you've seen or read (another writer's definition of *jazz*).

Begin exploring your subject by examining and listing its conventional meanings. An unabridged dictionary will provide meanings and give you synonyms and etymology. Also examine the differences of opinion about the word's meanings—the different ways, wrong or right, that you have heard or seen it used. Run through the other methods to see what fresh approaches to the subject they open up:

- *How can the subject be described?*
- *What are some examples?*
- *Can the subject be divided into qualities or characteristics?*
- *Can its functions help define it?*
- *Will comparing and contrasting it with something else help sharpen its meaning?*
- *Do its causes or effects help clarify its sense?*

Some of the questions may turn up nothing, but others may open your eyes to meanings you had not seen.

Forming a Thesis

When you have generated a good list of ideas about your subject, settle on the purpose of your definition. Do you mostly want to explain a word that is unfamiliar to readers? Do you want to express your own view so that readers see a familiar subject from a new angle? Do you want to argue in favor of a particular definition or perhaps persuade readers to look more critically at themselves or their surroundings? Try to work your purpose into a tentative thesis sentence that summarizes your definition and—just as important—asserts something about the subject. For example:

TENTATIVE THESIS STATEMENT The prevailing concept of *patriotism* is dangerously wrong.

REVISED THESIS STATEMENT Though generally considered entirely positive in meaning, *patriotism* also reflects selfish, childlike emotions that have no place in a global society, even one threatened by terrorism.

Note that the revised thesis statement not only summarizes the writer's definition and makes an assertion about the subject, but also identifies the prevailing definition she intends to counter in her essay.

With a thesis sentence formulated, reevaluate your ideas in light of it and pause to consider the needs of your readers:

- *What do readers already know about your subject*, and what do they need to be told in order to understand it as you do?
- *Are your readers likely to be biased for or against your subject?* If you were defining *patriotism*, for example, you might assume that your readers see the word as representing a constructive, even essential value that contributes to the strength of the country. If your purpose were to contest this view, as implied by the thesis above, you would have to build your case carefully to win readers to your side.

Organizing

The introduction to a definition essay should provide a base from which to expand and at the same time explain to readers why the forthcoming definition is useful, significant, or necessary. You may want to report the incident that prompted you to define, say why the subject itself is important, or specify the common understandings, or misunderstandings, about its meaning. Several devices can serve as effective beginnings: the etymology of the word; a quotation from another writer supporting or contradicting your definition; or an explanation of what the word does *not* mean (negation). (Try to avoid the overused opening that cites a dictionary: "According to the *American Heritage Dictionary*, ____ means . . ." Your readers have probably seen this opening many times before.) If it is not implied in the rest of your introduction, you may want to state your thesis so that readers know precisely what your purpose and point are.

The body of the essay should then proceed, paragraph by paragraph, to refine the characteristics or qualities of the subject, using the arrangement and methods that will distinguish it from anything similar and provide your perspective. For instance, you might try any of the following approaches:

- *Draw increasingly tight boundaries around the subject*, moving from broader, more familiar meanings to the one you have in mind.
- *Arrange your points in order of increasing drama.*
- *Begin with your own experience of the subject* and then show how you see it operating in your surroundings.

The conclusion to a definition essay is equally a matter of choice. You might summarize your definition, indicate its superiority to other definitions of the same subject, quote another writer whose view supports your own, or recommend that readers make some use of the information you have provided. The choice depends—as it does in any kind of essay—on your purpose and the impression you want to leave with readers.

Drafting

While drafting your extended definition, keep your subject vividly in mind. Say too much rather than too little about it to ensure that you capture its essence; you can always cut when you revise. And be sure to provide plenty of details and examples to support your view. Such evidence is particularly important when, as in the earlier example of patriotism, you seek to change readers' perceptions of your subject.

In definition the words you use are especially important. Abstractions and generalities cannot draw precise boundaries around a subject, so your words must be as concrete and specific as you can make them. You'll have chances during revising and editing to work on your words, but try during drafting to pin down your meanings. Use words and phrases that appeal directly to the senses and experiences of readers. When appropriate, use figures of speech to make meaning inescapably clear; instead of "Patriotism can be childlike," for example, you might say, "The blindly patriotic person is like a small child who sees his or her parents as gods, all-knowing, always right." The connotations of words—the associations called up in readers' minds by words like *home, ambitious,* and *generous*—can contribute to your definition as well. But be sure that connotative words trigger associations suited to your purpose. And when you are trying to explain something precisely, rely most heavily on words with generally neutral meanings. (For further discussion, consult the following entries in the Glossary: *abstract and concrete words, general and specific words, figures of speech,* and *connotation and denotation.*)

Revising and Editing

When you are satisfied that your draft is complete, revise and edit it using the following questions.

- *Have you surrounded your subject completely and tightly?* Your definition should not leave gaps, nor should the boundaries be so broadly drawn that the subject overlaps something else. For instance, a definition of *hype* that focuses on exaggerated and deliberately misleading claims should include all such claims (some political speeches, say, as well as some advertisements), and it should exclude appeals that do not fit the basic definition (some public-service advertising, for instance).

- *Does your definition reflect the conventional meanings of the word?* Even if you are providing a fresh slant on your subject, you can't change its meaning entirely or you will confuse your readers and perhaps undermine your own credibility. *Patriotism,* for example, could not be defined from the first as "hatred of foreigners," for that definition strays into an entirely different realm. The conventional meaning of "love of country" would have to serve as the starting point, though your essay might interpret the meaning in an original way.

JUDY BRADY

Judy Brady was born in 1937 in San Francisco, California. She attended the University of Iowa and graduated with a bachelor's degree in painting in 1962. Married in 1960, by the mid-1960s she was raising two daughters. She began working in the women's movement in 1969 and through it developed an ongoing concern with political and social issues, especially women's rights, cancer, and the environment. She believes that "as long as women continue to tolerate a society which places profits above the needs of people, we will continue to be exploited as workers and as wives." Besides the essay reprinted here, Brady has written articles for various magazines and edited 1 in 3: Women with Cancer Confront an Epidemic *(1991), motivated by her own struggle with the disease. She is also cofounder of the Toxic Links Coalition and serves on the board of Greenaction for Health and Environmental Justice.*

I Want a Wife

Writing after eleven years of marriage, and before divorcing her husband, Brady here pins down the meaning of the word wife *from the perspective of one person who lives the role. This essay was published in the first issue of* Ms. *magazine in December 1971, and it has since been reprinted widely. Is its harsh portrayal still relevant today?*

1   I belong to that classification of people known as wives. I am A Wife. And, not altogether incidentally, I am a mother.

2   Not too long ago a male friend of mine appeared on the scene fresh from a recent divorce. He had one child, who is, of course, with his ex-wife. He is looking for another wife. As I thought about him while I was ironing one evening, it suddenly occurred to me that I, too, would like to have a wife. Why do I want a wife?

3   I would like to go back to school so that I can become economically independent, support myself, and, if need be, support those dependent upon me. I want a wife who will work and send

me to school. And while I am going to school I want a wife to take care of my children. I want a wife to keep track of the children's doctor and dentist appointments. And to keep track of mine, too. I want a wife to make sure my children eat properly and are kept clean. I want a wife who will wash the children's clothes and keep them mended. I want a wife who is a good nurturant attendant to my children, who arranges for their schooling, makes sure that they have an adequate social life with their peers, takes them to the park, the zoo, etc. I want a wife who takes care of the children when they are sick, a wife who arranges to be around when the children need special care, because, of course, I cannot miss classes at school. My wife must arrange to lose time at work and not lose the job. It may mean a small cut in my wife's income from time to time, but I guess I can tolerate that. Needless to say, my wife will arrange and pay for the care of the children while my wife is working.

I want a wife who will take care of *my* physical needs. I want 4 a wife who will keep my house clean. A wife who will pick up after my children, a wife who will pick up after me. I want a wife who will keep my clothes clean, ironed, mended, replaced when need be, and who will see to it that my personal things are kept in their proper place so that I can find what I need the minute I need it. I want a wife who cooks the meals, a wife who is a *good* cook. I want a wife who will plan the menus, do the necessary grocery shopping, prepare the meals, serve them pleasantly, and then do the cleaning up while I do my studying. I want a wife who will care for me when I am sick and sympathize with my pain and loss of time from school. I want a wife to go along when our family takes a vacation so that someone can continue to care for me and my children when I need a rest and change of scene.

I want a wife who will not bother me with rambling com- 5 plaints about a wife's duties. But I want a wife who will listen to me when I feel the need to explain a rather difficult point I have come across in my course of studies. And I want a wife who will type my papers for me when I have written them.

I want a wife who will take care of the details of my social 6 life. When my wife and I are invited out by friends, I want a wife who will take care of the babysitting arrangements. When I meet people at school that I like and want to entertain, I want a wife who will have the house clean, will prepare a special meal, serve it to me and my friends, and not interrupt when I talk about things that interest me and my friends. I want a wife who will have arranged that the children are fed and ready for bed before my guests arrive so that the children do not bother us. I want a wife who takes care of the needs of my guests so that they feel comfortable, who makes sure that they have an ashtray, that they are passed the hors d'oeuvres, that they are offered a second helping of the food, that their wine glasses are replenished when necessary, that their coffee is served to them as they like it. And I want a wife who knows that sometimes I need a night out by myself.

I want a wife who is sensitive to my sexual needs, a wife who 7
makes love passionately and eagerly when I feel like it, a wife who makes sure that I am satisfied. And, of course, I want a wife who will not demand sexual attention when I am not in the mood for it. I want a wife who assumes the complete responsibility for birth control, because I do not want more children. I want a wife who will remain sexually faithful to me so that I do not have to clutter up my intellectual life with jealousies. And I want a wife who understands that *my* sexual needs may entail more than strict adherence to monogamy. I must, after all, be able to relate to people as fully as possible.

If, by chance, I find another person more suitable as a wife 8
than the wife I already have, I want the liberty to replace my present wife with another one. Naturally, I will expect a fresh, new life; my wife will take the children and be solely responsible for them so that I am left free.

When I am through with school and have a job, I want my 9
wife to quit working and remain at home so that my wife can more fully and completely take care of a wife's duties.

My God, who *wouldn't* want a wife?   10

Meaning

1. In one or two sentences, summarize Brady's definition of a wife. Consider not only the functions she mentions but also the relationship she portrays.

2. Brady provides many instances of a double standard of behavior and responsibility for the wife and the wife's spouse. What are the wife's chief responsibilities and expected behaviors? What are the spouse's?

Purpose and Audience

1. Why do you think Brady wrote this essay? Was her purpose to explain a wife's duties, to complain about her own situation, to poke fun at men, to attack men, to attack society's attitudes toward women, or something else? Was she trying to provide a realistic and fair definition of *wife*? What passages in the essay support your answers?

2. What does Brady seem to assume about her readers' gender (male or female) and their attitudes toward women's roles in society, relations between the sexes, and work inside and outside the home? Does she seem to write from the perspective of a particular age group or social and economic background? In answering these questions, cite specific passages from the essay.

3. Brady clearly intended to provoke a reaction from readers. What is *your* reaction to this essay: do you think it is realistic or exaggerated, fair or unfair to men, relevant or irrelevant to the present time? Why?

Method and Structure

1. Why would anybody need to write an essay defining a term like *wife*? Don't we know what a wife is already? How does Brady use definition in an original way to achieve her purpose?

2. Analyze Brady's essay as a piece of definition, considering its thoroughness, its specificity, and its effectiveness in distinguishing the subject from anything similar.

3. Analyze the introduction to Brady's essay. What function does paragraph 1 serve? In what way does paragraph 2 confirm Brady's definition? How does the question at the end of the introduction relate to the question at the end of the essay?

4. OTHER METHODS   Brady develops her definition primarily by classification. What does she classify, and what categories does she form? What determines her arrangement of these categories? What does the classification contribute to the essay?

Language

1. How would you characterize Brady's tone: whining, amused, angry, contemptuous, or what? What phrases in the essay support your answer? (If necessary, consult the Glossary under *tone*.)

2. Why does Brady repeat "I want a wife" in almost every sentence, often at the beginning of the sentence? What does this stylistic device convey about the person who wants a wife? How does it fit in with Brady's main idea and purpose?

3. Why does Brady never substitute the personal pronoun "she" for "my wife"? Does the effect gained by repeating "my wife" justify the occasionally awkward sentences, such as the last one in paragraph 3?

4. What effect does Brady achieve with the expressions "of course" (paragraphs 3, 7), "Needless to say" (3), "after all" (7), and "Naturally" (8)?

Writing Topics

1. Analyze a role that is defined by gender, such as that of a wife or husband, mother or father, sister or brother, daughter or son. First write down the responsibilities, activities, and relationships that define that role, and then elaborate your ideas, forming an essay to define this role as you see it. You could, if appropriate, follow Brady's model by showing how the role is influenced by the expectations of another person or people.

2. Combine the methods of definition and comparison in an essay that compares a wife or a husband you know with Brady's definition of either role. Be sure that the point of your comparison is clear and that you use specific examples to illustrate the similarities or differences you see.

3. Brady's essay was written in the specific cultural context of 1971. Undoubtedly, many cultural changes have taken place since then, particularly changes in gender roles. However, one could also argue that much remains the same. Write an essay in which you compare the stereotypical role of a wife now with the role Brady defines. In addition to your own observations and experiences, consider contemporary images of wives that the media present—for instance, in advertising or sitcoms.

GLORIA NAYLOR

An American novelist and essayist, Gloria Naylor was born in 1950 in New York City. She served as a missionary for Jehovah's Witnesses from 1967 to 1975 and then worked as a hotel telephone operator until 1981. That year she graduated from Brooklyn College of the City of New York with a BA and went on to do graduate work in African American studies at Yale University. Since receiving an MA from Yale, Naylor has published five novels dealing with the varied histories and lifestyles often lumped together as "the black experience": The Women of Brewster Place *(1982), about the lives of eight black women, which won the American Book Award for fiction and was made into a television movie;* Linden Hills *(1985), about a black middle-class neighborhood;* Mama Day *(1988), about a Georgian woman with visionary powers;* Bailey's Cafe *(1992), about a group of people whose lives are at crossroads; and* The Men of Brewster Place *(1997), about the men whose lives intersect those of the women of Brewster Place.*

The Meanings of a Word

Recalling an experience as a third grader leads Naylor to probe the meanings of a highly sensitive word. At the same time she explores how words acquire their meanings from use. This essay first appeared in the New York Times.

Language is the subject. It is the written form with which I've 1 managed to keep the wolf away from the door and, in diaries, to keep my sanity. In spite of this, I consider the written word inferior to the spoken, and much of the frustration experienced by novelists is the awareness that whatever we manage to capture in even the most transcendent passages falls far short of the richness of life. Dialogue achieves its power in the dynamics of a fleeting moment of sight, sound, smell, and touch.

I'm not going to enter the debate here about whether it is lan- 2
guage that shapes reality or vice versa. The battle is doomed to be
waged whenever we seek intermittent reprieve from the chicken
and egg dispute. I will simply take the position that the spoken
word, like the written word, amounts to a nonsensical arrangement of sounds or letters without a consensus that assigns "meaning." And building from the meanings of what we hear, we order
reality. Words themselves are innocuous; it is the consensus that
gives them true power.

I remember the first time I heard the word *nigger*.[1] In my third- 3
grade class, our math tests were being passed down the rows, and
as I handed the papers to a little boy in back of me, I remarked
that once again he had received a much lower mark than I did. He
snatched his test from me and spit out that word. Had he called
me a nymphomaniac or a necrophiliac, I couldn't have been more
puzzled. I didn't know what a nigger was, but I knew that whatever
it meant, it was something he shouldn't have called me. This was
verified when I raised my hand, and in a loud voice repeated what
he had said and watched the teacher scold him for using a "bad"
word. I was later to go home and ask the inevitable question that
every black parent must face—"Mommy, what does *nigger* mean?"

And what exactly did it mean? Thinking back, I realize that 4
this could not have been the first time the word was used in my
presence. I was part of a large extended family that had migrated
from the rural South after World War II and formed a close-knit
network that gravitated around my maternal grandparents. Their
ground-floor apartment in one of the buildings they owned in
Harlem was a weekend mecca for my immediate family, along
with countless aunts, uncles, and cousins who brought along
assorted friends. It was a bustling and open house with assorted
neighbors and tenants popping in and out to exchange bits of
gossip, pick up an old quarrel, or referee the ongoing checkers
game in which my grandmother cheated shamelessly. They were
all there to let down their hair and put up their feet after a week
of labor in the factories, laundries, and shipyards of New York.

---

[1]The author wants it understood that the use of the word *nigger* is reprehen-
sible in today's society. This essay speaks to a specific time and place when that
word was utilized to empower African Americans; today it is used to degrade
them even if spoken from their own mouths.

Amid the clamor, which could reach deafening propor- 5
tions—two or three conversations going on simultaneously,
punctuated by the sound of a baby's crying somewhere in the
back rooms or out on the street—there was still a rigid set of
rules about what was said and how. Older children were sent out
of the living room when it was time to get into the juicy details
about "you-know-who" up on the third floor who had gone and
gotten herself "p-r-e-g-n-a-n-t!" But my parents, knowing that I
could spell well beyond my years, always demanded that I follow the others out to play. Beyond sexual misconduct and death,
everything else was considered harmless for our young ears. And
so among the anecdotes of the triumphs and disappointments in
the various workings of their lives, the word *nigger* was used in
my presence, but it was set within contexts and inflections that
caused it to register in my mind as something else.

In the singular, the word was always applied to a man who 6
had distinguished himself in some situation that brought their
approval for his strength, intelligence, or drive:

"Did Johnny *really* do that?"   7

"I'm telling you, that nigger pulled in $6,000 of overtime last 8
year. Said he got enough for a down payment on a house."

When used with a possessive adjective by a woman—"my 9
nigger"—it became a term of endearment for her husband or
boyfriend. But it could be more than just a term applied to a
man. In their mouths it became the pure essence of manhood—a
disembodied force that channeled their past history of struggle
and present survival against the odds into a victorious statement
of being: "Yeah, that old foreman found out quick enough—you
don't mess with a nigger."

In the plural, it became a description of some group within 10
the community that had overstepped the bounds of decency as
my family defined it. Parents who neglected their children, a
drunken couple who fought in public, people who simply refused
to look for work, those with excessively dirty mouths or unkempt
households were all "trifling niggers." This particular circle
could forgive hard times, unemployment, the occasional bout of
depression—they had gone through all of that themselves—but
the unforgivable sin was a lack of self-respect.

A woman could never be a "nigger" in the singular, with its 11
connotation of confirming worth. The noun *girl* was its closest

equivalent in that sense, but only when used in direct address and regardless of the gender doing the addressing. *Girl* was a token of respect for a woman. The one-syllable word was drawn out to sound like three in recognition of the extra ounce of wit, nerve, or daring that the woman had shown in the situation under discussion.

"G-i-r-l, stop. You mean you said that to his face?"   12

But if the word was used in a third-person reference or short-   13
ened so that it almost snapped out of the mouth, it always involved some element of communal disapproval. And age became an important factor in these exchanges. It was only between individuals of the same generation, or from any older person to a younger (but never the other way around), that *girl* would be considered a compliment.

I don't agree with the argument that use of the word *nigger* 14
at this social stratum of the black community was an internalization of racism. The dynamics were the exact opposite: the people in my grandmother's living room took a word that whites used to signify worthlessness or degradation and rendered it impotent. Gathering there together, they transformed *nigger* to signify the varied and complex human beings they knew themselves to be. If the word was to disappear totally from the mouths of even the most liberal of white society, no one in that room was naive enough to believe it would disappear from white minds. Meeting the word head-on, they proved it had absolutely nothing to do with the way they were determined to live their lives.

So there must have been dozens of times that *nigger* was spo-   15
ken in front of me before I reached the third grade. But I didn't "hear" it until it was said by a small pair of lips that had already learned it could be a way to humiliate me. That was the word I went home and asked my mother about. And since she knew that I had to grow up in America, she took me in her lap and explained.

Meaning

1. Naylor writes that "the spoken word, like the written word, amounts to a nonsensical arrangement of sounds or letters without a consensus that assigns 'meaning'" (paragraph 2). Explain this statement in your own words. How did this statement apply to the word *nigger* for the young Naylor?

2. What is Naylor's main idea? Where does she express it?

3. In paragraph 14 Naylor disagrees with those who claim that the African American community's use of the term *nigger* constitutes "an internalization of racism." What alternative explanation does she offer? Do you agree with her interpretation? Why, or why not?

Purpose and Audience

1. What is Naylor's purpose or purposes in writing this essay: to express herself? to explain something? to convince readers of something? Support your answer by referring to passages from the essay.

2. Naylor's essay first appeared in the *New York Times*, a daily newspaper whose readers are largely middle-class whites. In what ways does she seem to consider and address this audience?

Method and Structure

1. Why is Naylor's choice of the method of definition especially appropriate given the point she is trying to make about language?

2. Naylor supports her main idea by defining two words, *nigger* and *girl*. What factors influence the various meanings of each word?

3. Naylor's essay is divided into sections, each contributing something different to the whole. Identify the sections and their functions.

4. OTHER METHODS   Like many writers of definition, Naylor employs a number of other methods of development: for instance, in paragraphs 4 and 5 she describes the atmosphere of her grandparents' apartment; in 8, 9, and 12 she cites examples of speech; and in 11–13 she compares and contrasts the two uses of *girl*. At two points in the essay Naylor relies on a narrative of the same incident. Where, and for what purpose?

Language

1. How would you describe the tone of Naylor's essay? Steady and reasoned, or impassioned? Is the style more academic or more informal? Do you find Naylor's tone and style appropriate given her subject matter? Why?

2. In paragraph 3 Naylor uses language to convey a child's perspective. For example, she seems to become the arrogant little girl who "remarked that once again he had received a much lower mark than I did." Locate three or four other uses of language in the essay that emphasize her separation from the world of adults. How does this perspective contribute to the effect of the essay?

3. In paragraph 14 Naylor concludes that her family used *nigger* "to signify the varied and complex human beings they knew themselves to be." This variety and complexity is demonstrated through the words and expressions she uses to describe life in her grandparents' home—"a weekend mecca," "a bustling and open house" (4). Cite five or six other examples of concrete, vivid language in this description.

Writing Topics

1. Using your own experiences as examples, write an essay modeled on Naylor's in which you define "the meanings of a word" (or words). The word you choose might be a stereotype based on ethnicity, gender, appearance, or income, for example. Have you found, like Naylor, that meaning varies with context? If so, make the variations clear.

2. A grassroots movement tried but failed to have the word *nigger* removed from dictionaries. Are there some words so hateful that they should be banned from the language? Or is such an attempt to control language even more objectionable? Write an essay that states and supports your answers, giving plenty of examples.

3. About African Americans' use of the word *nigger*, Naylor writes that "the people in my grandmother's living room took a word that whites used to signify worthlessness or degradation and rendered it impotent" (paragraph 14). Write an essay in which you discuss a symbol, a trait, or another word that has been used negatively by one group toward another but has been transformed by the targeted group to possess a positive meaning. Examples include the gay community's use of the word *queer* and the Jewish community's reclaiming of the Star of David after the Nazis used the symbol to stigmatize Jews. How did the definition of the symbol, trait, or word change from one community to another? Like Naylor, provide readers with examples that clarify your definitions.

AMY TAN

Amy Tan was born in 1952 in Oakland, California, the daughter of Chinese immigrants. She grew up in northern California and majored in English and linguistics at San Jose State University, where she received a BA and an MA. Tan's first career was as a business writer, crafting corporate reports and executives' speeches. Dissatisfied with her work, she began writing fiction. Her first book, The Joy Luck Club *(1989), a critical and popular success, is a series of interrelated stories about the bonds between immigrant Chinese mothers and their American-born daughters. Since* The Joy Luck Club *Tan has written four more novels:* The Kitchen God's Wife *(1991),* The Hundred Secret Senses *(1995),* The Bonesetter's Daughter *(2001), and* Saving Fish from Drowning *(2005). She has also published a collection of essays,* The Opposite of Fate *(2003), and two books for children.*

Mother Tongue

In this essay, Tan defines her sense of a mother tongue, exploring the versions of English that she has used as a daughter, a student, and a writer. The essay was first published in Threepenny Review.

I am not a scholar of English or literature. I cannot give you 1
much more than personal opinions on the English language and
its variations in this country or others.

I am a writer. And by that definition, I am someone who has 2
always loved language. I am fascinated by language in daily life.
I spend a great deal of my time thinking about the power of language—the way it can evoke an emotion, a visual image, a complex idea, or a simple truth. Language is the tool of my trade. And
I use them all—all the Englishes I grew up with.

Recently, I was made keenly aware of the different Englishes I 3
do use. I was giving a talk to a large group of people, the same talk
I had already given to half a dozen other groups. The nature of

the talk was about my writing, my life, and my book, *The Joy Luck Club*. The talk was going along well enough, until I remembered one major difference that made the whole talk sound wrong. My mother was in the room. And it was perhaps the first time she had heard me give a lengthy speech, using the kind of English I have never used with her. I was saying things like, "The intersection of memory upon imagination" and "There is an aspect of my fiction that relates to thus-and-thus"—a speech filled with carefully wrought grammatical phrases, burdened, it suddenly seemed to me, with nominalized forms, past perfect tenses, conditional phrases, all the forms of standard English that I had learned in school and through books, the forms of English I did not use at home with my mother.

Just last week, I was walking down the street with my mother, 4 and I again found myself conscious of the English I was using, and the English I do use with her. We were talking about the price of new and used furniture and I heard myself saying this: "Not waste money that way." My husband was with us as well, and he didn't notice any switch in my English. And then I realized why. It's because over the twenty years we've been together I've often used that same kind of English with him, and sometimes he even uses it with me. It has become our language of intimacy, a different sort of English that relates to family talk, the language I grew up with.

So you'll have some idea of what this family talk I heard 5 sounds like, I'll quote what my mother said during a recent conversation which I videotaped and then transcribed. During this conversation, my mother was talking about a political gangster in Shanghai who had the same last name as her family's, Du, and how the gangster in his early years wanted to be adopted by her family, which was rich by comparison. Later, the gangster became more powerful, far richer than my mother's family, and one day showed up at my mother's wedding to pay his respects. Here's what she said in part:

"Du Yusong having business like fruit stand. Like off the 6 street kind. He is like Du Zong—but not Tsung-ming Island people. The local people call putong, the river east side, he belong to that side local people. That man want to ask Du Zong father take him in like become own family. Du Zong father wasn't look down on him, but didn't take seriously, until that man big like become a mafia. Now important person, very hard to inviting him. Chinese way, came only to show respect, don't stay for dinner. Respect for making big celebration, he shows up. Mean gives lots of respect. Chinese custom. Chinese social life that way. If too important won't have to stay too long. He come to my wedding. I didn't see, I heard it. I gone to boy's side, they have YMCA dinner. Chinese age I was nineteen."

You should know that my mother's expressive command of 7 English belies how much she actually understands. She reads the *Forbes* report, listens to *Wall Street Week*, converses daily with her stockbroker, reads all of Shirley MacLaine's books with ease—all kinds of things I can't begin to understand. Yet some of my friends tell me they understand fifty percent of what my mother says. Some say they understand eighty to ninety percent. Some say they understand none of it, as if she were speaking pure Chinese. But to me, my mother's English is perfectly clear, perfectly natural. It's my mother tongue. Her language, as I hear it, is vivid, direct, full of observation and imagery. That was the language that helped shape the way I saw things, expressed things, made sense of the world.

Lately, I've been giving more thought to the kind of English 8 my mother speaks. Like others, I have described it to people as "broken" or "fractured" English. But I wince when I say that. It has always bothered me that I can think of no way to describe it other than "broken," as if it were damaged and needed to be fixed, as if it lacked a certain wholeness and soundness. I've heard other terms used, "limited English," for example. But they seem just as bad, as if everything is limited, including people's perceptions of the limited English speaker.

I know this for a fact, because when I was growing up, my 9 mother's "limited" English limited *my* perception of her. I was ashamed of her English. I believed that her English reflected the quality of what she had to say. That is, because she expressed them imperfectly her thoughts were imperfect. And I had plenty of empirical evidence to support me: the fact that people in department stores, at banks, and at restaurants did not take her seriously, did not give her good service, pretended not to understand her, or even acted as if they did not hear her.

My mother has long realized the limitations of her English 10 as well. When I was fifteen, she used to have me call people on the phone to pretend I was she. In this guise, I was forced to ask for information or even to complain and yell at people who had been rude to her. One time it was a call to her stockbroker in New York. She had cashed out her small portfolio and it just so happened we were going to go to New York the next week, our very first trip outside California. I had to get on the phone and say in an adolescent voice that was not very convincing, "This is Mrs. Tan."

And my mother was standing in the back whispering loudly, 11 "Why he don't send me check, already two weeks late. So mad he lie to me, losing me money."

And then I said in perfect English, "Yes, I'm getting rather 12 concerned. You had agreed to send the check two weeks ago, but it hasn't arrived."

Then she began to talk more loudly. "What he want, I come 13 to New York tell him front of his boss, you cheating me?" And I was trying to calm her down, make her be quiet, while telling the stockbroker, "I can't tolerate any more excuses. If I don't receive the check immediately, I am going to have to speak to your manager when I'm in New York next week." And sure enough, the following week there we were in front of this astonished stockbroker, and I was sitting there red-faced and quiet, and my mother, the real Mrs. Tan, was shouting at his boss in her impeccable broken English.

We used a similar routine just five days ago, for a situation 14 that was far less humorous. My mother had gone to the hospital for an appointment, to find out about a benign brain tumor a CAT scan had revealed a month ago. She said she had spoken very good English, her best English, no mistakes. Still, she said, the hospital did not apologize when they said they had lost the CAT scan and she had come for nothing. She said they did not seem to have any sympathy when she told them she was anxious to know the exact diagnosis, since her husband and son had both died of brain tumors. She said they would not give her any more information until the next time and she would have to make another appointment for that. So she said she would not leave until the doctor called her daughter. She wouldn't budge. And when the doctor finally called her daughter, me, who spoke in perfect English—lo and behold—we had assurances the CAT scan would be found, promises that a conference call on Monday would be held, and apologies for any suffering my mother had gone through for a most regrettable mistake.

I think my mother's English almost had an effect on limiting 15 my possibilities in life as well. Sociologists and linguists probably will tell you that a person's developing language skills are more influenced by peers. But I think that the language spoken in the family, especially in immigrant families which are more insular, plays a large role in shaping the language of the child. And I believe that it affected my results on achievement tests, IQ tests, and the SAT. While my English skills were never judged as poor, compared to math, English could not be considered my strong suit. In grade school I did moderately well, getting perhaps B's, sometimes B-pluses, in English and scoring perhaps in the sixtieth or seventieth percentile on achievement tests. But those scores were not good enough to override the opinion that my true abilities lay in math and science, because in those areas I achieved A's and scored in the ninetieth percentile or higher.

This was understandable. Math is precise; there is only one 16 correct answer. Whereas, for me at least, the answers on English tests were always a judgment call, a matter of opinion and personal experience. Those tests were constructed around items like fill-in-the-blank sentence completion, such as, "Even though Tom was _____, Mary thought he was _____." And the correct answer always seemed to be the most bland combinations of thoughts, for example, "Even though Tom was shy, Mary thought he was charming," with the grammatical structure "even though" limiting the correct answer to some sort of semantic opposites, so you wouldn't get answers like, "Even though Tom was foolish, Mary thought he was ridiculous." Well, according to my mother, there were very few limitations as to what Tom could have been and what Mary might have thought of him. So I never did well on tests like that.

The same was true with word analogies, pairs of words in 17 which you were supposed to find some sort of logical, semantic relationship—for example, "*Sunset* is to *nightfall* as _____ is to _____." And here you would be presented with a list of four possible pairs, one of which showed the same kind of relationship: *red* is to *stoplight, bus* is to *arrival, chills* is to *fever, yawn* is to *boring.* Well, I could never think that way. I knew what the tests were asking, but I could not block out of my mind the images already created by the first pair, "*sunset* is to *nightfall*"—and I would see a burst of colors against a darkening sky, the moon rising, the lowering of a curtain of stars. And all the other pairs of words—*red, bus, stoplight, boring*—just threw up a mass of confusing images, making it impossible for me to sort out something as logical as saying: "A sunset precedes nightfall" is the same as "a chill precedes a fever." The only way I would have gotten that answer right would have been to imagine an associative situation, for example, my being disobedient and staying out past sunset, catching a chill at night, which turns into feverish pneumonia as punishment, which indeed did happen to me.

I have been thinking about all this lately, about my mother's 18 English, about achievement tests. Because lately I've been asked, as a writer, why there are not more Asian Americans enrolled in creative writing programs. Why do so many Chinese students go into engineering? Well, these are broad sociological questions I can't begin to answer. But I have noticed in surveys—in fact, just last week—that Asian students, as a whole, always do significantly better on math achievement tests than in English. And this makes me think that there are other Asian American students whose English spoken in the home might also be described as "broken" or "limited." And perhaps they also have teachers who are steering them away from writing and into math and science, which is what happened to me.

Fortunately, I happen to be rebellious in nature and enjoy the 19 challenge of disproving assumptions made about me. I became an English major my first year in college, after being enrolled as premed. I started writing nonfiction as a freelancer the week after I was told by my former boss that writing was my worst skill and I should hone my talents toward account management.

But it wasn't until 1985 that I finally began to write fiction. 20 And at first I wrote using what I thought to be wittily crafted sentences, sentences that would finally prove I had mastery over the English language. Here's an example from the first draft of a story that later made its way into *The Joy Luck Club*, but without this line: "That was my mental quandary in its nascent state." A terrible line, which I can barely pronounce.

Fortunately, for reasons I won't get into today, I later decided 21
I should envision a reader for the stories I would write. And the
reader I decided upon was my mother, because these were stories about mothers. So with this reader in mind—and in fact
she did read my early drafts—I began to write stories using all
the Englishes I grew up with: the English I spoke to my mother,
which for lack of a better term might be described as "simple";
the English she used with me, which for lack of a better term
might be described as "broken"; my translation of her Chinese,
which could certainly be described as "watered down"; and what
I imagined to be her translation of her Chinese if she could speak
in perfect English, her internal language, and for that I sought to
preserve the essence, but neither an English nor a Chinese structure. I wanted to capture what language ability tests can never
reveal: her intent, her passion, her imagery, the rhythms of her
speech, and the nature of her thoughts.

Apart from what any critic had to say about my writing, I 22
knew I had succeeded where it counted when my mother finished
reading my book and gave me her verdict: "So easy to read."

Meaning

1. For Tan the phrase "mother tongue" has a special meaning. How
   would you summarize this meaning? Why does Tan feel so deeply
   about her "mother tongue"?
2. In what ways does the English that Tan's mother speaks affect how
   people outside the Chinese American community think of her? What
   examples does Tan give to demonstrate this fact of her mother's life?
3. In paragraph 15, Tan writes, "[M]y mother's English almost had an
   effect on limiting my possibilities in life as well." What does she
   mean? Why does she use the qualifier "almost"?

Purpose and Audience

1. Why do you suppose Tan wrote this essay? Does she have a purpose
   beyond changing readers' perceptions of her mother's "broken" English? What passages support your answer?
2. How can you tell that Tan is not writing primarily to an audience of
   Asian Americans? If Asian Americans were her primary audience,
   how might the essay be different?

Method and Structure

1. How does Tan develop her definition of her "mother tongue"? That is, how does she best help readers understand her mother's speech?

2. Tan divides her essay into three sections, the second beginning in paragraph 8 and the third beginning in paragraph 18. What is the focus of each section? Why do you think Tan divided the essay like this?

3. OTHER METHODS   In paragraph 2 and again in paragraph 21, Tan refers to "all the Englishes I grew up with." How does she classify these various "Englishes"?

Language

1. What troubles Tan about the labels "broken," "fractured," and "limited" for her mother's English (paragraph 8)? How do these labels contrast with the way she views her mother's speech?

2. In paragraphs 16 and 17, Tan writes about the kinds of vocabulary items that appear on standardized English tests. In contrast to the precision of the answers to mathematical questions, why were the answers to vocabulary questions "always a judgment call, a matter of opinion and personal experience" for her?

Writing Topics

1. Think about the language you speak with close friends or family members. What are some characteristics of this language that outsiders might find difficult to understand? Write an essay that focuses on the idea of "personal" language—that is, language that creates or reflects closeness among people. In developing your essay, you may call on your own experiences, your observations of others, and your reading (of both fiction and nonfiction). Be sure to provide as many specific examples of language use as you can.

2. How do you define "standard English" (paragraph 3)? To what extent do you believe that nonstandard English marks people as "limited"? On what occasions is standard English absolutely required? Are there any occasions when nonstandard English is entirely appropriate? In an essay, explain and illustrate both the drawbacks and the benefits of standard and nonstandard English. (The Glossary discusses both under *diction*.)

3. Tan writes that as a student she didn't do well on standardized English tests. In recent years, such standardized testing has grown increasingly prominent in evaluating students' achievement. In an

essay, discuss your ideas about standardized tests. How accurately do you think they assess students' academic abilities? How do you respond to the claim that many such tests are biased in favor of affluent white students? How, in your experience, have they affected classroom teaching strategies? You can consider any of these questions or other related ones that interest you.

DAGOBERTO GILB

A fiction writer and essayist, Dagoberto Gilb was born in 1950 in Los Angeles, California. After enrolling in junior college with some doubts about his academic ability, Gilb "just went nuts over books" and earned a BA in philosophy and an MA in religion from the University of California at Santa Barbara. He had difficulty finding work after college and for fifteen years scraped together a living with irregular construction jobs while keeping a journal on the side. The son of a Mexican mother and a German American father, Gilb celebrates mestizaje *(mixed) culture and often examines the experiences and perspectives of working-class Latinos in his work. He has published a collection of essays,* Gritos *(2003); two novels,* The Last Known Residence of Mickey Acuña *(1994) and* The Flowers *(2008); and four collections of short stories,* Winners on the Pass Line and Other Stories *(1985),* The Magic of Blood *(1993),* Woodcuts of Women *(2001), and* Before the End, After the Beginning *(2011). Gilb has received many honors and prizes, including the Hemingway Foundation/PEN Award, a* New York Times *notable book designation, and a Guggenheim Fellowship. He currently directs the Center for Mexican American Literature and Culture at the University of Houston–Victoria, where he is also the artist-in-residence.*

Pride

First published in It Ain't Braggin' if It's True, *the curator's catalog for an exhibit of uniquely Texan artifacts at the Texas State History Museum, "Pride" is also the closing essay of Gilb's* Gritos *(the title roughly translates as "shouts" and refers, the author explains, to the exuberant cries of triumph—or despair—common in mariachi singing). In the essay Gilb explores that sense of conflict by explaining the meaning of* pride *for one group of Mexican Americans.*

It's almost time to close at the northwest corner of Altura and 1
Copia in El Paso. That means it is so dark that it is as restful
as the deepest unremembering sleep, dark as the empty space

around this spinning planet, as a black star. Headlights that beam a little cross-eyed from a fatso American car are feeling around the asphalt road up the hill toward the Good Time Store, its yellow plastic smiley face bright like a sugary suck candy. The loose muffler holds only half the misfires, and, dry springs squeaking, the automobile curves slowly into the establishment's lot, swerving to avoid the new self-serve gas pump island. Behind it, across the street, a Texas flag—out too late this and all the nights—pops and slaps in a summer wind that finally is cool.

A good man, gray on the edges, an assistant manager in a 2 brown starched and ironed uniform, is washing the glass windows of the store, lit up by as many watts as Venus, with a roll of paper towels and the blue liquid from a spray bottle. Good night, m'ijo![1] he tells a young boy coming out after playing the video game, a Grande Guzzler the size of a wastebasket balanced in one hand, an open bag of Flaming Hot Cheetos, its red dye already smearing his mouth and the hand not carrying the weight of the soda, his white T-shirt, its short sleeves reaching halfway down his wrists, the whole XXL of it billowing and puffing in the outdoor gust.

A plump young woman steps out of that car. She's wearing a 3 party dress, wide scoops out of the top, front, and back, its hemline way above the knees.

Did you get a water pump? the assistant manager asks her. 4 Are you going to make it to Horizon City? He's still washing the glass of the storefront, his hand sweeping in small hard circles.

The young woman is patient and calm like a loving mother. I 5 don't know yet, she tells him as she stops close to him, thinking. I guess I should make a call, she says, and her thick-soled shoes, the latest fashion, slap against her heels to one of the pay phones at the front of the store.

Pride is working a job like it's as important as art or war, is 6 the happiness of a new high score on a video game, of a pretty new black dress and shoes. Pride is the deaf and blind confidence of the good people who are too poor but don't notice.

A son is a long time sitting on the front porch where he played 7 all those years with the squirmy dog who still licks his face, both puppies then, even before he played on the winning teams of

[1]Spanish slang: "my son." [Editors' note.]

Little League baseball and City League basketball. They sprint down the sidewalk and across streets, side by side, until they stop to rest on the park grass, where a red ant, or a spider, bites the son's calf. It swells, but he no longer thinks to complain to his mom about it — he's too old now — when he comes home. He gets ready, putting on the shirt and pants his mom would have ironed but he wanted to iron himself. He takes the ride with his best friend since first grade. The hundreds of moms and dads, abuelos y abuelitas, the tios and primos,[2] baby brothers and older married sisters, all are at the Special Events Center for the son's high school graduation. His dad is a man bigger than most, and when he walks in his dress eel-skin boots down the cement stairs to get as close to the hardwood basketball-court floor and ceremony to see — m'ijo! — he feels an embarrassing sob bursting from his eyes and mouth. He holds it back, and with his hands, hides the tears that do escape, wipes them with his fingers, because the chavalitos[3] in his aisle are playing and laughing and they are so small and he is so big next to them. And when his son walks to the stage to get his high school diploma and his dad wants to scream his name, he hears how many others, from the floor in caps and gowns and from around the arena, are already screaming it — could be any name, it could be any son's or daughter's: Alex! Vanessa! Carlos! Veronica! Ricky! Tony! Estella! Isa! — and sees his boy waving back to all of them.

Pride hears gritty dirt blowing against an agave whose stiff 8 fertile stalk, so tall, will not bend — the love of land, rugged like the people who live on it. Pride sees the sunlight on the Franklin Mountains in the first light of morning and listens to a neighbor's gallo[4] — the love of culture and history. Pride smells a sweet, musky drizzle of rain and eats huevos con chile[5] in corn tortillas heated on a cast-iron pan — the love of heritage.

Pride is the fearless reaction to disrespect and disregard. It is 9 knowing the future will prove that wrong.

Seeing the beauty: Look out there from a height of the moun- 10 tain and on the north and south of the Rio Grande, to the far

---

[2]Spanish: "grandfathers and grandmothers," "aunts and uncles," and "cousins." [Editors' note.]

[3]Spanish slang: "little kids." [Editors' note.]

[4]Spanish: "rooster." [Editors' note.]

[5]Traditional Mexican dish of eggs and peppers. [Editors' note.]

away and close, the so many miles more of fuzz on the wide horizon, knowing how many years the people have passed and have stayed, the ancestors, the ones who have medaled, limped back on crutches or died or were heroes from wars in the Pacific or Europe or Korea or Vietnam or the Persian Gulf, the ones who have raised the fist and dared to defy, the ones who wash the clothes and cook and serve the meals, who stitch the factory shoes and the factory slacks, who assemble and sort, the ones who laugh and the ones who weep, the ones who care, the ones who want more, the ones who try, the ones who love, those ones with shameless courage and hardened wisdom, and the old ones still so alive, holding their grandchildren, and the young ones in their glowing prime, strong and gorgeous, holding each other, the ones who will be born from them. The desert land is rock-dry and ungreen. It is brown. Brown like the skin is brown. Beautiful brown.

Meaning

1. In your own words, summarize Gilb's definition of *pride*.
2. How do paragraphs 8–10 contribute to Gilb's definition?
3. What point does Gilb make in his concluding paragraph? How does his final image serve as a sort of summary?

Purpose and Audience

1. What would you say is Gilb's purpose in this essay?
2. As noted in the headnote on page 271, this essay was originally written to accompany a historical exhibit at a Texas museum. What, then, could Gilb have reasonably assumed about his readers? How are those assumptions reflected in his essay?

Method and Structure

1. Why do you think Gilb opens the essay as he does? What impression does he create with the three people in the Good Time Store parking lot?
2. Following paragraphs 1–5, Gilb specifically defines the pride of the people about whom he has just written; however, after paragraph 7 his definition does not apply specifically to the father and son just described. Why do you think he varies his strategy here?

3. Analyze Gilb's development of paragraph 7. How would you describe its movement? its ultimate effect?
4. OTHER METHODS Paragraphs 1–5 rely heavily on description. Why do you think Gilb describes this scene in such detail?

Language

1. In paragraph 1 how does Gilb use specific language to create a distinct impression of the car that pulls into the store's parking lot?
2. What is striking about the verbs Gilb uses in paragraph 8?
3. The first sentence of paragraph 10 is unusually long. How does Gilb manage to maintain its clarity and readability?

Writing Topics

1. Using Gilb's essay as a model, write an essay of your own that defines *pride* or another human feeling or characteristic—*happiness,* for example, or *sadness* or *fear* or *courage.* As Gilb does, present a wide range of examples to suggest various aspects of your subject.
2. Research the current situation of Mexican Americans in the United States: population, incomes, living conditions, education levels, and so forth. Then write an essay in which you present your findings.
3. Write an essay in which you analyze Gilb's use of language in this essay or in a portion of it. What is the level of his diction? (For a definition of *diction,* see the Glossary.) What are some especially effective uses of language? What overall impression does Gilb give of himself based on the language he uses?

DEFINITION

Select one of the following topics, or any other topic they suggest, for an essay developed by definition. Be sure to choose a topic you care about so that definition is a means of communicating an idea, not an end in itself.

Personal Qualities

1. Ignorance
2. Selflessness or selfishness
3. Loyalty or disloyalty
4. Responsibility
5. Hypocrisy

Experiences and Feelings

6. A nightmare
7. A good teacher, coach, parent, or friend
8. Religious faith
9. A good joke or a tasteless joke
10. Freedom
11. Success or failure
12. An emotion such as fear, excitement, or shame

Social Concerns

13. Poverty
14. Education
15. Domestic violence
16. Substance abuse
17. Feminism
18. Prejudice

Art and Entertainment

19. Jazz or some other kind of music
20. A good novel, movie, or television program
21. Impressionism or some other art movement

Chapter 9

CAUSE-AND-EFFECT ANALYSIS

USING THE METHOD

Why did free agency become so important in professional baseball, and how has it affected the sport? What caused the recent warming of the Pacific Ocean, and how did the warming affect the earth's weather? We answer questions like these with **cause-and-effect analysis**, the method of dividing occurrences into their elements to find relationships among them. Cause-and-effect analysis is a specific kind of analysis, the method discussed in Chapter 4.

When we analyze **causes**, we discover which of the events preceding a specified outcome actually made it happen:

> What caused Adolf Hitler's rise in Germany?
>
> Why have herbal medicines become so popular?

When we analyze **effects**, we discover which of the events following a specified occurrence actually resulted from it:

> What do we do for (or to) drug addicts when we imprison them?
>
> What happens to our foreign policy when the president's advisers disagree over its conduct?

These are existing effects of past or current situations, but effects are often predicted for the future:

> How would a cure for cancer affect the average life expectancy of men and women?
>
> How might your decision to major in history affect your job prospects?

Causes and effects can also be analyzed together, as the questions opening this chapter illustrate.

Cause-and-effect analysis is found in just about every discipline and occupation, including history, social science, natural science, engineering, medicine, law, business, and sports. In any of these fields, as well as in writing done for college courses, your purpose in analyzing may be to explain or to persuade. In explaining why something happened or what its outcome was or will be, you try to order experience and pin down the connections in it. In arguing with cause-and-effect analysis, you try to demonstrate why one explanation of causes is more accurate than another or how a proposed action will produce desirable or undesirable consequences.

The possibility of arguing about causes and effects points to the main challenge of this method. Related events sometimes overlap, sometimes follow one another immediately, and sometimes connect over gaps in time. They vary in their duration and complexity. They vary in their importance. Analyzing causes and effects thus requires not only identifying them but also discerning their relationships accurately and weighing their significance fairly.

Causes and effects often do occur in a sequence, each contributing to the next in what is called a **causal chain**. For instance, an unlucky man named Jones ends up in prison, and the causal chain leading to his imprisonment can be outlined as follows: Jones's neighbor, Smith, dumped trash on Jones's lawn. In reprisal, Jones set a small brushfire in Smith's yard. A spark from the fire accidentally ignited Smith's house. Jones was prosecuted for the fire and sent to jail. In this chain, each event is the cause of an effect, which in turn is the cause of another effect, and so on to the unhappy conclusion.

Identifying a causal chain partly involves sorting out events in time:

- **Immediate** causes or effects occur nearest an event. For instance, the immediate cause of a town's high unemployment rate may be the closing of a large manufacturing plant where many townspeople work.
- **Remote** causes or effects occur further away in time. The remote cause of the town's unemployment rate may be a drastic

decline in the company's sales or (more remote) a weak regional or national economy.

Analyzing causes also requires distinguishing their relative importance in the sequence:

- **Major** causes are directly and primarily responsible for the outcome. For instance, if a weak economy is responsible for low sales, it is a major cause of the manufacturing plant's closing.
- **Minor** causes (also called **contributory** causes) merely contribute to the outcome. The manufacturing plant may have closed for the additional reason that the owners could not afford to make repairs to its machines.

As these examples illustrate, time and significance can overlap in cause-and-effect analysis: a weak economy, for instance, is both a remote and a major cause; the lack of funds for repairs is both an immediate and a minor cause.

Because most cause-and-effect relationships are complex, you should take care to avoid several pitfalls in analyzing and presenting them. One is a confusion of coincidence and cause — that is, an assumption that because one event preceded another, it must have caused the other. This error is nicknamed **post hoc**, from the Latin *post hoc, ergo propter hoc,* meaning "after this, therefore because of this." Superstitions often illustrate post hoc: a basketball player believes that a charm once ended her shooting slump, so she now wears the charm whenever she plays. But post hoc also occurs in more serious matters. For instance, the office of a school administrator is vandalized, and he blames the incident on a recent speech by the student-government president criticizing the administration. But the administrator has no grounds for his accusation unless he can prove that the speech incited the vandals. In the absence of proof, the administrator commits the error of post hoc by asserting that the speech caused the vandalism simply because the speech preceded the vandalism.

Another potential problem in cause-and-effect writing is **oversimplification**. You must consider not just the causes and effects that seem obvious or important but all the possibilities: remote as well as immediate, minor as well as major. One form of oversimplification confuses a necessary cause with a sufficient cause:

- A **necessary** cause, as the term implies, is one that must happen in order for an effect to come about; an effect can have more than one necessary cause. For example, if emissions from a factory cause a high rate of illness in a neighborhood, the emissions are a necessary cause.
- A **sufficient** cause, in contrast, is one that brings about the effect *by itself*. The emissions are not a sufficient cause of the illness rate unless all other possible causes—such as water pollution or infection—can be eliminated.

Oversimplification can also occur if you allow opinions or emotions to cloud the interpretation of evidence. Suppose that you are examining why a gun-control bill you opposed was passed by the state legislature. Some of your evidence strongly suggests that a member of the legislature, a vocal supporter of the bill, was unduly influenced by lobbyists. But if you attributed the passage of the bill solely to this legislator, you would be exaggerating the significance of a single legislator and you would be ignoring the opinions of the many others who also voted for the bill. To achieve a balanced analysis, you would have to put aside your own feelings and consider all possible causes for the bill's passage.

DEVELOPING AN ESSAY BY CAUSE-AND-EFFECT ANALYSIS

Getting Started

Assignments in almost any course or line of work ask for cause-and-effect analysis: What caused the Vietnam War? In the theory of sociobiology, what are the effects of altruism on the survival of the group? Why did costs exceed the budget last month? You can find your own subject for cause-and-effect analysis from your experiences, from observation of others, from your course work, or from your reading outside school. Anytime you find yourself wondering what happened or why or what if, you may be onto an appropriate subject.

Remember that your treatment of causes or effects or both must be thorough; thus your subject must be manageable within the constraints of time and space imposed on you. Broad subjects like those following must be narrowed to something whose complexities you can cover adequately.

BROAD SUBJECT Causes of the decrease in American industrial productivity

NARROWER SUBJECT Causes of decreasing productivity on one assembly line

BROAD SUBJECT Effects of cigarette smoke

NARROWER SUBJECT Effects of parents' secondhand smoke on small children

Whether your subject suggests a focus on causes or effects or both, list as many of them as you can from memory or from further reading. If the subject does not suggest a focus, then ask yourself questions to begin exploring it:

- *Why did it happen?*
- *What contributed to it?*
- *What were or are its results?*
- *What might its consequences be?*

One or more of these questions should lead you to a focus and, as you explore further, to a more complete list of ideas.

But you cannot stop with a simple list; you must arrange the causes or effects in sequence and weigh their relative importance: Do the events sort out into a causal chain? Besides the immediate causes and effects, are there also less obvious, more remote ones? Besides the major causes or effects, are there also minor ones? At this stage, you may find that diagramming relationships helps you see them more clearly. The following diagram illustrates the earlier example of the plant closing:

Though uncomplicated, the diagram does sort out the causes and effects and shows their relationships and sequence.

While you are developing a clear picture of your subject, you should also be anticipating the expectations and needs of your readers. As with the other methods of essay development, consider especially what your readers already know about your subject and what they need to be told:

- *Do readers require background information?*
- *Are they likely to be familiar with some of the causes or effects you are analyzing,* or should you explain each one completely?
- *Which causes or effects might readers already accept?*
- *Which ones might they disagree with?* If, for instance, the plant closing affected many of your readers—putting them or their relatives out of work—they might blame the company's owners rather than economic forces beyond the owners' control. You would have to address these preconceptions and provide plenty of evidence for your own interpretation.

Forming a Thesis

To help manage your ideas and information, try to develop a thesis sentence that states your subject, your perspective on it, and your purpose. For instance:

> EXPLANATORY THESIS SENTENCE Being caught in the middle of a family quarrel has affected not only my feelings about my family but also my relations with friends.

> PERSUASIVE THESIS SENTENCE Contrary to local opinion, the many people put out of work by the closing of Windsor Manufacturing were victims not of the owners' incompetence but of the nation's weak economy.

Notice that these thesis sentences reflect clear judgments about the relative significance of possible causes or effects. Such judgments can be difficult to reach and may not be apparent when you start writing. Often you will need to complete a draft of your analysis before you are confident about the relationship between cause and effect. And even if you start with an idea of how cause and effect are connected, you may change your mind after you've mapped out the relationship in a draft. That's fine: just remember to revise your thesis sentence accordingly.

Organizing

The introduction to a cause-and-effect essay can pull readers in by describing the situation whose causes or effects you plan to analyze, such as the passage of a bill in the legislature or a town's high unemployment rate. The introduction may also provide background, such as a brief narrative of a family quarrel; or it may summarize the analysis of causes or effects that the essay disputes, such as the townspeople's blaming the owners for a plant's closing. If your thesis is not already apparent in the introduction, stating it explicitly can tell readers exactly what your purpose is and which causes or effects or both you plan to highlight. But if you anticipate that readers will oppose your thesis, you may want to delay stating it until the end of the essay, after you have provided the evidence to support it.

The arrangement of the body of the essay depends primarily on your material and your emphasis. If events unfold in a causal chain with each effect becoming the cause of another effect, and if stressing these links coincides with your purpose, then a simple chronological sequence will probably be clearest. But if events overlap and vary in significance, their organization will require more planning. Probably the most effective way to arrange either causes or effects is in order of increasing importance. Such an arrangement helps readers see which causes or effects you consider minor and which major, while also reserving your most significant (and probably most detailed) point for last. The groups of minor or major events may then fit into a chronological framework.

To avoid being preoccupied with organization while you are drafting your essay, prepare some sort of outline before you start writing. The outline need not be detailed so long as you have written the details elsewhere or can retrieve them easily from your mind. But it should show all the causes or effects you want to discuss and the order in which you will cover them.

To conclude your essay, you may want to restate your thesis—or state it, if you deliberately withheld it for the end—so that readers are left with the point of your analysis. If your analysis is complex, readers may also benefit from a summary of the relationships you have identified. And depending on your purpose, you may want to specify why your analysis is significant, what use your readers can make of it, or what action you hope they will take.

Drafting

While drafting your essay, strive primarily for clarity—sharp details, strong examples, concrete explanations. To make readers see not only *what* you see but also *why* you see it, you can draw on just about any method of writing discussed in this book. For instance, you might narrate the effect of a situation on one person, analyze a process, or compare and contrast two interpretations of cause. Particularly if your thesis is debatable (like the earlier example asserting the owners' blamelessness for the plant's closing), you will need accurate, representative facts to back up your interpretation, and you may also need quotations from experts such as witnesses and scholars. If you do not support your assertions specifically, your readers will have no reason to believe them. (For more on evidence in persuasive writing, see pp. 320 and 325–26.)

Revising and Editing

While revising and editing your draft, consider the following questions to be sure your analysis is sound and clear.

- *Have you explained causes or effects clearly and specifically?* Readers will need to see the pattern of causes or effects—their sequence and relative importance. And readers will need facts, examples, and other evidence to understand and accept your analysis.
- *Have you demonstrated that causes are not merely coincidences?* Avoid the error of post hoc—of assuming that one event caused another just because it preceded the other. To be convincing, a claim that one event caused another must be supported with ample evidence.
- *Have you considered all the possible causes or effects?* Your analysis should go beyond what is most immediate or obvious so that you do not oversimplify the cause-and-effect relationships.

Your readers will expect you to present the relationships in all their complexity.

- *Have you represented the cause-and-effect relationships honestly?* Don't deliberately ignore or exaggerate causes or effects in a misguided effort to strengthen your essay. If a cause fails to support your thesis but still does not invalidate it, mention the cause and explain why you believe it to be unimportant. If a change you are proposing will have bad effects as well as good, mention the bad effects and explain how they are outweighed by the good. As long as your reasoning and evidence are sound, such admissions will not weaken your essay; on the contrary, readers will appreciate your fairness.

- *Have you used transitions to signal the sequence and relative importance of events?* Transitions between sentences can help you pinpoint causes or effects (*for this reason, as a result*), show the steps in a sequence (*first, second, third*), link events in time (*in the same month*), specify duration (*a year later*), and indicate the weights you assign events (*equally important, even more crucial*). (See also *transitions* in the Glossary.)

MALCOLM GLADWELL

Born in England in 1963 to an English father and a Jamaican mother, Malcolm Gladwell immigrated with his parents to Canada as a child. After receiving his bachelor's degree in history from the University of Toronto, Gladwell worked for the Washington Post *as a science and medicine reporter and later as chief of the* Post's *New York bureau. Gladwell is currently a staff writer at the* New Yorker, *where he is known for highly readable articles that synthesize complex research in the sciences and social sciences. In 2000 he published his first book* The Tipping Point: How Little Things Can Make a Big Difference, *an examination of why change occurs. The book was a breakout success and landed Gladwell on* Time *magazine's list of the 100 most influential people in the world. He has since followed it with three more bestsellers:* Blink *(2005), an argument for acting impulsively;* Outliers *(2008), an exploration of what makes some people more successful than others; and* What the Dog Saw *(2009), a collection of his* New Yorker *essays.*

The Tipping Point

In the introduction to The Tipping Point, *Gladwell writes that the "best way to understand the dramatic transformation of unknown books into bestsellers, or the rise of teenage smoking, or the phenomena of word of mouth, or any number of the other mysterious changes that mark everyday life is to think of them as epidemics. Ideas and products and messages and behaviors spread just like viruses do." The title of the book—and of this selection—comes from epidemiology. As Gladwell defined it in an interview, the* tipping point *is "the name given to that moment in an epidemic when a virus reaches critical mass." In this excerpt, Gladwell focuses on the dramatic decrease in New York City's violent crime rate during the 1990s. The decrease, Gladwell explains, was fueled in large part by strict policing of more minor crimes.*

During the 1990s violent crime declined across the United States 1
for a number of fairly straightforward reasons. The illegal trade
in crack cocaine, which had spawned a great deal of violence
among gangs and drug dealers, began to decline. The economy's
dramatic recovery meant that many people who might have been
lured into crime got legitimate jobs instead, and the general
aging of the population meant that there were fewer people in
the age range—males between eighteen and twenty-four—that is
responsible for the majority of all violence. The question of why
crime declined in New York City, however, is a little more complicated. In the period when the New York epidemic tipped down,
the city's economy hadn't improved. It was still stagnant. In fact,
the city's poorest neighborhoods had just been hit hard by the
welfare cuts of the early 1990s. The waning of the crack cocaine
epidemic in New York was clearly a factor, but then again, it had
been in steady decline well before crime dipped. As for the aging
of the population, because of heavy immigration to New York in
the 1980s, the city was getting younger in the 1990s, not older.
In any case, all of these trends are long-term changes that one
would expect to have gradual effects. In New York the decline
was anything but gradual. Something else clearly played a role in
reversing New York's crime epidemic.

The most intriguing candidate for that "something else" is 2
called the Broken Windows theory. Broken Windows was the
brainchild of the criminologists James Q. Wilson and George
Kelling. Wilson and Kelling argued that crime is the inevitable
result of disorder. If a window is broken and left unrepaired,
people walking by will conclude that no one cares and no one
is in charge. Soon, more windows will be broken, and the sense
of anarchy will spread from the building to the street on which
it faces, sending a signal that anything goes. In a city, relatively
minor problems like graffiti, public disorder, and aggressive panhandling, they write, are all the equivalent of broken windows,
invitations to more serious crimes:

> Muggers and robbers, whether opportunistic or professional, believe
> they reduce their chances of being caught or even identified if they
> operate on streets where potential victims are already intimidated by
> prevailing conditions. If the neighborhood cannot keep a bothersome

panhandler from annoying passersby, the thief may reason, it is even less likely to call the police to identify a potential mugger or to interfere if the mugging actually takes place.

This is an epidemic theory of crime. It says that crime is contagious—just as a fashion trend is contagious—that it can start with a broken window and spread to an entire community. The Tipping Point in this epidemic, though, isn't a particular kind of person—a Connector like Lois Weisberg or a Maven like Mark Alpert.[1] It's something physical like graffiti. The impetus to engage in a certain kind of behavior is not coming from a certain kind of person but from a feature of the environment.

In the mid-1980s Kelling was hired by the New York Transit 3 Authority as a consultant, and he urged them to put the Broken Windows theory into practice. They obliged, bringing in a new subway director by the name of David Gunn to oversee a multibillion-dollar rebuilding of the subway system. Many subway advocates, at the time, told Gunn not to worry about graffiti, to focus on the larger questions of crime and subway reliability, and it seemed like reasonable advice. Worrying about graffiti at a time when the entire system was close to collapse seems as pointless as scrubbing the decks of the *Titanic* as it headed toward the icebergs. But Gunn insisted. "The graffiti was symbolic of the collapse of the system," he says. "When you looked at the process of rebuilding the organization and morale, you had to win the battle against graffiti. Without winning that battle, all the management reforms and physical changes just weren't going to happen. We were about to put out new trains that were worth about ten million bucks apiece, and unless we did something to protect them, we knew just what would happen. They would last one day and then they would be vandalized."

Gunn drew up a new management structure and a precise set 4 of goals and timetables aimed at cleaning the system line by line, train by train. He started with the number seven train that connects Queens to midtown Manhattan, and began experimenting with new techniques to clean off the paint. On stainless-steel cars,

[1]In an earlier chapter of *The Tipping Point,* Gladwell discusses personality types who trigger major changes in society. Connectors have unusually large social circles, and Mavens are particularly knowledgeable about products, services, and prices. Lois Weisberg and Mark Alpert are two Americans whom Gladwell interviewed to illustrate these types. [Editors' note.]

solvents were used. On the painted cars, the graffiti were simply painted over. Gunn made it a rule that there should be no retreat, that once a car was "reclaimed" it should never be allowed to be vandalized again. "We were religious about it," Gunn said. At the end of the number one line in the Bronx, where the trains stop before turning around and going back to Manhattan, Gunn set up a cleaning station. If a car came in with graffiti, the graffiti had to be removed during the changeover, or the car was removed from service. "Dirty" cars, which hadn't yet been cleansed of graffiti, were never to be mixed with "clean" cars. The idea was to send an unambiguous message to the vandals themselves.

"We had a yard up in Harlem on One hundred thirty-fifth 5 Street where the trains would lay up over night," Gunn said. "The kids would come the first night and paint the side of the train white. Then they would come the next night, after it was dry, and draw the outline. Then they would come the third night and color it in. It was a three-day job. We knew the kids would be working on one of the dirty trains, and what we would do is wait for them to finish their mural. Then we'd walk over with rollers and paint it over. The kids would be in tears, but we'd just be going up and down, up and down. It was a message to them. If you want to spend three nights of your time vandalizing a train, fine. But it's never going to see the light of day."

Gunn's graffiti cleanup took from 1984 to 1990. At that point, 6 the Transit Authority hired William Bratton to head the transit police, and the second stage of the reclamation of the subway system began. Bratton was, like Gunn, a disciple of Broken Windows. He describes Kelling, in fact, as his intellectual mentor, and so his first step as police chief was as seemingly quixotic as Gunn's. With felonies—serious crimes—on the subway system at an all-time high, Bratton decided to crack down on fare-beating. Why? Because he believed that, like graffiti, fare-beating could be a signal, a small expression of disorder that invited much more serious crimes. An estimated 170,000 people a day were entering the system, by one route or another, without paying a token. Some were kids, who simply jumped over the turnstiles. Others would lean backward on the turnstiles and force their way through. And once one or two or three people began cheating the system, other people—who might never otherwise have considered evading the law—would join in, reasoning that if some people weren't going to pay, they shouldn't either, and the problem would snowball. The problem was exacerbated by the fact fare-beating was not easy to fight. Because there was only $1.25 at stake, the transit police didn't feel it was worth their time to pursue it, particularly when there were plenty of more serious crimes happening down on the platform and in the trains.

Bratton is a colorful, charismatic man, a born leader, and he 7 quickly made his presence felt. His wife stayed behind in Boston, so he was free to work long hours, and he would roam the city on the subway at night, getting a sense of what the problems were and how best to fight them. First, he picked stations where fare-beating was the biggest problem, and put as many as ten policemen in plainclothes at the turnstiles. The team would nab fare-beaters one by one, handcuff them, and leave them standing, in a daisy chain, on the platform until they had a "full catch." The idea was to signal, as publicly as possible, that the transit police were now serious about cracking down on fare-beaters. Previously, police officers had been wary of pursuing fare-beaters because the arrest, the trip to the station house, the filling out of necessary forms, and the waiting for those forms to be processed took an entire day—all for a crime that usually merited no more than a slap on the wrist. Bratton retrofitted a city bus and turned it into a rolling station house, with its own fax machines, phones, holding pen, and fingerprinting facilities. Soon the turnaround time on an arrest was down to an hour. Bratton also insisted that a check be run on all those arrested. Sure enough, one out of seven arrestees had an outstanding warrant for a previous crime, and one out of twenty was carrying a weapon of some sort. Suddenly it wasn't hard to convince police officers that tackling fare-beating made sense. "For the cops it was a bonanza," Bratton writes. "Every arrest was like opening a box of Cracker Jack. What kind of toy am I going to get? Got a gun? Got a knife? Got a warrant? Do we have a murderer here? . . . After a while the bad guys wised up and began to leave their weapons home and pay their fares." Under Bratton, the number of ejections from subway stations—for drunkenness, or improper behavior—tripled within his first few months in office. Arrests for misdemeanors, for the kind of minor offenses that had gone unnoticed in the past, went up fivefold between 1990 and 1994. Bratton turned the transit police into an organization focused on the smallest infractions, on the details of life underground.

After the election of Rudolph Giuliani as mayor of New York 8 in 1994, Bratton was appointed head of the New York City Police

Department, and he applied the same strategies to the city at large. He instructed his officers to crack down on quality-of-life crimes: on the "squeegee men" who came up to drivers at New York City intersections and demanded money for washing car windows, for example, and on all the other above-ground equivalents of turnstile-jumping and graffiti. "Previous police administration had been handcuffed by restrictions," Bratton says. "We took the handcuffs off. We stepped up enforcement of the laws against public drunkenness and public urination and arrested repeat violators, including those who threw empty bottles on the street or were involved in even relatively minor damage to property. . . . If you peed in the street, you were going to jail." When crime began to fall in the city—as quickly and dramatically as it had in the subways—Bratton and Giuliani pointed to the same cause. Minor, seemingly insignificant quality-of-life crimes, they said, were Tipping Points for violent crime.

Meaning

1. What is the Broken Windows theory? How does it explain increases or decreases in crime in particular communities?
2. As director of New York City's subways, why did David Gunn crack down on graffiti? What was the result?
3. How did William Bratton, first as chief of the transit police and later as chief of the New York City police, continue to apply Gunn's methods? Again, what was the result? What is the lesson to be drawn?

Purpose and Audience

1. Do you think that Gladwell achieves his purpose here? Is his explanation for the dramatic reduction of crime in New York City convincing? Why, or why not?
2. Throughout his essay, Gladwell includes quotations from David Gunn and William Bratton. What effect do you suppose he hoped these quotations would have on readers?

Method and Structure

1. Given its subject and purpose, why is cause-and-effect analysis the most appropriate method for this essay?

2. Gladwell opens his essay by showing why the decrease in New York City crime is "more complicated" than the national decline in crime. Why do you think he chose to begin in this way?

3. OTHER METHODS   Why is Gladwell's early definition of the Broken Window theory (paragraph 2) crucial to the development of his essay as a whole?

Language

1. In paragraph 2, Gladwell writes that "crime is contagious—just as a fashion trend is contagious." In what way is the word *contagious* appropriate in this context?

2. Gladwell generally maintains a reporter's neutral tone throughout the essay. In paragraph 3, however, he writes, "Worrying about graffiti at a time when the entire system was close to collapse seems as pointless as scrubbing the decks of the *Titanic* as it headed toward the icebergs." Why do you think Gladwell made this shift in tone?

Writing Topics

1. It is clear that Gladwell agrees with James Q. Wilson and George Kelling that bad behavior, if left unchecked, spreads among people—that "once one or two or three people began cheating the system, other people—who might never otherwise have considered evading the law—would join in" (paragraph 6). Drawing on your own experiences and observations, write an essay that considers how widespread you believe this phenomenon to be. Be sure to include examples that support your point.

2. Do you agree with William Bratton that even minor infractions of the law deserve harsh penalties? For example, should subway fare-beaters be handcuffed and arrested? Should teenagers who engage in minor vandalism, such as graffiti, be treated as criminals? In an essay, consider the extent to which you believe that minor crimes should have major consequences.

3. Gladwell notes in his opening paragraph that "males between eighteen and twenty-four" are responsible for most violent crime in the United States. Brainstorm some reasons why you think this might be the case. Then analyze your reasons, and develop them with brief explanations. Finally, draft an essay in which you explain the possible causes of high crime rates among young men. (If you wish, you may do some research to augment your own ideas, but be sure to acknowledge your sources.)

STEVEN PINKER

Steven Pinker is an influential evolutionary psychologist who studies language and cognition. He was born in 1954 in Montreal, Canada, and received a BA from McGill University before continuing for a PhD from Harvard University. Currently a professor at Harvard, Pinker has also taught at Stanford, MIT, and the University of California at Santa Barbara. A frequent contributor to both scholarly journals and popular magazines, and chair of the usage panel of the American Heritage Dictionary, *he has written six books for general readers:* The Language Instinct *(1994),* How the Mind Works *(1997),* Words and Rules *(1999),* The Blank Slate *(2002),* The Stuff of Thought *(2007), and* The Better Angels of Our Nature *(2011), the last a controversial analysis of what Pinker argues has been a decline in human violence in recent centuries.*

Mind Over Mass Media

In this essay Pinker joins his primary writing interests, science and philosophy, as he dismisses growing concerns that reliance on the Internet and other electronic technologies is lowering human intelligence. The essay first appeared in the New York Times *in 2010.*

New forms of media have always caused moral panics: the printing press, newspapers, paperbacks, and television were all once denounced as threats to their consumers' brainpower and moral fiber. 1

So too with electronic technologies. *PowerPoint*, we're told, is reducing discourse to bullet points. Search engines lower our intelligence, encouraging us to skim on the surface of knowledge rather than dive to its depths. *Twitter* is shrinking our attention spans. 2

But such panics often fail basic reality checks. When comic books were accused of turning juveniles into delinquents in the 1950s, crime was falling to record lows, just as the denunciations 3 of video games in the 1990s coincided with the great American crime decline. The decades of television, transistor radios and rock videos were also decades in which IQ scores rose continuously.

For a reality check today, take the state of science, which 4 demands high levels of brainwork and is measured by clear benchmarks of discovery. These days scientists are never far from their e-mail, rarely touch paper and cannot lecture without *PowerPoint*. If electronic media were hazardous to intelligence, the quality of science would be plummeting. Yet discoveries are multiplying like fruit flies, and progress is dizzying. Other activities in the life of the mind, like philosophy, history and cultural criticism, are likewise flourishing, as anyone who has lost a morning of work to the Web site *Arts & Letters Daily*[1] can attest.

Critics of new media sometimes use science itself to press 5 their case, citing research that shows how experience can change the brain. But cognitive neuroscientists roll their eyes at such talk. Yes, every time we learn a fact or skill the wiring of the brain changes; it's not as if the information is stored in the pancreas. But the existence of neural plasticity does not mean the brain is a blob of clay pounded into shape by experience.

Experience does not revamp the basic information-process- 6 ing capacities of the brain. Speed-reading programs have long claimed to do just that, but the verdict was rendered by Woody Allen after he read *War and Peace* in one sitting: "It was about Russia."[2] Genuine multitasking, too, has been exposed as a myth, not just by laboratory studies but by the familiar sight of an SUV undulating between lanes as the driver cuts deals on his cellphone.

Moreover, as the psychologists Christopher Chabris and 7 Daniel Simons show in their new book *The Invisible Gorilla: And Other Ways Our Institutions Deceive Us*, the effects of experience are highly specific to the experiences themselves. If you train people to do one thing (recognize shapes, solve math puzzles, find hidden words), they get better at doing that thing, but almost

[1]A hyperlinked roundup of notable essays, articles, and book reviews, maintained by the *Chronicle of Higher Education*. [Editors' note.]
[2]Woody Allen is an American comedian and filmmaker. *War and Peace* (1869) is an epic novel by Russian writer Leo Tolstoy. [Editors' note.]

nothing else. Music doesn't make you better at math, conjugating Latin doesn't make you more logical, brain-training games don't make you smarter. Accomplished people don't bulk up their brains with intellectual calisthenics; they immerse themselves in their fields. Novelists read lots of novels, scientists read lots of science.

The effects of consuming electronic media are also likely to 8
be far more limited than the panic implies. Media critics write as if the brain takes on the qualities of whatever it consumes, the informational equivalent of "you are what you eat." As with primitive peoples who believe that eating fierce animals will make them fierce, they assume that watching quick cuts in rock videos turns your mental life into quick cuts or that reading bullet points and *Twitter* postings turns your thoughts into bullet points and *Twitter* postings.

Yes, the constant arrival of information packets can be dis- 9
tracting or addictive, especially to people with attention deficit disorder. But distraction is not a new phenomenon. The solution is not to bemoan technology but to develop strategies of self-control, as we do with every other temptation in life. Turn off e-mail or *Twitter* when you work, put away your BlackBerry at dinner time, ask your spouse to call you to bed at a designated hour.

And to encourage intellectual depth, don't rail at *PowerPoint* 10
or *Google*. It's not as if habits of deep reflection, thorough research and rigorous reasoning ever came naturally to people. They must be acquired in special institutions, which we call universities, and maintained with constant upkeep, which we call analysis, criticism and debate. They are not granted by propping a heavy encyclopedia on your lap, nor are they taken away by efficient access to information on the Internet.

The new media have caught on for a reason. Knowledge is 11
increasing exponentially; human brainpower and waking hours are not. Fortunately, the Internet and information technologies are helping us manage, search and retrieve our collective intellectual output at different scales, from *Twitter* and previews to e-books and online encyclopedias. Far from making us stupid,[3] these technologies are the only things that will keep us smart.

---

[3]Pinker is alluding to a widely read 2008 *Atlantic* magazine article by Nicholas Carr, titled "Is Google Making Us Stupid?" [Editors' note.]

Meaning

1. What connection does Pinker make between new media and intelligence? Express his main idea in a sentence or two of your own.

2. What does Pinker mean by "neural plasticity" (paragraph 5)? What does the concept have to do with the effects of using electronic technologies?

Purpose and Audience

1. What seems to be the author's primary purpose in this essay: to discredit other writers? to reassure users of communication technologies? to advance a scientific theory? Do you think Pinker accomplishes his purpose? Why, or why not?

2. What assumptions does Pinker seem to make about the readers of this essay? Are the assumptions correct in your case?

Method and Structure

1. Identify at least three types of evidence that Pinker uses to support his cause-and-effect analysis. How effective do you find this evidence? Is any one type more persuasive than the others? Why do you think so?

2. List the major concerns that Pinker dismisses as groundless. How does he arrange his responses to such concerns?

3. OTHER METHODS   Pinker opens his cause-and-effect analysis with a discussion of "moral panics" (paragraph 1) and "reality checks" (3). Analyze his use of comparison and contrast in the introduction and explain what it contributes to the essay.

Language

1. How would you characterize Pinker's tone in this essay, particularly when he is describing the concerns expressed by media critics? To what extent does the tone influence your receptiveness to his argument?

2. An accomplished linguist, Pinker uses many figures of speech. Locate at least one use each of metaphor, simile, and hyperbole (review these terms under *figures of speech* in the Glossary.) In what ways do these instances of inventive language reinforce—or undermine—the author's point?

Writing Topics

1. Pinker writes on a topic that has been the subject of some controversy. Where do you stand on the issue? Do electronic media make people dumber—or smarter? Draft a narrative account of an experience you have had using a medium such as *Google*, *Facebook*, or *Microsoft Word*, in an attempt to discover whether you believe such tools affect intelligence for better or worse. Then expand your narrative to explain your assessment of the cause-and-effect relationship between media and intelligence, being sure to define what you mean by *intelligence*.

2. Write an essay in which you compare and contrast two related types of communication or entertainment media: for example, print books and e-readers, television and *YouTube*, radio and streaming music services. Your approach may be either lighthearted or serious, but make sure you come to some conclusion about your subjects. Which technology do you favor? Why?

3. Ask the reference librarian at your library to help you find information about the initial fears sparked by one of the new developments Pinker cites in his introduction: "the printing press, newspapers, paperbacks, and television" (paragraph 1); comic books, radios, and music videos (3). With your research in hand, write an essay describing what those fears were and explaining when, how, and to what extent they proved to be accurate. (Be sure to cite your sources.) How does the history of that earlier medium shed light on contemporary fears about electronic technologies?

BARBARA EHRENREICH

*Barbara Ehrenreich was born in 1941 in Butte, Montana. She gradu-
ated from Reed College, received a PhD in biology from Rockefeller University, and taught for a while at the State University of New York at
Old Westbury. As a journalist and activist focused on issues of social
justice, she has written feature articles, reviews, and essays for a wide
range of publications, including the* Washington Post Magazine, *the*
Wall Street Journal, Esquire, *the* Atlantic, Harper's Magazine, *the*
New Republic, Social Policy, Vogue, *and* Z Magazine. *She is currently
a contributing writer at the* Nation *and the* Progressive. *Ehrenreich's
books include* Complaints and Disorders: The Sexual Politics of
Sickness *(1973),* Fear of Falling: The Inner Life of the Middle Class
(1989), Nickel and Dimed: On (Not) Getting By in America *(2001),*
This Land Is Their Land: Reports from a Divided Nation *(2008), and*
Bright-Sided: How the Relentless Promotion of Positive Thinking
Has Undermined America *(2009).*

Cultural Baggage

*After struggling to identify her "ethnic genes," Ehrenreich looks to the
spirit of her parents, whose unofficial motto was "new things [are] better than old." This essay from the* New York Times Magazine *presents
an unorthodox understanding of cultural heritage: a celebration of lin-
eage free from the shackles of "poverty, superstition, and grief."*

An acquaintance was telling me about the joys of rediscovering 1
her ethnic and religious heritage. "I know exactly what my ancestors were doing 2,000 years ago," she said, eyes gleaming with
enthusiasm, "and *I can do the same things now*." Then she leaned
forward and inquired politely, "And what is your ethnic background, if I may ask?"

"None," I said, that being the first word in line to get out of my 2
mouth. Well, not "none," I backtracked. Scottish, English, Irish—

298

that was something, I supposed. Too much Irish to qualify as a WASP; too much of the hated English to warrant a "Kiss Me, I'm Irish" button; plus there are a number of dead ends in the family tree due to adoptions, missing records, failing memories and the like. I was blushing by this time. Did "none" mean I was rejecting my heritage out of Anglo-Celtic self-hate? Or was I revealing a hidden ethnic chauvinism in which the Britannically derived served as a kind of neutral standard compared with the ethnic "others"?

Throughout the 60s and 70s, I watched one group after 3 another—African Americans, Latinos, Native Americans—stand up and proudly reclaim their roots while I just sank back ever deeper into my seat. All this excitement over ethnicity stemmed, I uneasily sensed, from a past in which *their* ancestors had been trampled upon by *my* ancestors, or at least by people who looked very much like them. In addition, it had begun to seem almost un-American not to have some sort of hyphen at hand, linking one to more venerable times and locales.

But the truth is, I was raised with none. We'd eaten ethnic 4 foods in my childhood home, but these were all borrowed, like the pasties, or Cornish meat pies, my father had picked up from his fellow miners in Butte, Montana. If my mother had one rule, it was militant ecumenism in all matters of food and experience. "Try new things," she would say, meaning anything from sweetbreads to clams, with an emphasis on the "new."

As a child, I briefly nourished a craving for tradition and 5 roots. I immersed myself in the works of Sir Walter Scott.[1] I pretended to believe that the bagpipe was a musical instrument. I was fascinated to learn from a grandmother that we were descended from certain Highland clans and longed for a pleated skirt in one of their distinctive tartans.

But in *Ivanhoe*, it was the dark-eyed "Jewess" Rebecca I iden- 6 tified with, not the flaxen-haired bimbo Rowena. As for clans: Why not call them "tribes," those bands of half-clad peasants and warriors whose idea of cuisine was stuffed sheep gut washed

[1]Scott (1771–1832) was a Scottish poet and novelist. His novel *Ivanhoe* (next paragraph) is a historical romance set in medieval times. The Jewish Rebecca falls in love with the Christian Ivanhoe, but it is Lady Rowena, the upper-class Saxon, who wins Ivanhoe's love. [Editors' note.]

down with whisky? And then there was the sting of Disraeli's[2] remark—which I came across in my early teens—to the effect that his ancestors had been leading orderly, literate lives when my ancestors were still rampaging through the Highlands daubing themselves with blue paint.

Motherhood put the screws on me, ethnicity-wise. I had 7 hoped that by marrying a man of Eastern European–Jewish ancestry I would acquire for my descendants the ethnic genes that my own forebears so sadly lacked. At one point, I even subjected the children to a Seder[3] of my own design, including a little talk about the flight from Egypt and its relevance to modern social issues. But the kids insisted on buttering their matzohs and snickering through my talk. "Give me a break, Mom," the older one said. "You don't even believe in God."

After the tiny pagans had been put to bed, I sat down to brood 8 over Elijah's wine.[4] What had I been thinking? The kids knew that their Jewish grandparents were secular folks who didn't hold Seders themselves. And if ethnicity eluded me, how could I expect it to take root in my children, who are not only Scottish-English-Irish, but Hungarian-Polish-Russian to boot?

But, then, on the fumes of Manischewitz,[5] a great insight 9 took form in my mind. It was true, as the kids said, that I didn't "believe in God." But this could be taken as something very different from an accusation—a reminder of a genuine heritage. My parents had not believed in God either, nor had my grandparents or any other progenitors going back to the great-great level. They had become disillusioned with Christianity generations ago—just as, on the in-law side, my children's other ancestors had shaken off their Orthodox Judaism. This insight did not exactly furnish me with an "identity," but it was at least something to work with: we are the kind of people, I realized—whatever our distant ancestors' religions—who do *not* believe, who

---

[2]Benjamin Disraeli (1804–81), British statesman, writer, and prime minister, was of Jewish descent. [Editors' note.]

[3]A Jewish ceremonial meal, eaten on the first or second day of Passover, that celebrates the release of the Jews from captivity in Egypt. [Editors' note.]

[4]A special cup of wine placed on the Seder table as an offering to the Hebrew prophet Elijah. [Editors' note.]

[5]The brand name of a kosher wine often served during Passover. [Editors' note.]

do not carry on traditions, who do not do things just because someone has done them before.

The epiphany went on: I recalled that my mother never   10 introduced a procedure for cooking or cleaning by telling me, "Grandma did it this way." What did Grandma know, living in the days before vacuum cleaners and disposable toilet mops? In my parents' general view, new things were better than old, and the very fact that some ritual had been performed in the past was a good reason for abandoning it now. Because what was the past, as our forebears knew it? Nothing but poverty, superstition and grief. "Think for yourself," Dad used to say. "Always ask why."

In fact, this may have been the ideal cultural heritage for my   11 particular ethnic strain—bounced as it was from the Highlands of Scotland across the sea, out to the Rockies, down into the mines and finally spewed out into high-tech, suburban America. What better philosophy, for a race of migrants, than "Think for yourself"? What better maxim, for people whose whole world was rudely inverted every thirty years or so, than "Try new things"?

The more tradition-minded, the newly enthusiastic celebrants   12 of Purim and Kwanzaa and Solstice,[6] may see little point to survival if the survivors carry no cultural freight—religion, for example, or ethnic tradition. To which I would say that skepticism, curiosity and wide-eyed ecumenical tolerance are also worthy elements of the human tradition and are at least as old as such notions as "Serbian" or "Croatian," "Scottish" or "Jewish." I make no claims for my personal line of progenitors except that they remained loyal to the values that may have induced all of our ancestors, long, long ago, to climb down from the trees and make their way into the open plains.

A few weeks ago, I cleared my throat and asked the children,   13 now mostly grown and fearsomely smart, whether they felt any stirrings of ethnic or religious identity, etc., which might have been, ahem, insufficiently nourished at home. "None," they said, adding firmly, "and the world would be a better place if nobody else did, either." My chest swelled with pride, as would my mother's, to know that the race of "none" marches on.

[6]Purim is a Jewish festival also known as the Feast of Lots. Kwanzaa is a holiday that celebrates the cultural heritage of African Americans. Solstice, occurring on the shortest day of the year, is an ancient pagan celebration welcoming the return of the sun. [Editors' note.]

Meaning

1. What personal heritage does Ehrenreich embrace? How does she feel this heritage was passed down to her?
2. At the end of paragraph 2, Ehrenreich asks herself whether, by claiming no ethnic background, she was "revealing a hidden ethnic chauvinism in which the Britannically derived served as a kind of neutral standard compared with the ethnic 'others.'" What does she mean? Why might this make her feel guilty?
3. In what ways does Ehrenreich attempt to assert an ethnic identity for herself? Why do her efforts fail?

Purpose and Audience

1. Ehrenreich's thesis does not become clear until paragraphs 12 and 13. What is her thesis?
2. What seems to be Ehrenreich's main purpose in this essay? To defend her lack of ethnic identity? To persuade her readers that some traditions are more important than ethnic traditions? To explore the evolution of her own sense of tradition and cultural identity? Something else? Why do you think so?
3. Is Ehrenreich writing primarily for those with a strong ethnic identity, for those—like herself—without one, or for both? How can you tell? What other assumptions does she seem to make about her audience?

Method and Structure

1. What are the two main cause-and-effect relationships that Ehrenreich explores in this essay? How are these central to her purpose for writing?
2. Ehrenreich opens and closes her essay with two anecdotes. How is the dialogue in these anecdotes connected?
3. Ehrenreich poses a number of questions (for example, in paragraphs 2, 8, 10, 11, and 13). Why are such questions particularly appropriate in this essay?
4. OTHER METHODS   In paragraphs 3 and 12, Ehrenreich brings in comparison and contrast. What are her subjects in each case? What point does comparison and contrast help her make?

Language

1. How would you describe Ehrenreich's tone in this essay? Is it consistent throughout?

2. Why does Ehrenreich italicize the words "I can do the same things now" when quoting her friend in paragraph 1? Does this phrase have a larger point in the essay?

3. Why does Ehrenreich link "Purim and Kwanzaa and Solstice" in paragraph 12? What is her point?

4. In her final sentence Ehrenreich refers to "the race of 'none.'" Why does she use the word *race* in this context?

Writing Topics

1. Write an essay in which you evaluate the importance you assign to any outward symbols of your heritage: food, music, holidays, customs, religious services, clothing, and the like. For example, do such signs serve to strengthen your cultural identity? If you don't have such signs, how important is their absence?

2. By referring in paragraph 12 to Serbs and Croats—two ethnic groups that fought each other in the 1990s—Ehrenreich suggests the potentially negative consequences of ethnic pride or religious zeal. In an essay, consider when people's cultural identity can be a source of conflict, even violence. Is there any way such conflicts can be avoided or resolved? You may wish to think globally about this issue, but be sure to bring your essay down to earth by focusing primarily on what you've experienced or witnessed closer to home.

3. The United States is a country of immigrants, and each group has made an indelible mark on American identity. For example, consider just foods: salsa outsells ketchup, tacos are to be found everywhere, and cappuccino and sushi are now everyday food items for many Americans who have no Italian or Japanese heritage. Write an essay about the effects of immigration on your daily life: the food you consume, the music you listen to, the dress styles you prefer, and so forth. Include personal examples to bring your ideas to life.

STEPHEN JAY GOULD

One of the best-known science writers of the twentieth century, Stephen Jay Gould was born in New York City in 1941 and attended Antioch College and Columbia University. Though he wrote scholarly articles and taught biology, geology, and history of science courses at Harvard, his essays, including a long-running column for Natural History *magazine, made science accessible to a popular audience. He won the National Book Award for* The Panda's Thumb *(1980) and the National Book Critics Circle Award for* The Mismeasure of Man *(1981). His essays were collected in many books, including* The Panda's Thumb, The Flamingo's Smile *(1985),* Dinosaur in a Haystack *(1995), and* I Have Landed *(2002). His last book,* The Structure of Evolutionary Theory *(2002), is the culmination of his more than twenty years of writing and thinking on Darwinism. Gould died in 2002 at the age of sixty.*

Sex, Drugs, Disasters, and the Extinction of Dinosaurs

This essay originally appeared in Discover *magazine and was republished in Gould's collection* The Flamingo's Smile. *Gould attempts to explain why dinosaurs disappeared, speculating on the chain of events that most likely led to their extinction.*

Science, in its most fundamental definition, is a fruitful mode of 1 inquiry, not a list of enticing conclusions. The conclusions are the consequence, not the essence.

My greatest unhappiness with most popular presentations of 2 science concerns their failure to separate fascinating claims from the methods that scientists use to establish the facts of nature. Journalists, and the public, thrive on controversial and stunning statements. But science is, basically, a way of knowing—in P. B. Medawar's apt words, "the art of the soluble." If the growing corps of popular science writers would focus on *how* scientists develop and defend those fascinating claims, they would make their greatest possible contribution to public understanding.

Consider three ideas, proposed in perfect seriousness to explain ₃ that greatest of all titillating puzzles—the extinction of dinosaurs. Since these three notions invoke the primally fascinating themes of our culture—sex, drugs, and violence—they surely reside in the category of fascinating claims. I want to show why two of them rank as silly speculation, while the other represents science at its grandest and most useful.

Science works with testable proposals. If, after much compila- ₄ tion and scrutiny of data, new information continues to affirm a hypothesis, we may accept it provisionally and gain confidence as further evidence mounts. We can never be completely sure that a hypothesis is right, though we may be able to show with confidence that it is wrong. The best scientific hypotheses are also generous and expansive: They suggest extensions and implications that enlighten related, and even far distant, subjects. Simply consider how the idea of evolution has influenced virtually every intellectual field.

Useless speculation, on the other hand, is restrictive. It gen- ₅ erates no testable hypothesis, and offers no way to obtain potentially refuting evidence. Please note that I am not speaking of truth or falsity. The speculation may well be true; still, if it provides, in principle, no material for affirmation or rejection, we can make nothing of it. It must simply stand forever as an intriguing idea. Useless speculation turns in on itself and leads nowhere; good science, containing both seeds for its potential refutation and implications for more and different testable knowledge, reaches out. But, enough preaching. Let's move on to dinosaurs, and the three proposals for their extinction.

1. *Sex.* Testes function only in a narrow range of temperature (those of mammals hang externally in a scrotal sac because internal body temperatures are too high for their proper function). A worldwide rise in temperature at the close of the Cretaceous period caused the testes of dinosaurs to stop functioning and led to their extinction by sterilization of males.

2. *Drugs.* Angiosperms (flowering plants) first evolved toward the end of the dinosaurs' reign. Many of these plants contain

psychoactive agents, avoided by mammals today as a result of their bitter taste. Dinosaurs had neither means to taste the bitterness nor livers effective enough to detoxify the substances. They died of massive overdoses.

3. *Disasters.* A large comet or asteroid struck the earth some 65 million years ago, lofting a cloud of dust into the sky and blocking sunlight, thereby suppressing photosynthesis and so drastically lowering world temperatures that dinosaurs and hosts of other creatures became extinct.

Before analyzing these three tantalizing statements, we must establish a basic ground rule often violated in proposals for the dinosaurs' demise. *There is no separate problem of the extinction of dinosaurs.* Too often we divorce specific events from their wider contexts and systems of cause and effect. The fundamental fact of dinosaur extinction is its synchrony with the demise of so many other groups across a wide range of habitats, from terrestrial to marine.

The history of life has been punctuated by brief episodes 6 of mass extinction. A recent analysis by University of Chicago paleontologists Jack Sepkoski and Dave Raup, based on the best and most exhaustive tabulation of data ever assembled, shows clearly that five episodes of mass dying stand well above the "background" extinctions of normal times (when we consider all mass extinctions, large and small, they seem to fall in a regular 26-million-year cycle). The Cretaceous debacle, occurring 65 million years ago and separating the Mesozoic and Cenozoic eras of our geological time scale, ranks prominently among the five. Nearly all the marine plankton (single-celled floating creatures) died with geological suddenness; among marine invertebrates, nearly 15% of all families perished, including many previously dominant groups, especially the ammonites (relatives of squids in coiled shells). On land, the dinosaurs disappeared after more than 100 million years of unchallenged domination.

In this context, speculations limited to dinosaurs alone ignore 7 the larger phenomenon. We need a coordinated explanation for a system of events that includes the extinction of dinosaurs as one component. Thus it makes little sense, though it may fuel our desire to view mammals as inevitable inheritors of the earth, to guess that dinosaurs died because small mammals ate their eggs (a perennial favorite among untestable speculations). It seems most unlikely that some disaster peculiar to dinosaurs befell these massive beasts—and that the debacle happened to strike just when one of history's five great dyings had enveloped the earth for completely different reasons.

The testicular theory, an old favorite from the 1940s, had its 8 root in an interesting and thoroughly respectable study of temperature tolerances in the American alligator, published in the staid *Bulletin of the American Museum of Natural History* in 1946 by three experts on living and fossil reptiles—E. H. Colbert, my own first teacher in paleontology; R. B. Cowles; and C. M. Bogert.

The first sentence of their summary reveals a purpose beyond 9 alligators: "This report describes an attempt to infer the reactions of extinct reptiles, especially the dinosaurs, to high temperatures as based upon reactions observed in the modern alligator." They studied, by rectal thermometry, the body temperatures of alligators under changing conditions of heating and cooling. (Well, let's face it, you wouldn't want to try sticking a thermometer under a 'gator's tongue.) The predictions under test go way back to an old theory first stated by Galileo in the 1630s—the unequal scaling of surfaces and volumes. As an animal, or any object, grows (provided its shape doesn't change), surface areas must increase more slowly than volumes—since surfaces get larger as length squared, while volumes increase much more rapidly, as length cubed. Therefore, small animals have high ratios of surface to volume, while large animals cover themselves with relatively little surface.

Among cold-blooded animals lacking any physiological 10 mechanism for keeping their temperatures constant, small creatures have a hell of a time keeping warm—because they lose so much heat through their relatively large surfaces. On the other hand, large animals, with their relatively small surfaces, may lose heat so slowly that, once warm, they may maintain effectively constant temperatures against ordinary fluctuations of climate. (In fact, the resolution of the "hot-blooded dinosaur" controversy that burned so brightly a few years back may simply be that, while large dinosaurs possessed no physiological mechanism for constant temperature, and were not therefore warm-blooded in the technical sense, their large size and relatively small surface area kept them warm.)

Colbert, Cowles, and Bogert compared the warming rates of 11
small and large alligators. As predicted, the small fellows heated
up (and cooled down) more quickly. When exposed to a warm
sun, a tiny 50-gram (1.76-ounce) alligator heated up one degree
Celsius every minute and a half, while a large alligator, 260 times
bigger at 13,000 grams (28.7 pounds), took seven and a half
minutes to gain a degree. Extrapolating up to an adult 10-ton
dinosaur, they concluded that a one-degree rise in body temperature would take eighty-six hours. If large animals absorb heat so
slowly (through their relatively small surfaces), they will also be
unable to shed any excess heat gained when temperatures rise
above a favorable level.

The authors then guessed that large dinosaurs lived at or 12
near their optimum temperatures; Cowles suggested that a rise in
global temperatures just before the Cretaceous extinction caused
the dinosaurs to heat up beyond their optimal tolerance—and,
being so large, they couldn't shed the unwanted heat. (In a most
unusual statement within a scientific paper, Colbert and Bogert
then explicitly disavowed this speculative extension of their
empirical work on alligators.) Cowles conceded that this excess
heat probably wasn't enough to kill or even to enervate the great
beasts, but since testes often function only within a narrow range
of temperature, he proposed that this global rise might have ster-
ilized all the males, causing extinction by natural contraception.

The overdose theory has recently been supported by UCLA 13
psychiatrist Ronald K. Siegel. Siegel has gathered, he claims,
more than 2,000 records of animals who, when given access,
administer various drugs to themselves—from a mere swig of
alcohol to massive doses of the big H. Elephants will swill the
equivalent of twenty beers at a time, but do not like alcohol in
concentrations greater than 7%. In a silly bit of anthropocentric
speculation, Siegel states that "elephants drink, perhaps, to forget
[. . .] the anxiety produced by shrinking rangeland and the competition for food."

Since fertile imaginations can apply almost any hot idea to 14
the extinction of dinosaurs, Siegel found a way. Flowering plants
did not evolve until late in the dinosaurs' reign. These plants also
produced an array of aromatic, amino-acid-based alkaloids—the
major group of psychoactive agents. Most mammals are "smart"

enough to avoid these potential poisons. The alkaloids simply don't taste good (they are bitter); in any case, we mammals have livers happily supplied with the capacity to detoxify them. But, Siegel speculates, perhaps dinosaurs could neither taste the bitterness nor detoxify the substances once ingested. He recently told members of the American Psychological Association: "I'm not suggesting that all dinosaurs OD'd on plant drugs, but it certainly was a factor." He also argued that death by overdose may help explain why so many dinosaur fossils are found in contorted positions. (Do not go gentle into that good night.)

Extraterrestrial catastrophes have long pedigrees in the pop- 15 ular literature of extinction, but the subject exploded again in 1979, after a long lull, when the father-son, physicist-geologist team of Luis and Walter Alvarez proposed that an asteroid, some 10 km in diameter, struck the earth 65 million years ago. (Comets, rather than asteroids, have since gained favor. Good science is self-corrective.)

The force of such a collision would be immense, greater by 16 far than the megatonnage of all the world's nuclear weapons. In trying to reconstruct a scenario that would explain the simultaneous dying of dinosaurs on land and so many creatures in the sea, the Alvarezes proposed that a gigantic dust cloud, generated by particles blown aloft in the impact, would so darken the earth that photosynthesis would cease and temperatures drop precipitously. (Rage, rage against the dying of the light.) The single-celled photosynthetic oceanic plankton, with life cycles measured in weeks, would perish outright, but land plants might survive through the dormancy of their seeds (land plants were not much affected by the Cretaceous extinction, and any adequate theory must account for the curious pattern of differential survival). Dinosaurs would die by starvation and freezing; small, warm-blooded mammals, with more modest requirements for food and better regulation of body temperature, would squeak through. "Let the bastards freeze in the dark," as bumper stickers of our chauvinistic neighbors in sunbelt states proclaimed several years ago during the Northeast's winter oil crisis.

All three theories, testicular malfunction, psychoactive over- 17 dosing, and asteroidal zapping, grab our attention mightily. As pure phenomenology, they rank about equally high on any hit parade of primal fascination. Yet one represents expansive science, the others restrictive and untestable speculation. The proper criterion lies in evidence and methodology; we must probe behind the superficial fascination of particular claims.

How could we possibly decide whether the hypothesis of testicular frying is right or wrong? We would have to know things that the fossil record cannot provide. What temperatures were optimal for dinosaurs? Could they avoid the absorption of excess heat by staying in the shade, or in caves? At what temperatures did their testicles cease to function? Were late Cretaceous climates ever warm enough to drive the internal temperatures of dinosaurs close to this ceiling? Testicles simply don't fossilize, and how could we infer their temperature tolerances even if they did? In short, Cowles's hypothesis is only an intriguing speculation leading nowhere. The most damning statement against it appeared right in the conclusion of Colbert, Cowles, and Bogert's paper, when they admitted: "It is difficult to advance any definite arguments against this hypothesis." My statement may seem paradoxical—isn't a hypothesis really good if you can't devise any arguments against it? Quite the contrary. It is simply untestable and unusable. 18

Siegel's overdosing has even less going for it. At least Cowles extrapolated his conclusion from some good data on alligators. And he didn't completely violate the primary guideline of siting dinosaur extinction in the context of a general mass dying—for rise in temperature could be the root cause of a general catastrophe, zapping dinosaurs by testicular malfunction and different groups for other reasons. But Siegel's speculation cannot touch the extinction of ammonites or oceanic plankton (diatoms make their own food with good sweet sunlight; they don't OD on the chemicals of terrestrial plants). It is simply a gratuitous, attention-grabbing guess. It cannot be tested, for how can we know what dinosaurs tasted and what their livers could do? Livers don't fossilize any better than testicles. 19

The hypothesis doesn't even make any sense in its own context. Angiosperms were in full flower ten million years before dinosaurs went the way of all flesh. Why did it take so long? As for the pains of a chemical death recorded in contortions of fossils, I regret to say (or rather I'm pleased to note for the dinosaurs' 20 sake) that Siegel's knowledge of geology must be a bit deficient: Muscles contract after death and geological strata rise and fall with motions of the earth's crust after burial—more than enough reason to distort a fossil's pristine appearance.

The impact story, on the other hand, has a sound basis in evi- 21 dence. It can be tested, extended, refined, and, if wrong, disproved. The Alvarezes did not just construct an arresting guess for public consumption. They proposed their hypothesis after laborious geochemical studies with Frank Asaro and Helen Michael had revealed a massive increase of iridium in rocks deposited right at the time of extinction. Iridium, a rare metal of the platinum group, is virtually absent from indigenous rocks of the earth's crust; most of our iridium arrives on extraterrestrial objects that strike the earth.

The Alvarez hypothesis bore immediate fruit. Based origi- 22 nally on evidence from two European localities, it led geochemists throughout the world to examine other sediments of the same age. They found abnormally high amounts of iridium everywhere—from continental rocks of the western United States to deep sea cores from the South Atlantic.

Cowles proposed his testicular hypothesis in the mid-1940s. 23 Where has it gone since then? Absolutely nowhere, because scientists can do nothing with it. The hypothesis must stand as a curious appendage to a solid study of alligators. Siegel's overdose scenario will also win a few press notices and fade into oblivion. The Alvarezes' asteroid falls into a different category altogether, and much of the popular commentary has missed this essential distinction by focusing on the impact and its attendant results, and forgetting what really matters to a scientist—the iridium. If you talk just about asteroids, dust, and darkness, you tell stories no better and no more entertaining than fried testicles or terminal trips. It is the iridium—the source of testable evidence—that counts and forges the crucial distinction between speculation and science.

The proof, to twist a phrase, lies in the doing. Cowles's hypoth- 24 esis has generated nothing in thirty-five years. Since its proposal in 1979, the Alvarez hypothesis has spawned hundreds of studies, a major conference, and attendant publications. Geologists are fired up. They are looking for iridium at all other extinction boundaries. Every week exposes a new wrinkle in the scientific press. Further evidence that the Cretaceous iridium represents extraterrestrial impact and not indigenous volcanism continues to accumulate. As I revise this essay in November 1984 (this paragraph will be out of date when [it] is published), new data include chemical "signatures" of other isotopes indicating unearthly provenance, glass spherules of a size and sort produced by impact and not by volcanic eruptions, and high-pressure varieties of silica formed (so far as we know) only under the tremendous shock of impact.

My point is simply this: Whatever the eventual outcome (I 25 suspect it will be positive), the Alvarez hypothesis is exciting, fruitful science because it generates tests, provides us with things to do, and expands outward. We are having fun, battling back and forth, moving toward a resolution, and extending the hypothesis beyond its original scope.

As just one example of the unexpected, distant cross-fertiliza- 26 tion that good science engenders, the Alvarez hypothesis made a major contribution to a theme that has riveted public attention in the past few months—so-called nuclear winter. In a speech delivered in April 1982, Luis Alvarez calculated the energy that a ten-kilometer asteroid would release on impact. He compared such an explosion with a full nuclear exchange and implied that all-out atomic war might unleash similar consequences.

This theme of impact leading to massive dust clouds and 27 falling temperatures formed an important input to the decision of Carl Sagan and a group of colleagues to model the climatic consequences of nuclear holocaust. Full nuclear exchange would probably generate the same kind of dust cloud and darkening that may have wiped out the dinosaurs. Temperatures would drop precipitously and agriculture might become impossible. Avoidance of nuclear war is fundamentally an ethical and political imperative, but we must know the factual consequences to make firm judgments. I am heartened by a final link across disciplines and deep concerns—another criterion, by the way, of science at its best: A recognition of the very phenomenon that made our evolution possible by exterminating the previously dominant dinosaurs and clearing a way for the evolution of large mammals, including us, might actually help to save us from joining those magnificent beasts in contorted poses among the strata of the earth.

Meaning

1. According to Gould, what constitutes a scientific hypothesis? What constitutes useless speculation? Where in the essay do you find his definitions of these terms?

2. State, in your own words, the thesis of this essay.

3. What does Gould perceive to be the major flaws in the testicular malfunction and drug overdose theories about the extinction of dinosaurs? Cite his specific reasons for discrediting each theory.

4. What is the connection between nuclear holocaust and the extinction of dinosaurs? (See the essay's last paragraph.)

Purpose and Audience

1. Overall, do you find Gould's essay effective in explaining a specialized subject to an audience of nonspecialists? Why, or why not?

2. Paragraphs 14 and 16 contain references to Dylan Thomas's poem "Do Not Go Gentle into That Good Night." (The poem's title is used in paragraph 14; "Rage, rage against the dying of the light," one of the poem's refrains, appears in paragraph 16.) If you are not familiar with the poem, look it up. Is it necessary to know the poem to understand Gould's use of these lines? What is the effect of these allusions? (If necessary, see the Glossary under *allusion*.)

Method and Structure

1. In explaining the Alvarezes' hypothesis about the causes of the dinosaurs' extinction, Gould outlines a causal chain. Draw a diagram to illustrate this chain.

2. OTHER METHODS   How does the process analysis in paragraphs 4–5, 9–12, 14, and 16 help Gould analyze the possible causes of dinosaur extinction? What would the essay lack without these paragraphs?

Language

1. How do you understand the phrases "hit parade of primal fascination" (paragraph 17) and "the hypothesis of testicular frying" (18)? Is the tone here somber, silly, whimsical, ironic, or what? (If necessary, see the definition of *tone* in the Glossary.)

2. What do you take the following sentence to mean: *"There is no separate problem of the extinction of dinosaurs"* (paragraph 5)? Separate from what? According to Gould, then, what *is* the problem being discussed?

Writing Topics

1. In an essay, explore the causes of a situation that affects you directly—a breakup with a close friend or significant other, a course you are having difficulties with, a problem you face at work, or the like. Make sure to give your audience a clear sense of the situation. You may want to rely on narration, telling the story of the circumstances.

2. As Gould himself predicts (paragraph 24), his summary of the research into the Alvarez hypothesis is now dated: more data have accumulated; the hypothesis has been challenged, tested, revised. Do research in the library to find articles written over the past several years about the extinction of the dinosaurs. Write an essay updating Gould's in which you summarize the significant evidence for and against the Alvarez hypothesis.

3. Apply Gould's distinction between hypothesis and speculation (paragraphs 4–5) in an area you know well—for instance, Civil War battles, dance, basketball, waste recycling, carpentry, nursing. What, in your area, is the equivalent of the useful hypothesis? What is the equivalent of the useless speculation? Be as specific as possible so that a reader outside the field can understand you.

CAUSE-AND-EFFECT ANALYSIS

Select one of the following questions, or any question they suggest, and answer it in an essay developed by analyzing causes or effects. The question you choose should concern a topic you care about so that your analysis of causes or effects is a means of communicating an idea, not an end in itself.

People and Their Behavior

1. Why is a past or present politician, athlete, police officer, or fire fighter considered a hero?
2. Why does a sound body contribute to a sound mind?
3. Why is a particular friend or relative always getting into trouble?
4. Why do people root for the underdog?
5. How does a person's alcohol or drug dependency affect others?

Work

6. At what age should a person start working for pay, and why?
7. What effects do you expect your education to have on your choice of career and your performance in it?
8. What effect has the job market had on you and your friends?
9. Why would a man or a woman enter a field that has traditionally been filled by the opposite sex, such as nursing or engineering?

Art and Entertainment

10. How has the Internet changed the music industry?
11. What makes a professional sports team succeed in a new city?
12. Why is (or was) a particular television show, movie, or Web site so popular?

Contemporary Issues

13. Why does the United States spend so much money on health care?
14. How can a long period of involuntary unemployment affect a person?
15. Is a college education worth the expense?
16. Why do marriages between teenagers fail more often than marriages between people in other age groups?
17. Why might someone resort to a public act of violence, such as bombing a building?

Chapter 10

ARGUMENT AND PERSUASION

USING THE METHOD

Since we argue all the time—with relatives, with friends, with the auto mechanic or the shop clerk—a chapter devoted to argument and persuasion may at first seem unnecessary. But arguing with an auto mechanic over the cost of repairs is quite a different process from presenting an argument over a complex issue to readers. In both cases we are trying to find common ground with our audience, perhaps to change someone's views or even to compel people to act as we wish. But the mechanic is in front of us; we can shift our tactics in response to his or her gestures, expressions, and words. The reader, in contrast, is "out there"; we have to anticipate those gestures, expressions, and words in the way we structure the argument, the kinds of evidence we use to support it, even the way we conceive of the subject.

A great many assertions that are worth making are debatable on some level—whether over the facts on which the assertions are based or over the values they imply. Two witnesses to an accident cannot agree on what they saw; two scientists cannot agree on what an experiment shows; two economists cannot agree on what measures will reduce unemployment; two doctors cannot agree on what constitutes life or death. We see such disagreements play out in writing all the time, whether we're reading an accident report, a magazine article claiming the benefits of unemployment rates, or an editorial responding to a Supreme Court decision.

Technically, argument and persuasion are two different processes:

- **Argument** appeals mainly to an audience's sense of reason in order to negotiate a common understanding or to win agreement with a claim. It is the method of a columnist who defends a president's foreign policy on the grounds of economics and defense strategy.
- **Persuasion** appeals mainly to an audience's feelings and values in order to compel some action, or at least to win support for an action. It is the method of a mayoral candidate who urges voters to support her because she is sensitive to the poor.

But argument and persuasion so often mingle that we will use the one term *argument* to mean a deliberate appeal to an audience's reason and emotions in order to create compromise, win agreement, or compel action. Making an effective case for our opinions requires upholding certain responsibilities and attending to several established techniques of argumentation, most of them dating back to ancient Greece.

The Elements of Argument

All arguments share certain elements:

- *The core of any argument is an **assertion** or **proposition**,* a debatable claim about the subject. Generally you express this assertion as your thesis statement. It may defend or attack a position, suggest a solution to a problem, recommend a change in policy, or challenge a value or belief. Here are a few examples:

   The college should give first priority for on-campus jobs to students who need financial aid.

   School prayer has been rightly declared unconstitutional and should not be reinstituted in any form.

   Smokers who wish to poison themselves should be allowed to do so, but not in any place where their smoke will poison others.

- *The central assertion is broken down into subclaims,* each one supported by evidence.
- *Significant opposing arguments are raised and dispensed with,* again with the support of evidence.

- *The parts of the argument are organized into a clear, logical structure that pushes steadily toward the conclusion.*

You may draw on classification, comparison, or any other rhetorical method to develop the entire argument or to introduce evidence or strengthen your conclusion. For instance, in a paper arguing for raising a college's standards of admission, you might contrast the existing standards with the proposed standards, analyze a process for raising the standards over a period of years, and predict the effects of the new standards on future students' preparedness for college work.

Appeals to Readers

In arguing you are appealing to readers: you want them to listen to what you have to say, judge your words fairly, and, as much as they can, agree with you. Most arguments combine three kinds of appeals to readers: ethical, emotional, and rational.

Ethical Appeal

The **ethical appeal** is often not explicit in an argument, yet it pervades the whole. It is the sense you convey of your expertise and character, projected by the reasonableness of the argument, by the use of evidence, and by tone. A rational argument shows readers that you are thinking logically and fairly. Strong evidence establishes your credibility. And a sincere, reasonable tone demonstrates your balance and goodwill.

Emotional Appeal

The **emotional appeal** in argument aims directly for readers' hearts—for the complex of beliefs, values, and feelings deeply embedded in all of us. We are just as often motivated by these ingrained ideas and emotions as by our intellects. Even scientists, who stress the rational interpretation of facts above all else, are sometimes influenced in their interpretations by emotions deriving from, say, competition with other scientists. And the willingness of a nation's citizens to go to war may result more from their fear and pride than from their reasoned considerations of risks and gains. An emotional appeal in argument attempts to tap such feelings for any of several reasons:

- *To heighten the responsiveness of readers*
- *To inspire readers to new beliefs*
- *To compel readers to act*
- *To assure readers that their values remain unchallenged*

An emotional appeal may be explicit, as when an argument against capital punishment appeals to readers' religious values by citing the Bible's Sixth Commandment, "Thou shalt not kill." But an emotional appeal may also be less obvious, because individual words may have connotations that elicit emotional responses from readers. For instance, one writer may characterize an environmental group as "a well-organized team representing diverse interests," while another may call the same group "a hodgepodge of nature lovers and irresponsible businesspeople." The first appeals to readers' preference for order and balance, the second to readers' fear of extremism and disdain for unsound business practices. (See the Glossary for more on *connotation*.)

The use of emotional appeals requires care:

- *The appeal must be directed at the audience's actual beliefs and feelings.*
- *The appeal must be presented dispassionately* enough that readers have no reason to doubt your fairness in the rest of the argument.
- *The appeal must be appropriate to the subject and to the argument.* In arguing against a pay raise for city councilors, for example, you might be tempted to appeal to readers' resentment and distrust of wealthy people by pointing out that two of the councilors are rich enough to work for no pay. But such an appeal would divert attention from the issue of whether the pay raise is justified for all councilors on the basis of the work they do and the city's ability to pay the extra cost.

Carefully used, emotional appeals have great force, particularly when they contribute to an argument based largely on sound reasoning and evidence. The appropriate mix of emotion and reason in a given essay is entirely dependent on the subject, your purpose, and the audience. Emotional appeals are out of place in most arguments in the natural and social sciences, where rational interpretations of factual evidence are all that will convince readers of the truth of an assertion. But emotional appeals may be essential when you want an audience to support or take an action, for emotion is a stronger motivator than reason.

Rational Appeal

A **rational appeal** addresses the capacity of readers to reason logically about a problem. You establish the truth of a proposition or claim by moving through a series of related subclaims, each supported by evidence. In doing so, you follow processes of reasoning that are natural to all of us and thus are expected by readers. These processes are induction and deduction.

Inductive reasoning moves from the particular to the general, from evidence to a generalization or conclusion about the evidence. It is a process we begin learning in infancy and use daily throughout our lives: a child burns herself the three times she touches a stove, so she concludes that stoves burn; we have liked four movies produced by Guillermo del Toro, so we form the generalization that Guillermo del Toro makes good movies. Inductive reasoning is also very common in argument: you might offer facts showing that chronic patients in the state's mental hospitals receive only drugs as treatment and then conclude that the state's hospitals rely exclusively on drugs to treat chronic patients.

The movement from particular to general is called an **inductive leap** because you must make something of a jump to conclude that what is true of some instances (the chronic patients whose records were available) is also true of all other instances in the class (the rest of the chronic patients). In an ideal world we could perhaps avoid the inductive leap by pinning down every conceivable instance, but in the real world such thoroughness is usually impractical and often impossible. Instead, we gather enough evidence to make our generalizations probable.

The evidence for induction may be of several kinds:

- *Facts*: statistics or other hard data that are verifiable or attested to by reliable sources (the number of drug doses per chronic patient, derived from hospital records).
- *Opinions* of recognized experts who have drawn conclusions based on research and observation (the testimony of an experienced hospital doctor).
- *Examples* illustrating the evidence (the treatment history of one patient).

A sound inductive generalization can form the basis for the second reasoning process, **deductive reasoning**. Working from the general to the particular, you start with such a generalization and apply it to a new situation in order to draw a conclusion about that situation. Like induction, deduction is a process we use constantly to order our experience. The child who learns from three experiences that all stoves burn then sees a new stove and concludes that this stove also will burn. The child's thought process can be written in the form of a **syllogism**, a three-step outline of deductive reasoning:

> All stoves burn me.
> This is a stove.
> Therefore, this stove will burn me.

The first statement, the generalization derived from induction, is called the **major premise**. The second statement, a more specific assertion about some element of the major premise, is called the **minor premise**. And the third statement, an assertion of the logical connection between premises, is called the **conclusion**. The following syllogism takes the earlier example about mental hospitals one step further:

> MAJOR PREMISE The state hospitals' treatment of chronic patients relies exclusively on drugs.
>
> MINOR PREMISE Drugs do not cure chronic patients.
>
> CONCLUSION Therefore, the state hospitals' treatment of chronic patients will not cure them.

Unlike an inductive conclusion, which requires a leap, the deductive conclusion derives necessarily from the premises: as long as the reasoning process is valid and the premises are accepted as true, then the conclusion must also be true. To be valid, the reasoning must conform to the process outlined above. The following syllogism is *not* valid, even though the premises are true:

> All radicals want to change the system.
> Georgia Allport wants to change the system.
> Therefore, Georgia Allport is a radical.

The flaw in this syllogism is that not *only* radicals want to change the system, so Allport does not *necessarily* fall within the class of radicals just because she wants to change the system. The conclusion, then, is invalid.

A syllogism can be valid without being true if either of the premises is untrue. For example:

> All people who want political change are radicals.
> Georgia Allport wants political change.
> Therefore, Georgia Allport is a radical.

The conclusion here is valid because Allport falls within the class of people who want political change. But the conclusion is untrue because the major premise is untrue. As commonly defined, a radical seeks extreme change, often by revolutionary means. But other forms and means of change are also possible; Allport, for instance, may be interested in improving the delivery of services to the poor and in achieving passage of tougher environmental-protection laws—both political changes, to be sure, but neither radical.

In arguments, syllogisms are rarely spelled out as neatly as in these examples. Sometimes the order of the statements is reversed, as in this sentence paraphrasing a Supreme Court decision:

> The state may not imprison a man just because he is too poor to pay a fine; the only justification for imprisonment is a certain danger to society, and poverty does not constitute certain danger.

The buried syllogism can be stated thus:

> MAJOR PREMISE The state may imprison only those who are a certain danger to society.
>
> MINOR PREMISE A man who is too poor to pay a fine is not a certain danger to society.
>
> CONCLUSION Therefore, the state cannot imprison a man just because he is too poor to pay a fine.

Often one of a syllogism's premises, or even its conclusion, is implied but not expressed. Each of the following sentences omits one part of the same syllogism:

All five students cheated, so they should be expelled. [Implied major premise: cheaters should be expelled.]

Cheaters should be punished by expulsion, so all five students should be expelled. [Implied minor premise: all five students cheated.]

Cheaters should be punished by expulsion, and all five students cheated. [Implied conclusion: all five students should be expelled.]

Fallacies

Inappropriate emotional appeals and flaws in reasoning—called **fallacies**—can trap you as you construct an argument. Watch out for the following, which your readers will find if you don't:

- **Hasty generalization**: an inductive conclusion that leaps to include *all* instances when at best only *some* instances provide any evidence. Hasty generalizations form some of our worst stereotypes:

  Physically challenged people are mentally challenged, too.

  African Americans are good athletes.

  Italian Americans are volatile.

- **Oversimplification**: an inductive conclusion that ignores complexities in the evidence that, if heeded, would weaken the conclusion or suggest an entirely different one. For example:

  The newspaper folded because it couldn't compete with the Internet.

  Although the Internet may have taken some business from the paper, other papers continue to thrive; thus the Internet could not be the only cause of the paper's failure.

- **Begging the question**: assuming a conclusion in the statement of a premise, and thus begging readers to accept the conclusion—the question—before it is proved. For example:

  We can trust the president not to neglect the needy because he is a compassionate man.

  This sentence asserts in a circular fashion that the president is not uncompassionate because he is compassionate. He may indeed be compassionate, but the question that needs addressing is what will he do for the needy.

- **Ignoring the question**: introducing an issue or consideration that shifts the argument away from the real issue. Offering an emotional appeal as a premise in a logical argument is a form of ignoring the question. The following sentence, for instance, appeals to pity, not to logic:

  The mayor was badly used by people he loved and trusted, so we should not blame him for the corruption in his administration.

- **Ad hominem** (Latin for "to the man"): a form of ignoring the question by attacking the opponents instead of the opponents' arguments. For example:

  O'Brien is married to a convict, so her proposals for prison reform should not be taken seriously.

- **Either-or**: requiring that readers choose between two interpretations or actions when in fact the choices are more numerous.

  Either we imprison all drug users, or we will become their prisoners.

  The factors contributing to drug addiction, and the choices for dealing with it, are obviously more complex than this statement suggests. Not all either-or arguments are invalid, for sometimes the alternatives encompass all the possibilities. But when they do not, the argument is false.

- **Non sequitur** (Latin for "it does not follow"): a conclusion derived illogically or erroneously from stated or implied premises. For instance:

  Young children are too immature to engage in sex, so they should not be taught about it.

  This sentence implies one of two meanings, both of them questionable: only the sexually active can learn anything about sex, or teaching young children about sex will cause them to engage in it.

- **Post hoc** (from the Latin *post hoc, ergo propter hoc*, "after this, therefore because of this"): assuming that because one thing preceded another, it must have caused the other. For example:

After the town banned smoking in closed public places, the incidence of vandalism went up.

Many things may have caused the rise in vandalism, including improved weather and a climbing unemployment rate. It does not follow that the ban on smoking, and that alone, caused the rise.

DEVELOPING AN ARGUMENTATIVE AND PERSUASIVE ESSAY

Getting Started

You will have many chances to write arguments—from defending or opposing a policy such as progressive taxation in an economics course to justifying a new procedure at work to persuading a company to refund your money for a bad product. To choose a subject for an argumentative essay, consider a behavior or policy that irks you, an opinion you want to defend, a change you would like to see implemented, a way to solve a problem. The subject you pick should meet certain criteria:

- *It should be something you have some knowledge of,* from your own experience or observations, from class discussions, or from reading, although you may need to do further research as well.

- *It should be limited to a topic you can treat thoroughly in the space and time available to you*—for instance, the quality of computer instruction at your school rather than in the whole nation.

- *It should be something that you feel strongly about* so that you can make a convincing case. (However, it's best to avoid subjects that you cannot view with some objectivity, seeing the opposite side as well as your own; otherwise, you may not be open to flaws in your argument, and you may not be able to represent the opposition fairly.)

Once you have selected a subject, do some preliminary research to make sure that you will have enough evidence to support your opinion. This step is especially important with issues like welfare cheating or tax advantages for the wealthy—which we all tend to have opinions about whether we know the facts or not. Where to seek evidence depends on the nature of your argument.

- *For an argument derived from your own experiences and observations,* such as a recommendation that all students work part-time for the education if not for the money, gathering evidence will be primarily a matter of searching your own thoughts and also uncovering opposing views, perhaps by consulting others.

- *For some arguments derived from personal experience,* you can strengthen your evidence with judicious use of facts and opinions from other sources. An essay arguing in favor of vegetarianism, for instance, could mix the benefits you or others you have interviewed have felt with those demonstrated by scientific data.

- *For an argument on a nonpersonal or a controversial subject,* you will have to gather the evidence of other sources. Though you might strongly favor or oppose a massive federal investment in solar-energy research, your opinions would count little if they were not supported with facts and the opinions of experts.

In addition to evidence, knowledge of readers' needs and expectations is absolutely crucial in planning an argument. In explanatory writing, detail and clarity alone may accomplish your purpose, but you cannot hope to move readers in a certain direction unless you have some idea of where they stand. You need a sense of their background in your subject, of course. But even more, you need a good idea of their values and beliefs, their attitudes toward your subject—in short, their willingness to be convinced. In a composition class, your readers will probably be your instructor and your classmates, a small but diverse group. A good target when you are addressing a diverse audience is the reader who is neutral or mildly biased one way or the other toward your subject. You can hope to influence this person as long as your argument is reasonable, your evidence is thorough and convincing, your treatment of opposing views is fair, and your appeals to readers' emotions are appropriate to your purpose, your subject, and especially your readers' values and feelings.

Forming a Thesis

With your subject and some evidence in hand, you should develop a tentative thesis. But don't feel you have to prove your thesis at this early stage; fixing it too firmly may make you unwilling to reshape it if further evidence, your audience, or the structure of your argument so demands.

Stating your thesis in a preliminary thesis statement can help you form your idea. Make this sentence as clear and specific as possible. Don't resort to a vague generalization or a nondebatable statement of fact. Instead, state the precise opinion you want readers to accept or the precise action you want them to take or support. For instance:

> VAGUE Computer instruction is important.
>
> NONDEBATABLE The school's investment in computer instruction is less than the average investment of the nation's colleges and universities.
>
> PRECISE Money designated for new dormitories and athletic facilities should be diverted to constructing computer facilities and hiring first-rate computer faculty.
>
> VAGUE Cloning research is promising.
>
> NONDEBATABLE Scientists have been experimenting with cloning procedures for many years.
>
> PRECISE Those who oppose cloning research should consider the potentially valuable applications of the research for human health and development.

Since the thesis is essentially a conclusion from evidence, you will probably need to do some additional reading to ensure that you have a broad range of facts and opinions supporting not only your view of the subject but also any opposing views. Though it may be tempting to ignore your opposition in the hope that readers know nothing of it, it is dishonest and probably futile to do so. Acknowledging and, whenever possible, refuting significant opposing views will enhance your credibility with readers. If you find that some counterarguments damage your own argument too greatly, then you will have to rethink your thesis.

Organizing

Once you have formulated your thesis and evaluated your reasons and evidence against the needs and expectations of your audience, begin planning how you will arrange your argument. The introduction to your essay should draw readers into your framework, making them see how the subject affects them and predisposing them to consider your argument. Sometimes a forthright approach works best, but an eye-opening anecdote or quotation can also be effective. Your thesis sentence may end your introduction. But if you think readers will not even entertain your thesis until they have seen some or all of your evidence, then withhold your thesis for later.

The main part of the essay consists of your reasons and your evidence for them. The evidence you generated or collected should suggest the reasons that will support the claim of your thesis—essentially the minor arguments that bolster the main argument. In an essay favoring federal investment in solar-energy research, for instance, the minor arguments might include the need for solar power, the feasibility of its widespread use, and its cost and safety compared with the cost and safety of other energy sources. It is in developing these minor arguments that you are most likely to use induction and deduction consciously—generalizing from specifics or applying generalizations to new information. Thus the minor arguments provide the entry points for your evidence, and together they should encompass all the relevant evidence.

Unless the minor arguments form a chain, with each growing out of the one before, their order should be determined by their potential effects on readers. In general, it is most effective to arrange the reasons in order of increasing importance or strength so as to finish powerfully. But to engage readers in the argument from the start, try to begin with a reason that they will find compelling or that they already know and accept; that way, the weaker reasons will be sandwiched between a strong beginning and an even stronger ending.

The views opposing yours can be raised and dispensed with wherever it seems most appropriate to do so. If a counterargument pertains to just one of your minor arguments, then dispose of it at that point. But if the counterarguments are more basic, pertaining to your whole thesis, you should dispose of them either after the introduction or shortly before the conclusion. Use the former strategy if the opposition is particularly strong and you fear that readers will be disinclined to listen unless you address their concerns first. Use the latter strategy when the counterarguments are generally weak or easily dispensed with once you've presented your case.

In the conclusion to your essay, you may summarize the main point of your argument and state your thesis for the first time, if you have saved it for the end, or restate it from your introduction. An effective quotation, an appropriate emotional appeal, or a call for support or action can often provide a strong finish to an argument.

Drafting

While you are drafting the essay, work to make your reasoning clear by showing how each bit of evidence relates to the reason or minor argument being discussed, and how each minor argument relates to the main argument contained in the thesis. In working through the reasons and evidence, you may find it helpful to state each reason as the first sentence in a paragraph and then support it in the following sentences. If this scheme seems too rigid or creates overlong paragraphs, you can always make changes after you have written the draft. Draw on a range of methods to clarify your points. For instance, define specialized terms or those you use in a special sense, compare and contrast one policy or piece of evidence with another, or carefully analyze causes or effects.

Revising and Editing

When your draft is complete, use the following questions to guide your revision and editing.

- *Is your thesis debatable, precise, and clear?* Readers must know what you are trying to convince them of, at least by the end of the essay if not up front.
- *Is your argument unified?* Does each minor claim support the thesis? Do all opinions, facts, and examples provide evidence for a minor claim? On behalf of your readers, question every

sentence you have written to be sure it contributes to the point you are making and to the argument as a whole.

- *Is the structure of your argument clear and compelling?* Readers should be able to follow easily, seeing when and why you move from one idea to the next.

- *Is the evidence specific, representative, and adequate?* Facts, examples, and expert opinions should be well detailed, should fairly represent the available information, and should be sufficient to support your claim.

- *Have you slipped into any logical fallacies?* Detecting fallacies in your own work can be difficult, but your readers will find them if you don't. Look for the following fallacies discussed earlier (pp. 323–25): hasty generalization, oversimplification, begging the question, ignoring the question, ad hominem, either-or, non sequitur, and post hoc. (All of these are also listed in the Glossary under *fallacies*.)

BILL McKIBBEN

One of the world's foremost environmental writers and activists, Bill McKibben was born in Palo Alto, California, in 1960 and grew up in suburban Lexington, Massachusetts. After graduating from Harvard University in 1982, McKibben landed a job as a staff writer for the New Yorker *and wrote the magazine's "Talk of the Town" column for five years before setting off as a freelance journalist. A frequent contributor to magazines such as the* Atlantic, Orion, Grist, *and* Outside, *he has written more than a dozen books about the environment, starting with* The End of Nature *(1989) and including* Maybe One: A Case for Smaller Families *(1998),* Enough: Staying Human in an Engineered Age *(2003), and* Eaarth: Making a Life on a Tough New Planet *(2010). In addition to writing, McKibben has launched multiple grassroots campaigns and organized thousands of rallies to draw attention to the problem of climate change, to demand political action, and to encourage people to embrace earth-friendly lifestyles. He lives in Ripton, Vermont, and is scholar in residence at Middlebury College.*

Waste Not, Want Not

One problem about which McKibben has been particularly outspoken is a global economy that depends on consumer spending for continued growth. A vocal critic of consumption, McKibben has devoted most of his career to warning that the planet cannot survive human abuses of natural resources. In this essay, first published in Mother Jones *in 2009, he presents his argument in favor of simple living for the sake of the environment. The essay after this one, by Derrick Jensen (p. 339), rejects McKibben's proposal by insisting that individual actions are meaningless.*

Once a year or so, it's my turn to run recycling day for our tiny town. Saturday morning, nine to twelve, a steady stream of people show up to sort out their plastics (No. 1, No. 2, etc.), their corrugated cardboard (flattened, please), their glass (and their returnable glass, which goes to benefit the elementary school),

their Styrofoam peanuts, their paper, their cans. It's quite satisfying—everything in its place.

But it's also kind of disturbing, this waste stream. For one, a   2
town of 550 sure generates a lot—a trailer load every couple of
weeks. Sometimes you have to put a kid into the bin and tell her
to jump up and down so the lid can close.

More than that, though, so much of it seems utterly unneces-   3
sary. Not just waste, but wasteful. Plastic water bottles, one after
another—80 million of them get tossed every day. The ones I'm
stomping down are being "recycled," but so what? In a country
where almost everyone has access to clean drinking water, they
define waste to begin with. I mean, you don't have a mug? In fact,
once you start thinking about it, the category of "waste" begins to
expand, until it includes an alarming percentage of our economy.
Let's do some intellectual sorting:

There's old-fashioned waste, the dangerous, sooty kind. You're   4
making something useful, but you're not using the latest technology, and so you're spewing: particulates into the air, or maybe sew-
age into the water. You wish to keep doing it, because it's cheap,
and you block any regulation that might interfere with your right
to spew. This is the kind of waste that's easy to attack; it's obvious
and obnoxious and a lot of it falls under the Clean Air Act and
Clean Water Act and so on. There's actually less of this kind of
waste than there used to be—that's why we can swim in most of
our rivers again.

There's waste that comes from everything operating as it   5
should, only too much so. If carbon monoxide (carbon with one
oxygen atom) exemplifies pollution of the first type, then carbon
dioxide (carbon with two oxygen atoms) typifies the second. Carbon monoxide poisons you in your garage and turns Beijing's
air brown, but if you put a catalytic converter on your tailpipe
it all but disappears. Carbon dioxide doesn't do anything to you
directly—a clean-burning engine used to be defined as one that
released only CO_2 and water vapor—but in sufficient quantity it
melts the ice caps, converts grassland into desert, and turns every
coastal city into New Orleans.

There's waste that comes from doing something that mani-   6
festly doesn't need doing. A hundred million trees are cut every
year just to satisfy the junk-mail industry. You can argue about cutting trees for newspapers, or magazines, or Bibles, or symphony

scores—but the cascade of stuffporn that arrives daily in our mailboxes? It wastes forests, and also our time. Which, actually, is precious—we each get about 30,000 days, and it makes one a little sick to calculate how many of them have been spent opening credit card offers.

Or think about what we've done with cars. From 1975 to 7 1985, fuel efficiency for the average new car improved from 14 to 28 miles per gallon. Then we stopped worrying about oil and put all that engineering talent to work on torque. In the mid-1980s, the typical car accelerated from 0 to 60 mph in 14.5 seconds. Today's average (even though vehicles are much heavier) is 9.5 seconds. But it's barely legal to accelerate like that, and it makes you look like an idiot, or a teenager.

Then there's the waste that comes with doing something 8 maybe perhaps vaguely useful when you could be doing something actually useful instead. For instance: Congress is being lobbied really, really hard to fork over billions of dollars to the nuclear industry, on the premise that it will fight global warming. There is, of course, that little matter of nuclear waste—but lay that aside (in Nevada or someplace). The greater problem is the wasted opportunity: That money could go to improving efficiency, which can produce the same carbon reductions for about a fifth of the price.

Our wasteful habits wouldn't matter much if there were just 9 a few of us—a Neanderthal hunting band could have discarded six plastic water bottles apiece every day with no real effect except someday puzzling anthropologists. But the volumes we manage are something else. Chris Jordan is the photographer laureate of waste—his most recent project, "Running the Numbers," uses exquisite images to show the 106,000 aluminum cans Americans toss every 30 seconds, or the 1 million plastic cups distributed on US airline flights every 6 hours, or the 2 million plastic beverage bottles we run through every 5 minutes, or the 426,000 cell phones we discard every day, or the 1.14 million brown paper supermarket bags we use each hour, or the 60,000 plastic bags we use every 5 seconds, or the 15 million sheets of office paper we use every 5 minutes, or the 170,000 Energizer batteries produced every 15 minutes. The simple amount of stuff it takes—energy especially—to manage this kind of throughput makes it daunting to even think about our waste problem. (Meanwhile, the next time someone tells you that population is at the root of our troubles, remind them that the average American uses more energy between the stroke of midnight on New Year's Eve and dinner on January 2 than the average, say, Tanzanian consumes in a year. Population matters, but it *really* matters when you multiply it by proximity to Costco.)

Would you like me to go on? Americans discard enough 10 aluminum to rebuild our entire commercial air fleet every three months—and aluminum represents less than 1% of our solid waste stream. We toss 14% of the food we buy at the store. More than 46,000 pieces of plastic debris float on each square mile of ocean. And—oh, forget it.

These kinds of numbers get in the way of figuring out how 11 much we really waste. In recent years, for instance, 40% of Harvard graduates have gone into finance, consulting, and business. They had just spent four years with the world's greatest library, some of its finest museum collections, an unparalleled assemblage of Nobel-quality scholars, and all they wanted to do was go to lower Manhattan and stare into computer screens. What a waste! And when they got to Wall Street, of course, they figured out extravagant ways to waste the life savings of millions of Americans, which in turn required the waste of taxpayer dollars to bail them out,[1] money that could have been spent on completely useful things: trains to get us where we want to go—say, new national parks.

Perhaps the only kind of waste we've gotten good at cutting 12 is the kind we least needed to eliminate: An entire industry of consultants survives on telling companies how to get rid of inefficiencies—which generally means people. And an entire class of politicians survives by railing about government waste, which also ends up meaning programs for people: Health care for poor children, what a boondoggle.

Want to talk about government waste? We're going to end up 13 spending north of a trillion dollars on the war in Iraq, which will go down as one of the larger wastes of money—and lives—in

[1]In 2009 the Obama administration passed the American Recovery and Reinvestment Act, an attempt to jump-start a stalled economy by distributing nearly a trillion dollars in stimulus money to businesses, states, and cities struggling through a deep recession. [Editors' note.]

our history.[2] But we spend more than half a trillion a year on the military anyway, more than the next ten nations combined. That almost defines profligacy.

We've gotten away with all of this for a long time because 14 we had margin, all kinds of margin. Money, for sure—we were the richest nation on Earth, and when we wanted more we just borrowed it from China. But margin in other ways as well: We landed on a continent with topsoil more than a foot thick across its vast interior, so the fact that we immediately started to waste it with inefficient plowing hardly mattered. We inherited an atmosphere that could buffer our emissions for the first 150 years of the Industrial Revolution. We somehow got away with wasting the talents of black people and women and gay folks.

But our margin is gone. We're out of cash, we're out of atmo- 15 sphere, we're out of luck. The current economic carnage is what happens when you waste—when the CEO of Merrill Lynch thinks he needs a $35,000 commode, when the CEO of Tyco thinks it would be fun to spend a million dollars on his wife's birthday party, complete with an ice sculpture of Michelangelo's *David* peeing vodka.[3] The melted Arctic ice cap is what you get when everyone in America thinks he requires the kind of vehicle that might make sense for a forest ranger.

Getting out of the fix we're in—if it's still possible—requires 16 in part that we relearn some very old lessons. We were once famously thrifty: Yankee frugality, straightening bent nails, saving string. We used to have a holiday, Thrift Week, which began on Ben Franklin's birthday: "Beware of little expenses; a small leak will sink a great ship," said he. We disapproved of frippery, couldn't imagine wasting money on ourselves, made do or did without. It took a mighty effort to make us what we are today—in

[2]The war began in 2003 and officially ended on December 15, 2011. Analysts' estimates put the price tag at roughly $1 trillion in direct expenses, with 4,500 American lives and 100,000 Iraqi lives lost. [Editors' note.]

[3]When John Thain took leadership of the financial group Merrill Lynch in the midst of the financial crisis of 2008, he had his office suite redecorated at an estimated cost of $1.22 million and was promptly fired. Dennis Kozlowski, the former head of the global manufacturing corporation Tyco, is serving a twenty-five-year prison sentence for misappropriating company funds for personal use; the 2001 party was used as evidence toward his conviction. [Editors' note.]

fact, it took a mighty industry, advertising, which soaks up plenty more of those Harvard grads and represents an almost total waste.

In the end, we built an economy that depended on waste, and 17 boundless waste is what it has produced. And the really sad part is, it felt that way, too. Making enough money to build houses with rooms we never used, and cars with engines we had no need of, meant wasting endless hours at work. Which meant that we had, on average, one-third fewer friends than our parents' generation. What waste that! "Getting and spending, we lay waste our powers," wrote Wordsworth.[4] We can't say we weren't warned.

The economic mess now transfixing us will mean some kind 18 of change. We can try to hang on to the status quo—living a Walmart life so we can buy cheaply enough to keep the stream of stuff coming. Or we can say uncle. There are all kinds of experiments in postwaste living springing up: Freecycling, and Craigslisting, and Dumpster diving, and car sharing (those unoccupied seats in your vehicle—what a waste!), and open sourcing. We're sharing buses, and going to the library in greater numbers. Economists keep hoping we'll figure out a way to revert—that we'll waste a little more, and pull us out of the economic doldrums. But the psychological tide suddenly runs the other way.

We may have waited too long—we may have wasted our last 19 good chance. It's possible the planet will keep warming and the economy keep sinking no matter what. But perhaps not—and we seem ready to shoot for something nobler than the hyperconsumerism that's wasted so much of the last few decades. Barack Obama said he would "call out" the nation's mayors if they wasted their stimulus money. That's the mood we're in, and it's about time.

Meaning

1. McKibben focuses on two issues related to waste: the environment and the economy. Which of his arguments deal with the first issue, and which the second? How is each issue related to his thesis?
2. What reasons does McKibben give for our wastefulness? What examples does he provide for this kind of behavior?

[4]William Wordsworth (1770–1850) was an English poet. The line is from his 1807 sonnet "The World Is Too Much with Us." [Editors' note.]

3. McKibben doesn't get to his proposed solution until the end of the essay. What solution does he propose? What action does he ask readers to take?

Purpose and Audience

1. Does McKibben seem to expect his audience to agree or disagree with his position? In answering this question, consider his use of pronouns (*we* and *you* especially): what audience reaction does he seem to be seeking in his presentation of examples?
2. In the next essay, which rejects McKibben's proposed solution, Derrick Jensen suggests that advocates of simple living miss the point: "Consumer culture and the capitalist mindset have taught us to substitute acts of personal consumption (or enlightenment) for organized political resistance" (paragraph 2, p. 339). Does McKibben's purpose in this essay seem entirely focused on the personal? Does he ignore culture and politics, as Jensen implies? How do you think McKibben might respond to Jensen's criticism?

Method and Structure

1. Locate examples of emotional, ethical, and rational appeals in McKibben's argument. Which appeals do you consider most effective? Least effective? Why?
2. McKibben's overall argument is based on a syllogism. Express his major premise, minor premise, and conclusion in your own words. Is his reasoning valid, in your opinion?
3. Where and how does McKibben address objections or opposing arguments? Do you find his strategy of counterargument effective? Why, or why not?
4. OTHER METHODS   How does McKibben use classification to sort out the different kinds of waste he sees in the contemporary world? What categories of waste does he identify? Why do the distinctions matter?

Language

1. Notice McKibben's frequent use of informal language and colloquial phrases, such as "oh, forget it" (paragraph 10). What does he achieve with this attitude? Do you find his tone appropriate, given the seriousness of the subject?
2. What does "stuffporn" (paragraph 6) mean? What about "throughput" (9)? Locate other examples of business jargon in the essay and explain their effect. Why does McKibben use these words?

Writing Topics

1. Using the Internet, research an environmental organization such as Greenpeace or McKibben's 350.org. In an essay summarize the global vision the organization outlines in its mission statement, which may include goals met to date as well as plans for the future. Then discuss whether you agree with the organization's assessment of the current environmental situation, its proposed solutions, and its methods for achieving those solutions. (You may need to narrow this discussion to a particular environmental problem.)

2. McKibben makes the point that the United States is more wasteful than other countries are: "the average American uses more energy between the stroke of midnight on New Year's Eve and dinner on January 2 than the average, say, Tanzanian consumes in a year" (paragraph 9). Write an essay that defends or argues against the relative resource consumption of the United States. Do geography, cultural ideas, product output, or other characteristics somehow make the United States more needful or deserving of resources than other nations? In formulating your answer, consider also how a person from another country might respond—a resident of, say, Tanzania or Italy or China.

3. McKibben suggests that consumer culture leads to unhappiness: "Making enough money to build houses with rooms we never used, and cars with engines we had no need of, meant wasting endless hours at work. Which meant that we had, on average, one-third fewer friends than our parents' generation. What waste that!" (paragraph 17). And yet for many Americans those hours at work could be said to improve the quality of life—by paying for a vacation, or a new sofa, or even bare necessities such as food and health care. Write an essay arguing for or against McKibben's statement, based on your own experiences and observations.

DERRICK JENSEN

Born in 1960, Derrick Jensen is a writer and environmental activist known for his radical stances against capitalism and Western civilization. "All of my work," he has said, is part of his life's mission to "stop this culture from killing the planet." Jensen received a BS in mineral engineering and physics from the Colorado School of Mines in 1983 and attempted to make a living as a beekeeper before finishing an MFA in creative writing from Eastern Washington University in 1991. He has written fifteen books of nonfiction, among them Listening to the Land *(1995),* A Language Older than Words *(2000),* The Culture of Make Believe *(2002), and* Resistance Against Empire *(2010). Jensen is also the author of two novels:* Songs of the Dead *(2009) and* Lives Less Valuable *(2010). His articles on environmental politics have appeared in the* New York Times Magazine, Audubon, Orion, *and the* Sun.

Forget Shorter Showers

This essay was published in Orion *magazine in 2009, one month after Bill McKibben's "Waste Not, Want Not" (p. 331). Responding (indirectly) to his fellow* Orion *contributor, Jensen lays out his own argument against consumption, but with a decidedly different focus.*

Would any sane person think Dumpster diving would have stopped 1
Hitler, or that composting would have ended slavery or brought about the eight-hour workday, or that chopping wood and carrying water would have gotten people out of Tsarist prisons, or that dancing naked around a fire would have helped put in place the Voting Rights Act of 1957 or the Civil Rights Act of 1964? Then why now, with all the world at stake, do so many people retreat into these entirely personal "solutions"?

Part of the problem is that we've been victims of a campaign 2
of systematic misdirection. Consumer culture and the capitalist mindset have taught us to substitute acts of personal consumption (or enlightenment) for organized political resistance.

An Inconvenient Truth[1] helped raise consciousness about global warming. But did you notice that all of the solutions presented had to do with personal consumption—changing light bulbs, inflating tires, driving half as much—and had nothing to do with shifting power away from corporations, or stopping the growth economy that is destroying the planet? Even if every person in the United States did everything the movie suggested, US carbon emissions would fall by only 22%. Scientific consensus is that emissions must be reduced by at least 75% worldwide.

Or let's talk water. We so often hear that the world is running out 3 of water. People are dying from lack of water. Rivers are dewatered from lack of water. Because of this we need to take shorter showers. See the disconnect? *Because I take showers, I'm responsible for drawing down aquifers?* Well, no. More than 90% of the water used by humans is used by agriculture and industry. The remaining 10% is split between municipalities and actual living breathing individual humans. Collectively, municipal golf courses use as much water as municipal human beings. People (both human people and fish people) aren't dying because the world is running out of water. They're dying because the water is being stolen.

Or let's talk energy. Kirkpatrick Sale[2] summarized it well: 4 "For the past fifteen years the story has been the same every year: individual consumption—residential, by private car, and so on—is never more than about a quarter of all consumption; the vast majority is commercial, industrial, corporate, by agribusiness and government [he forgot military]. So, even if we all took up cycling and wood stoves it would have a negligible impact on energy use, global warming, and atmospheric pollution."

Or let's talk waste. In 2005, per-capita municipal waste pro- 5 duction (basically everything that's put out at the curb) in the US was about 1,660 pounds. Let's say you're a die-hard simple-living activist, and you reduce this to zero. You recycle everything. You bring cloth bags shopping. You fix your toaster. Your toes poke out of old tennis shoes. You're not done yet, though. Since municipal waste includes not just residential waste, but also waste from government offices and businesses, you march to those offices,

[1] A 2006 documentary film based on the book of the same name, both by former US Vice-President Al Gore. [Editors' note.]
[2] Kirkpatrick Sale is an American journalist who often writes about environmental issues, economics, and politics. [Editors' note.]

waste reduction pamphlets in hand, and convince them to cut down on their waste enough to eliminate your share of it. Uh, I've got some bad news. Municipal waste accounts for only 3% of total waste production in the United States.

I want to be clear. I'm not saying we shouldn't live simply. I 6 live reasonably simply myself, but I don't pretend that not buying much (or not driving much, or not having kids) is a powerful political act, or that it's deeply revolutionary. It's not. Personal change doesn't equal social change.

So how, then, and especially with all the world at stake, have 7 we come to accept these utterly insufficient responses? I think part of it is that we're in a double bind. A double bind is where you're given multiple options, but no matter what option you choose, you lose, and withdrawal is not an option. At this point, it should be pretty easy to recognize that every action involving the industrial economy is destructive (and we shouldn't pretend that solar photovoltaics,[3] for example, exempt us from this: they still require mining and transportation infrastructures at every point in the production processes; the same can be said for every other so-called green technology). So if we choose option one—if we avidly participate in the industrial economy—we may in the short term think we win because we may accumulate wealth, the marker of "success" in this culture. But we lose, because in doing so we give up our empathy, our animal humanity. And we really lose because industrial civilization is killing the planet, which means everyone loses. If we choose the "alternative" option of living more simply, thus causing less harm, but still not stopping the industrial economy from killing the planet, we may in the short term think we win because we get to feel pure, and we didn't even have to give up all of our empathy (just enough to justify not stopping the horrors), but once again we really lose because industrial civilization is still killing the planet, which means everyone still loses. The third option, acting decisively to stop the industrial economy, is very scary for a number of reasons, including but not restricted to the fact that we'd lose some of the luxuries (like electricity) to which we've grown accustomed, and the fact that those in power might try to kill us if we seriously impede their ability to exploit the

[3]A method of absorbing sunlight with film-coated panels and using the stored energy to generate electricity. [Editors' note.]

world—none of which alters the fact that it's a better option than a dead planet. Any option is a better option than a dead planet.

Besides being ineffective at causing the sorts of changes nec- 8 essary to stop this culture from killing the planet, there are at least four other problems with perceiving simple living as a political act (as opposed to living simply because that's what you want to do). The first is that it's predicated on the flawed notion that humans inevitably harm their landbase. Simple living as a political act consists solely of harm reduction, ignoring the fact that humans can help the Earth as well as harm it. We can rehabilitate streams, we can get rid of noxious invasives, we can remove dams, we can disrupt a political system tilted toward the rich as well as an extractive economic system, we can destroy the industrial economy that is destroying the real, physical world.

The second problem—and this is another big one—is that it 9 incorrectly assigns blame to the individual (and most especially to individuals who are particularly powerless) instead of to those who actually wield power in this system and to the system itself. Kirkpatrick Sale again: "The whole individualist what-you-can-do-to-save-the-Earth guilt trip is a myth. We, as individuals, are not creating the crises, and we can't solve them."

The third problem is that it accepts capitalism's redefinition 10 of us from citizens to consumers. By accepting this redefinition, we reduce our potential forms of resistance to consuming and not consuming. Citizens have a much wider range of available resistance tactics, including voting, not voting, running for office, pamphleting, boycotting, organizing, lobbying, protesting, and, when a government becomes destructive of life, liberty, and the pursuit of happiness, we have the right to alter or abolish it.

The fourth problem is that the endpoint of the logic behind 11 simple living as a political act is suicide. If every act within an industrial economy is destructive, and if we want to stop this destruction, and if we are unwilling (or unable) to question (much less destroy) the intellectual, moral, economic, and physical infrastructures that cause every act within an industrial economy to be destructive, then we can easily come to believe that we will cause the least destruction possible if we are dead.

The good news is that there are other options. We can follow 12 the examples of brave activists who lived through the difficult times I mentioned—Nazi Germany, Tsarist Russia, antebellum United

States—who did far more than manifest a form of moral purity; they actively opposed the injustices that surrounded them. We can follow the example of those who remembered that the role of an activist is not to navigate systems of oppressive power with as much integrity as possible, but rather to confront and take down those systems.

Meaning

1. What is the thesis of Jensen's argument? Where is this thesis stated most clearly? What is the relationship between Jensen's thesis and McKibben's thesis in the previous essay (beginning on p. 331)?
2. On what points does Jensen seem to agree with McKibben? On what points does he disagree? To what extent do the two writers' perspectives explain their difference of opinion?
3. What does Jensen mean by a "double bind" (paragraph 7)? Why does he believe that the industrial economy creates an impossible situation? What is his preferred solution to the problem?

Purpose and Audience

1. Given his effort to convince readers that simple living is not a solution to environmental problems, why does Jensen make a point of explaining that he's "not saying we shouldn't live simply" (paragraph 6)?
2. Whom does Jensen seem to be addressing in this essay: general readers? politicians? business leaders? some other group? (Hint: look up *Orion* magazine's mission and history.) What influence does he apparently hope to have on his readers' behavior? To what extent did he influence your opinions of simple living and of McKibben's argument supporting it?
3. Compare Jensen's and McKibben's depictions of municipal solid waste, or trash (paragraph 5 in Jensen; paragraphs 9–10, pp. 333–34, in McKibben). Which is more detailed? How does each author's use of detail—and the details themselves—reflect his emphasis?

Method and Structure

1. To what extent does Jensen use rational appeal in refuting the effectiveness of simple living? ethical appeal? emotional appeal? Identify examples of each in your answer.
2. Why, in an essay about the environment, does Jensen open and close with examples of Hitler, American slaves, Russian prison camps, and rights movements? What point is he making with these examples?
3. Jensen suggests that some of his opponents' arguments are based on faulty reasoning. What logical fallacies does he implicitly or

344   ARGUMENT AND PERSUASION

explicitly identify? Does Jensen lapse into any logical fallacies himself? If so, where?

4. OTHER METHODS   Much of Jensen's argument is developed by cause-and-effect analysis. Why is this method particularly effective for countering McKibben's proposal, given Jensen's main point?

Language

1. How would you characterize Jensen's tone in this essay—for instance, worried, condescending, frustrated, dismissive, eager, angry, militant, reassuring, serious, irritated, flippant? Is it consistent throughout? Give examples to support your analysis.

2. Take a close look at the first sentences of paragraphs 3–5. What is distinctive about them? What effect do they produce?

3. Why do you suppose Jensen quotes Kirkpatrick Sale twice? What does he achieve by using another writer's words to explain his points?

Writing Topics

1. Jensen's proposal to "stop the industrial economy" is extremely radical, and as he says, "very scary for a number of reasons" (paragraph 7). How do you react to his argument? Do you agree with him that revolution is necessary to save the planet, or do you find his concerns overblown, his suggestions unrealistic? Write an essay of your own responding to Jensen's essay. Be sure to include evidence to support your view.

2. Like McKibben, Jensen objects to the levels of personal consumption encouraged by industrial economy. Write an essay that defends or argues against consumption for its own sake, making a point of explaining what, in your mind, constitutes a necessity and what is a luxury. Do we have a right—even an obligation—to spend money on things we don't truly need? Why, or why not?

3. Both Jensen and McKibben take global warming as a given, but some observers dispute the notion that the planet is in trouble. Write a brief essay about your view of one aspect of the state of the environment. Do you regard waste and climate change as critical problems? Do you believe that the government is taking adequate steps to protect the environment? Do you believe that the actions of individuals can make a difference? Your essay may but need not be an argument: that is, you could explain your answer to any of these questions or argue a specific point. Either way, choose a narrow focus and use examples and details to support your ideas.

VIRGINIA POSTREL

Virginia Postrel (born 1960) is a journalist who writes about commercial culture. She is also a sought-after speaker who lectures for business and university audiences. A graduate of Princeton University, Postrel began her career as a reporter for the Wall Street Journal *and* Inc. *She was the editor of* Reason *magazine from 1989 to 2000 and has written columns and feature articles for the* Atlantic, Forbes, *the* New York Times, *the* Washington Post, *and* Bloomberg View. *She has also written two influential books:* The Future and Its Enemies: The Growing Conflict Over Creativity, Enterprise, and Progress *(1998), and* The Substance of Style: How the Rise of Aesthetic Value Is Remaking Commerce, Culture, and Consciousness *(2003). Since donating a kidney to psychologist and writer Sally Satel in 2006, Postrel has become an outspoken critic of laws and cultural norms that restrict living organ donations. She is currently researching a book on glamour.*

In Praise of Chain Stores

A libertarian, Postrel is a strong believer in free markets and individual choice. In this essay from the Atlantic, *she dismisses complaints that national retailers destroy local character and argues, instead, that their sameness from one town to another benefits communities.*

Every well-traveled cosmopolite knows that America is mind-numbingly monotonous—the most boring country to tour, because "everywhere looks like everywhere else," as the columnist Thomas Friedman once told Charlie Rose.[1] Boston has the same stores as Denver, which has the same stores as Charlotte or Seattle or Chicago. We live in a "Stepford world,"[2] says Rachel

---

[1] Thomas Friedman writes about foreign affairs for the *New York Times*. Charlie Rose is a television talk-show host. [Editors' note.]

[2] *The Stepford Wives* was a 1975 science-fiction movie, based on Ira Levin's 1972 novel about Connecticut suburbanites (possibly robots) who are eerily submissive. [Editors' note.]

Dresbeck, the author of *Insiders' Guide to Portland, Oregon.* Even Boston's historic Faneuil Hall, she complains, is "dominated by the Gap, Anthropologie, Starbucks, and all the other usual suspects. Why go anywhere? Every place looks the same." This complaint is more than the old worry, dating back to the 1920s, that the big guys are putting Mom and Pop out of business. Today's critics focus less on what isn't there—Mom and Pop—than on what is. Faneuil Hall actually has plenty of locally owned businesses, from the Geoclassics store selling minerals and jewelry, to Pizzeria Regina ("since 1926"). But you do find the same chains everywhere.

The suburbs are the worst. Take Chandler, Arizona, just south 2 of Phoenix. At Chandler Fashion Center, the area's big shopping mall, you'll find P. F. Chang's, California Pizza Kitchen, Chipotle Mexican Grill, and the Cheesecake Factory. Drive along Chandler's straight, flat boulevards, and you'll see Bed Bath & Beyond and Linens-n-Things; Barnes & Noble and Borders; PetSmart and Petco; Circuit City and Best Buy; Lowe's and Home Depot; CVS and Walgreens. Chandler has the Apple Store and Pottery Barn, the Gap and Ann Taylor, Banana Republic and DSW, and, of course, Target and Walmart, Starbucks and McDonald's.[3] For people allergic to brands, Chandler must be hell—even without the 110-degree days.

One of the fastest-growing cities in the country, Chandler is 3 definitely the kind of place urbanists have in mind as they intone, "When every place looks the same, there is no such thing as place anymore." Like so many towns in America, it has lost much of its historic character as a farming community. The annual Ostrich Festival still honors one traditional product, but these days Chandler raises more subdivisions and strip malls than ostrich plumes or cotton, another former staple. Yet it still refutes the common assertion that national chains are a blight on the landscape, that they've turned American towns into an indistinguishable "geography of nowhere."

The first thing you notice in Chandler is that, as a broad 4 empirical claim, the cliché that "everywhere looks like everywhere else" is obvious nonsense. Chandler's land and air and foliage are peculiar to the desert Southwest. The people dress differ-

---

[3]Since this essay was published in 2006, Linens-n-Things, Circuit City, and Borders have gone out of business. [Editors' note.]

ently. Even the cookie-cutter housing developments, with their xeriscaping[4] and washed-out desert palette, remind you where you are. Forget New England clapboard, Carolina columns, or yellow Texas brick. In the intense sun of Chandler, the red-tile roofs common in California turn a pale, pale pink.

Stores don't give places their character. Terrain and weather and culture do. Familiar retailers may take some of the discovery out of travel — to the consternation of journalists looking for obvious local color — but by holding some of the commercial background constant, chains make it easier to discern the real differences that define a place: the way, for instance, that people in Chandler come out to enjoy the summer twilight, when the sky glows purple and the dry air cools.

Besides, the idea that America was once filled with wildly varied business establishments is largely a myth. Big cities could, and still can, support more retail niches than small towns. And in a less competitive national market, there was certainly more variation in business efficiency — in prices, service, and merchandise quality. But the range of retailing *ideas* in any given town was rarely that great. One deli or diner or lunch counter or cafeteria was pretty much like every other one. A hardware store was a hardware store, a pharmacy a pharmacy. Before it became a ubiquitous part of urban life, Starbucks was, in most American cities, a radically new idea.

Chains do more than bargain down prices from suppliers or divide fixed costs across a lot of units. They rapidly spread economic discovery — the scarce and costly knowledge of what retail concepts and operational innovations actually work. That knowledge can be gained only through the expensive and time-consuming process of trial and error. Expecting each town to independently invent every new business is a prescription for real monotony, at least for the locals. Chains make a large range of choices available in more places. They increase local variety, even as they reduce the differences from place to place. People who mostly stay put get to have experiences once available only to frequent travelers, and this loss of exclusivity is one reason why frequent travelers are the ones who complain. When Borders was a unique Ann Arbor institution, people in places like Chandler — or, for that matter, Philadelphia and Los Angeles — didn't have much

5

6

7

[4]Landscape design using plants that require little or no water. [Editors' note.]

in the way of bookstores. Back in 1986, when California Pizza Kitchen was an innovative local restaurant about to open its second location, food writers at the LA *Daily News* declared it "the kind of place every neighborhood should have." So what's wrong if the country has 158 neighborhood CPKs instead of one or two?

The process of multiplication is particularly important for 8 fast-growing towns like Chandler, where rollouts of established stores allow retail variety to expand as fast as the growing population can support new businesses. I heard the same refrain in Chandler that I've heard in similar boomburgs elsewhere, and for similar reasons. "It's got all the advantages of a small town, in terms of being friendly, but it's got all the things of a big town," says Scott Stephens, who moved from Manhattan Beach, California, in 1998 to work for Motorola. Chains let people in a city of 250,000 enjoy retail amenities once available only in a huge metropolitan center. At the same time, familiar establishments make it easier for people to make a home in a new place. When Nissan recently moved its headquarters from Southern California to Tennessee, an unusually high percentage of its Los Angeles–area employees accepted the transfer. "The fact that Starbucks are everywhere helps make moving a lot easier these days," a rueful Greg Whitney, vice president of business development for the Los Angeles County Economic Development Corporation, told the *Los Angeles Times* reporter John O'Dell. Orth Hedrick, a Nissan product manger, decided he could stay with the job he loved when he turned off the interstate near Nashville and realized, "You could really be Anywhere, USA. There's a great big regional shopping mall, and most of the stores and restaurants are the same ones we see in California. Yet a few miles away you're in downtown, and there's lots of local color, too."

Contrary to the rhetoric of bored cosmopolites, most cit- 9 ies don't exist primarily to please tourists. The children toddling through the Chandler mall hugging their soft Build-A-Bear animals are no less delighted because kids can also build a bear in Memphis or St. Louis. For them, this isn't tourism; it's life—the experiences that create the memories from which the meaning of a place arises over time. Among Chandler's most charming sights are the business-casual dads joining their wives and kids for lunch in the mall food court. The food isn't the point, let alone whether it's from Subway or Dairy Queen. The restaurants merely provide the props and setting for the family time. When those kids grow up, they'll remember the food court as happily as an older generation recalls the diners and motels of Route 66[5]—not because of the businesses' innate appeal but because of the memories they evoke.

The contempt for chains represents a brand-obsessed view 10 of place, as if store names were all that mattered to a city's character. For many critics, the name on the store really *is* all that matters. The planning consultant Robert Gibbs works with cities that want to revive their downtowns, and he also helps developers find space for retailers. To his frustration, he finds that many cities actually turn away national chains, preferring a moribund downtown that seems authentically local. But, he says, the same local activists who oppose chains "want specialty retail that sells exactly what the chains sell—the same price, the same fit, the same qualities, the same sizes, the same brands, even." You can show people pictures of a Pottery Barn with nothing but the name changed, he says, and they'll love the store. So downtown stores stay empty, or sell low-value tourist items like candles and kites, while the chains open on the edge of town. In the name of urbanism, officials and activists in cities like Ann Arbor and Fort Collins, Colorado, are driving business to the suburbs. "If people like shopping at the Banana Republic or the Gap, if that's your market—or Payless Shoes—why not?" says an exasperated Gibbs. "Why not sell the goods and services people want?"

Meaning

1. Why, according to Postrel, do so many critics object to chain stores? On what grounds does she reject the validity of their objections?

2. In Postrel's view, how does opposition to chain stores hurt the very communities critics mean to protect?

Purpose and Audience

1. What is a "cosmopolite" (paragraphs 1, 9), and what other words and phrases in the essay carry similar meaning? What does Postrel's use of these words reveal about the audience she imagines?

[5]One of the first interstate highways, Route 66 is a system of two-lane roads that run between Chicago and Los Angeles. It was famed in the mid-twentieth century for its quirky roadside businesses and attractions. [Editors' note.]

2. Postrel spends most of this essay expounding on the benefits of chain stores in general, but her last paragraph suggests a more focused purpose. How would you characterize that purpose?

Method and Structure

1. If Postrel disagrees with those who complain that "every place looks the same" (paragraph 1), why does she devote her first three paragraphs to sharing the complaint as if it were her own?
2. List the reasons Postrel gives in support of her claim that chain stores benefit communities. How persuasive do you find them?
3. OTHER METHODS   What does Postrel mean by "character" (paragraphs 3, 5, 10)? How is her definition of this term central to her point?

Language

1. Point out instances of irony in the essay. (For a definition of *irony*, see the Glossary.) Is the irony effective? Why, or why not?
2. Analyze Postrel's use of quotations. Whom does she quote, and where? How do the quotations themselves, and the differences among them, support her argument?

Writing Topics

1. Write an essay expressing your opinion of Postrel's essay. For instance, how did you react to her depiction of chain-store critics as "frequent travelers . . . who complain" (paragraph 7) and "bored cosmopolites" (9)? Do you think she is too critical or dismissive of her opponents? Does she seem to ignore any important considerations about economy, culture, or environment? Agree or disagree with Postrel, supporting your opinion with your own examples.
2. Of the chain stores Postrel mentions, Walmart is the largest and the most controversial. How do you feel about the retail giant? Are you a fan of the store, do you shop there reluctantly, or do you go out of your way to avoid the place? Have you, or has somebody you know, ever worked there? In an essay, take a position on the ongoing debate over the chain's impact: Is Walmart good or bad for the economy? In what ways might the store's overwhelming success affect our way of life? Why do you think so? (If you wish, you may research and quote expert opinion to support your argument, as Postrel does in her consideration of chain stores in general. Be sure to cite your sources if you do.)
3. In pointing out that "familiar establishments make it easier for people to make a home in a new place" (paragraph 8), Postrel reminds

us that Americans tend to be mobile. Very few people live in the same place their whole lives anymore. Why is that? And what impacts do frequent moves have on individuals, families, and communities? In an essay that draws on your own experience and observations, write a cause-and-effect analysis that examines the rootlessness of American life (you may want to narrow your focus to one family or one neighborhood). As you write, consider whether you think increased mobility is a positive or negative development, and whether it is inevitable or avoidable. Why do you think so?

SHERRY TURKLE

Sherry Turkle was born in New York City in 1948, completed her PhD at Harvard University in 1976, and has taught at the Massachusetts Institute of Technology ever since. She is regarded as the leading expert in the psychology and sociology of electronic media, a subject she has explored in her best-selling books Life on the Screen: Identity in the Age of the Internet *(1995),* The Second Self: Computers and the Human Spirit *(2005), and* Alone Together: Why We Expect More from Technology and Less from Each Other *(2011). A frequent guest on television and radio programs, Turkle is a licensed clinical psychologist and the founding director of MIT's Initiative on Technology and Self, a group of scholars who study the interactions between people and machines from a social perspective. She lives in Boston.*

Privacy Has a Politics

Turkle's Alone Together *draws on laboratory research and hundreds of interviews with users of technology to assess the impact that robotics, artificial intelligence, and digital connectivity have had on human interaction. In this self-contained section from the book, Turkle argues that despite the many opportunities and advantages inherent in social networking, the Internet also poses a potential threat to democracy.*

It has become commonplace to talk about all the good the Web 1 has done for politics. We have new sources of information, such as news of political events from all over the world that comes to us via photographs and videos taken by the cameras on cell phones. There is organizing and fund-raising; ever since the 2004 primary run of Howard Dean, online connections have been used as a first step in bringing people together physically. The Barack Obama campaign transformed the Dean-era idea of the "meet up" into a tool for bringing supporters out of the virtual and into each other's homes or onto the streets.[1] We diminish none of these very positive developments if we attend to the troubling realities of the Internet when it comes to questions of privacy. Beyond passivity and resignation, there is a chilling effect on political speech.

When they talk about the Internet, young people make a dis-   2 turbing distinction between embarrassing behavior that will be forgiven and political behavior that might get you into trouble. For high school and college students, stalking and anything else they do to each other fall into the first category. Code such antics as embarrassing. They believe that you can apologize for embarrassing behavior and then move on. Celebrity culture, after all, is all about transgression and rehabilitation. (These young people's comfort with "bullying" their peers is part of this pattern—something for which they believe they will be forgiven.) But you can't "take back" political behavior, like signing a petition or being at a demonstration. One eighteen-year-old puts it this way: "It [the Internet] definitely makes you think about going to a protest or something. There would be so many cameras. You can't tell where the pictures could show up."

Privacy has a politics. For many, the idea "we're all being   3 observed all the time anyway, so who needs privacy?" has become a commonplace. But this state of mind has a cost. At a Webby Awards ceremony, an event to recognize the best and most influential websites, I was reminded of just how costly it is. The year I attended the Webbies, the ceremonies took place just as a government wiretapping scandal dominated the press. When the question of illegal eavesdropping arose, a common reaction among the gathered "Weberati" was to turn the issue into a nonissue. There was much talk about "all information being good information," "information wanting to be free," and "if you have nothing to hide, you have nothing to fear." At a pre-awards cocktail party, one Web luminary spoke to me with animation about the wiretapping controversy. To my surprise, he cited Michel Foucault on

---

[1]Early in the 2004 campaign, Howard Dean used *Meetup.com*, an early social networking site built around message boards, to reach out to voters and collect donations. Four years later, Barack Obama's team tapped the interactive and streaming abilities of Web 2.0 to organize and galvanize supporters on a scale that most observers described as revolutionary. [Editors' note.]

the panopticon² to explain why he was not worried about privacy on the Internet.

For Foucault, the task of the modern state is to reduce its 4 need for actual surveillance by creating a citizenry that will watch itself. A disciplined citizen minds the rules. Foucault wrote about Jeremy Bentham's design for a panopticon because it captured how such a citizenry is shaped. In the panopticon, a wheel-like structure with an observer at its hub, one develops the sense of always being watched, whether or not the observer is actually present. If the structure is a prison, inmates know that a guard can potentially always see them. In the end, the architecture encourages self-surveillance.

The panopticon serves as a metaphor for how, in the mod- 5 ern state, every citizen becomes his or her own policeman. Force becomes unnecessary because the state creates its own obedient citizenry. Always available for scrutiny, all turn their eyes on themselves. By analogy, said my Webby conversation partner, on the Internet, someone might always be watching, so it doesn't matter if, from time to time, someone actually is. As long as you are not doing anything wrong, you are safe. Foucault's critical take on disciplinary society had, in the hands of this technology guru, become a justification for the US government to use the Internet to spy on its citizens. All around us at the cocktail party, there were nods of assent. We have seen that variants of this way of thinking, very common in the technology community, are gaining popularity among high school and college students.

If you relinquish your privacy on *MySpace* or *Facebook* about 6 everything from your musical preferences to your sexual hang-ups, you are less likely to be troubled by an anonymous government agency knowing whom you call or what websites you frequent. Some are even gratified by a certain public exposure; it feels like validation, not violation. Being seen means that they are not insignificant or alone. For all the talk of a generation empowered by the Net, any discussion of online privacy generates claims of resignation and impotence. When I talk to teenagers about the

---

²Michel Foucault (1926–84) was a French philosopher. He discusses his theory of the panopticon in *Discipline and Punish: The Birth of the Prison* (1979). [Editors' note.]

certainty that their privacy will be invaded, I think of my very different experience growing up in Brooklyn in the 1950s.

As the McCarthy era swirled about them, my grandparents 7 were frightened.[3] From Eastern European backgrounds, they saw the McCarthy hearings not as a defense of patriotism but as an attack on people's rights. Joseph McCarthy was spying on Americans, and having the government spy on its citizens was familiar from the old world. There, you assumed that the government read your mail, which never led to good. In America, things were different. I lived with my grandparents as a young child in a large apartment building. Every morning, my grandmother took me downstairs to the mailboxes. Looking at the gleaming brass doors, on which, she noted, "people were not afraid to have their names listed, for all to see," my grandmother would tell me, as if it had never come up before, "In America, no one can look at your mail. It's a federal offense. That's the beauty of this country." From the earliest age, my civics lessons at the mailbox linked privacy and civil liberties. I think of how different things are today for children who learn to live with the idea that their e-mail and messages are shareable and unprotected. And I think of the Internet guru at the Webby awards who, citing Foucault with no apparent irony, accepted the idea that the Internet has fulfilled the dream of the panopticon and summed up his political position about the Net as follows: "The way to deal is to just be good."

But sometimes a citizenry should not simply "be good." You 8 have to leave space for dissent, real dissent. There needs to be technical space (a sacrosanct mailbox) and mental space. The two are intertwined. We make our technologies, and they, in turn, make and shape us. My grandmother made me an American citizen, a civil libertarian, a defender of individual rights in an apartment lobby in Brooklyn. I am not sure where to take my eighteen-year-old daughter, who still thinks that *Loopt* (the application that uses the GPS capability of the iPhone to show her

[3]Spurred by fears of Soviet expansion, Senator Joseph McCarthy, the FBI, and the House Un-American Activities Committee led a campaign through the 1950s accusing government employees, actors, teachers, union members, and others of engaging in communist activities or being sympathetic to communist ideals. Thousands of Americans who fell under suspicion lost their jobs or their reputations; others were sent to jail. [Editors' note.]

where her friends are) seems "creepy" but notes that it would be hard to keep it off her phone if all her friends had it. "They would think I had something to hide."

In democracy, perhaps we all need to begin with the assump- 9 tion that everyone has something to hide, a zone of private action and reflection, one that must be protected no matter what our techno-enthusiasms. I am haunted by the sixteen-year-old boy who told me that when he needs to make a private call, he uses a pay phone that takes coins and complains how hard it is to find one in Boston. And I am haunted by the girl who summed up her reaction to losing online privacy by asking, "Who would care about me and my little life?"

I learned to be a citizen at the Brooklyn mailboxes. To me, 10 opening up a conversation about technology, privacy, and civil society is not romantically nostalgic, not Luddite in the least. It seems like part of democracy defining its sacred spaces.

Meaning

1. How does Turkle account for young people's willingness to reveal personal information on the Web? What reasons does she give to discourage such behavior?
2. Where does Turkle place the blame for the average American's reluctance to participate in political activities?
3. By what means does the author bring her argument around to the subject of civil liberties?

Purpose and Audience

1. What thesis does Turkle attempt to support? What is her purpose?
2. Judging from the allusions made in this essay, would you say that Turkle is writing for a highly specialized audience or an educated but nonspecialized general audience? (If necessary, see the definition of *allusion* in the Glossary.)

Method and Structure

1. What does the author accomplish by opening with examples of the political good that has been done by the Internet?
2. Is this essay an example of appeal to emotion or reasoned argument or both? Give evidence for your answer.

3. OTHER METHODS   Turkle includes as evidence two narratives of her personal experiences. What is the point of the narrative about her grandmother (paragraph 7)?

Language

1. What is a *panopticon*? Why does the metaphor trouble Turkle? (If necessary, see the definition of *metaphor* in the Glossary under *figures of speech*.)
2. What is Turkle talking about when she insists that her position is "not Luddite in the least" (paragraph 10)?
3. Examine Turkle's tone. How would you characterize her attitude toward young people in particular? As a student, how do you respond to that attitude?

Writing Topics

1. Write an essay about one moment when you either did something embarrassing or witnessed someone else's embarrassment online. What motivated the behavior, and what were the consequences? Was the mistake forgiven? Why, or why not? Narrate this incident to help explain why you believe that a personal Web presence is risky—or beneficial.
2. "We make our technologies, and they, in turn, make and shape us," writes Turkle in paragraph 8. What does she mean? And do you agree? In an essay, develop one example of a technology—such as television, smartphones, or GPS navigation—that, in your opinion, has (or has not) affected society or culture in a meaningful way. As you write, consider the original purposes for the technology, the ways it came to be used, and its intended and unintended effects on individual behavior.
3. Write a paper in which you analyze and evaluate any one of Turkle's ideas. For instance: Do the people you know distinguish between personal and political activities online (paragraph 2)? Are we as resigned to lack of privacy as she says (6)? Do we really need privacy in the first place? Support your view with evidence from your experience, observation, or reading.

MARTIN LUTHER KING, JR.

Born in 1929 in Atlanta, Georgia, the son of a Baptist minister, Martin Luther King, Jr., was a revered and powerful leader of the black civil rights movement during the 1950s and 1960s. He was ordained in his father's church before he was twenty and went on to earn degrees at Morehouse College (BA in 1948), Crozer Theological Seminary (BD in 1951), and Boston University (PhD in 1955). In 1955 and 1956, while he was pastor of a church in Montgomery, Alabama, King attracted national attention to the plight of Southern blacks by leading a boycott that succeeded in desegregating the city's buses. He was elected the first president of the Southern Christian Leadership Conference and continued to organize demonstrations for equal rights in other cities. By the early 1960s his efforts had helped raise the national consciousness so that the landmark Civil Rights Act of 1964 and Voting Rights Act of 1965 could be passed by Congress. In 1964 King was awarded the Nobel Peace Prize. When leading sit-ins, boycotts, and marches, King always insisted on nonviolent resistance "because our end is a community at peace with itself." But his nonviolence often met with violent opposition. Over the years he was jailed, beaten, stoned, and stabbed. His house in Montgomery was bombed. And on April 4, 1968, at a motel in Memphis, Tennessee, he was assassinated. He was not yet forty years old.

I Have a Dream

On August 28, 1963, one hundred years after Abraham Lincoln's Emancipation Proclamation had freed the slaves, 200,000 Americans marched on Washington, DC, to demand equal rights for blacks. It was the largest crowd ever to assemble in the capital for a cause, and the high point of the day was this speech delivered by King on the steps of the Lincoln Memorial (he revised it slightly for print publication). Always an eloquent and inspirational speaker, King succeeded in articulating the frustrations and aspirations of America's blacks in a way that gave hope to the oppressed and opened the eyes of many oppressors.

Five score years ago, a great American, in whose symbolic shadow 1
we stand, signed the Emancipation Proclamation. This momen-
tous decree came as a great beacon light of hope to millions of
Negro slaves who had been seared in the flames of withering
injustice. It came as a joyous daybreak to end the long night of
captivity.

But one hundred years later, we must face the tragic fact that 2
the Negro is still not free. One hundred years later, the life of the
Negro is still sadly crippled by the manacles of segregation and
the chains of discrimination. One hundred years later, the Negro
lives on a lonely island of poverty in the midst of a vast ocean of
material prosperity. One hundred years later, the Negro is still
languishing in the corners of American society and finds himself
an exile in his own land. So we have come here today to drama-
tize an appalling condition.

In a sense we have come to our nation's capital to cash a 3
check. When the architects of our republic wrote the magnificent
words of the Constitution and the Declaration of Independence,
they were signing a promissory note to which every American
was to fall heir. This note was a promise that all men—yes, black
men as well as white men—would be guaranteed the unalienable
rights of life, liberty, and the pursuit of happiness.

It is obvious today that America has defaulted on this promis- 4
sory note insofar as her citizens of color are concerned. Instead
of honoring this sacred obligation, America has given the Negro
people a bad check, a check which has come back marked "insufficient funds." But we refuse to believe that there are insufficient
funds in the great vaults of opportunity of this nation. So we have
come to cash this check—a check that will give us upon demand
the riches of freedom and the security of justice. We have also
come to this hallowed spot to remind America of the fierce urgency
of *now*. This is no time to engage in the luxury of cooling off or
to take the tranquilizing drugs of gradualism. *Now* is the time to
make real the promises of Democracy. *Now* is the time to rise from
the dark and desolate valley of segregation to the sunlit path of
racial justice. *Now* is the time to open the doors of opportunity to
all of God's children. *Now* is the time to lift our nation from the
quicksands of racial injustice to the solid rock of brotherhood.

It would be fatal for the nation to overlook the urgency of the 5
moment and to underestimate the determination of the Negro.

This sweltering summer of the Negro's legitimate discontent will not pass until there is an invigorating autumn of freedom and equality; 1963 is not an end, but a beginning. Those who hope that the Negro needed to blow off steam and will now be content will have a rude awakening if the nation returns to business as usual. There will be neither rest nor tranquility in America until the Negro is granted his citizenship rights. The whirlwinds of revolt will continue to shake the foundations of our nation until the bright day of justice emerges.

But there is something that I must say to my people who 6 stand on the warm threshold which leads into the palace of justice. In the process of gaining our rightful place we must not be guilty of wrongful deeds. Let us not seek to satisfy our thirst for freedom by drinking from the cup of bitterness and hatred. We must forever conduct our struggle on the high plane of dignity and discipline. We must not allow our creative protest to degenerate into physical violence. Again and again we must rise to the majestic heights of meeting physical force with soul force. The marvelous new militancy which has engulfed the Negro community must not lead us to a distrust of all white people, for many of our white brothers, as evidenced by their presence here today, have come to realize that their destiny is tied up with our destiny and their freedom is inextricably bound to our freedom. We cannot walk alone.

And as we walk, we must make the pledge that we shall march 7 ahead. We cannot turn back. There are those who are asking the devotees of civil rights, "When will you be satisfied?" We can never be satisfied as long as the Negro is the victim of the unspeakable horrors of police brutality. We can never be satisfied as long as our bodies, heavy with the fatigue of travel, cannot gain lodging in the motels of the highways and the hotels of the cities. We cannot be satisfied as long as the Negro's basic mobility is from a smaller ghetto to a larger one. We can never be satisfied as long as a Negro in Mississippi cannot vote and a Negro in New York believes he has nothing for which to vote. No, no, we are not satisfied, and we will not be satisfied until justice rolls down like waters and righteousness like a mighty stream.

I am not unmindful that some of you have come here out of 8 great trials and tribulations. Some of you have come fresh from narrow jail cells. Some of you have come from areas where your quest for freedom left you battered by the storms of persecution and staggered by the winds of police brutality. You have been the veterans of creative suffering. Continue to work with the faith that unearned suffering is redemptive.

Go back to Mississippi, go back to Alabama, go back to South 9 Carolina, go back to Georgia, go back to Louisiana, go back to the slums and ghettos of our northern cities, knowing that somehow this situation can and will be changed. Let us not wallow in the valley of despair.

I say to you today, my friends, that in spite of the difficulties 10 and frustrations of the moment I still have a dream. It is a dream deeply rooted in the American dream.

I have a dream that one day this nation will rise up and live 11 out the true meaning of its creed: "We hold these truths to be self-evident, that all men are created equal."

I have a dream that one day on the red hills of Georgia the 12 sons of former slaves and the sons of former slaveowners will be able to sit down together at the table of brotherhood.

I have a dream that one day even the state of Mississippi, a 13 desert state sweltering with the heat of injustice and oppression, will be transformed into an oasis of freedom and justice.

I have a dream that my four little children will one day live in 14 a nation where they will not be judged by the color of their skin but by the content of their character.

I have a dream today. 15

I have a dream that one day the state of Alabama, whose 16 governor's lips are presently dripping with the words of interposition and nullification, will be transformed into a situation where little black boys and black girls will be able to join hands with little white boys and white girls and walk together as sisters and brothers.

I have a dream today. 17

I have a dream that one day every valley shall be exalted, every 18 hill and mountain shall be made low, the rough places will be made plain, and the crooked places will be made straight, and the glory of the Lord shall be revealed, and all flesh shall see it together.[1]

This is our hope. This is the faith with which I return to the 19 South. With this faith we will be able to hew out of the mountain

---

[1]This paragraph quotes the Bible, Isaiah 40:4–5. [Editors' note.]

of despair a stone of hope. With this faith we will be able to transform the jangling discords of our nation into a beautiful symphony of brotherhood. With this faith we will be able to work together, to pray together, to struggle together, to go to jail together, to stand up for freedom together, knowing that we will be free one day.

This will be the day when all of God's children will be able to   20
sing with new meaning

> My country, 'tis of thee,
> Sweet land of liberty,
>   Of thee I sing:
> Land where my fathers died,
> Land of the pilgrims' pride,
> From every mountainside,
>   Let freedom ring.

So let freedom ring from the prodigious hilltops of New   21
Hampshire. Let freedom ring from the mighty mountains of New York. Let freedom ring from the heightening Alleghenies of Pennsylvania. Let freedom ring from the snowcapped Rockies of Colorado. Let freedom ring from the curvaceous peaks of California.

But not only that. Let freedom ring from Stone Mountain   22
of Georgia. Let freedom ring from Lookout Mountain of Tennessee. Let freedom ring from every hill and molehill of Mississippi. From every mountainside, let freedom ring.

When we let freedom ring, when we let it ring from every vil-   23
lage and every hamlet, from every state and every city, we will be able to speed up that day when all of God's children, black men and white men, Jews and Gentiles, Protestants and Catholics, will be able to join hands and sing in the words of the old Negro spiritual, "Free at last! Free at last! Thank God almighty, we are free at last!"

Meaning

1. In a sentence, state the main point of King's speech.
2. How does King depict the general condition of the nation's African Americans? What specific injustices does he cite?
3. What reasons does King give for refusing to resort to violence? What comfort does he offer those who have been jailed or beaten?

4. Summarize the substance of King's dream. What does he mean when he says, "It is a dream deeply rooted in the American dream" (paragraph 10)?

Purpose and Audience

1. What do you think King wanted to achieve with this speech? How does each part of the speech relate to his purpose?

2. What group of people does King seem to be addressing primarily in this speech? Where does he seem to assume that they agree with his ideas? Where does he seem to assume that they have reservations or need reassurance?

3. What about King's purpose and audience leads him to rely primarily on emotional appeal? Where does he appeal specifically to his listeners' pride and dignity? to their religious beliefs? to their patriotism?

4. Where does King seem to suppose that doubters and opponents of the civil rights movement might also hear his speech? What messages about the goals and determination of the movement does he convey to these hearers?

Method and Structure

1. Analyze the organization of King's speech. What is the main subject of paragraphs 3–5? 6–9? 10–23? How does this structure suit King's purpose?

2. Why does King's first paragraph refer to the hope generated by Lincoln's Emancipation Proclamation? Is the contrast King develops in paragraphs 1 and 2 an effective introduction to the speech? Why, or why not?

3. OTHER METHODS   Paragraph 3 and the first half of paragraph 4 are developed by comparison and contrast. What are the main points of comparison, and what purpose do they serve? Do you think King's use of comparison is effective? Why, or why not?

Language

1. In paragraph 6 King says, "Let us not seek to satisfy our thirst for freedom by drinking from the cup of bitterness and hatred." To what extent in this speech does King follow his own suggestion? How would you characterize his attitudes toward oppression and segregation? Choose words and phrases in the speech to support your answer.

2. King's speech abounds in metaphors, such as "manacles of segregation" and "chains of discrimination" (paragraph 2). Locate as many
metaphors as you can (consulting the Glossary under *figures of
speech* if necessary), and analyze what five or six of them contribute
to King's meaning. Which metaphors are repeated or restated, and
how does this repetition help link portions of the speech?

Writing Topics

1. King's speech had a tremendous impact when it was first delivered
in 1963, and it remains influential to this day. Pick out the elements
of the speech that seem most remarkable and powerful to you: ideas,
emotional appeals, figures of speech, repetition and parallelism, or
whatever you choose. Write an essay in which you cite these elements and analyze their effectiveness.

2. Reread paragraph 6, where King outlines a strategy for achieving
racial justice. In an essay, briefly explain an unjust situation that
affects you directly—in school, in your family, at work, in your community—and propose a strategy for correcting the injustice. Be specific about the steps in the strategy, and explain how each one relates
to the final goal you want to achieve.

3. King says that his dream is "deeply rooted in the American dream"
(paragraph 10). Write an essay in which you provide your own
definition of the American dream. Draw on the elements of King's
dream as you see fit. Make your definition specific with examples
and details from your experiences, observations, and reading.

JONATHAN SWIFT

Jonathan Swift was an Anglican priest, a poet, and a political pamphleteer, but he is best known as a satirist with a sharp wit and a sense of outrage at human folly and cruelty. He was born in 1667 in Dublin, Ireland, to English parents. After receiving a diploma from Trinity College in Dublin, he went to England in 1689 and there became involved in the political and literary life of London. He was ordained in the Church of Ireland in 1694 and in 1713 became dean of St. Patrick's Cathedral in Dublin, where he served until his death in 1745. Several of Swift's works, including The Tale of a Tub *and* The Battle of the Books *(both 1704), ridicule the religious extremism and literary pretensions of his day.* Gulliver's Travels *(1726), his most famous book, is often abridged for children into a charming fantasy about tiny people and giants and a wise race of horses; but unabridged it takes a bitter swipe at humankind's lack of humanity and abuse of reason.*

A Modest Proposal

In Swift's time Ireland had already suffered almost two centuries of exploitation by the English. Mostly from abroad, the English controlled much of Ireland's farmland, exacted burdensome taxes from the Irish, and repressed the people in countless other ways. Swift, who had often lashed out at the injustices he saw, was moved in 1729 to his most vicious attack. Several years of crop failures had resulted in widespread starvation among the Irish poor, yet the government of England, the English landowners, and the well-to-do Irish had done nothing to help. In response, Swift wrote "A Modest Proposal." The essay is a model of satire, the combination of wit and criticism to mock or condemn human foolishness or evil. Like much satire, the essay is also heavily ironic, saying one thing but meaning another. (Satire and irony are both explained more fully in the Glossary.) Assuming the role of a thoughtful and sympathetic observer, Swift proposes a solution to the troubles of the Irish that, in the words of the critic Gilbert Highet, is "couched in terms of blandly persuasive logic, but so atrocious that no one could possibly take it as serious."

*For Preventing the Children of the Poor People in Ireland
from Being a Burden to Their Parents or Country,
and for Making Them Beneficial to The Public*

It is a melancholy object to those who walk through this great 1
town[1] or travel in the country, when they see the streets, the
roads, and cabin doors, crowded with beggars of the female sex,
followed by three, four, or six children, all in rags and importun-
ing every passenger for an alms. These mothers, instead of being
able to work for their honest livelihood, are forced to employ all
their time in strolling to beg sustenance for their helpless infants,
who, as they grow up, either turn thieves for want of work, or
leave their dear native country to fight for the Pretender in Spain,
or sell themselves to the Barbados.[2]

I think it is agreed by all parties that this prodigious number 2
of children in the arms, or on the backs, or at the heels of their
mothers, and frequently of their fathers, is in the present deplor-
able state of the kingdom a very great additional grievance; and
therefore whoever could find out a fair, cheap, or easy method of
making these children sound, useful members of the commonwealth would deserve so well of the public as to have his statue
set up for a preserver of the nation.

But my intention is very far from being confined to provide 3
only for the children of professed beggars; it is of a much greater
extent, and shall take in the whole number of infants at a certain
age who are born of parents in effect as little able to support them
as those who demand our charity in the streets.

As to my own part, having turned my thoughts for many 4
years upon this important subject, and maturely weighed the
several schemes of other projectors,[3] I have always found them
grossly mistaken in their computation. It is true, a child just
dropped from its dam may be supported by her milk for a solar
year, with little other nourishment; at most not above the value of
two shillings,[4] which the mother may certainly get, or the value

[1]Dublin [Editors' note.]

[2]The Pretender was James Stuart (1688–1766). He laid claim to the English
throne from exile in Spain, and many Irishmen joined an army in support of his
cause. Irishmen also shipped out for the British colony of Barbados, in the Carib-
bean, exchanging several years' labor there for their passage. [Editors' note.]

[3]People who develop projects or schemes. [Editors' note.]

[4]A shilling was then worth less than twenty-five cents. [Editors' note.]

in scraps, by her lawful occupation of begging; and it is exactly at one year that I propose to provide for them in such a manner as instead of being a charge upon their parents or the parish, or wanting food and raiment for the rest of their lives, they shall on the contrary contribute to the feeding, and partly to the clothing, of many thousands.

There is likewise another great advantage in my scheme, that 5 it will prevent those voluntary abortions, and that horrid practice of women murdering their bastard children, alas, too frequent among us, sacrificing the poor innocent babes, I doubt, more to avoid the expense than the shame, which would move tears and pity in the most savage and inhuman breast.

The number of souls in this kingdom being usually reckoned 6 one million and a half, of these I calculate there may be about two hundred thousand couples whose wives are breeders; from which number I subtract thirty thousand couples who are able to maintain their own children, although I apprehend there cannot be so many under the present distress of the kingdom; but this being granted, there will remain an hundred and seventy thousand breeders. I again subtract fifty thousand of those women who miscarry, or whose children die by accident or disease within the year. There only remain an hundred and twenty thousand children of poor parents annually born. The question therefore is, how this number shall be reared and provided for, which, as I have already said, under the present situation of affairs, is utterly impossible by all the methods hitherto proposed. For we can neither employ them in handicraft or agriculture; we neither build houses (I mean in the country) nor cultivate land. They can very seldom pick up a livelihood by stealing till they arrive at six years old, except where they are of towardly parts;[5] although I confess they learn the rudiments much earlier, during which time they can however be looked upon only as probationers, as I have been informed by a principal gentleman in the country of Cavan, who protested to me that he never knew above one or two instances under the age of six, even in a part of the kingdom so renowned for the quickest proficiency in that art.

I am assured by our merchants that a boy or a girl before 7 twelve years old is no salable commodity; and even when they

[5]Natural abilities. [Editors' note.]

come to this age they will not yield above three pounds; or three pounds and half a crown at most on the Exchange;[6] which cannot turn to account either to the parents or the kingdom, the charge of nutriment and rags having been at least four times that value.

I shall now therefore humbly propose my own thoughts, 8 which I hope will not be liable to the least objection.

I have been assured by a very knowing American of my 9 acquaintance in London, that a young healthy child well nursed is at a year old a most delicious, nourishing, and wholesome food, whether stewed, roasted, baked, or boiled; and I make no doubt that it will equally serve in a fricassee or a ragout.

I do therefore humbly offer it to public consideration that of 10 the hundred and twenty thousand children, already computed, twenty thousand may be reserved for breed, whereof only one fourth part to be males, which is more than we allow to sheep, black cattle, or swine; and my reason is that these children are seldom the fruits of marriage, a circumstance not much regarded by our savages, therefore one male will be sufficient to serve four females. That the remaining hundred thousand may at a year old be offered in sale to the persons of quality and fortune through the kingdom, always advising the mother to let them suck plentifully in the last month, so as to render them plump and fat for a good table. The child will make two dishes at an entertainment for friends; and when the family dines alone, the fore or hind quarter will make a reasonable dish, and seasoned with a little pepper or salt will be very good boiled on the fourth day, especially in winter.

I have reckoned upon a medium that a child just born will 11 weigh twelve pounds, and in a solar year if tolerably nursed increaseth to twenty-eight pounds.

I grant this food will be somewhat dear, and therefore very 12 proper for landlords, who, as they have already devoured most of the parents, seem to have the best title to the children.

Infant's flesh will be in season throughout the year, but more 13 plentiful in March, and a little before and after. For we are told by a grave author, an eminent French physician,[7] that fish being

---

[6]A pound consisted of twenty shillings; a crown consisted of five shillings. [Editors' note.]

[7]François Rabelais, a sixteenth-century French humorist. [Editors' note.]

a prolific diet, there are more children born in Roman Catholic countries about nine months after Lent than at any other season; therefore, reckoning a year after Lent, the market will be more glutted than usual, because the number of popish infants is at least three to one in this kingdom; and therefore it will have one other collateral advantage, by lessening the number of Papists among us.

I have already computed the charge of nursing a beggar's 14 child (in which list I reckon all cottagers, laborers, and four-fifths of the farmers) to be about two shillings per annum, rags included; and I believe no gentleman would repine to give ten shillings for the carcass of a good fat child, which, as I have said, will make four dishes of excellent nutritive meat, when he hath only some particular friend or his own family to dine with him. Thus the squire will learn to be a good landlord, and grow popular among the tenants; the mother will have eight shillings net profit, and be fit for work till she produces another child.

Those who are more thrifty (as I must confess the times 15 require) may flay the carcass; the skin of which artifically[8] dressed will make admirable gloves for ladies, and summer boots for fine gentlemen.

As to our city of Dublin, shambles[9] may be appointed for this 16 purpose in the most convenient parts of it, and butchers we may be assured will not be wanting; although I rather recommend buying the children live, and dressing them hot from the knife as we do roasting pigs.

A very worthy person, a true lover of his country, and whose 17 virtues I highly esteem, was lately pleased in discoursing on this matter to offer a refinement upon my scheme. He said that many gentlemen of his kingdom, having of late destroyed their deer, he conceived that the want of venison might be well supplied by the bodies of young lads and maidens, not exceeding fourteen years of age nor under twelve, so great a number of both sexes in every county being now ready to starve for want of work and service; and these to be disposed of by their parents, if alive, or otherwise by their nearest relations. But with due deference to so excellent a friend and so deserving a patriot, I cannot be altogether in

[8]Artfully. [Editors' note.]
[9]Slaughterhouses. [Editors' note.]

his sentiments; for as to the males, my American acquaintance assured me from frequent experience that their flesh was generally tough and lean, like that of our schoolboys, by continual exercise, and their taste disagreeable; and to fatten them would not answer the charge. Then as to the females, it would, I think with humble submission, be a loss to the public, because they soon would become breeders themselves; and besides, it is not improbable that some scrupulous people might be apt to censure such a practice (although indeed very unjustly) as a little bordering upon cruelty; which, I confess, hath always been with me the strongest objection against any project, how well soever intended.

But in order to justify my friend, he confessed that this 18 expedient was put into his head by the famous Psalmanazar,[10] a native of the island Formosa, who came from thence to London above twenty years ago, and in conversation told my friend that in his country when any young person happened to be put to death, the executioner sold the carcass to persons of quality as a prime dainty; and that in his time the body of a plump girl of fifteen, who was crucified for an attempt to poison the emperor, was sold to his Imperial Majesty's prime minister of state, and other great mandarins of the court, in joints from the gibbet, at four hundred crowns. Neither indeed can I deny that if the same use were made of several plump young girls in this town, who without one single groat to their fortunes cannot stir abroad without a chair,[11] and appear at the playhouse and assemblies in foreign fineries which they never will pay for, the kingdom would not be the worse.

Some persons of desponding spirit are in great concern 19 about the vast number of poor people who are aged, diseased, or maimed, and I have been desired to employ my thoughts what course may be taken to ease the nation of so grievous an encumbrance. But I am not in the least pain upon the matter, because it is very well known that they are every day dying and rotting by cold and famine, and filth and vermin, as fast can be reasonably expected. And as to the younger laborers, they are now in almost as hopeful a condition. They cannot get work, and conse-

---

[10]Georges Psalmanazar was a Frenchman who gulled London society into thinking he was an exotic Formosan. [Editors' note.]

[11]A groat was a coin worth a few pennies. In a sedan chair, one person is carried about by two others on foot. [Editors' note.]

quently pine away for want of nourishment to a degree that if any time they are accidentally hired to common labor, they have not strength to perform it; and thus the country and themselves are happily delivered from the evils to come.

I have too long digressed, and therefore shall return to my 20 subject. I think the advantages by the proposal which I have made are obvious and many, as well as of the highest importance.

For first, as I have already observed, it would greatly lessen 21 the number of Papists, with whom we are yearly overrun, being the principal breeders of the nation as well as our most dangerous enemies; and who stay at home on purpose to deliver the kingdom to the Pretender, hoping to take their advantage by the absence of so many good Protestants, who have chosen rather to leave their country than to stay at home and pay tithes against their conscience to an Episcopal curate.

Secondly, the poorer tenants will have something valuable of 22 their own, which by law may be made liable to distress,[12] and help to pay their landlord's rent, their corn and cattle being already seized and money a thing unknown.

Thirdly, whereas the maintenance of an hundred thousand 23 children, from two years old and upwards, cannot be computed at less than ten shillings a piece per annum, the nation's stock will be thereby increased fifty thousand pounds per annum, besides the profit of a new dish introduced to the tables of all gentlemen of fortune in the kingdom who have any refinement in taste. And the money will circulate among ourselves, the goods being entirely of our own growth and manufacture.

Fourthly, the constant breeders, besides the gain of eight shil 24 lings sterling per annum by the sale of their children, will be rid of the charge of maintaining them after the first year.

Fifthly, this food would likewise bring great custom to tav 25 erns, where the vintners will certainly be so prudent as to procure the best receipts[13] for dressing it to perfection, and consequently have their houses frequented by all the fine gentlemen, who justly value themselves upon their knowledge in good eating; and a skillful cook, who understands how to oblige his guests, will contrive to make it as expensive as they please.

[12]Seizure for payment of debts. [Editors' note.]
[13]Recipes. [Editors' note.]

Sixthly, this would be a great inducement to marriage, which 26
all wise nations have either encouraged by rewards or enforced
by laws and penalties. It would increase the care and tenderness
of mothers toward their children, when they were sure of a set-
tlement for life to the poor babes, provided in some sort by the
public, to their annual profit instead of expense. We should see
an honest emulation among the married women, which of them
could bring the fattest child to the market. Men would become
as fond of their wives during the time of their pregnancy as they
are now of their mares in foal, their cows in calf, or sows when
they are ready to farrow; nor offer to beat or kick them (as is too
frequent a practice) for fear of a miscarriage.

Many other advantages might be enumerated. For instance, 27
the addition of some thousand carcasses in our exportation of
barreled beef, the propagation of swine's flesh, and improvements
in the art of making good bacon, so much wanted among us by
the great destruction of pigs, too frequent at our tables, which
are no way comparable in taste or magnificence to a well-grown,
fat, yearling child, which roasted whole will make a considerable
figure at a lord mayor's feast or any other public entertainment.
But this and many others I omit, being studious of brevity.

Supposing that one thousand families in this city would be 28
constant customers for infants' flesh, besides others who might
have it at merry meetings, particularly weddings and christenings,
I compute that Dublin would take off annually about twenty thousand carcasses, and the rest of the kingdom (where probably they
will be sold somewhat cheaper) the remaining eighty thousand.

I can think of no one objection that will possibly be raised 29
against this proposal, unless it should be urged that the number
of people will be thereby much lessened in the kingdom. This I
freely own, and it was indeed one principal design in offering
it to the world. I desire the reader will observe, that I calculate
my remedy for this one individual kingdom of Ireland and for
no other that ever was, is, or I think ever can be upon earth.
Therefore let no man talk to me of other expedients: of taxing
our absentees at five shillings a pound: of using neither clothes
nor household furniture except what is of our own growth and
manufacture: of utterly rejecting the materials and instruments
that promote foreign luxury: of curing the expensiveness of pride,
vanity, idleness, and gaming in our women: of introducing a vein

of parsimony, prudence, and temperance: of learning to love our country, in the want of which we differ even from Laplanders and the inhabitants of Topinamboo:[14] of quitting our animosities and factions, nor acting any longer like the Jews, who were murdering one another at the very moment their city was taken:[15] of being a little cautious not to sell our country and conscience for nothing: of teaching landlords to have at least one degree of mercy toward their tenants: lastly, of putting a spirit of honesty, industry, and skill into our shopkeepers; who, if a resolution could not be taken to buy only our native goods, would immediately unite to cheat and exact upon us in the price, the measure, and the goodness, nor could ever yet be brought to make one fair proposal of just dealing, though often and earnestly invited to it.

Therefore I repeat, let no man talk to me of these and the like 30 expedients, till he hath at least some glimpse of hope that there will be some hearty and sincere attempt to put them in practice.

But as to myself, having been wearied out for many years 31 with offering vain, idle, visionary thoughts, and at length utterly despairing of success, I fortunately fell upon this proposal, which, as it is wholly new, so it hath something solid and real, of no expense and little trouble, full in our own power, and whereby we can incur no danger in disobliging England. For this kind of commodity will not bear exportation, the flesh being of too tender a consistence to admit a long continuance in salt, although perhaps I could name a country which would be glad to eat up our whole nation without it.

After all, I am not so violently bent upon my own opinion 32 as to reject any offer proposed by wise men, which shall be found equally innocent, cheap, easy, and effectual. But before something of that kind shall be advanced in contradiction to my scheme, and offering a better, I desire the author or authors will be pleased maturely to consider two points. First, as things now stand, how they will be able to find food and raiment for an hundred thousand useless mouths and backs. And secondly, there being a round million of creatures in human figure throughout

[14]Lapland is the northernmost part of Scandinavia, above the Arctic Circle. The primitive tribes of Topinamboo, in Brazil, were notorious in Swift's day for their savagery. [Editors' note.]

[15]Jerusalem was seized by the Romans in AD 70. [Editors' note.]

this kingdom, whose sole subsistence put into a common stock would leave them in debt two millions of pounds sterling, adding those who are beggars by profession to the bulk of farmers, cottagers, and laborers, with their wives and children who are beggars in effect; I desire those politicians who dislike my overture, and may perhaps be so bold to attempt an answer, that they will first ask the parents of these mortals whether they would not at this day think it a great happiness to have been sold for food at a year old in this manner I prescribe, and thereby have avoided such a perpetual scene of misfortunes as they have since gone through by the oppression of landlords, the impossibility of paying rent without money or trade, the want of common sustenance, with neither house nor clothes to cover them from the inclemencies of the weather, and the most inevitable prospect of entailing the like or greater miseries upon their breed forever.

I profess, in the sincerity of my heart, that I have not the least 33 personal interest in endeavoring to promote this necessary work, having no other motive than the public good of my country, by advancing our trade, providing for infants, relieving the poor, and giving some pleasure to the rich. I have no children by which I can propose to get a single penny; the youngest being nine years old, and my wife past childbearing.

Meaning

1. In your own words, explain Swift's "modest proposal," the chief problems it is designed to solve, and how it proposes to solve those problems.
2. What reasonable solutions does Swift mention to Ireland's problems? Why does he reject these solutions in favor of his outrageous one?

Purpose and Audience

1. Like all satirists, Swift writes on two levels: as his narrator, the *I* of the essay, and as himself. What is the narrator's purpose? What is Swift's real purpose? Where do these two purposes overlap? Where do they diverge?
2. Ever since this essay was first published, many readers have failed to grasp its irony and have condemned Swift for his inhumanity. Yet Swift provides clues that make his true intentions clear, as in his statement that the landlords, "as they have already devoured most of the

parents, seem to have the best title to the children" (paragraph 12). What other such clues do you find after that point? Why do you think Swift provides them?

3. What was your own reaction to Swift's essay? Did you appreciate the irony? To what extent—and in what ways—did the repulsiveness of the proposal affect your willingness to accept his argument? What do your own responses and those of your classmates suggest about the advantages and disadvantages of satire as a technique of argument?

Method and Structure

1. Swift casts his essay in a fairly standard argumentative structure. Outline the essay roughly to see its parts, and analyze what each part contributes to the whole.

2. What steps does Swift take to establish the ethical appeal of his narrator? Cite sentences or passages that seem designed to gain the reader's trust and confidence in the author.

3. OTHER METHODS   Swift furthers his argument through skillful use of several methods of development, including process analysis and cause-and-effect analysis. Locate one example of each of these methods, and explain what each contributes to the persuasiveness of the argument.

Language

1. Locate several passages where Swift's irony strikes you as particularly apt or intriguing, and explain the contrast between their ironic and literal meanings. At whom is the ironic barb directed? Is it bitter or humorous? (If necessary, consult the Glossary for a definition of *irony*.)

2. Swift refers to the poor people of Ireland in terms normally reserved for livestock—for example, "breeders" (paragraph 6) and "fore or hind quarter" (10). Locate other expressions or sentences in this vein. What do they lend to the satire?

3. How would you characterize Swift's writing style? Give examples to support your answer. To what extent does his style contribute to or detract from your appreciation of the essay, and why? (See *style* in the Glossary if you need a definition.)

Writing Topics

1. Just as Swift was outraged by conditions in Ireland, you may be similarly moved by some current condition—perhaps terrorism, increasing crime, a newly discovered health hazard, or a dangerous traffic intersection the authorities persist in ignoring. Imitate Swift's

strategy and write a "modest proposal" to end the condition. Like Swift's, your proposal should be fairly simple and argued with the most careful and detailed logic you can muster.

2. Ireland's problems did not end with the publication of Swift's essay but in fact have endured. Find an overview of the history of Ireland and its relations with England from Swift's time until the present. Focus on one of the specific problems Swift mentions—prejudices against "Papists," for example, or food shortages or absentee landlords— and research it in several other sources. Write an essay explaining the origins of the problem, the extent of its persistence, the attempts to resolve it, and the results of those attempts.

3. In analyzing Swift's essay, you have observed many of the elements of good satire. Using what you now know about satire, write an essay examining the strategy and effectiveness of one of the other satiric essays in this book, such as Jessica Mitford's "Embalming Mr. Jones" (p. 197) or Judy Brady's "I Want a Wife" (p. 251).

Writing with the Method

ARGUMENT AND PERSUASION

Select one of the following statements, or any other statement they suggest, and support or refute it in an argumentative essay. The statement you choose should concern a topic you care about so that argument is a means of convincing readers to accept an idea, not an end in itself.

Popular Culture

1. Pornographic magazines and films should be banned.
2. Advertisements serve useful purposes.
3. Music recordings should be labeled if their lyrics contain violent or sexual references.
4. Professional athletes should not be allowed to compete in the Olympics.

Health and Technology

5. Terminally ill people should have the right to choose when to die.
6. Private automobiles should be restricted in cities.
7. Laboratory experiments on dogs, cats, and primates are necessary.
8. Smoking should be banned in all public places, including outdoors.

Education

9. Students caught in any form of academic cheating should be expelled.
10. The school's costly athletic programs should be eliminated in favor of improving the academic curriculum.
11. Like high-school textbooks, college textbooks should be purchased by the school and loaned to students for the duration of a course.

Social and Political Issues

12. Corporate executives are overpaid.
13. Private institutions should have the right to make rules that would be unconstitutional outside those institutions.
14. Public libraries should provide free, unlimited access to the Internet for all.
15. When adopted children turn eighteen, they should have free access to information about their birth parents.

Glossary

Abstract and concrete words An **abstract** word refers to an idea, quality, attitude, or state that we cannot perceive with our senses: *democracy, generosity, love, grief.* It conveys a general concept or impression. A **concrete** word, in contrast, refers to an object, person, place, or state that we can perceive with our senses: *lawnmower, teacher, Chicago, moaning.* Concrete words make writing specific and vivid. See also *general and specific words.*

Ad hominem argument See *fallacies.*

Allusion A brief reference to a real or fictitious person, place, object, or event. An allusion can convey considerable meaning with few words, as when a writer describes a movie as "potentially this decade's *Star Wars*" to imply both that the movie is a space adventure and that it may be a blockbuster. But to be effective, the allusion must refer to something readers know well.

Analysis (also called **division**) The method of development in which a subject is separated into its elements or parts and then reassembled into a new whole. See Chapter 4 on division or analysis, p. 221.

Anecdote A brief narrative that recounts an episode from a person's experience. See, for instance, Peck, paragraph 1, p. 221. See also Chapter 2 on narration, p. 62.

Argument The form of writing that appeals to readers' reason and emotions in order to win agreement with a claim or to compel some action. This definition encompasses both argument in a narrower sense—the appeal to reason to win agreement—and persuasion—the appeal to emotion to compel action. See Chapter 10 on argument and persuasion, p. 316.

Assertion A debatable claim about a subject; the central idea of an argument.

Audience A writer's audience is the group of readers for whom a particular work is intended. To communicate effectively, the writer should estimate readers' knowledge of the subject, their interests in it, and their biases toward it and should then consider these needs and expectations in choosing what to say and how to say it. For further discussion of audience, see pp. 2, 9–10, 13–14.

Begging the question See *fallacies*.

Body The part of an essay that develops the main idea. See also pp. 18–19.

Cause-and-effect analysis The method of development in which occurrences are divided into their elements to find what made an event happen (its causes) and what the consequences were (its effects). See Chapter 9 on cause-and-effect analysis, p. 277.

Chronological order A pattern of organization in which events are arranged as they occurred over time, earliest to latest. Narratives usually follow a chronological order; see Chapter 2, p. 62.

Classification The method of development in which the members of a group are sorted into classes or subgroups according to shared characteristics. See Chapter 5 on classification, p. 148.

Cliché An expression that has become tired from overuse and that therefore deadens rather than enlivens writing. Examples: *in over their heads, turn over a new leaf, march to a different drummer, as heavy as lead, as clear as a bell.*

Climactic order A pattern of organization in which elements—words, sentences, examples, ideas—are arranged in order of increasing importance or drama.

Coherence The quality of effective writing that comes from clear, logical connections among all the parts, so that the reader can follow the writer's thought process without difficulty. See also *parallelism, repetition and restatement*, and *transitions*.

Colloquial language The language of conversation, including contractions *(don't, can't)* and informal words and expressions *(hot* for new or popular, *boss* for employer, *ad* for advertisement, *get away with it, flunk the exam)*. Most dictionaries label such words and expressions *colloquial* or *informal*. Colloquial language is inappropriate when the writing situation demands precision and formality, as a college term paper or a business report usually does. But in other situations it can be used selectively to relax a piece of writing and reduce the distance between writer and reader. (See, for instance, Hughes, p. 69.) See also *diction*.

Comparison and contrast   The method of development in which the similarities and differences between subjects are examined. Comparison examines similarities and contrast examines differences, but the two are generally used together. See Chapter 7 on comparison and contrast, p. 208.

Conclusions   The endings of written works—the sentences that bring the writing to a close. A conclusion provides readers with a sense of completion, with a sense that the writer has finished. Sometimes the final point in the body of an essay may accomplish this purpose, especially if it is very important or dramatic (for instance, see Eighner, p. 194). But usually a separate conclusion is needed to achieve completion. It may be a single sentence or several paragraphs, depending on the length and complexity of the piece of writing. And it may include one of the following, or a combination, depending on your subject and purpose:

- A summary of the main points of the essay (see Visser, p. 131)
- A statement of the main idea of the essay, if it has not been stated before (see Klass, p. 105), or a restatement of the main idea incorporating information from the body of the essay (see Naylor, p. 259)
- A comment on the significance or implications of the subject (see Dillard, p. 78; Gould, p. 312)
- A call for reflection, support, or action (see Quindlen, p. 110; Ericsson, p. 170)
- A prediction for the future (see King, pp. 361–62)
- An example, anecdote, question, or quotation that reinforces the point of the essay (see Brady, p. 253; Ehrenreich, p. 301)

Excluded from this list are several endings that should be avoided because they tend to weaken the overall effect of an essay: (1) an example, fact, or quotation that pertains to only part of the essay; (2) an apology for your ideas, for the quality of the writing, or for omissions; (3) an attempt to enhance the significance of the essay by overgeneralizing from its ideas and evidence; (4) a new idea that requires the support of an entirely different essay.

Concrete words   See *abstract and concrete words.*

Connotation and denotation A word's **denotation** is its literal meaning: *famous* denotes the quality of being well known. A word's **connotations** are the associations or suggestions that go beyond its literal meaning: *notorious* denotes fame but also connotes sensational, even unfavorable, recognition.

Contrast   See *comparison and contrast.*

Critical reading   Reading that looks beneath the surface of a work, seeking to uncover both its substance and the writer's interpretation of the substance.

Deductive reasoning   The method of reasoning that moves from the general to the specific. See Chapter 10 on argument and persuasion, especially pp. 321–23. See also *syllogism*.

Definition   An explanation of the meaning of a word. An extended definition may serve as the primary method of developing an essay. See Chapter 8 on definition, p. 244.

Denotation   See *connotation and denotation*.

Description   The form of writing that conveys the perceptions of the senses—sight, hearing, smell, taste, touch—to make a person, place, object, or state of mind vivid and concrete. See Chapter 1 on description, p. 22.

Diction   The choice of words you make to achieve a purpose and make meaning clear. Effective diction conveys your meaning exactly, emphatically, and concisely, and it is appropriate to your intentions and audience. **Standard English**, the written language of educated native speakers, is expected in all writing for college, business and the professions, and publication. The vocabulary of standard English is large and varied, encompassing, for instance, both *comestibles* and *food* for edible things, both *paroxysm* and *fit* for a sudden seizure. In some writing situations, standard English may also include words and expressions typical of conversation (see *colloquial language*). But it excludes other levels of diction that only certain groups understand or find acceptable. Most dictionaries label expressions at these levels as follows:

- **Nonstandard**: words spoken among particular social groups, such as *ain't*, *them guys*, *hisself*, and *nowheres*.
- **Obsolete**: words that have passed out of use, such as *cleam* for smear.
- **Regional** or **dialect**: words spoken in a particular region but not in the country as a whole, such as *poke* for a sack or bag, *holler* for a hollow or small valley.
- **Slang**: words that are usually short-lived and that may not be understood by all readers, such as *tanked* for drunk, *bling* for jewelry or money, and *honcho* for one in charge.

See also *connotation and denotation* and *style*.

Division or analysis   See *analysis*.

Dominant impression The central ideal or feeling conveyed by a description of a person, place, object, or state of mind. See Chapter 1 on description, especially p. 23.

Effect See *cause-and-effect analysis.*

Either-or See *fallacies.*

Emotional appeal In argumentative and persuasive writing, the appeal to readers' values, beliefs, or feelings in order to win agreement or compel action. See pp. 318–20.

Essay A prose composition on a single nonfictional topic or idea. An essay usually reflects the personal experiences and opinions of the writer.

Ethical appeal In argumentative and persuasive writing, the sense of the writer's expertise and character projected by the reasonableness of the argument, the use and quality of evidence, and tone. See p. 318.

Evidence The details, examples, facts, statistics, or expert opinions that support any general statement or claim. See pp. 320 and 325–26 on the use of evidence in argumentative writing.

Example An instance or representative of a general group or an abstract concept or quality. One or more examples may serve as the primary method of developing an essay. See Chapter 3 on example, p. 96.

Exposition The form of writing that explains or informs. Most of the essays in this book are primarily expository, and some essays whose primary purpose is self-expression or persuasion employ exposition to clarify ideas.

Fallacies Flaws in reasoning that weaken or invalidate an argument. Some of the most common fallacies are listed below (the page numbers refer to further discussion in the text).

- **Ad hominem** ("to the man") **argument**, attacking an opponent instead of the opponent's argument: *She is just a student, so we need not listen to her criticisms of foreign policy* (p. 324).
- **Begging the question**, assuming the truth of a conclusion that has not been proved: *Acid rain does not do serious damage, so it is not a serious problem* (p. 323).
- **Either-or**, presenting only two alternatives when the choices are more numerous: *If you want to do well in college, you have to cheat a little* (p. 324).
- **Hasty generalization**, leaping to a conclusion on the basis of inadequate or unrepresentative evidence: *Every one of the twelve students*

polled supports the change in the grading system, so the administration should implement it (p. 323).

- **Ignoring the question,** shifting the argument away from the real issue: *A fine, churchgoing man like Charles Harold would make an excellent mayor* (p. 324).

- **Non sequitur** ("It does not follow"), deriving a wrong or illogical conclusion from stated premises: *Because students are actually in school, they should be the ones to determine our educational policies* (p. 324).

- **Oversimplification,** overlooking or ignoring inconsistencies or complexities in evidence: *If the United States banned immigration, our unemployment problems would be solved* (p. 323).

- **Post hoc** (from *post hoc, ergo propter hoc,* "after this, therefore because of this"), assuming that one thing caused another simply because it preceded the other: *Two students left school in the week after the new policies were announced, proving that the policies will eventually cause a reduction in enrollments* (pp. 324–325).

Figures of speech   Expressions that imply meanings beyond or different from their literal meanings in order to achieve vividness or force.

Some figures of speech involve comparisons of two unlike objects:

- A **metaphor** compares two unlike things by saying that one is the other: *Bright circles of ebony, her eyes smiled back at me.*

- A **simile** equates two unlike things using *like* or *as*: *The crowd was restless, like bees in a hive.*

- **Personification** gives human qualities to things or abstractions: *The bright day smirked at my bad mood.*

Other figures of speech consist of deliberate misrepresentations:

- **Hyperbole** is a conscious overstatement or exaggeration: *The desk provided an acre of work surface.* (The opposite of hyperbole is understatement, discussed under *irony.*)

- A **paradox** is a seemingly self-contradictory statement that, on reflection, makes sense: *Children are the poor person's wealth* (wealth can be monetary, or it can be spiritual). *Paradox* may also refer to a situation that is inexplicable or contradictory, such as the restriction of one group's rights to secure the rights of another group.

Formal style   See *style.*

Freewriting   A technique for discovering ideas for writing: writing for a fixed amount of time without stopping to reread or edit. See p. 15.

General and specific words A **general** word refers to a group or class: *car, mood, book.* A **specific** word refers to a particular member of a group or class: *Toyota, irritation, dictionary.* Usually, the more specific a word is, the more interesting and informative it will be for readers. See also *abstract and concrete words.*

Generalization A statement about a group or a class derived from knowledge of some or all of its members: for instance, *Dolphins can be trained to count* or *Television news rarely penetrates beneath the headlines.* The more examples the generalization is based on, the more accurate it is likely to be. A generalization is the result of inductive reasoning; see p. 320.

Hasty generalization See *fallacies.*

Hyperbole See *figures of speech.*

Ignoring the question See *fallacies.*

Image A verbal representation of sensory experience—that is, of something seen, heard, felt, tasted, or smelled. Images may be literal: *Snow stuck to her eyelashes; The red car sped past us.* Or they may be figures of speech: *Her eyelashes were snowy feathers; The car rocketed past us like a red missile.* Through images, a writer touches the readers' experiences, thus sharpening meaning and adding immediacy. See also *abstract and concrete words.*

Inductive reasoning The method of reasoning that moves from the particular to the general. See Chapter 10 on argument and persuasion, especially p. 320.

Informal style See *style.*

Introductions The openings of written works, the sentences that set the stage for what follows. An introduction to an essay identifies and restricts the subject while establishing your attitude toward it. Accomplishing these purposes may require anything from a single sentence to several paragraphs, depending on your purpose and how much readers need to know before they can begin to grasp the ideas in the essay. The introduction often includes a thesis sentence stating the main idea of the essay (see pp. 16–17). To set up the thesis sentence, or as a substitute for it, any of the following openings, or a combination, may be effective:

- Background on the subject that establishes a time or place or that provides essential information (see de Zengotita, p. 134; Swift, p. 366)
- An anecdote or other reference to the writer's experience that forecasts or illustrates the main idea or that explains what prompted the essay (see Dillard, p. 74; Brady, p. 251)

- An explanation of the significance of the subject (see Naylor, p. 256)
- An outline of the situation or problem that the essay will address, perhaps using interesting facts or statistics (see King, p. 359)
- A statement or quotation of an opinion that the writer will modify or disagree with (see Postrel, p. 345)
- An example, quotation, or question that reinforces the main idea (see Klass, p. 102)

A good introduction does not mislead readers by exaggerating the significance of the subject or the essay, and it does not bore readers by saying more than is necessary. In addition, a good introduction avoids three openings that are always clumsy: (1) beginning with *The purpose of this essay is . . .* or something similar; (2) referring to the title of the essay in the first sentence, as in *This is not as hard as it looks* or *This is a serious problem;* and (3) starting too broadly or vaguely, as in *Ever since humans walked upright . . .* or *In today's world. . . .*

Irony   In writing, irony is the use of words to suggest a meaning different from their literal meaning. Swift's "A Modest Proposal" presents an ironic statement relying on reversal: he says the opposite of what he really means (pp. 365–74). But irony can also derive from understatement (saying less than is meant) or hyperbole (exaggeration). Irony can be witty, teasing, biting, or cruel. At its most humorless and heavily contemptuous, it becomes **sarcasm:** *Thanks a lot for telling Dad we stayed out all night; that was really bright of you.*

Metaphor   See *figures of speech.*

Narration   The form of writing that tells a story, relating a sequence of events. See Chapter 2 on narration, p. 62.

Non sequitur   See *fallacies.*

Nonstandard English   See *diction.*

Oversimplification   See *fallacies.*

Paragraph   A group of related sentences, set off by an initial indentation, that develops an idea. By breaking continuous text into units, paragraphing helps the writer manage ideas and helps the reader follow those ideas. Each paragraph makes a distinct contribution to the main idea governing the entire piece of writing. The idea of the paragraph itself is often stated in a topic sentence, and it is supported with sentences containing specific details, examples, and reasons. Like the larger piece of writing to which it contributes, the paragraph should be unified, coherent, and well developed.

Parallelism   The use of similar grammatical form for ideas of equal importance. Parallelism occurs within sentences: *The doctor recommends swimming, bicycling, or walking.* It also occurs among sentences: *Strumming her guitar, she made listeners feel her anger. Singing lines, she made listeners believe her pain.*

Personification   See *figures of speech*.

Persuasion   See *argument*.

Point of view   The position of the writer in relation to the subject. In description, point of view depends on the writer's physical and psychological relation to the subject (see pp. 23–24). In narration, point of view depends on the writer's place in the story and on his or her relation to it in time (see p. 63). More broadly, point of view can also mean the writer's particular mental stance or attitude. For instance, an employee and employer might have different points of view toward the employee's absenteeism or the employer's sick-leave policies.

Post hoc   See *fallacies*.

Premise   The generalization or assumption on which an argument is based. See *syllogism*.

Process analysis   The method of development in which a sequence of actions with a specified result is divided into its component steps. See Chapter 6 on process analysis, p. 180.

Proposition   A debatable claim about a subject; the central idea of an argument.

Purpose   The reason for writing, the goal the writer wants to achieve. The purpose may be primarily to explain the subject so that readers understand it or see it in a new light; to convince readers to accept or reject an opinion or to take a certain action; to entertain readers with a humorous or exciting story; or to express the thoughts and emotions triggered by a revealing or instructive experience. The writer's purpose overlaps the main idea—the particular point being made about the subject. In effective writing, the two together direct and control every choice the writer makes. See also pp. 9–10, 13, *thesis*, and *unity*.

Rational appeal   In argumentative and persuasive writing, the appeal to readers' rational faculties—to their ability to reason logically—in order to win agreement or compel action. See pp. 320–23.

Repetition and restatement   The careful use of the same words or close parallels to clarify meaning and tie sentences together.

Revision The stage of the writing process devoted to "re-seeing" a draft, divided into fundamental changes in content and structure (revision) and more superficial changes in grammar, word choice, and the like (editing). See pp. 19–21.

Rhetoric The art of using words effectively to communicate with an audience, or the study of that art. To the ancient Greeks, rhetoric was the art of the *rhetor*—orator, or public speaker—and included the art of persuasion. Later the word shifted to mean elegant language, and a version of that meaning persists in today's occasional use of *rhetoric* to mean pretentious or hollow language, as in *Their argument was mere rhetoric*.

Sarcasm See *irony*.

Satire The combination of wit and criticism to mock or condemn human foolishness or evil. The intent of satire is to arouse readers to contempt or action, and thus it differs from comedy, which seeks simply to amuse. Much satire relies on irony—saying one thing but meaning another (see *irony*).

Simile See *figures of speech*.

Slang See *diction*.

Spatial organization A pattern of organization that views an object, scene, or person by paralleling the way we normally scan things—for instance, top to bottom or near to far. See also p. 25.

Specific words See *general and specific words*.

Standard English See *diction*.

Style The *way* something is said, as opposed to *what* is said. Style results primarily from a writer's characteristic word choices and sentence structures. A person's writing style, like his or her voice or manner of speaking, is distinctive. Style can also be viewed more broadly as ranging from formal to informal. A very **formal style** adheres strictly to the conventions of standard English (see *diction*); tends toward long sentences with sophisticated structures; and relies on learned words, such as *malodorous* and *psychopathic*. A very **informal style**, in contrast, is more conversational (see *colloquial language*); tends toward short, uncomplicated sentences; and relies on words typical of casual speech, such as *smelly* or *crazy*. Among the writers represented in this book, King (p. 358) writes quite formally, Hughes (p. 69) quite informally. The formality of style may often be modified to suit a particular audience or occasion: a college term paper, for instance, demands a more formal style than an essay narrating a personal experience. See also *tone*.

Syllogism   The basic form of deductive reasoning, in which a conclusion derives necessarily from proven or accepted premises. For example: *The roof always leaks when it rains* (the major premise). *It is raining* (the minor premise). *Therefore, the roof will leak* (the conclusion). See Chapter 10 on argument and persuasion, especially pp. 321–23.

Symbol   A person, place, or thing that represents an abstract quality or concept. A red heart symbolizes love; the Golden Gate Bridge symbolizes San Francisco's dramatic beauty; a cross symbolizes Christianity.

Thesis   The main idea of a piece of writing, to which all other ideas and details relate. The main idea is often stated in a **thesis sentence** (or sentences), which asserts something about the subject and conveys the writer's purpose. The thesis sentence is often included near the beginning of an essay. Even when the writer does not state the main idea and purpose, however, they govern all the ideas and details in the essay. See also pp. 16–17 and *unity*.

Tone   The attitude toward the subject, and sometimes toward the audience and the writer's own self, expressed in choice of words and sentence structures as well as in what is said. Tone in writing is similar to tone of voice in speaking, from warm to serious, amused to angry, joyful to sorrowful, sympathetic to contemptuous. For examples of strong tone in writing, see White (p. 28), Mitford (p. 197), Brady (p. 251), and King (p. 358).

Transitions   Links between sentences and paragraphs that relate ideas and thus contribute to clarity and smoothness. Transitions may be sentences beginning paragraphs or brief paragraphs that shift the focus or introduce new ideas. They may also be words and phrases that signal and specify relationships. Some of these words and phrases—by no means all—are listed below:

- **Addition or repetition:** again, also, finally, furthermore, in addition, moreover, next, that is
- **Cause or effect:** as a result, consequently, equally important, hence, then, therefore, thus
- **Comparison:** also, in the same way, likewise, similarly
- **Contrast:** but, even so, however, in contrast, on the contrary, still, yet
- **Illustration:** for example, for instance, specifically, that is
- **Intensification:** indeed, in fact, of course, truly
- **Space:** above, below, beyond, farther away, here, nearby, opposite, there, to the right
- **Summary or conclusion:** all in all, in brief, in conclusion, in short, in summary, therefore, thus

• **Time:** afterward, at last, earlier, later, meanwhile, simultaneously, soon, then

Understatement   See *irony*.

Unity   The quality of effective writing that occurs when all the parts relate to the main idea and contribute to the writer's purpose: the sentences build the central idea of their paragraphs, and the paragraphs build the central idea of the whole essay. Readers do not have to wonder what the essay is about or what a particular paragraph has to do with the rest of the piece.

Acknowledgments

Jennifer Finney Boylan. "In the Early Morning Rain." From *It Gets Better* by Dan Savage. Copyright © 2012 by Jennifer Finney Boylan. Reprinted with the permission of International Creative Management, Inc.

Judy Brady. "I Want a Wife." From *Ms. Magazine*, Vol. 1, No. 1, Dec. 31, 1971. Copyright © 1971 by Judy Brady. Reprinted with the permission of the author.

Judith Ortiz Cofer. "Silent Dancing." From *Silent Dancing: A Partial Remembrance of a Puerto Rican Childhood* by Judith Ortiz Cofer. Copyright © 1990 by Judith Ortiz Cofer. Reprinted with the permission of Arte Público Press.

Thomas de Zengotita. "*American Idol* Worship." From *The Los Angeles Times*, Feb. 12, 2006. Copyright © 2006 by Thomas de Zengotita. Reprinted with the permission of Thomas de Zengotita, teacher at New York University and author of *Mediated,* which won the Marshall McLuhan Award in 2006.

Joan Didion. "The Santa Ana." From "Los Angeles Notebook" in *Slouching Towards Bethlehem* by Joan Didion. Copyright © 1996 by Joan Didion. Reprinted with the permission of Farrar, Straus and Giroux.

Annie Dillard. "The Chase." Pages 45–49 from *An American Childhood* by Annie Dillard. Copyright © 1987 by Annie Dillard. Reprinted with the permission of HarperCollins Publishers.

Firoozeh Dumas. "Sweet, Sour, and Resentful." From *Gourmet,* 2008. Copyright © 2008 Condé Nast. All rights reserved. Reprinted with the permission of Condé Nast.

Barbara Ehrenreich. "Cultural Baggage." From *The New York Times*, 1992. Copyright © 1992 by Barbara Ehrenreich. Reprinted with the permission of *The New York Times*.

Lars Eighner. "Dumpster Diving." From *Travels with Lizbeth* by Lars Eighner, St. Martin's Press. Copyright © 1993 by Lars Eighner. Reprinted with the permission of Holtzbrink Publishers.

Index of Authors and Titles